C000127942

CONTENTS.

Page

CONTENTS. xxi.

ABSTRACTS OF YORKSHIRE INQUISITIONS.

I. CONCERNING LOSS SUSTAINED BY THE MEN OF YORK BY THE ENLARGING OF A DITCH.

[25 HEN. III. No. 18.]

Writ dated at Westminster, 3 May, 25th year (1241), directing inquiry to be made what damage the King's men of York have suffered by the purpresture which Geoffrey, formerly King's Chamberlain, made in enlarging the ditch *(fossatum)* of the city for its safeguarding in war-time.

INQUISITION made by the oath of Paul de Mubray, Walter Basi, Ralph *de Muro*, Henry de Fiskergate, William Tanner, Philip de Acum, Roger Kinseman, Thomas son of Uting, Robert son of Baldewyn, Robert brother of Walter, Herbert Tanner, Thomas de Acum, to inquire how much damage the honest men of the City of York have suffered by the purpresture which Geoffrey, formerly the King's Chamberlain, made to widen the ditch of the City of York, and for the guarding of the same in time of war, and how much is lost yearly thereby. They say that Herbert de Holdernes had seven houses upon the bank* of the ditch of Ploxwangate,ᵃ which were thrown down by the said Geoffrey to widen the ditch in time of war, and he lost the annual rent of 20s. Also Robert de Merston had one plot upon the ditch-bank *(super duwam fossati)* of Mikellit,ᵇ which was thrown down for the same cause, and he lost the annual rent of 12d. Also the following, viz. :

Roger Ithny	for one plot *(placeâ)* lost	2s.
Robert de Hayton	„	„ 12d.
Franco Clerk	„	, 3s.
Rayner Palmer *(Palmerius)*	„	, 3s.

ᵃ Blossomgate.   ᵇ Micklegate.

1

John de Bagergate[a]   .   for one plot *(placeâ)* lost 18*d.*
Nicholas de Hunsingouer   „   „   3*s.*
Paul de Mubray   .   two   „   4*s.*
Stephen Lurdenan .   .   one   „   18*d.*
Robert de Hoton   .   „   „   3*s.*
Matthew Tailor *(Cissor)*   „   „   3*s.*
William Sergeant *(Serviens)*   „   „   12*d.*
John Blunde[b] lost annual rent of 7*s.* from two houses. William
Ferur lost annual rent of 2*s.* from one plot.

II.   RALPH DE FETHERESTAN.   *Inq. p. m.*

[28 HEN. III. No. 16.]

Writ dated at Rochester, 14 Jan., 28th year (1243-4).

EXTENT of land which was of Ralph de Fetherestan in
Fetherestan,[c] made by the oath of William de Bretton,
John de Sothulle, John de Seyville, Stephen de Sutkirkeby,
Eudo de Sutthone, John de Smitheton, Ralph son of Hugh,
William son of Roger of Fetherestan, Adam de Preston, Alan
son of Josiana, William *de Assartis,* and Robert *le Daungerus,*
who say that the said Ralph had in demesne in Fetherestan
thirty acres of land of which every acre is worth by the year 4*d.*,
also one messuage 2*s.*, five acres of meadow, every acre 6*d.*, a
certain pasture, 14*s.* by the year.   He had also in villenage two
bovates of land and three parts of one bovate, every bovate by
the year worth 4*s.*, in rent of free men in Fetherestan 49*s.* 3½*d.* ;
in the town of Chevet[d] rent of assize one marc ; and in Stubbes[e]
3*d.*   Sum 102*s.* 4½*d.*   He had besides in Fetherestan one pound
of pepper and two pounds of cumin *(cimini).*

Olive, daughter of Ralph, who is aged sixteen years and a
half, is his heir, because before marriage he had by one Emma
with whom he lived for ten years, a son Richard, and after marriage contracted between them, the said Olive.[f]

[a] *John de Bagergate, i.e.,* Beggar-gate (Drake's *Ebor.,* pp. 246-7).

[b] A John Blund was Chancellor of York, 124—. *(Ibid.,* p. 555.)

[c] Featherstone, in the Wapentake of Osgoldcross, two miles from Pontefract.

[d] In the parish of Royston, near Wakefield.

[e] Stubbs Walden, in the parish of Womersley.

[f] The finding of the jury is in these words :—" Dicunt eciam quod intelligunt
quod Oliva filia predicti Rad[ulf]i propinquior heres ejus est, que est de etate sex-
decim annorum et dimidii, quia idem Rad's tenuit quandam feminam, nomine
Emmam, antequam matrimonium fuit inter eos contractum per decem annos, et
genuit ex ea Ricardum filium suum, et post matrimonium inter eos contractum
genuit ex eadem Emma dictam Olivam."

III.   HENRY DE MERSTON, *a fugitive.*

[28 HEN. III. No. 4.]

Writ dated at Creyke, 28 July, 28th year (1244).

INQUISITION—whether six bovates of land in Cnapeton[a] held by Henry de Merstone, who fled [for robbery done to foreign merchants[b]] were his own inheritance, or frank marriage of Agnes his wife—made by Lambert de Billeburc, Thomas *le Lardiner*, Henry Bastard, Richard Hamelin, John de Ekestone, Thomas de Cnapeton, Alemot *(Alemotum)* de Merstone, Ranulf de Bilum, William son of Alexander of Merstone, William Whichard of Calton, John de Cnapeton, Robert Marshal *(Marescallum)* of Aketon, who say upon their oath that the said six bovates were frank marriage of Agnes wife of Henry de Merstone and not his own inheritance.[c]

IV.   THOMAS DE AUNO.   *Inq. p. m.*

[30 HEN. III. No. 32.]

Writ dated at Westminster, 15 Jan., 30th year (1245-6).

INQUISITION made by Bartholomew de Eskelby, Robert Arundel, Walter de Sinderby, John de Favell', Robert son of Geoffrey of Pichalle, Pigot de Neuton, Elias de Tanefelde, Hugh de Bardelby, Alan de Eskelby, Richard de Dunum in Carthorpe, John son of Elias of Synderby, and Thomas de Bindedenilde, who say that Thomas de Auno held in the town of Carthorpe[d] four score and ten acres of arable land in demesne (9*d.*), 23 acres of meadow (2*s.* 6*d.*), and pasture for six score sheep and twenty beasts *(averia)* which is worth by the year half a marc.   Sum of the demesne with meadow and pasture, £6 11*s.* 8*d.*

He had also there in villenage 22 bovates of land which yield yearly £6 4*s.*, thirty-six hens (3*s.*), and 300 eggs (9*d.*). The villains do no works beyond rendering the farm aforesaid; but they pay yearly 26*s.* 6*d.* to do foreign service *(ad faciendum forinsecum)*, which money the said Thomas was wont to retain for his own use.   Cottages *(cotagia)* yield yearly 18*s.* 10*d.*, 60 eggs and six hens which are worth by the year 7½*d.*   Sum of villenage with cottages, £8 13*s.* 8½*d.*

---

a Knapetone in the writ.

b " Qui fugit pro roboria facta mercatoribus de partibus transmarinis " by the writ.

c "Fuerunt liberum maritagium Agnetis uxoris dicti Henrici de Merstone, et non hereditas ipsius Henrici."

d In the parish of Burneston.

Rent of free tenants 5s. 3d., pannage worth yearly 6d. The aids of men in Brinestone[a] to plough and reap in autumn are yearly worth 5s. 9d. Sum of the sums, £15 16s. 10½d.[b]

V. CONCERNING RENTS GRANTED BY WILLIAM DE PERCY IN TADCASTER.

[30 HEN. III. No. 12.]

Writ dated at Gudeforde (Guildford), 30 Jan., 30th year (1245-6).

INQUISITION made by the oath of Robert *le Butelir*, William de Bengrant, Henry *filius Magistri*, Robert Marescall of Metum, Thomas Marescall at the Cross, Maurice [de] Wilton, Thomas [M]arescall, Adam *le Wineter*, Philip de Oscum, Hugh Chaplain of Sutton, Robert Fatting', and Richard de Linton, who say that William de Percy[c] gave to Roger Maudit and Robert his son, and the issue of Robert, twenty shillings rent to be received yearly in the mills *(molendinis)* of Tadecastre, and they were in seisin for two years before his death. He also gave to the Prior of (Helagh) Park *(Priori de Parco)* in pure and perpetual almoigne two marcs, and to Thomas *le Lardiner* sixteen shillings rent by the year in the said mill (before plural, but here "*in dicto molendino*") until he (William) or his heirs shall make an exchange with the said Thomas and his heirs, that is to say, two bovates of land and one toft in Tadecastre.

[a] Burneston, a parish near Bedale.

[b] There are two Inquisitions for Lincolnshire, in which the name is written " Thomas de Aunou " and " Thomas de Alnov." In neither of these is any mention of the heir of this Thomas. He was dead before 11 July, 1244, on which day the King commanded the Sheriff of Lincolnshire, after taking security from his executors for payment of what was due to himself, to allow them free administration of all his goods in order to perform the testament of the said Thomas.— (*Excerpta è Rotulis Finium*, vol. i., p. 420.)

[c] William de Percy, son of Henry de Percy and Isabella, daughter of Adam de Brus of Skelton, and grandson of Joceline of Louvain and Agnes de Percy. He married Joan, daughter of William de Briwerre, by whom he appears to have had only daughters ; and secondly Elen (in Dodsworth simply Sibilla), daughter of Ingelram de Balliol, with whom he had Dalton Percy. She survived her husband, and was the mother of his son and heir. In 8 Hen. III. (1223-4) he had a grant of a market every Friday at Spofforth (Dugdale's *Baronage*, vol. i., p. 271, quoting *Close Roll*, 8 Hen. III., m. 20, and *Whitby Chartulary*, vol. ii., p. 685). On 15 Sept., 1244, he paid homage to the King at Windsor for the lands of his uncle, Richard de Percy, saving the dower of Richard's widow, and the King's right in the manor of Topcliffe. On the 28th July in the following year, the Sheriff of Sussex was ordered to take into the King's hand all the lands in his bailiwick late belonging to William de Percy (*Excerpta è Rotulis Finium*, vol. i., pp. 423, 440). He was buried at Sawley Abbey. The custody of his son and heir Henry, was granted on 29 March, 1246, to Isabel, widow of Henry (*lege* Richard) de Percy, and on 17 Jan., 1248-9, the young man paid the King a fine of £900 for having his lands and marrying whom he would (*Ibid.*, vol. i., p. 450, and vol. ii., p. 47). See No. XLVI.

VI. ROBERT DE HORTON. *Inq. p. m.*

[30 HEN. III. No. 22.]

Writ dated at Canterbury, 18 May, 30th year (1246).

INQUISITION made by Roger de Thornton,[a] Elias de Oxenhope, John de Howrde,[b] Henry de Ocwrde,[c] Robert de Bollinge,[d] Godfrey de Wylsindene,[e] Hugh de Clayton, Adam de Clayton, Simon of the same, Henry de Clayton, Swain de Horton, and William son of William of Braforde, who say by their oath, that Robert de Horton had in demesne in Horton and in Clayton[f] fifty-four acres of land (price of the acre 4*d.*). Sum, 18*s.* He had in villenage 25 acres (acre 4*d.*), 9*s.* ; in service of free men eleven bovates of land and fivescore and eight acres, worth 37*s.* 5*d.*

He held his land of J. de Lacy, formerly Earl of Lincoln, by the service of the third part of one knight's fee; and Hugh de Horton is his next heir and of full age.

VII. ROBERT DE CHANCY. *Inq. p. m.*

[30 Hen. III. No. 37.]

No writ.

INQUISITION[g] concerning the lands of Robert de Chancy[h] which may escheat by reason of any dower or inheritance, made by Richard Trussebut, Thomas de Lutton, Walter Wacelin, Eudo de Coleville, John de Barkethorppe, William [de Toraldeby],

[a] Lord of the manor of Thornton, near Bradford, witness to a grant of land by Hugh de Horton to Byland Abbey (James's *History of Bradford*, pp., 344, 349, 350).

[b] Haworth.

[c] Oakworth, in the parish of Keighley. Acurde in Domesday.

[d] Robert de Bollinge, *i.e.* Bowling, near Bradford. He died 43 Hen. III. *(Ibid.,* p. 309).

[e] Wilsden, near Bradford. In the thirteenth century Thomas de Thornton gave all his land in Wilsden to Byland, with the service and homage of Godfrey de Wilesden and his heirs *(Ibid.,* p. 373).

[f] Horton and Clayton, near Bradford. Robert de Horton *alias* de Stapleton had a grant from Robert de Lacy of four carucates in Horton and Clayton, by the service of a third part of one knight's fee. His son Hugh de Horton made a grant of land to Byland in 1239 *(Ibid.,* p. 333). As this Robert de Horton is said in the Inquisition to have held his land of John de Lacy, he must have died before 22 July, 1240, the date of the latter's death.

[g] This document is imperfect, being torn completely down one side.

[h] The Chancy, Chauncy, or Cancy family was settled from an early period at Skirpenbeck, which they held in chief of the King. Walter de Canci and Anfrid his son gave the church there to Whitby Abbey before 1180 (*Whitby Chartulary*, vol. i., pp. 5, 159, 302). The following extracts from the *Excerpta è Rotulis Finium* give an account of the family at this period. On 4 Jan., 1228-9, the land of Walter

Jordan of the same, Ralph de Gaugi, Walter Rispaud, John Brun, Walter de Lutton, and Adam de Diuelkeby,[a] who say upon their oath that after the death of Robert de Chancy there fell into the King's hand in fifteen days [? after the Annuncia]tion of Blessed Mary in the 30th year of the King's reign (8 April 1246) a dower, in which a lady named Matilda Murdoc had in demesne ten bovates of land (10s. the bovate), 16 acres of meadow (2s.), in bondage six bovates (at 10s.), in rents . . . . marcs by the year, and in rents of cottars with the capital messuage of the same lady, 23s. 6d.   She also had in Toraldeby[b] of farm by the year 6s.

Another lady, who was mother of the said Robert, ... in good prosperity of living *(que est in bona prosperitate vivendi)* holds in dower ten bovates of land, of which every bovate is worth by the year (10s.), 16 acres of meadow (at 2s.), her capital messuage worth by the year . . . . has [nothing] in rents, bondages, or in cottars.

There is nothing to escheat by reason of dower or inheritance except the aforesaid, so far as they know.

de Chauncy, lately dead, was seised by the Sheriff of Yorkshire, and the King commanded him to keep it until further notice (vol. i., p. 180).   On 20 March following, the King informed the Sheriff that he had taken the homage of Roger de Chauncy for five knight's fees, which his brother Walter de Chauncy (whose heir he (Roger) was) held in chief, having taken security for £25 to be paid for his relief, he was to give Roger seisin of all the lands which came to him by inheritance (vol. i., p. 182).   On 18 Dec., 1238, the King commanded Roger de Essex to hold the lands of Roger de Chauncy, which had been taken into the King's hand, until otherwise ordered (vol. i., p. 317).   On 2nd March following, the King took the homage of Robert son of Roger de Chauncy for five knight's fees, which his father held of him in chief; and also reduced his relief from £25 to 25 marcs, which sum he was to pay at the rate of five marcs a year.   The Sheriff of Yorkshire was commanded to take security for the payment of the 25 marcs, and then to give him seisin of his father's lands (vol. i., p. 321).   On 21 July, 1246, the King granted to Robert de Creppinge, for his service and for a fine of £100, the wardship of the land and heir of Robert de Chauncy and also his marriage (vol. i., p. 458).   On 5 May, 1249, the Sheriff of Yorkshire is commanded to take into the King's hand twelve bovates of land in Fridaythorpe, of which Margery Basset who held them by knight's service of Thomas son and heir of Robert de Chauncy, now in ward to the King, died seised in fee, and to keep them safely until otherwise ordered (vol. ii., p. 53).   On 24 Sept., 1268, the King took the homage of Thomas de Chauncy, son and heir of Robert de Chauncy, for all the lands and tenements which his father held of the King in chief on the day of his death, and restored to him those lands and tenements.   John de Reygate, Escheator *citra Trentam*, was commanded to give full seisin to Thomas of all lands which his father held in fee (vol. ii., p. 478).   From their holding in chief the Chaunceys were called the Barons of Skirpenbeck.   In a Roll of Arms published in the *Antiquary* (vol. ii., p. 241) Le Baron de Skirpenbecke bore gules a cross pateè argent, on a chief azure a lion passant or.

    [a] Probably a corruption of Duggleby.   In Domesday Difgelibi and Dighelibi.
    [b] Thoraldby, in the parish of Bugthorpe, near Pocklington.

VIII. ROBERT DE CANCY OR CHANCY. *Inq. p. m.*

[30 HEN. III. No. 45.]
No Writ.

INQUISITION (undated) made by John de Barketorp, William de Toraldeby, Jordan of the same, Walter Risspalde, Ralph Guagy, William de Langetoft, William *le Surays*, John *le Brun*, William Borard, William Basset, William son of Eudo, Robert son of Roger of Berretorp, who say upon their oath that Robert de Chancy held in Skerpingbec in demesne eleven bovates of land (at 11*s.*), and one bovate (at 8*s.*), six acres, one rood and a half (worth per annum 5*s.* 3¾*d.*), sixteen acres of meadow (at 2*s.*), one mill worth by the year four marcs, and a capital messuage with gardens and vivaries 40*s.* He had in Skerbinbec and in Toraldeby six bondmen who hold twelve bovates of land in bondage (every bovate worth yearly 10*s.*), and fifteen cottars who hold fifteen tofts and half an acre of land, yielding by the year 34*s.* 8*d.*

Hugh son of William holds one bovate for 6*s.* a year, and does foreign service *(et facit forinsecum)* whereof ten carucates of land make one knight's fee. Walter Risspald holds two bovates for foreign service only *(pro forinseco tantum)*, and two tofts for fourpence. Hugh Bascy holds two bovates for 2*s.* a year, and does foreign service *(et facit forinsecum)*. The same Hugh holds two tofts, and a third part of one toft, and one marsh for 6*d.* yearly. Thomas Bretun [yields] for one toft 3*s.*; Robert son of Deacon *(Rob' fil' Diaconi)* for one toft 5*s.*; Roger Burdun for one toft 2*s.*; Roger de Skyrpinbeke for one toft 8*d.* and one pound of cumin; Thomas Burdun for one toft a penny; and Jordan de Toraldeby 12*d.* by the year.

Thomas son of Robert de Cancy is his next heir, and he will be two years old at the feast of the Invention of the Holy Cross in the 30th year of King Henry son of King John. (3 May, 1246).

Robert de Cancy used to render to the lord William de Ros for the aforesaid land 15*s.* by the year, but how or by what right the jurors know not. Margaret,[a] who was wife of Robert, has a third part of all the aforesaid lands, rents, villenages, and other farms.

Sum of the value of the whole land held by Robert of the King in chief in the county of York, and of which he was seised in fee on the day of his death, in demesnes, rents, villenages, and

[a] On 2 Feb., 1245-6, the King, then at Reading, commanded Robert de Crepping to assign dower to Margaret, who was wife of Robert de Chauncy, in the lands of her late husband. *(Close Rolls, 30 Hen. III., m. 19.)*

all issues of the land, £21 3s. 10¾d.; of which the said Margaret his wife has a third part as aforesaid.

Moreover,[a] after Robert de Chancy died, a certain lady who was wife of the lord Walter de Chancy (uncle of Robert) died, whereby her whole dower fell into the King's hand by reason of wardship, which dower is worth yearly, as the jurors say upon oath, in demesnes, villenages, and all other issues of the land, £11 17s. 2d. in the whole.

IX. ALICE HAGET.[b] *Inq. p. m.*

[31 HEN. III. No. 33.]

Writ dated at Windsor, 3 Feb., 31st year (1246-7).

INQUISITION made by Henry *del Grene*, Ralph de Federstan, William *del Grene*, Simon Marshal *(Marscall')*, William Russel, Peter *le Passur* Adam Chamberlain *(Camerar')*, Richard son of Robert, Adam son of Ralph, Simon son of Terry *(Terrici)*, Adam de Bukedene, and Robert de Scultorpe, who say by their oath that Alice Haget had in demesne at Fristone and Feri[c] ten-score acres of land (6d. the acre). Sum, 100s. There are in demesne meadow *(in dominico prato)* 26½ acres (3s.). Sum, 79s. 6d. In bondage 15 bovates of land (each by the year 2s.), 30s.; and the men render for quitclaim of their works 43s. 9d. There are six cottars *(cotar')* who render nothing of farm, but do works which are worth 8s. 3d. There are four other tenants who render 2s. 10d., and fifteen free tenants who render by the year 54s. A windmill there yields yearly 26s. Also in farm of Marton 6s. At Frikeley in demesne 64½ acres [of land] (4d. the acre), 21s. 6d.; in demesne meadow two acres, 2s.; in bondage eleven bovates of land (5s. the bovate), 55s.; and the men render in their works 22d. Also there are in cottages five acres which yield 5s., four free tenants who render yearly 12s. 7½d., and three women who render yearly 23d. Sum of the whole, £22 10s. 2½d.

a This addition is written on the back of the Inquisition.

b Geoffrey Haget, founder of the Priory of Helagh Park, near Tadcaster, and son of Bertram Haget, had four sisters, Lucia, wife of Peter Turet, Gundreda, died unmarried, one whose name is unknown, the wife of Alan Fitz Brian, and Alice, wife of John de Friston and mother of the above-named Alice Haget, who seems to have preferred her mother's maiden name. This last named Alice Haget married Jordan de Sancta Maria, and had two daughters, Elizabeth, mother of Richard Waleys, and Nicholaa. These facts will be found in the Helagh Park Chartulary, now in the British Museum.—(*Cott. MSS.*, *Vesp.*, *A. iv.*) chiefly on the first folio.

c Ferry Fryston, near Pontefract.

The said Alice had two heirs, viz.: Richard Waleys *(Wallensem)* son of her first daughter, and Nicholaa her other daughter.[a]

X. AS TO THE LIABILITY OF DAVID LARDENER TO REPAIR THE KING'S GAOL OF THE FOREST IN YORK.

[31 HEN. III. No. 40.]

Writ dated at Westminster, 13 Feb., 31st year (1246-7).

INQUISITION whether the King's gaol of the forest, which is in the keeping of David *le Lardiner* in the city of York, ought to be made *(fieri debeat)* at the King's cost or at that of David, because he has that custody of fee, made by William de Barton, William de Yolton, Gervase de Routheclyve, Odo de Ofyatesutton,[b] John Wandelarde, William de Lillinge, William *le Establer* of Hoton, William *le Bret*, Adam Gaoler *(Gaolarium)*, William Bonifice, William *Romanum*, and Richard *de Camera*, who say upon their oath that the King has had his said gaol in the city of York for keeping incarcerated those who were taken for trespass of his forest, which gaol David le Lardener[c] has now in his keeping of fee. Before David or any of his antecessors were enfeoffed by the King's charter of custody of the said gaol, repair was made at the King's cost, and never after was it necessary to renew it; but in the time of Geoffrey de Nevill, Chamberlain of England, who was keeper of the forest, Sheriff of Yorkshire,[d] and keeper of the King's castles in the same county, the said gaol was repaired in some part; so, that is to say, that the timber used was taken in the King's forest of Galtris by him (Geoffrey) and the repairs made at the King's cost. For this reason the jurors say that the gaol ought to be repaired at the King's cost, and not at the cost of the said David.

---

[a] The Sheriff of the County was commanded by writ, dated 26 April, 1247, to give seisin to the heirs of Alice Haget, after taking security for their relief of two knights' fees held of J., formerly Earl of Lincoln.—*(Excerpta è Rotulis Finium,* vol. ii., p. 11.)

[b] This name occurs as Ougate Sutton in a North Riding Subsidy Roll for 30 Edward I. It is probably the same as Sutton-on-the-Forest.

[c] See Nos. XIV. and LXIX. for other Inquisitions about him.

[d] 2-7 Hen. III., that is, 28 Oct., 1217—27 Oct., 1223.

2

XI.   AGATHA TRUSSEBUT.   *Inq. p. m.*

[31 HEN. III.   No. 21.]

Writ dated at Windsor, 28 Feb., 31st year (1246-7).

INQUISITION made by Robert *le Butiller*, Nigel his brother, Nigel de Stockeld, Geoffrey Dagun, Peter de Colethorp, Adam the Tailor *(le Taillur)* of the same, Alan Carpenter of the same, William son of Swain of the same, Henry son of Walter of Dicton, John Clerk of the same, John son of Ivo *(fil' Yvony)* of Werreby, and Adam de Bilton of the same, concerning the value of the manor of Dicton,[a] which Agatha Trussebut held of the King in chief. The said manor with appurtenances is worth in all issues by the year £44 of silver. By what service save royal service it was held they know not.

William de Ros is the next heir of Agatha.[b]

---

[a] Kirk Deighton near Wetherby.

[b] The deed by which the Trussebut estates were partitioned amongst the three sisters and co-heiresses of Robert Trussebut, is entered on a Curia Regis Roll attributed to Trinity Term, 5 Richard I., 1194 (*Curia Regis*, No. 1., m. 2). To the share of Roesia de Ros fell Ribbestein, Hunsinghour (Hunsingore), Walleford', with the mills, Wargebi, or perhaps Wengebi, with the soke, which are worth £62. The knights' fees pertaining to the share are £23 13s. 5d. in Watre (Wartre), and a third part of the wood throughout the whole inheritance. Sum of all £62. These are the knights: Richard Trussebut holds two knights' fees, William Burdet half a knight's fee, Reginald de Cherpunville half a virgate, P(eter) de Becheringes a fourth part of a knight's fee. John Burdet a fourth part. Sum, three and a half knights' fees. The share of Hillaria de Builers: Melton, Copegrava (Copgrave), Copmonistorp (Copmanthorpe), Fulleford (Fulford), Stivelingflet (Stillingfleet), Cotingwic. In the City of York three marcs and 3d., and in Watra £15 2s. 8d., and a third part of the wood throughout the whole inheritance. Sum of all, £62 6s. These are knights: Godefrid de Burun and Hugh de Noville, a knight's fee a-piece, Geoffrey de Colebi, Nicholas de Chavingcurt, and Alan de Neville, each half a knight's fee. Sum, three and a half knights' fees. Share of Agatha Meinfelin: Didton (Kirk Deighton), with the soke, Chahale (Cattal), and one marc in Tocwic', Hulesbi, Grahingham, and in Wartre £15 4s., and a third part of the wood. Sum of all, £62 6s. Knights: Matthew de Brenna, and Bernard de Rippele, each half a knight's fee, James de Benesle, one knight's fee, in Braken one knight's fee, Walter de Hainville half a knight's fee. Sum, three knights' fees and a half. On another Curia Regis Roll (No. 36. mm. 3[d], 5), attributed to 6 or 7 John, is the record of a suit about the manor of Wicton or Wicham in Yorkshire, which Robert de Ros, William de Aubenni and Agatha his wife, and Eularia or Eilaria Trussebut, claimed against Henry de Puteaco, as the inheritance which had come to them from their ancestor Gaufrid, son of Pagan, who was seised thereof in the time of Henry I.; from Gaufrid the right descended to William Trussebut; and from William to Gaufrid Trussebut; and from Gaufrid to Robert Trussebut, grandfather of the said Robert, and father of Agatha and Eularia. And this they, the plaintiffs, offer to prove by their freeman, William de Copland, who is willing to prove it by his body, as of the sight and hearing of Ulfkill his father *(Et hoc offer[un]t dirationare versus eum per quendam liberum hominem suum, scilicet, Willelmum de Copland; qui hoc offert per corpus suum, etc., ut de visu et auditu Ulfkill' patris sui, etc.).* The defendant, however, preferred to rest his title on a grant by Henry II., which had been confirmed by Richard I. and John. The case was adjourned to Michaelmas Term, when Pudsey was to produce his charters before the King. From the above Inquisition, it appears that the two sisters,

XII. CONCERNING RENT IN EASINGWOLD

[31 HEN. III. No. 19.]

Writ of the King, dated at Windsor the first day of June, 31st year (1247), and directed to Thomas de Stamforde and Robert de Creppinges, his Escheators, commanding enquiry to be made, whether seven marcs, which Robert Bon and his parceners of Heyton[a] used to render from three carucates of land held by them in Esingwalde, ought to be rendered to the farm of that manor from those three carucates, or from the whole township.

INQUISITION made by the King's writ concerning seven marcs yearly given for increase of rent in Esingwalde.

Jurors. Thomas de Coleville, Simon de Lillinge, William Boniface, William de Lillinge, William de Jolton, Michael of the same, Nicholas de Alne, William[b] *Stabularius*, William *le Grant*, Robert de Rascel, John de Hoby, William de Everley, William Frost.

They say by their oath that the whole township *(villata)* of Esingwalde offered the said seven marcs to the King, and fined for increase of rent; and all are bound in payment of the same *(omnes comuniter tenentur in solucione)*.

And they say that in the town *(villa)* of Esingwalde there are eleven carucates of land in bondage of the King *(de bondagio domini Regis)*, of which three carucates have paid seven marcs for ten years at the feast of S. Michael next to come, by compulsion of the bailiffs, and eight carucates for the same time have been quit, but unjustly.

Hillaria, wife of Robert de Builers or Budlers, who were both living in 1200 *(Rotuli de Oblatis et Finibus*, 102, and *Excerpta è Rotulis Finium*, vol. i., p. 341 *),* the above named Agatha Trussebut, wife of William de Albeni or Aubenni (*Ibid.*, vol. i., p. 303), died without issue. William de Ros, Agatha's heir, was her grandnephew, being the son of Robert de Ros, called Fursan, who was the son of Everard de Ros and Roesia Trussebut (*Rievaulx Chartulary*, p. 360). It is very probable that the family of Ros got the water-bougets or buts, their well known bearing, from the Trussebuts.

   [a] This name seems to have entirely disappeared. No place with a similar name occurs amongst the places which were in the soke of Easingwold in *Domesday*, except a certain Hotterne which is probably Hutton Sessay. At a later period, towards the end of the twelfth century, a Bernard Milner *(Molendinarius)* gave the Priory of Durham two bovates in *villa de Hetona*, which Marmeduc Darel had given him for his homage and service ; a gift which was confirmed by Marmeduc's grandson Marmeduc de Arell', with the addition of a toft and rent of twelve pence *(Durham Charters*, 3[ois] 1[ma], *Ebor.*, Nos. 6 and 7*)*. Bernard's seal, which is attached to another deed in the same collection (No. 5) about land at Thirsk, is very curious. It is circular, 1½ inches in diameter, and bears a hand issuing from the sinister, holding a mill pick, with a square object on either side like a cushion with a mark (a knob ?) in the centre, + SIGILL' BERNARDI PVGILIS. The two S's are reversed. From his seal it would appear he was a prize-fighter as well as a miller. The place is not mentioned in *Kirkby's Inquest*, but it was still known in Tudor times, as it is named more than once in the *Yorkshire Fines (Tudor)*, vol. i., pp. 45, 117, 259, and 302. In No. XL. a Thomas Maunsel of Heton is mentioned among the assailants of the Abbot of Byland's Grange, at Wilden.

   [b] William the "Establer" of Hoton, in No. x.

XIII.   IDONEA DE VIPONT.[a]   *Custody of Lands.*

[31 HEN. III. No. 35.]

Writ dated at Windsor, 3 June, 31st year (1247).

INQUISITION made by Roger de Stockewell, Richard de Barneby, Thomas *de Aula* of the same, Richard Pluket, Adam de Scauceby, William Talun, Alexander de Stocbrig', Thomas de Annington, Osbert be Luversal, Richard de Lenneder, Oto of the same, and William de Elleres, who say that Peter de Mauley *(Malo lacu)* on his departure from the parts of York, when he took his journey to the Holy Land, granted to Sir Gerard la Grue the first wardship or escheat which should fall to him, and enjoined one Reginald, his steward, that he should cause him to have such when time and place offered. And when the lady Idonea de Vipont deceased, Reginald put Gerard in seisin of the lands of Westerfeud[b] and Bautre, because the custody of the said lands ought to appertain to the said Peter. Gerard was in seisin eight days, and then came the bailiff of Sir Nicholas de Molis, then Sheriff, and he removed Gerard and his men from the custody of the land. Gerard had the seisin aforesaid on All Saints' day in the 26th year (1 Nov., 1241), and at the Circumcision of Our Lord following (6 Jan., 1241-2), the King's bailiffs took seisin of the lands which were of Sir Peter de Mauley.[c]

In Westerfeud there are five bovates of land in demesne and one bovate in villenage, every one of which is worth by the year half a marc, and in rent of assize 16s. 3d. In Bautre no demesne, but in rent of assize eight marcs; also a mill, a market, and all manner of other casual profit *(aventure)*, which are worth yearly twelve marcs. Sum, £16 2s. 11d.

[a] Daughter and heiress of John de Busli, and widow of Robert de Vipont. She and her husband claimed the Honour of Tickhill against Alice Countess of Eu *(Yorkshire Archæological Journal*, vol. ix, p. 290*)*. On 2nd March, 1228, the Sheriff of Yorkshire was ordered to inquire what had become of the chattels of Robert de Vipont, which were sold after his death, and into whose possession they had come, and to cause Idonea, his widow, to recover the same and have them valued, after taking security for her answering to the King for their price when called upon *(Excerpta è Rotulis Finium*, vol. i., p. 168*)*. On 19 Oct., 1241, the Sheriff of Buckinghamshire was ordered to seize the lands lately belonging to her, both those she held in inheritance, and those she held in dower *(Ibid.*, vol. i., p. 357*)*. On 13 March following, Alice, Countess of Eu (Comitissa Augi), made a fine with the King of one hundred marcs, for having the custody of the lands of Idonea de Vipont, which were of her (the Countess's) fee, to the lawful age of the heirs of the said Idonea *(Ibid.*, vol. i., p. 371*)*. She granted considerable privileges to Bawtry, which she had inherited from her father *(Hunter's South Yorkshire*, vol. i., p. 70*)*, and was buried at Roche Abbey *(Burton's Monasticon*, and Aveling's *Roche Abbey*, p. 140*)*.

[b] Austerfield in the parish of Blyth, near Bawtry.

[c] Matthew Paris *(Chronica Majora*, vol. iv., p. 89*)* states that among the nobles who went to the Holy Land in the year 1241 was Peter de Mauley, a Poitevin by

XIV. AS TO THE LIABILITY OF DAVID LARDENER TO REPAIR
THE KING'S GAOL OF THE FOREST IN YORK[a].

[31 HEN. III. No. 57.]

Writ dated at Wodestoke, 25 July, 31 year (1247).

INQUISITION—if David Lardener, who has of fee the keeping of
the King's gaol of the forest in the county of York, ought
to construct and repair it at his own cost, or whether this should
be done at the cost of the King—made by William Boniface,
William de Yolton, Richard *de Camera*, Michael de Yolton,
William *le Stabeler*, William de Galmethorpe, William Luvel,
Nicholas de Alene, Gervase de Routheclive, William *le Bret*, and
Ralph de Graynesby, who say upon their oath that the gaol
was constructed by the King at his own cost long before any
antecessor of the said David was enfeoffed of the custody; and
always before, as need arose, the goal was repaired at the King's
cost, as well in David's time as in that of his antecessors. So
they say that the gaol ought to be constructed and repaired,
when necessary, at the cost of the King.

XV. PHILIPPA DE TILLI. *Extent.*

[33 HEN. III. No. 14.]

Writ dated at Bugden' (Buckden, Co. Huntingdon[b]), 25 Nov., 33rd year
(1248).

EXTENT of the land of Phillipa de Tilli (Tylly in writ) in
Meltun, made by William de Insula, Robert de Rihil,
Hugh de Schouceby[c], Robert of the same, Adam Paynel, Jordan
de Pikebourne, Jordan de Mar, Richard de Meltun, William
Joie, William de Hanggnethwayt, William Clerk of Awike, Wilfrid de Hikeltun, who say by their oath that the said Philippa
had in demesne in the town of Meltun[d] five-score acres of land

nation, who was for a long time brought up and enriched under the patronage of
King John. William de Fortibus, Earl of Albemarle, John Hansard, and Alexander
de Hilton went at the same time. In 1242 the King let to Gerard La Grue the
lands formerly belonging to Peter de Mauley, at an annual rent of five hundred
marcs, he keeping up the Castle of Mulgrave (Mulegrive) at his own cost. The
next year he was ordered to surrender the lands to Guido de Russilun, who had a
grant of them until the majority of the heir *(Excerpta è Rotulis Finium*, vol. i., pp.
379, 409).

[a] See Nos. X. and LXIX.

[b] Henry is shewn in the Chancery Rolls to have been on the same day at
Huntingdon, which is four miles distant.

[c] Reading doubtful.

[d] Melton-on-the-Hill near Doncaster.

(every acre worth by the year 6*d.*), and in villenage seven bovates of land (every bovate worth by the year 9*s.*), and in free men 8*s.* 6*d.*; also of hall and court *(de aula et curia)* 5*s.*, and of wood 20*s.* by the year.

She was born in England, and had land in Normandy but left it for her own land in England; and they understand her to have been English rather than Norman.[a]   Sum total, £7 6*s.* 6*d.*

XVI.   ALEXANDER DE RYVILLE.

[33 HEN. III. No. 71.]

Writ dated at Winchester, 27 May, 33rd year (1249).

INQUISITION, whether Alexander de Ryvill taken and detained in the King's prison at York for the death of John de Neusum, of which Adam de Neusum appeals him, is appealed because he is guilty, or by malice and hatred *(odio et atia)* and if not guilty who is guilty, made by Philip de Mileforde, John de Mileforde, Hugh de Ecclesthorpe, William de Gunnulton, Robert de Langewaythe, Ralph de Mileforde, Hugh Gernun, William son of Alexander, Robert de Clifforde, Nicholas de Hoylwode(?),[b] William son of William of Fenton, and Roger de Leuenaton, who say upon their oath that Alexander de Ryvill is not guilty of the death of John de Neusum, and that he is appealed by Adam de Neusum, through the malice and hatred of Brother Nicholas de Aske manager *(Husbandi)* of the Grange of Lede, who procured Adam to appeal him out of revenge, because Alexander obstructed the water of the grange-mill of Lede, wherefrom *(un[de])* the master and brethren of the Hospital of S. Leonard in York removed the said mill; and because Alexander hindered the said Brother Nicholas from raising a hedge in the common of Lede *(Et quia idem Alexander impedivit dictum fratrem Nicholaum levare quandam hayam in communa de Lede).* And they say that Thomas Stan, born in Notton, slew the said John de Neusum.

[a] "Item dicunt predicti juratores, quod dicta Philippa nata fuit in Anglia, et quod terram habuit in Normannia, et illam reliquit pro terra sua in Anglia: et melius intelligunt quod dicta Philippa Anglica fuit quam Normann [ica]." No. XXXVI., also refers to her.   Hunter *(South Yorkshire*, vol. i., p. 363) says, "This was during the troubles between Lewis and Henry. Lewis expelled all the English from France, and Henry confiscated all the lands of the French in England. Philippa de Tilli appears to have brought the question to issue with the King, and to have been finally unsuccessful, for from this time the name of Tilli disappears from the district, a family which had very great possessions, whose cross is still one of the ornaments of Doncaster, but of whom we should probably have known more had not their allegiance been divided between the crowns of England and France."

[b] Perhaps Heselwude.

XVII. ALEXANDER DE NEVILL. *Inq. p. m.*

[33 HEN. III. No. 50.]

Writ dated at Westminster, 12 July, 33rd year (1249).

INQUISITION made by Nicholas de Erdeslawe, John of the same, John de Batelay, Hugh de Muhaut, Nicholas de Mirefeld, John *de Alta Ripa*, Thomas de Heden, John del Hil', Sampson de Gilhusum, Robert son of Richard of Mirfeud, Alexander of the same, Roger Alayn, and John de Birstal, who say that Alexander de Nevill[a] had in Nunington two carucates and two bovates of land in demesne, which he held of the Abbot of S. Mary's, York ; of which every bovate contains seven acres, and is worth by the year 6s. Sum, 108s. There is a capital messuage with two gardens, one toft and one dovehouse, which are worth yearly 17s. 10d. Free tenants render 7s. 7½d. Sum total, £6 13s. 5½d.; of which paid to the Abbot 11s., and so there remains the true sum, £6 2s. 5½d.

He held of Edmund de Lascy in the town of Mirfeud two carucates of land in demesne, worth by the year 40s. Pasture there, one marc ; five acres of meadow, 10s. yearly. There is one mill worth by the year 16 marcs ; also two carucates of land in bondage (the bovate 8s.), £6 8s. ; and from service of free tenants, £8 13s. 9½d. Sum, £28 18s. 5½d., of which to Edmund de Lascy yearly half a marc, and the fees of two knights. So there remains the true sum, £28 11s. 9½d.

He held nothing of the King in demesne in this county ; and Alexander his son is his next heir, aged twelve years and more.[b]

[a] Mr. J. C. Brook, *Rouge Croix*, in a letter to the Rev. J. Ismay, Vicar of Mirfield, dated 13 Jan., 1775, after stating that he had made large collections for the History of the West Riding of Yorkshire, says that after the Conquest Sweyn the son of Aluric obtained a regrant of the Manor of Mirfield (having previously been the possessor), to be held of Ilbert de Lacy as of his Honour of Pontefract. " He, Sweyn, had a son Adam, who had two daughters, who divided his estate, and Mirfield fell to the share of Amabilia, who was married, first to Wm. Neville, secondly to Simon de Crevequer ; by the first she had a daughter, Sarah, married to Thomas de Burgh, whose posterity enjoyed an estate in Mirfield, and had the patronage of the living. By Crevequer she had also one daughter called Cecilia, married to Walter de Neville, who in her right became Lord of Mirfield. These Nevilles possessed it several generations, but they became extinct temp. Hen. III., when Alexander de Neville died *sine prole* 37 of that reign, leaving five sisters, who married Neville, Folenfant, Newmarshe, Tyas, and Heton. Neville and Folenfant quit claimed their shares of the Manor of Mirfield to one Adam de Pomfret, as appears by writings in my possession, who, I take it, was the same person with Adam de Newmarshe, who married the fourth daughter . . . and the same person or his posterity probably afterwards took the name of Mirfield, for Pomfret's share came to that family. Tyas's moiety went by marriage of two co-heirs to the families of Rockley, of Rockley near Barnsley, and Wentworth, of North Elmsall. The family of Mirfield who inherited Pomfret's share, continued at Mirfield many generations, but at last expired in an heir female, married first to

XVIII. CONCERNING RENT IN EASINGWOLD[a].

[33 Hen. III. No. 44.]

Writ dated at Woodstock, 23 July, 33rd year (1249).

INQUISITION—if seven marcs of increment which were addition-ally imposed upon *(adaucte fuerunt)* the men of the manor of Esingwalde, come from three carucates of land which were the King's demesne, or not, and who now hold the land—made by William Haget, Richard Mansel, William de Galmethorp, Nicholas de Alne, William *le Estabiler*, Richard de Rivers *(Ripariis)*, John de Hoby, Robert de Raschelfe, Walter de Thormodby, Nicholas *fil' Ode*, Walter de Thouethorpe, and William de Lillinge, who say upon their oath that the seven marcs come wholly from three carucates of land which were the

Eland, secondly to Jenkinson, and she transferred all her interest in Mirfield to Sir John Wentworth, of North Elmsall, in exchange for the Manor of Dighton."

The following notes bear on the same subject :

King's Court at York on Tuesday next after the Octave of St. Martin, 4 John (1202). Final Agreement between Robert son of Ulric de Mirfeld, demandant, and William de Nevill and Amabel his wife and Richard the son of Wimund de Mirfeld, tenants, of a bovate of land in Mirfeld.

Close Rolls, 38 Hen. III. (1253-4), Mem : 15. Because the King hath received the homage of John de Heton, who married Joan, the fifth daughter and one of the heirs of Alex. de Nevill, for the fifth part of three knights' fees (de quintâ parte feodorum trium militum) which the same Alex[r] held of the King in chief, the King will not that by occasion of taking the lands which belonged to the said William into the King's hand and which he held of others than the King, they should detain from the aforesaid John and Joan the portion belonging to the same John and Joan by hereditary right, of the lands which the aforesaid Alex[r] held of others than the King in his bailiwick. Mandate to Thomas de Stamford, Escheator beyond Trent, to deliver to the said John and Joan full seisin of the right portion (rectâ porcione) belonging to the said Joan by hereditary right of the aforesaid Alexander's lands in Nuningetone and Mirefeld.

The following are from the *De Banco Rolls* :

Easter Term, 1 Edw. II. (1308). Mem : 126[d]. Ebor. Matilda, formerly wife of Adam de Hopton, claims in dower from Thomas de Mukton of Holand the third part of certain premises in Westheton, and from Thomas de Heton the third part of premises in Mirfield.

Trinity Term, 1 Edw. II. (1308). Mem : 108. Ebor. The same Matilda claims against Thomas de Burgh her dower of premises in Myrfelde, Lepton, and Walton, and Thomas, by his attorney, comes and says that Matilda, immediately after the death of the aforesaid Adam her husband, seized John his son and heir (whose wardship and marriage belonged to the same Thomas) and carried him off. And he (Thomas) says that if Matilda will return the heir to him he will give her her dower, &c.

Mem : 148. Ebor. Adam de Pontefract of Mirfeld claims against Adam the son of Robert Newmarshe *(de Novo Mercato)* that he keep the agreement made between them for lands, &c., in Mirfeld and Hopton.

There are several notes about Alexander de Nevill in Dodsworth's *Wapentake of Agbrigg (Yorkshire Archæological Journal*, vol. vii.).

[b] On 15 March, 1249-50, the Escheators for Lincolnshire are commanded to let his widow Matelcon' have a third part of his chattels (*Excerpta è Rotulis Finium*, vol. ii., p. 74.)

[a] See No. XII.

King's demesne in Esingwald, and not from other eight carucates which are of socage in the same town. Moreover they say that Roger Chaplain holds of the aforesaid three carucates, two bovates; Oda[a] daughter of Ralph *(Oda fil' Rad'i)* holds one; William son of Adam, one; William son of Hugh, two; Robert son of Ralph, one; Gerard Bosse, two; Ragenild daughter of Matilda *(Ragenild' fil' Matild')*, one; William son of Uctred, one; Adam son of William, one; Jordan son of Basil, one; Hugh son of Henry, one; Robert May, half; Reginald son of Richard, half; Robert Bonde, two; William son-in-law *(gen')* of Gamel, one; John Eem, one; Ralph Hert, one; William Kempe, one; Megge, Agnes, and Agnes, sisters, two; Alan son of Ingelot, one bovate.

XIX. EMERIC LE BUTILLER. *Extent.*

[33 HEN. III. No. 35].

Writ[b] dated at Chertsey, 16 Sept., 33rd year (1249).

EXTENT of the land which was of Emerik[c] in Kolton[d]. [No jurors' names.] There is a capital messuage and garden which are worth by the year 4*s.*; 36 acres of land in demesne (11*d.* the acre), 33*s.*; two acres and one rood of meadow, 4*s.* 6*d.*,; 9 bovates of land (7*s.* the bovate), 63*s.* There are two tofts worth 6*s.*, and two others worth 3*s.* by the year; one piece of land, worth 8*d.*, and another small piece, worth 4*d.* by the year. There is also rent in a windmill 4*s.* 5¼*d.*, and rent of three bushels of nuts,[e] worth yearly sixpence. Moreover in Apilton, land of the same Emeric in demesne, twelve acres (every acre 8*d.*), 8*s.* by the year. Sum, £6 7*s.* 5¼*d.*

ᵃ Perhaps Eda.

ᵇ The writ, addressed to the Sheriff of the County, directs that land in Colton to be extended which was of Emeric le Butiller by the King's gift *(extendi facias terram que fuit Emerici le Butiller* de dono nostri *in Colton).*

ᶜ Mr. Roberts reads the name " Endric vel Eudric " *(Cal. Gen.* vol. i., p. 23*)*. The *Calender Inq.-p. m.* has " Endricus." He was probably a son of Amauricus Pincerna or le Butiller, son of William Pincerna, who had lands in Nottinghamshire and Lincolnshire. Amauricus died about 1235, when the wardship of his land and heirs was granted to William Earl of Ferrars for £100 *(Excerpta è Rotulis Finium.* vol. i., pp. 251, 288).

ᵈ Colton and Nun Appleton, in the parish of Bolton Percy.

ᵉ Nuts were of more value than now. In 1242, Peter de Brus gave the Canons of Guisborough leave to gather nuts in his wood of Great Moorsholm *(Guisborough Chartulary.* vol. i., p. 117*)*.

3

XX. SIR THEOBALD LE BUTELLER. *Inq. p. m.*

[33 HEN. III. No. 49.]

Writ dated at Geytinton, 6 July, 33rd year (1249).

SCHEPLAY,[a] co. York. EXTENT made of the land of Sir *(d'ni)* Theobald *le Buteller*, in the town of Scheplay, on the eve of S. Matthew Apostle, 33 Hen. (20 Sept., 1249), by twelve men sworn, viz.: Adam son of John of Scheplay, Roger son of William of the same, Roger son of Thomas, Gilbert son of John, Henry son of John, William son of Wynfrid', Richard son of Thomas, Richard Milner, Hugh de Grena, Alan Coly, John son of Thomas, Thomas son of John. They say that in the said town is a capital messuage worth by the year 2s. There is no land in demesne, but one land called Rodes, worth by the year 20s. There are fourteen free tenants who hold 24 bovates of land and give *(dant)* for the same yearly £6; also nine cottars *(Cotarii)* who give 6s. 10d. One mill in common years is worth 20s. There is a small wood, the herbage and pasture of which are common to the said town of Scheplay, and the men there ought to have husbote and haybote [by the view][b] and livery of the foresters. The pannage of the wood is worth sometimes more, sometimes less, but this year 5s.

Sum of the whole extent, £8 13s. 10d.[c]

XXI. ROBERT LE MOYGNE, CHAPLAIN. *Ad quod damnum.*

[33 HEN. III. No. 12.]

Writ dated at Westminster, 7 Oct., 33rd year (1249).

INQUISITION—whether it would be to the damage of the city of York or not, if the King should grant to Robert le Moygne, chaplain, a certain lane called " Patricpol "[d] to enlarge his place in York ; and whether, in case of fire (which God forbid)

---

^a Shepley, in the parish of Kirkburton, Wapentake of Agbrigg.

^b Here the document is injured, but the context suggests the words supplied. " Et homines de predicta villa debent habere in predicto bosco Husbote et Haybote [per visum] et liberacionem forestar'," etc.

^c There are two extents made about the same time in co. Norfolk, by one of which it is found that the heir of the said Theobald is aged six years. There are also three extents of land in Lancashire. The custody of Theobald's lands in Ireland was committed to Peter de Bermingham by writ dated 5 Nov., 1248; and subsequently, for a fine of 3,000 marcs, the King granted the wardship of his land and heir to John fitzGeoffrey, Justice of Ireland, 21 January, 1250-1 *(Excerpta è Rotulis Finium*, vol. ii., pp. 44, 96 *)*.

^d *Patricpol*, Patrick pool, Old Swine-gate (Drake, p. 322).

breaking out, water for extinguishing it could as expeditiously be brought from elsewhere as by that lane—made by Hugh de Menthorpe, Walter his brother, Hobekin, Martin Butcher, Ralph the Seler, Jordan Goldsmith, Robert de Driffelde, Richard de Scelton *(Sceltona)*, John Scot *(de Scocia)*, Hugh de Clerevall', Roger Hayrun, and William de Ottelay, who say that the taking in *(opcuracio)* of that lane, called Patricpol, so far as the place of Robert le Moygne extends near it, is not to the damage of the city of York; because if fire chanced there *(in finibus illis)*, water could be as expeditiously brought by another lane, since this is so deep and unused that no one can pass through it.

XXII. RICHARD DE MARISCO. *Year and day.*

[33 HEN. III. No. 75.]

Writ dated at Westminster, 7 Oct., 33rd year (1249).

INQUISITION—whether eight acres and a half of land with the appurtenances in Oteringham, held by Richard *de Marisco*, who was hanged for the death of Matilda Halfkarl, his mother, have been in the King's hand for a year and day or not—made by William *le Vavasur*, Stephen de Colestainthorpe, Robert son of Walter, Richard de Holme, Stephen son of Gedric (or Godric) of Pahil,[a] Geoffrey son of Mariot of Halsam, Thomas de Meusum,[b] Simon de Meusum,[b] Stephen *le Brokur*, Stephen de Hoteringham, Philip de Rule,[c] and John son of the Chaplain of Wynestede, who say upon their oath that the said land was in the King's hand for a year and a day after the felony done by the aforesaid Richard, and that he held that land of William de Laceles.

XXIII. MICHAEL SON OF DENIS OF ELMESWELL. *Year and day.*

[33 HEN. III. No. 85.]

Writ dated at Westminster, 25 Oct., 33rd year (1249).

INQUISITION—whether one bovate of land and half a toft with the appurtenances in Garton[d] which Michael son of Denis

---

[a] Paull or Paghill. *Domesday*, Pagele and Paghel.

[b] A mistake for Neusum, now Newsham, in the parish of Wressle.

[c] Perhaps the modern Rowley, near Beverley.

[d] Garton-on-the-Wolds, near Emswell, in the parish of Great Driffield, from which the felon took his name.

(Dionis) of Elmeswell, who was outlawed for the death of
Roger de Elmeswell, held, have been in the King's hand for a
year and a day or not, and of whom Michael held the same
when he committed felony—made by Walter de Garton, Ralph
de Grendale, Marmeduke de Garton, Richard *le Ferur*, Peter
Pollard, Paulin de Garton, William de Hoton, William Gilot,
William de Cayton, Amfrey (Amfr') de Pokethorpe, Walter
Perunel, and Anselm de Thirnum, who say upon their oath, that
the said land and half-toft with the appurtenances in Garton'
have been in the King's hand for a year and a day, and that
Michael when outlawed, held the same of Joan daughter of
Denis *(fil' Dionisii)*, who is dead without issue, and that Adam
de Neusum married Elizabet, sister and heir of Joan ; and they
say that he committed felony at Christmas, 32 Henry (1247).

XXIV.   ROGER DE CLERE AND MATILDA HIS WIFE. *Inq. p. m.*

[34 HEN. III.   No. 44.]

Writ dated at Westminster, 6 Jan., 34th year (1249-50), and addressed to
Thomas de Stanford and his co-escheator in the county of York.

INQUISITION made at Pikeringe of the lands which were of
Sir Roger de Clere and Matilda his wife, before T. de
Stanford, Escheator of the King, and J. de Hamerton, his co-
escheator in the county of York, 34 Hen. son of John, by
William *Romanum*, Peter de Neville, William Malekake, John
de Neuton, Ralph de Loket[on], John de Alvestan, William de
Alvestan, Robert de Karbi, Thomas son of Adam of Pikering,
William Archebaud, Robert son of Walter of Thornet[on],
John Campiun of the same, sworn, who say that Sir Roger de
Clere and Matilda *(Matildis)* his wife held nothing in chief or
otherwise of the King in the County of York or elsewhere to
their knowledge *(ut sciunt)*, but said Roger held a moiety of
the manor of Brumelay " *in Com' de Ledred' juxta London'*,"[a] of
the inheritance of the lady Matilda his wife, but by what service
they know not.   He held of his own inheritance on the day of
his death one bovate of land in Sivelington,[b] of lord Roger

---

[a] In 1223 homage was taken of John, son and heir of Ralph de Fay, for one
knight's fee which he held of the King at Bromlegh in Surrey *(Excerpta è Rotulis
Finium,* vol. i., p. 102).   *Ledred'* is Leatherhead, co. Surrey.

[b] Sinnington near Pickering.   Matilda, wife of Roger de Clere, was a daughter
of Ralph de Fay, and eldest sister and co-heiress of John de Fay *(Ibid.,* vol. i., pp.
102, 352).   Their grand-daughter, Alice, named above, married Richard de Breuse
or Braiosa, who in 1272, together with his wife, entered into an agreement with
the Nuns of Yeddingham about service at the Chapel of St. Michael of Sinnington
(Dodsworth MSS., xcv., 31[b]).

Bigot, the King's Marshal, by knight's service, and that land is worth by the year 5s. He had one daughter and heir named Agathea, whom William *le Rus* married, and begat on her one daughter, Alice by name, who is heir to him and Matilda his wife, and she is now, as they believe, aged two years and more.

Moreover, the said Roger and Matilda his wife at some time held in demesne, as the inheritance of Roger de Clere, five carucates of land in Sivelington, of lord Roger le Bigot, by knight's service, every carucate by the year 40s. Sum, £10. They had also service of two carucates in the town of Mart[on],[a] that is to say, foreign service only, and this of the fee of lord Roger le Bigot; and held at some time of the same fee in the town of Wilton[b] six carucates by knight's service, every carucate by the year £4. Sum, £24.

They formerly held in demesne, of the fee of the Earl of Albemarle, two carucates and two bovates in the town of Edestone,[c] by knight's service, every carucate by the year 40s. Sum, £4 10s.

The said Roger de Clere gave and sold all the lands beforenamed, so that he retained in his own hand or had nothing save only that bovate of land before mentioned in the town of Sivelington.[d]

XXV. THE KING *v.* THE ABBOT OF CITEAUX ABOUT PROPERTY AT SCARBOROUGH.

[34 HEN. III. No. 37.]

Writ dated at Oxford, 3 June, 34th year (1250).

INQUISITION made, concerning eight messuages with the appurtenances claimed by the King as his demesne from the Abbot of Citeaux in Scardeburge, by William Malecake, Peter de Nevile, Thomas de Edbristone, William son of William Malecake, Richard de Angotebi, Ralph son of Peter of Roston, Robert de Haulay, Ralph .... ton, John de Neuton, William de Morpathe, Adam de Rouceby, and Richard *le Paumer* of

[a] Marton, in the parish of Sinnington.

[b] Wilton, in the parish of Ellerburn, four miles from Pickering.

[c] Edston, near Kirkby Moorside.

[d] By another writ, dated at Clarendon, 20 Dec., 34th year (1249), and addressed to Henry de Wengham and his co-escheator in the County of Surrey, an extent was made of the land of Matilda de Clere, which showed that she held of the King in chief a moiety of the Manor of Bromle, by the service of one knight's fee and a half. The jurors found that Alice, daughter of William le Rus, whom he had by Agatha his wife, daughter of Matilda, was her heir, and aged two years.

Aton, who being sworn, say that the Abbot holds eight messuages with the appurtenances which the King claims against
him as his demesne, where the capital messuage of the Abbot is
situate, and he renders to the King yearly in the name of
gabelage sixpence. The said eight messuages, while they were
separate, yielded to the King in gabelage by the year 3s. 10d. ;
but now, as they are included in one messuage, they ought,
according to the custom of the borough, to yield in the name of
one gabelage *(nomine unius Gabulagii)* sixpence ; for the custom
of the borough is such, that if any burgess inclose in one eight
messuages or more yielding gablage severally, he shall yield one
gablage only, that is 6d. As to how much the King would lose
in rents, services, &c., by granting to the Abbot the eight messuages appears by the aforesaid. As to the pleas which the
Abbot holds in his court of Scardeburg' they are worth by the
year 4s. As to how long the Abbot and his predecessors have
held those pleas, they say that they have done so from the time
that King Richard enfeoffed them of the church of the said
borough.

XXVI. JOHN DE WALKINGHAM. *Inq. p. m.*
[35 HEN. III. No. 62.]
Writ dated at Clarendon, 12 Dec., 35th year (1250).

INQUISITION made of the lands which were of John de Walkingham,[a] in the County of York, on Thursday, the morrow
of S. Paul, 35 Henry (26 Jan., 1250-1), before Thomas de Stanforde.

Names of the jurors—Nicholas de Burton, Gerard Clerk,
Ralph de Scotton, Robert de Hopton, Roger (or Richard)
de Bosco, Peter de Burton, Robert de Midilton, Adam de
Feringeby, Adam *del Tentur*, Adam *de Tolus*, Laurence son of
Laurence, William Kaym.

John de Walkingham held in chief of the King in the town
of Givildale[b] by service of serjeanty, three carucates and a half
of land, one small watermill, and two tofts, which yield by the
year in all issues of the land £4 0s. 7d *(preter partem domine)*,
saving the share of the lady [for dower]. Sum, £4 0s. 7d.

He also held the manor of Walkingham[c] of the Earl
Richard in the Honour of Cnarisburge, where there are in
demesne, beside the third part of the lady, ninety-six acres, one
rood, and two parts of one rood of arable land (acre 6d.). Sum,
48s. 2½d.

ᵃ Wokingham in the writ.   ᵇ Givendale, near Ripon.

ᶜ Walkingham Hill, between Knaresborough and Boroughbridge.

There are three acres of poor *(debilis)* meadow (acre 8*d.*), 2*s.*; a curtilage and garden with herbage, worth by the year 6*s.* 8*d.* In villenage six bovates and two parts of one bovate of land (bovate 5*s.* 3½*d.*), 35*s.* 3*d.* Two cottars pay yearly 4*s.* A watermill there is worth by the year 26*s.* 8*d.* Sum of the extent,[a] £6 2*s.* 9½*d.* Sum of the whole, £10 3*s.* 4½*d.*

John de Walkingham, son of the said John, is his next heir and nearly eighteen years old. He is in ward to the Earl Richard.[b]

XXVII. EMMA WASTHOSE[c]. *Inq. p. m.*

[35 HEN. III. No. 42.]

Writ wanting.

INQUISITION made by Thomas de Stanford at York, on Monday after the Octave of the Purification B.V.M. 35th year (13 Feb., 1250-1).

Names of Jurors—John de Clif, Hugh de Mar, John son of William of Berley, Roger *le Wowere* of Hatheleshay, John de Ackewrde, John *le Fraunkeleyn* of Duffelde, Ithelard de Snayth, Roger de Arnenest of Duffeude, Roger de Birum, William son of Simon of Snaith, Adam de Bladewrthe, and Hugh son of Alan of Poulington.

They say upon their oath that a certain knight named Rodes, who had Emma Wasthose to wife, and the same Emma held of the King in chief in the soke of Snayth, by the service of serjeanty of one haubergeon *(haubergoni)* in the King's army, a tenement of her inheritance, of which an ancestor of hers was enfeoffed by a former King, ancestor of the now King, which tenement was afterwards a pure escheat of the now King on account of a certain trespass done by the said Rodes and Emma.

---

[a] In every item the words "preter partem domine."

[b] Richard, Earl of Cornwall, brother of Henry III., elected King of the Romans in 1256.

[c] According to the *Whitby Chartulary* (vol. i., pp. 125, 126), she married Henry de Ormesby, who joined with her in giving half a carucate of land in Filingdales to that Abbey. The knight named Rodes must have been her second husband. Emma, daughter of Alan Wasthose, and Ralph her husband, a servant of King John, confirmed a gift her father had made to the Priory of Drax of an oxgang of land at Folkerby, a toft, the men who dwelt upon it, with their families, and free passage over the river Dun *(History of Hemingburgh,* p. 213*).* The lands of Ralph de Rodes were ordered to be taken into the King's hand on 25 July, 1241, and on 4 Sept. following, the Sheriff of Nottinghamshire was ordered to restore the lands Ralph held in his bailiwick, to Gerard de Rodes, his son and heir *(Excerpta è Rotulis Finium,* vol. i., pp. 349, 352*).*

Subsequently, the King of his grace granted to Emma after the death of her husband that she might hold the said tenement in Snaith for her life, so that after her death it should be a pure escheat of the King to do therewith as it pleased him.

The said Emma has nothing in demesne of the tenement aforesaid, but the whole is worth in rents, services, and other things, by the year £8 3s. 9½d.

XXVIII. OF WASTE DONE IN SNAITH AND COWICK BY JOHN TALEBOT AND GERARD HIS BROTHER.

[35 HEN. III. No. 19.]

Writ tested by R. de Thurkelby, at Wodestoke, 10 July, 35th year (1251).

INQUISITION,[a] what damages Edmund de Lacy had by reason of the waste, sale, and removal *(exilii)* made by John Talebot and Gerard his brother,[b] in the houses and woods which they had of the King's demise and grant, being of the inheritance of the said Edmund in Snayt[c] and Kuwyke, made by Sir Richard de Berlay, Alan de Smytheton, Stephen de Lyours, William Scorthebous, Eudo de Sutton, Adam Paynel, Thomas *ad stangnum de Smythetona*, William de Goldale, Peter of Kuwyc moor *(de Mora de Kuwyc)*, Hilary *(Ilarium)* de Snayt, Ranulf Godnese, and James de Hesele, who, being sworn, say upon their oath that the said John and Gerard Talebot made waste of two houses in Kuwyke to the damage and disherison *(exheredacionem)* of the said Edmund of one marc of silver; also of fifty-seven oaks (4s. the oak), £11 8s.; thirty-nine young oaks (12d.), 39s.; nineteen *(pomariis boscy)*[d] crabtrees (4d.), 6s. 4d.; forty-nine ash-trees (6d.), 24s. 6d.; fifteen white-thorns (½d.), 7½d. Sum of the damage, £15 11s. 9½d.

---

a The Inquisition is not dated, but the Sheriff was commanded to send it to the King's Justices at Westminster in fifteen days from Michaelmas (*i.e.*, 13 Oct., 1251). This, no doubt, was done.

b On 22 April, 1258, the King pardoned Gerard Talebot ten marcs, which John brother of the same Gerard owed the King for a loan, and which the King had given him for the exequies and burial of William de Abetot, Gerard's kinsman, who had been slain long before in the King's service at the siege of the castle of Ewyas in Wales *(Excerpta è Rotulis Finium, vol. ii., p. 276)*.

c " Snaythe " and " Cowyke " in the writ.

d Compare " pomme de bois," a crab or wilding (Cotgrave).

XXIX. ROGER DE MUBRAY. *Ad q. d.*

[35 HEN. III. No. 14.]

Writ of the King dated at Havering, 24 Aug., 35th year (1251), and directed to Thomas de Stanforde and his co-escheator in Co. York. Inquiry to be made how much the Wapentake of Ewcross, which Alice de Stavele held of the King to farm, is worth by the year. What barons, magnates, and knights owe suit to the same Wapentake. If it would be to the damage or advantage of the King to let it to farm to Roger de Mumbray.

INQUISITION made by twelve lawful men of the Wapentake of Yucros, viz.: Ralph de Depedale, Richard *de Burg*', Adam de Stagheside, Richard Clerk of Horton, Walter de Milleburne, Walter de Loukelandes, Adam de Twyselton, John de Mirewra, William de Bentham, William de Clapeham, Adam Grenehed, and John de Siggeswike, who, being sworn, say that the said Wapentake is worth by the year with all issues, twenty marcs, and scarcely so much. They say also that lord[a] Roger de Mubray, Sir Henry fitz Ranulf *(d'n's Henr' fil' Rann'),* Sir[a] John de Cancefeud, and all free tenants of the same Wapentake, that is to say, of nine towns, owe suit to the same, viz. at the next court after Michaelmasday only, and not more. It is rather to the advantage than to the loss of the King that the Wapentake be demised to lord Roger de Mubray to farm, and especially at such rate, because it is very dear *(et maxime ad talem firmam quia valde cara est).*

XXX. ADA DE BALLIOL.[b] *Inq. p. m.*

[35 HEN. III. No. 51.]

Writ dated at Guildford, 16 Sept., 35th year (1251).

INQUISITION made before the Escheator of the County of York by Walter de Staynesby, William de Mubray, Richard de Waussand, John de Normanneby, John de Pothou, Simon *le Bret*, Roger de Sturmy, Thomas de Hurthewrde, William de Piketon, Robert de Skutherskelf, Thomas de Salecoke, Elias

[a] The prefix is " dominus."

[b] Daughter of Hugh de Balliol and grand-daughter of Bernard de Balliol. Her brother John founded, in 1263, Baliol College, Oxford. She married John Fitz Robert, third Baron of Warkworth. In 2 Henry III., he obtained a charter for a fair in his manor of Stokesley, to be held yearly on the festival (Dec. 29), of St. Thomas the Martyr. Sheriff of Northumberland, 1224 to 1227. Died 1240. Their eldest son, Roger Fitz John, became the fourth Baron of Warkworth and was ancestor of the Clavering family. The two younger sons, Hugh and Robert, assumed the name of Eure, and from them were respectively descended the Lords Eure and the Eures of Belton and Washingborough, Co. Lincoln (Foster's *Visitations of Yorkshire*, p. 609).

de Marroil, who say upon their oath that lord Hugh de Balloil gave the manor of Stokesley with the appurtenances to Ada his daughter in frank marriage, and that she after the death of her husband enfeoffed Hugh and Robert her sons of the said manor with appurtenances, on Sunday before the feast of Saint Barnabas Apostle, 34 Henry (5 June, 1250). They were in full seisin as of fee from the said day to three weeks after the feast of S. Michael in the same year (20 October, 1250), so that each of them appointed a new steward and reeves for keeping his share, and deposing the said lady's steward and reeves, held courts for the time aforesaid and received amercements from many persons. They took homages of freemen and farm at the term of S. John Baptist, also multure of mill; they sold part of a meadow and caused the other part to be carried, they had corn reaped in autumn and carried. In all other things they did as their own up to three weeks after the feast of Saint Michael, when they delivered the manor to their mother to farm to hold for her life, yielding to them (Hugh and Robert) forty shillings yearly, with remainder after her death to themselves and their heirs for ever.

Also they say that the said lady Ada died at Stokesley, on Saturday after the feast of S. James Apostle, in the 35th year (29 July, 1251), as farmer of the said Hugh and Robert. Their attorneys put themselves in seisin of the manor after the death of the lady and before she was buried, and on the morrow after her burial, Hugh came and entered in his own name and that of his brother and held seisin . . . .[a] until he was expelled through the King's letters by the whole country who came with the Sheriff and Escheators . . . .[a] Bartholomew in the same year (August, 1251).[b]

XXXI. WALTER BISET. *Inq. p. m.*
[36 HEN. III. No. 58.]
Writ dated at Wallingeforde, 30 Oct., 36th year (1251).

INQUISITION made before Thomas de Stanforde, Escheator, William de Harun and Robert Ingram, Coroners of the County of York, concerning the manor of Ulvington.[c]

Names of the jurors—Gerard de Manefelde, Alan de Laton, Laurence de Girlington, Henry de Laton, Geoffrey de Karleton,

[a] The document is here torn.

[b] Accompanying the above is an extent of lands and tenements which were of Ada de "Bayloł" in the County of Northumberland, and held in dower as well as by marriage. The King's writ is dated at Windsor, 8 Sept., 35th year (1251).

[c] Ovington on the Tees. *Domesday*, Ulfeton.

William de Appleby, Roger de Melsaneby, William of the same, John *le Norreys*, Geoffrey de Caudewelle, Richard de Scirewithe, John son of Peter of Dalton.

They say upon their oath that Walter Biset was seised in fee of the manor of Ulvington with the appurtenances for many years in his lifetime; but they do not know if he was seised or not at the time of his death, because they neither know, nor can know, the day of his decease, for he died far away in Scotland, in an island called Araan. Some say that he died at vespers on Tuesday before, others on Tuesday after Michaelmas-day,[a] but the certainty is not yet known. On Tuesday before Michaelmas-day there came a messenger from Walter Biset to Ulvington with letters patent of his lord, directed to Gerard de Boghes, his bailiff there, in which it was contained : that Walter had given to Thomas Biset, his nephew, his manor of Ulvington with the appurtenances, and that Gerard should put him in full seisin of the manor. But Gerard was not found in those parts, for he had taken his journey to the Court [for the hearing] of a plea which he had before the King *(coram domino Rege)* in eight days of S. Michael; and he not being found, the messenger showed the letters to many of the country of Ulvington, and waited the return of Gerard, who came back from the Court on the Sunday following a fortnight from Michaelmas-day. Having received and inspected those letters, he (Gerard) said he dared not by them give seisin of the manor to any one without seeing the said Thomas in his proper person. Notwithstanding, he consented that Thomas Biset's attorney should stay there together with Walter Biset's reeve until he should hear further. On the Friday following, that is to say, in three weeks after Michaelmas-day (Oct. 20), Thomas Biset came to Ulvington and lodged there. Immediately before dinner he sent for Gerard, Walter Biset's bailiff, who was at the next town, and demanded of him the seisin for which he had warrant by his lord's letters patent. Then, two free men, one villain, and the reeve of the town being at once called together, Gerard gave him seisin, saving the right of every one, and straightway departed.

The said Thomas stated that his uncle was then in good health, and he received from the reeve his uncle's farm for Whitsuntide term last, and likewise the tallage laid in his uncle's time, which the reeve had yet in his hands and custody. So with the said money he went away. Soon after a rumour being heard in the County of York that Walter was dead, the King's Escheators came thither and seized the manor into the King's hand; and they yet hold it.

[a] In 1251, Michaelmas (29 Sept.) fell on a Friday, so the Tuesday before would be Sept. 26, and the Tuesday after Oct. 3.

XXXII. As to Customs in the Woods of Pickering
Forest in the time of King John.

[35 Hen. III. No. 58.]

Writ dated at Westminster, 13 May, 35th year (1251).

INQUISITION made at Pikeringe, on Monday after the Epiphany, 36 Henry son of John (8 Jan., 1251-2), before Sir Geoffrey de Langele, Justice of the forest, by the King's command—as to what commons and for what kind of cattle the men of the King's demesne in Pikeringe, were wont to have of right in the woods of Pikeringe forest in the time of King John, that is to say, in the year before war broke out between him and his barons; what easements they had of right in the said woods, and what customs and services they did to the King for having such easements—made by the oath of Peter de Nevile, Thomas de Edbreston, Roger Moraynt (or Moraunt), Ralph [son] of Peter of Roston, Richard *le Brun*, John *le Chaumpiun*, William son of Robert of Roston, John de Alverstane, Bartholomew de Scalleby, Richard de Berg', John de Hagwrdingham, and William de Habeton, who say upon their oath that the men of the King's demesne of Pikeringe in the year before the war broke out between King John and his barons, had common of pasture for all kinds of cattle save goats. in all the King's woods appertaining to the manor of Pikeringe (except the Hay of Blaundeby and the Hay of Daleby with their vallies, which do not appertain to the manor), and mast *(pessonem)* for their hogs without rendering pannage. As to easements, they had green and dead wood *(viride et mortuum boscum)* for husbote by livery of the foresters, and dry wood *(siccum)* without livery for burning (which woods are now wasted) ; and in other woods appertaining to the manor (except the Hay of Blaundeby and the Hay of Daleby with vallies), haybote and walling *(walluram)* for their houses, and "harz" for their ploughs, and enclosure *(clausturam)* for the hedges round their field, by view and livery of the foresters, and drywood lying on the ground *(siccum per terram jacentem)* with drywood which they could knock down by crooks *(cum sicco quod potuerunt prosternere per crocos)*. All these things they had by the will of the King and by the sufferance of the bailiffs of the forest without other right.

As to customs and services which they did for having the aforesaid, they used to give to the foresters for every bovate of land one halfpenny every year, when the foresters made livery to them for making their hedges.

XXXIII. AS TO CUSTOMS IN THE WOODS OF GALTRES
FOREST IN THE TIME OF KING JOHN.

[35 HEN. III. No. 43.]

Writ dated at Westminster, 30 May, 35th year (1250).

INQUISITION made at Sutton,[a] on Monday after the Epiphany,
36 Hen. son of John (8 Jan., 1251-2), before Sir Geoffrey de
Langele, Justice of the forest, as to what commons and for what
kind of cattle the men of the King's demesne in Esingwald and
Hoby used to have of right in the King's forest of Gautris, in
the time of the late King John, in the year before war broke out
between him and his barons, and what easements by right they
had of taking vert and dry wood *(de viridi et sicco capiend')* in
the King's demesne woods in the said forest, what customs and
services they did to the King or his bailiffs for such commons
and easements, by the oath of Thomas de Colevile, Simon de
Lillinge, Nicholas de Routheclive, and Richard de Thorner,
verderers. also of Robert Chaumbard, Gervase de Routheclive,
William de Lillinge, Tebin de Syupton,[b] Ralph *de Camera*, Marmaduke Darel, Robert *le Despenser*, Stephen son of Clement of
Sutton, William *le Stabeler*, Peter son of Everard, Richard
Plaice, and William de Galmetorpe, who say that the men of
Esingwald and Hoby in the time of King John were wont to
have common for oxen and cows, horses and mares, and for their
hogs the whole year except in the fence month *(in mense vetito)*,
so that they rendered for every hog *(porco)* over a year old, one
penny yearly for pannage whether the King's woods were agisted
or not, and for a hog under a year old a half-penny, or a tithe
pig *(decimum porcum)* in the name of pannage, at the will and
choice of the agistors. The said men at the time aforesaid
never had, and they ought not to have of right, common for
their sheep *(bidentes)* or goats *(capras)* within the covert of the
forest. Nor at any time used they to take or have any vert
(virid') in the forest for husbote, or even for building new
houses, when the towns of Esingwald and Hoby by misadventure
were burnt, as many times happened, without the special command of the King or of his Justice, or for making or repairing
their hedges, unless they gave to the King's bailiffs of their own
(de suo), which very often they did in the time of King John,
as well as in the time of the lord Henry now King.

---

[a] Sutton-on-the-Forest, and Huby in that parish.
[b] Probably Shipton, in the parish of Overton.

XXXIV. CONCERNING A PETITION OF PETER DE
MAULEY TO HAVE LANDS TO FARM.

[36 HEN. III. No. 47.]

Writ dated at York, 8 Jan., 36th year (1251-2), and directed to Geoffrey de
Langele, Justice of the King's forest, that Peter de Mauley *(Malo lacu)*
had petitioned that the whole wood and moor in Wheldale,[a] which the
King had demanded against him, and which Peter had then rendered
as the King's right, should be granted in fee-farm to him. Inquiry to
be made as to the annual value of the wood and moor, etc.

Another writ, also dated at York, but on the sixth of January, in the same
year, and directed to the same Geoffrey, commanding him to inquire if
it would be to the King's loss if he were to grant the forty acres of moor
and wood in Weldale, lately rendered to the King as his right, to Peter
de Mauley to farm *(ad firmam)*.

INQUISITION made at Pikeringe, on Thursday next after the
Epiphany, 36 Henry (11 Jan., 1251-2), before Sir Geoffrey
de Langele, Justice of the forest, by the oath of Peter de
Neville, Thomas de Edbricton, Roger Morant, Ralph son of
Peter of Rouston, Richard *le Brun*, John *le Chaumpiun*, John
de Alvesteyn, William son of Robert of Ruston, William de
Morpathe, William de Habeton, Bartholomew de Scalleby,
Ralph de Loketon, and Hugh de Loketon, who say that the
wood and moor in Wheldale, before Geoffrey de Langele and
his fellow Justices in eyre, at their last hearing of pleas of the
forest at York, were found by the oath of foresters, verderers,
regarders, and thirty-six knights, to be the proper demesne and
forest of the King, and not of Peter de Mauley as he said.
They contain five hundred acres and more, as it seems to them
by estimation, which are enclosed by these metes and bounds,
namely : as the sike which descends from Shonerhom as far as
the beck *(rivulum)* of Welledale, and to the place where it falls

---

[a] Wheeldale is a piece of high moorland immediately to the south of the
parish of Egton. Shonerhom the starting point of the boundaries, called in the
Guisbrough Chartulary (vol. i., p. 104) Senerhou, and now Shunner Howe, is a
tumulus, where the boundaries of the parishes of Glaisdale, Egton, and Rosedale
meet. The next point, proceeding in an easterly direction. is the beck of Welledale, the stream flowing along the Wheeldale Gill, which falls into the Murk Esk.
Here the boundary must go south, as it ascends the Gaytskilhewicbeke, apparently
the modern Wheeldale Beck, to Blawath, and then up a runnel or sike called Aykesike, probably the modern Blawath Beck, to a large stone standing on Huntereshuses, from whence it goes by a high ridge called Waldalerig, now Wardle Rigg,
as far as Flathou, possibly the tumulus at Brown Howe, then westwards to a stone,
which seems lost, and by a dike coming to Snouerou, probably wrongly written
for Shonerhou, the starting point. The amount contained in these boundaries is
far more than five hundred acres, more like two thousand. Waldalerig may be the
rapidly rising ground on the west side of the Wheeldale and Rutmoor Becks, as
the modern Wardle Rigg seems too far to the south. Hunt House, near the junction
of the Wheeldale Gill and Wheeldale Beck, preserves a reminiscence of Huntereshuses. Has Gaytskilhewicbeke anything to do with Gale Hill Rig, or does it refer
to the Roman road, which still exists on the east of Wheeldale?

into Mirke Eske, and ascending the length of the beck called Gaytskilhewicbeke and up to the place called Blawath, and so by the sike *(siketum)* called Aykesike up to the stone standing upon Huntereshuses, and so from the said stone by a high ridge called Waldalerig as far as Flathou, and so to the stone standing towards the West, and thence to the dike which descends from Snouerou *(sic)*, and falls into the beck called Wheldalebec, where it began.

They say also that the said wood and moor are worth by the year in all issues, as in herbage, pannage, and other things, ten marcs; as they understand: and it would be to the King's advantage if he were to commit them in fee-farm to Peter de Mauley for the said ten marcs, so that the wood and moor remain forest of the King, and within regard as used of old time.

Those forty acres which the King demanded, and which Peter rendered to the King as his right, are contained within the five hundred, and it would not be to the advantage *(commodum)* of the King to commit to him the forty acres unless the whole wood and moor were also committed, because by entering those forty acres he would have easement of the whole residue of wood and moor, and the King would have no profit therefrom. Moreover, they say that half of the five hundred acres is covered with wood, part good, part indifferent.

XXXV.   RALPH DE BOLBEKE.   *Inq. p. m.*

[36 HEN. III. No. 36.]

Writ dated at Windsor, 7 April, 36th year (1252), and directed to Thomas de Stanford, Escheator.

INQUISITION concerning the lands which Ralph de Bolbeke, forester of the fee of Pikering, held in chief of the King and of others in Levestham, Loketon, Scalleby, and elsewhere in the County of York, made at Levesȝham, on Monday before the feast of S. Mark Evangelist, 36 Henry (22 April, 1252), by Ralph de Loketon, John the younger of Neuton, John de Hagwrdingham, Walter son of Jordan of Rouceby, Everard son of Robert of Neuton, Hugh de Loketon, Adam de Rouceby, Robert de Kareby, Yon *(Yonem)* de Aslageby,[a] Richard Boye of the same, Peter de Saldene, Robert Clerk son of Ralph de Kintorp, who say upon their oath that the said Ralph de Bolbeke held in chief of the King, six bovates of land in the town of

[a] Amongst the Jurors of No. LI. is a Eudo de Aslakeby, who may be the same person as the above-named Yon de Aslageby.

Leves3ham, in the socage *(in socagio)* of Pikering (bovate 5*s.*), for which he paid yearly to the King 18*s.* 8*d.* He held of the fee of the Earl of Albemarle in the same, twenty bovates (bovate 5*s.*), yielding foreign service to the Earl and to the King for fine of the wapentake 2*s.* 6*d.*, and of the same fee other six bovates which free men held of the said Ralph for 18*s.* 7*d.* yearly. In cottage also there 9*s.* 4½*d.* The mill of Leves3ham is worth by the year ten marcs, and a meadow there 32*s.* The whole baili-wick of the King's forest which he had, is worth yearly 100*s.*, of which he paid to the King at the Exchequer four marcs. He had of free rents one pound of pepper and one pound and a half of cumin *(cimini).* He was patron of the church, worth by the year eight marcs, of which Robert le Bel is rector by his gift. His wife has not yet had dower of the lands, rents, and other things abovesaid. He had a brother named Osebert, who is his next heir and of full age, but where he is now, or in what country, the jurors know not.

INQUISITION made before Robert de Creppinge, Sheriff of Yorkshire, by William Malecake the elder, Peter de Nevile, Thomas de Edbriston, William Malecake the younger, John de Alvestain, William his brother, William son of Robert of Roston, Ralph son of Peter of the same, Richard *le Brun* of Thorneton, Robert son of Walter of the same, John Campiun of the same, and Adam de Rouceby, who say upon their oath that Ralph de Bollebec held in the town of Levesham, of the King in chief, six bovates of land with the appurtenances, and his capital messuage of socage of the King *(de socagio domini Regis)* of Pik[ering] by service of 16*s.* yearly (every bovate 6*s.* 8*d.*), 40*s.* He held also of the Earl of Albemarle 25 bovates of land and one water-mill in Levesham. Every bovate is worth by the year 6*s.* 8*d.*, and the mill, ten marcs. He held of the same Earl in Loketon 16 bovates, doing to him for the lands and mill in Levesham, as well as the lands in Loketon, the service of a fourth part of one knight's fee, where twenty caru-cates make one fee. Every bovate in Loketon is worth yearly 5*s.* Sum of lands and mill held of the Earl, £19.

The same Ralph held in Scalleby of bondage of the King *(de bondagio domini Regis)*, four bovates (bovate 5*s.*), 20*s.* by the year.

Osbert de Bolbec, brother of Ralph, is his next heir, aged thirty years and more.[a]

---

[a] By an inquisition taken in the county of Lincoln, mention is made of dower held by " Elena," mother of Ralph de Bulebeke; and his brother and heir, Osbert, is here said to be forty years old. *"Item dicunt [quod] Osbertus frater predicti Rad' est propinquior heres et est etatis xl. annorum."* See No. XLIII.

XXXVI. CONCERNING PHILIPPA DE TILLY, AND THE
MANOR OF MELTON (OR MEAUTON).[a]

[36 HEN. III. No. 56.]

Writ dated at Windsor, 15 June, 36th year (1252), and directed to Thomas
de Stanford, Escheator, commanding him to take with him the bailiff
of Tikehull, and to have extents made of the manor of Upton, co.
Nottingham, and of the manor of Meauton, co. York.

INQUISITION of Methylton, made at Meauton, before Thomas
de Stanford, and Ivo, Constable of Tikhile. Names of the
jurors—Robert de Wikerley, knight, Robert Bastarde, William
de Wintewrde, Jordan de Mar, Alexander de Stolkebrigge,
Richard de Lanweder, Otho *(Oto)* de Waddewrde, Robert de
Ryhil, Walter de Herlington, Otho *(Oto)* de Athewyke, Hugh
de Wythor[es], Henry Aubur of Mekesburge.

A moiety of Meauton is the inheritance of the son and heir
of Roger de Cressy, who is in ward to the lord Edward, the
King's son, by reason of the Honour of Tikhil, to which the said
wardship appertains. The other moiety of the manor was of
the lady Philippa de Tilhy, who died about the feast of S. Peter
in the chair, in the 32nd year of the now King (22 Feb., 1247-8),
and had sons and daughters who live in Normandy,[b] and are not
lieges of the King, wherefore the land is the King's escheat, and
appertains to the Honour of Tikhil, which lord Edward has of
the King's gift, nor is there any one who has any right in that
moiety.

There are in the said moiety in demesne six-score acres
of arable land (acre 6½d.), 65s.; six bovates and a half in bondage (bovate 9s.), 58s. 6d. The court *(curia)* with houses and
garden is worth by the year 5s. The issues and herbage of the
little wood *(bosculi)* appertaining to the moiety are worth in
common years 20s. There are five free men who hold five
bovates and a half, and they render yearly for all 19s. 6d., and
do foreign service. Also William de Stanton holds two bovates
by doing foreign service only. Sum of the aforesaid moiety,
which was of the said lady Philippa, £8 8s.

---

[a] See No. xv.

[b] By another Inquisition taken at Upton, co. Nottingham, it is found in like
manner that the lady Philippa de Tilly, died on the feast of S. Peter in the chair,
32 Hen. (22 Feb., 1247-8), leaving sons and daughters who live in Normandy. The
land in Upton is therefore an escheat of the King, and appertains to the Honour
of Tikhull, which the lord Edward has of the King's gift, and there is no other who
has any right in the said land.

5

XXXVII. CONCERNING LIBERTIES CLAIMED BY PETER OF
SAVOY AND HIS BAILIFFS IN RICHMONDSHIRE.ᵃ

[36 HEN. III. No. 14.]

Writ dated at Hertford, 23 Sept., 36th year (1252).

INQUISITION made by Robert Chaumbard, Robert de Sprox-
ton, Roger de Neusum, William de Barton, Richard *de
Camera*, Stephen de Katton, William de Skippton, William de
Karleton, John de Frytheby, William Boniface, John de Caum-
pedene, William de Lillinge, William de Rydal, and John de
Hoby, who, being sworn, say that the bailiffs of the lord P[eter]
of Savoy will not permit the King's bailiffs to enter within the
limits of Richemondskyre to do anything which appertains to
the King, nor will they permit any one of Richemondskyre to
come before the Sheriff or his bailiffs to execute the King's
command beyond the limits of the same place. Also they will
not do anything unless they have the original writ of the King
just as sent to the Sheriff of Yorkshire ; and that if it be written
to any one of Richemondskyre by writ of right "that he shall
hold full right to the demandant, and unless he do so, the Sheriff
shall do it," and the default of court of him to whom it is written
shall be sufficiently proved, they will not make that summons,
unless the original writ of right first come in the court of
Richem', just as in a county *(sicut et in Comit').*ᵇ

Also they say that the said lord Peter has appropriated,
and yet appropriates to himself, one wapentake which is within
the limits of Richemondskyre, and used to appertain to the
County of York, namely, the Wapentake of Bulemer.

Moreover they plead all pleas usual in the county of York,
as well of withernam *(nami vetito)* as others.

ᵃ Peter de Dreux, Earl of Richmond, having forfeited his Earldom for adherence
to the King of France, the Honour or County of Richmond was given by King
Henry to Peter of Savoy, uncle to Queen Eleanor. The patent, 1 May, 1241, did
not express the grant of an Earldom. He died 1268, and in pursuance of a power
given to him by the King, 1262, bequeathed the Honour to Queen Eleanor ; and
it was not until the Queen had accepted an annuity of 2,000 marcs, that the King
was enabled to grant the Earldom to John de Dreux, son of Peter de Dreux, in
July, 1268 (Courthope). See No. LXXVIII.

ᵇ Dicunt eciam quod [si] scribatur alicui de Richem'skyre per breve de recto,
quod petenti plenum rectum teneat, et nisi fecerit (fec') Vicecomes faciat, et defalta
curie ipsius cui scribitur sufficienter fuerit probata, illam summonicionem nolunt
facere, nisi breve de recto originale prius veniat in curia de Richem' sicut et in
Comitatu. The bailiffs claim, in effect, that Richmondshire is an independent
county, of which they are the Sheriffs.

XXXVIIa. ROBERT FITZ MILDRED.[a]

[37 HEN. III. No. 53.]

THE manors of Raskell and Sutton, and lands, etc., in Ethe-
richewerke, Skett, and Askmundby.

XXXVIII. CONCERNING LANDS IN KINTHORP, SUPPOSED
TO BE OF THE KING'S SERJEANTY OF PICKERING.

[37 HEN. III. No. 20.]

Writ dated at Chertsey, 23 Oct., 36th year (1252).

INQUISITION whether six bovates of land with the appurtenances in Kinthorp,[b] whereof .Roger son of Stephen of
Kinthorp holds four bovates of land, and William son of Gamel
two bovates, are of the King's serjeanty of Pikering or not; and
whether the predecessors of Roger and William were enfeoffed
by the King's predecessors, before the feoffment of the said
serjeanty or after; and whether the six bovates are of the
King's socage of Pikering or not; and by which of the King's
predecessors the rent of the six bovates was assigned to ser-
jeanty, made on Sunday, the morrow of S. Thomas Apostle, 37
Henry (22 Dec., 1252) before John de Reygate, Sheriff of Yorkshire, by the oath of William Malecake the elder, Thomas de
Edbristone, Peter de Nevile, William Malecake the younger,
Thomas de Pikeringe, Richard *le Brun*, Adam de Rouceby,
Robert son of Walter, John de Neuton the younger, Robert de
Brunton, William son of Matilda *(filium Matildis)* of Pikering,
Roger de Kirkedale in Edbriston, Alan Hert of Farmaneby,
John son of Reginald of Thorneton, Walter de Rouceby, Hugh
at the gate of Pikering, and John de Castre, who, being sworn,
say that the six bovates in Kinthorp, whereof Roger son of
Stephen of Kinthorp holds four, and William son of Gamel
holds two, are not of the King's serjeanty of Pikering, and the
predecessors of Roger and William were enfeoffed by the King's
predecessors before the feoffment of the said serjeanty. The six
bovates of land are of the King's socage of Pikering, and the
rent of the same was assigned to the said serjeanty by the King.

---

[a] Wanting in 1830.
[b] Kingthorpe, in the parish of Pickering.

XXXIX. ROBERT SON OF THOMAS DE CRAYSTOKE.

Inq. p. m.

[38 HEN. III. No. 42.]

Writ dated at Westminster, 4 May, 38th year (1254).

E XTENT made at Brunnum,[a] in the County of York, on Friday before the ascension of our Lord, 38 Henry (15 May, 1254), of the lands and tenements which were lord Robert's, son of Thomas de Craystoke,[b] before Alan de Audefeud, co-escheator *(quo excaetore)* of Sir Thomas de Stanforde, by Bartholomew de Brunnum, Henry de Hundegate of the same, Thomas son of Simon of the same, William Clere of the same, William de Catton, Thomas de Tansterne of Hayton, Ace de Flixton, Ranulf de Folketon, Robert D[aunc]e of Brunnum, Thomas son of Peter of Brunneby, Adam Bacun of Brunnum, Richer son of Robert of the same, who say that the said Robert held of the King in chief by knight's service in Brunnum, two knights' fees and a fourth part of one fee.

Demesne Land　A capital messuage which contains two acres, 5s. per annum.　In demesne twelve bovates of land (each seven acres and worth 4s.), 48s.; no meadow but a pasture, 4s; and a water mill, 40s.　Sum, £4 17s.

Villains.　Fourteen villains hold eighteen bovates (of which every bovate yields 2s.), and do other services worth yearly 15d.　Sum (with hens and eggs), £2 18s. 6d.

Cottars.　Seven cottars yield 7s., and they all do other services valued at 3s. 4½d.　Sum, 10s. 4½d.

Freemen.　One Bartholomew holds by knight's service, 2½ carucates of land, of which 19½ carucates make one knight's fee. He does nothing but foreign service.

---

[a] Nunburnholme, Brunham in *Domesday*, and Brunom in Kirkby's *Inquest*.

[b] There is an extent of lands in Cumberland written on two sides of a membrane. On the dorse, below the sum total of issues (£85 14s. 7d.) in Cumberland, as follows: " Et dicunt dicti Jur', quod Willelmus filius Thome de Craystoke, frater predicti Roberti, est propinquior heres predicti Roberti, et est etatis xxx. annorum." This information as to the heir (who is seen to have been a brother, William, aged 30), is wanting in the extent made for Yorkshire.　On 20 June, 1247, the King took the homage of Robert de Craystock, son and heir of Thomas Fitz William, for all the lands and tenements which the same Thomas held of the King in chief *(Excerpta è Rotulis Finium*, vol. ii., p. 14*).*　On 10 May, 1254, Elena, widow of Robert son of Thomas de Creystok', paid the King £20 for leave to marry whom she would *(Ibid.*, vol. ii., p. 186*).*　On 13 June following, William de Creystok', brother and heir of Robert de Creistok', paid fealty *(fidelitatem)* to the King for all the lands and tenements the said Robert held of the King in chief *(Ibid.*, vol. i., p. 190*).* It will be noticed it is always Creistok' or some such form, and never as nowadays Greystoke.

One Azo de Flixton holds eight bovates of land. Thomas de Tansterne holds 8 bovates. Each does nothing but foreign service. A woman, Helewise daughter of Reginald, holds 7½ bovates by charter, and yields 7s. 11½d. Henry de Hundegate holds 2½ bovates by charter for 22½d. William de Catton holds two bovates by charter for 18d. One Cristiana holds one toft and croft by charter for 3s. 4d. Thomas son of Simon holds by charter one toft with four acres of land for 3s. 6d. Sum, 18s. 2d.

Knights' Fees. The Prior of Wartre[a] holds 6 bovates, worth by the year 24s.; the Prioress of Brunn'[a] half a carucate, 16s.; Philip de la Leye[a] in Milinton and in Gripthorp,[b] half a knight's fee, 100s.; William son of Ralph[a] half a carucate of land in Wapplington,[c] 16s.; Remigius de Poclinton half a carucate of land in Sethon,[d] 20s.; Ranulf de Folketon three carucates in Folketon[e] and one mill, by the fifth part of one fee worth 10 marcs, and he pays yearly 16s. 8d., and does foreign service; William the Dispenser[a] *(Dispensator)* holds in Flixton[e] two bovates, 8s., and yields of farm yearly 2s., and does foreign service *(Et facit for').*

Sir *(D'n's)* William de Ergum holds one culture in Flixton[e] marsh and pays yearly 6d. Lady Isabella de Boythorp holds two bovates of land in Flixton, worth 8s. per annum, and does nothing but foreign service.

Sir *(D'n's)* Peter de la Haye holds half a fee in Spaldington of the Barony of Mubraye, and pays yearly 6s. 8d. That land is worth five marcs.

Sir *(D'n's)* Gerard Salvein holds three carucates of land in Thorp, of the fee of S. Mary, York, and pays yearly 12d. at Christmas *(ad Natale).*

The Prior of the Hospital of S. John of Jerusalem holds in the town of Brunnum one bovate worth yearly 4s., and he does nothing but foreign service. Sum, 18s. 10d. Sum total, £19 12s. 10½d.[f]

---

[a] Of all these it is said, that each does nothing but foreign service:—"Et nichil facit nisi forinsecum."

[b] Millington, in the parish of Great Givendale, and Gristhorp in that of Filey. The latter is called Grisetorp in *Domesday*, and Grispthorp and Grysthorp in Kirkby's *Inquest.*

[c] Waplington, near Pocklington.

[d] Seaton Ross, five miles from Pocklington (Kirkby's *Inquest*, p. 85).

[e] Folkton, nine miles from Scarborough, and Flixton, in that parish.

[f] The total cannot be well made out.

XL. INQUIRY CONCERNING THE PERPETRATORS OF
DAMAGE DONE TO TWO GRANGES BELONGING TO BYLAND
ABBEY.

[38 HEN. III. No. 25.]

Writ dated 10 Sept., 38th year (1254).

WYLDON GRANGE.[a]

INQUISITION concerning the foss of the Abbot of Byland
thrown down at Wyldone, made by William de Neuby,
William de Karleton, William son of Oliver of Dalton, William
Ke of the same, Roger de Crachalle, William son of Oliver of
Everesle, Richard Fountain *(de fonte)*, William de Maundeville,
Adam the Despenser, Henry de Karleton, Geoffrey de Ampel-
ford, Robert son of Alan of Trilleby, and William de Salecoc,
who say upon their oath that Ralph *del Bratino* of Carlton,
Walter son of Richard of the same, Robert Kirkyard *(de Cimi-
terio)*, William son of Hugh, Hugh son of Alice, Ingald son of
Walter, William son of Roger, Richard son of Matilda, Adam
de Hustwayt, Stephen son of William, Hugh son of Mariota,
Hugh son of William, Richard son of William, Walter Burry,
Hugh son of Roger, Roger the Reeve[b] *(prepositus)*, Hugh son of
Richard, Thomas son of Erm' (or Erin'), Paulin, William son of
......, Martin Tasker, Ernisius, Walter de Bellande, Henry
keeper of the animals *(custos animalium)*, Roger son of Ralph,
Thomas son of William, Hugh son of William, Hugh son of
Ingald, Adam son of Hugh, William son of Henry, John son of
Ingald of Hustwayt, Stephen Reeve, Simon son of Richard,
William son of Richard, John son of Hawyse, Ingald Reeve,
John Osmund's man, Richard son of John, John son of Osmund,
Benvenut, Thomas son of William, Robert son of Mariota,
Gilbert son of Hugh, Thomas at townhead *(ad capud ville)*,
Eustace son of Richard, Walter Scot, Ingram, Thomas son of
Reginald, Thomas son of Hugh, William son of Roger, Thomas
son of John, William son of Maud, Robert son of Adam Smith,
William son of Robert, Thomas the Carter, Roger Bruning,
Ingald Forester, and William Forester, came to the foss *(fossa-
tum)* of the Abbey of Byland, *(Bellalanda)* at Wyldon, on the
eve of S. Laurence (9 August) in the present year, at night, and
by force and arms threw down that foss against the peace of the
King (as the writ says), and whilst the house had no Abbot
(dummodo abbacia vacabat abbati).

[a] Wilden Grange, in the parish of Coxwold.
[b] The writ mentions Roger, reeve of Carleton, as the ringleader.

FALDINGTON GRANGE.[a]

INQUISITION made concerning the foss thrown down and hedge rooted up *(de fossato prostrato et sepe eradicata)*, and a certain parcel *(quadam parte)* of hay [carried away] and bars of the gate at the Grange of Faldinton in the moor called Pilemor, by William de Galmethorpe, Thomas Maunsel of Heton, . . . y, Walter de Thormodeby, Alan son of William of the same, Robert de Haumelake, Gilbert de Yserbeke, William de Percy of Bulmer (Bulem'), William de . . . dale, Robert de Brudeford, William son of Bartholomew of Thorny, and Osebert de Raskelfe, who say upon their oath that Richard de [Riparia], Henry his brother, Arundel servant of Richard, Simon *Bercar'*, Serlo his brother, Walter son of Meg *(fil' Megge)*, Robert Hod, Richard at town-end *(ad exitum ville)*, W . . . son of Richard Reeve *(Ric'i prepositi)*, William Ossemund, Arundel the little *(le Petit)*, Adam Smith, Thomas Fisher *(le Peschur)*, Walter his son, Richard [his] brother, ... starde, Thomas Blerimund, Nicholas Edolf, John Servant (or Serjeant, *serviens)*, of Neuburg', Robert Kirkland *(de terra ecclesie)*, Robert de Honington, . . Henry P . . . . of Theobald, Reginald de Brafferton, Adam son of Peter, Adam de Burton, Richard son of Peter, . . . Richard . . . William son of William Long, Richard son of Al . . . . aunceys, Stephen de Husthwait . . . , William *le Fevre*, Thomas Trutes, Thomas at town-end *(ad exitum ville)*, Peter son of Alice, A . chur, John Trute, William son of Maud *(Matill')*, . . Geoffrey the Carpenter, Thomas the Carter, Ri . . . tute the younger, Thomas son of Richard de Rypar[ia], Henry Wal . . . . . . , Robert *le Messor*, Simon de Esingwald, Reeve, Peter the Carter, Ralph *Garcifer* of Richard de Ripar[ia] John del . . , William son of Richard, ... elington, Thomas the Brewer *(Braciator)*, Richard son of Thomas Belle, Stephen the Carter, John de Wald, Geoffrey . . Robert del Hil, E . . . . the Carpenter, Richard son of Serlo, Ranulph, Robert the Cowherd *(vaccar')* Robert *Mercator*, Walter the Tailor, Thomas the Potter, William de Canc . . , William son of Ralph of Brandesby, John Burell, William son of Herbert, Robert Neubonde, Gernan Reeve, Richard son of Juliana, Henry son of Hugh Reeve *(prepositi)*, Geoffrey the Carpenter, Walter son of Thurstan, Adam de Crambun, Thomas Marshal, William Nyni, William Gardiner, John son of William Reeve *(prepositi)*, William son of Sigrim, Hugh de Lillinge, Richard son of Herbert, and Geoffrey Milner, came with force and arms against the peace of the King,

---

[a] Fawdington and Pill Moor, in the parish of Brafferton.

while the Abbey of Byland was void, to the Grange of Falding-
ton, and threw down a certain foss raised in Pilemor and rooted
up a certain hedge. They say that as to bars carried away and
hay carried away they know nothing and can make no inquiry.[a]

XLI. EXTENT OF THE LANDS OF JOHN DE LUNGVYLERS,
KNIGHT.[b]

No Writ.

[39 HEN. III. No. 39.]

EXTENT of all the lands which were of Sir John de Lungvy-
lers, made before Sir Thomas de Stanford, on Thursday,
the eve of S. Leonard, 39 Henry (5 Nov., 1254), at Hoton in
Richemundsire, by Warin de Bereford, William de Parva
Hoton, John de Rokeby, John son of . . . , John de Mileforde
of Kyrkeby, Robert de Mileforde, Thomas son of Samson of
Farnelay, Ivo son of David, John son of Mariot, Peter le
Norrays, William de Farnelay, Adam son of Adam of the same.

HOTON.[c]	Value per annum.		
	£	s.	d.
A capital messuage with garden and curtilage, containing two acres	0	6	8
A dovehouse situate within the court . .	0	3	0
In demesne 16 bovates of arable land (each bovate 7 acres at 12d. the acre), 112 acres	5	12	0

[a] The following are the terms in which the writ directs inquiry to be made:—
"qui una cum Ricardo de Riparia et aliis pluribus, dum abbacia de Bella landa
vacabat, vi et armis venerunt ad Grangiam predicte abbacie de Faldintone, et quoddam fossatum in Pilemore levatum prostraverunt, et quamdam sepem eradicaverunt,
et barras porte et quamdam partem feni asportaverunt, contra pacem nostram et
contra tenorem proteccionis nostre quam monachis predicte abbacie concessimus.
Diligenter eciam inquiras . . . . qui una cum Rogero preposito de Carletone noc-
tanter prostaverunt tempore predicte vacacionis quoddam fossatum predicte abbacie
apud Wyldon' contra pacem nostram et contra tenorem proteccionis nostre pre
dicte . . . Teste R. Comite Cornub. fratre nostro apud Sanctum Albanum, ʌ. die
Septembris anno regni nostri xxxviii."

[b] Son of Sir Eudo de Longvillers by Clemencia, daughter of Thomas de
Montbegon of Hornby in Lancashire, and sister and coheir of Roger de Montbegon (Harrison's History of Yorkshire, vol. i., p. 444). On 11 June, 1246, the King
took the homage of John, son and heir of Clemencia de Lungvilers, for half a
knight's fee in Lincolnshire, which Clemencia held in chief, and also for two
knights' fees in Yorkshire which J., formerly Earl of Lincoln, whose son and
heir was in ward to the King (Excerpta è Rotulis Finium, vol. i., p. 454). On
14 Feb., 1257-8, Elena, widow of John de Lungvilers, claimed land in Horneby
and Mellyng in Lancashire (Ibid. vol. ii., p. 271). The son and heir of the above
mentioned Sir John was another Sir John, who is stated in the Lincolnshire
Inquisition taken at this time, to have been twenty-four years old (Calendarium
Genealogicum, vol. i., p. 56). Margaret, the only child of this latter Sir John,
married Geoffrey de Neville, a brother of Robert de Neville of Raby.

[c] Hutton Magna, or Hutton Longvilers, near Greta Bridge.

Value per annum.
£ s. d.

In demesne 10 acres of meadow at 3s. . . 1 10 0
There is no pasture after corn and hay are carried,
and no fence *(defensum)*, because all the neighbouring townships have common.
Pasture for 300ᵃ sheep by the long hundred, valued
for every score at 3d. 0 6 0
A watermill let to farm for 40s. at three terms of the
year, viz., Martinmas 13s. 4d., Ash Wednesday 13s.
4d., and Pentecost, 13s. 4d. . . . 2 0 0
Ten bondmen *(bondi)* hold 16 bovates of land, every
bovate contains 7 acres with meadow, by the
perch of 20 feet, and they pay at Martinmas and·
Pentecost 4 0 0
Their works and customs by the year . . 1 1 0
Eleven cottars hold eleven cottages and 7 acres of
land divided between them by roods, and pay in
money at the terms aforesaid . . . 0 4 10
Their works and customs by the year 0 9 0
A brewhouse *(bracina)* by the year 0 1 0
Six free tenants hold 10 bovates of land and pay
yearly at the said terms . . . 2 10 0
One Eudo son of Norman holds four bovates of land
so freely that he yields nothing but ward and relief.

The said John held this manor of Hoton in chief of lord
Roger de Mubray, and a moiety of the town of Appelby in
Lindesye of the King in chief, and Hugh de Nevil the other
moiety; by reason of which tenure the other lands of the said
Hugh were taken into the King's hand as well as the lands of
the said John.

Sum of the whole extent of this manor of Hoton. £18 3 6

KYRKEBY UPON WERF.

Value per annum.
£ s. d.

A capital messuage with garden and curtilage containing 3 acres 0 6 8
In demesne 16 bovates of arable land (every bovate
8 acres, by the perch of 18 feet, at 6d. the acre),
6 score 8 acres . . . 3 4 0
Twelve acres of meadow in demesne at 2s. 6d. . 1 10 0
Six cottars hold six tofts with four acres of land, and
pay yearly at Martinmas and Pentecost . 1 0 8
Their works are valued at 11d. . . 0 0 11

ᵃ In order to make six shillings, the sheep should be four hundred in number.

6

Value per annum.
£ s. d.

Thomas de Ulfscelfe holds one toft and croft by
charter, and gives yearly one pound of cumin
John de Mileforde holds one carucate of land by
knight service, and pays in money at the said
terms . . . . I 0 0
Robert de Mileforde holds two bovates of land by
knight service, and pays at the same terms . . 0 4 0
The parson of the town of Kyrkeby holds one toft
by charter, and pays yearly at the same terms 19*d*. 0 1 7
The said John held this manor of Kyrkebi of Edmund de Lassi.
Sum of the whole extent of this manor of Kyrkebi. £7 7 10
And one pound of cumin.

FARNELAY.[a]

Value per Annum.
£ s. d.

A capital messuage with garden and curtilage containing 2 acres 0 6 8
In demesne four bovates of arable land (every bovate
15 acres by the perch of 20 feet at 4*d*. the acre),
60 acres . . . . I 0 0
Two acres of meadow in demesne, at 2*s*. . . 0 4 0
A watermill, of which the Abbot of Kyrkestal has
yearly 12*s*., and the lady of Wrydelesforde[b] half a
marc, and the share of the lord by the year . 0 11 4
A park of 4 score acres in wood and plain, able to
sustain bucks and does in number six score, and
beside the support of these beasts the value by
the year 0 6 8
A wood, a league in length, and half a league in
width, the pannage and perquisites by the year . 0 15 0
The whole land is warren, and the perquisites of the
said warren by the year 0 6 8
Six bondmen hold six tofts and 77 acres of land,
and they pay at Martinmas and Pentecost yearly I 11 0
Their works and customs are worth by the year 8*s*.
They give merchet and legewyt, but they ought
not to be talliated 0 8 0
Fifteen tenants, to wit, gresmen and cottars, hold 15
tofts and 35 acres 3 roods of land, and they pay
at the terms aforesaid . . . . I 9 8½
Six tenants hold by chirograph 6 tofts and 29 acres
of land, and they pay at the same terms . 0 18 I

[a] Near Leeds.
[b] Woodlesford, in the parish of Rothwell, near Leeds.

Value per annum.
£ s. d.

Three tenants hold by charter 40 acres of land ; of
whom one renders at Christmas a pound of pepper
or 4*d.*, and at Easter a pair of gilt spurs or 8*d.*;
another renders at Christmas twenty horse-shoes
with nails or 6*d.*; and the third, 16*d.* yearly at
Martinmas and Pentecost . . . 0 2 10
Thomas son of Samson holds four bovates of land
by knight's service, pays yearly 18*d.*, and does
service valued at 8*d.* 0 2 2
Isabella de Wrydelesford holds in the town of Farnelay for life, 5 bovates 10½ acres of land with 9
tofts and, pays at the before-named two terms 18*d.*
After her decease the land will revert to the heirs
of the said John de Lungevylers, and it is worth
in common years 60*s.* 0 1 6
Sum of the whole extent of the town of Farnelay, by the year
£8 3 7½

AKANESCALE.[a]

Value per annum.
£ s. d.

No capital messuage or demesne land ; but there are
ten bondmen who hold ten bovates of land (the
bovate 12 acres), and yield yearly in money at the
terms before named 3 6 8
They do works and customs worth by the year 8*s.* 4*d.*,
and owe merchet and lechewyt ; and they ought
to be talliated by the year 0 8 4
There are seven tenants, to wit gresmen and cottars
who hold 7 tofts and 30 acres of land, and yield
yearly at the said terms 0 18 6
Two free tenants hold by charter two bovates of
land, and yield yearly 18*d.*; and they answer for
foreign service 0 1 6
Two tenants hold one bovate of land by chirograph,
and yield yearly 0 6 8
Sum of the whole extent of Akanescale by the year. £5 1 8

HETUN.[b]

Value per annum.
£ s. d.

A capital messuage with two bovates of demesne land 0 12 6
A moiety of one mill, out of which the Abbot of
Kyrkestal has by gift of the father of the said
John with his body 5*s.*, and the share of said John. 0 8 4

a Oakenshaw, in the township of Cleckheaton and parish of Birstall.

b Cleckheaton. In 1302-3, Margaret de Nevill had three carucates of land in
Heton Clack, and in 1315-16 she was returned as the owner of Heton Cleck
(Kirkby's *Inquest*, pp. 224, 361).

Value per annum.
£ s. d.

Three bondmen hold five bovates with 3 tofts, and
yield at Martinmas and Pentecost . . . 1 0 0
They do works and customs valued at 2s. 3d., and
they owe merchet and letherwit, and ought to be
talliated at the will of the lord . . . . 0 2 3·
One bovate lies waste 0 4 0
Five tenants hold five bovates by chirograph, and
yield 0 13 6
Richard de Thonhil [*Thornhil*] holds two bovates
by knight's service—that land is worth 10s. by the
year—and gives 0 4 0
Henry de Hyperum holds eight bovates—that land
is worth by the year 40s.—and yields . . . 0 1 6
William Piper holds one bovate—that land is worth
by the year 5s.—and renders yearly on Christmas
day one pound of cumin.
William de Sutton and William de Stodlay hold five
bovates of land in Armelay by knight's service,
and that land is worth by the year 20s.
Sum of the whole extent of this town of Heton by the year—
66s. 1d. and one pound of cumin; but out of this the Abbot
and Convent of Kyrkestal have yearly 26s. 8d. for one pit-
tance by the gift of the said John: and so there remains—
39s. 5d.[a]

[*By endorsement.*] Extent of lands which were of Sir John
de Lungevileres, in the County of York.

XLII. CONCERNING THE DIVERSION OF A ROAD BETWEEN
BILBROUGH AND STEETON.

[39 HEN. III. No. 5.]

Writ dated at York, 15 Aug., 39th year (1255).

INQUISITION, whether it would be to the damage or injury
(*nocumentum*) of the King, or of the parts adjacent, if the
King were to grant that the street which extends from Bilburg'
towards Aynesty,[b] beyond the field of Styveton, should be obstructed and turned into the ancient street [which extends from

---

a The remainder of this Inquisition is illegible. It relates to the following
property:—Manors—Brerley, Colling [Cowling], Farnlay, and Kirkby; Fees in
Cuniglaye [Conondley], Farhull [Farnhill], Gergrave [Gargrave], Heton, Neuson
[Newsome], and Oston [Owston]. See *Calendar*, vol. i., p. 14.
b " De Bewebrug' versus Eynesty " in the writ.

the southern head *(australi capite)* of Kayrton Wood, between Styveton Moor and Kayrton Moor towards Eynesty],[a] made by John de Merxton, William de Walton, William de Dunesford, Robert son of Richard of Tocwyth, William son of Nicholas of the same, Robert Page of the same, Thomas son of William of Merston, Thomas Aloes of the same, William Clerk of the same, Adam de Etton, John Cote of Bilton, Richard de Kolton, Lambert de Bilburg', Adam Tailor *(cissorem)* of Kolthorp, who say upon their oath that the way *(chiminum)* would be *ad nocumentum* if it were turned to the ancient street, because it would require that there should be in the ancient street two bridges and one causeway a quarentene in length. If to the old street there were two bridges and a causeway, as to the new street, it would not be *ad nocumentum*, save only that that street .. [here torn] .... of the proper land of Sir Richard de Styveton, at whose petition the inquisition was made.

XLIII. CONCERNING LANDS ALLEGED TO HAVE BEEN SOLD BY OSBERT DE BOLLEBEC TO HUGH LE BIGOT, IN LEVISHAM, NEWTON, ETC.[b]

[40 HEN. III. No. 30.]

Writ dated at Westminster, 3 Nov., 40th year (1255).

INQUISITION—whether it would be to the damage of the King if he should confirm to Hugh le Bigot the land which Osbert de Bollebec held of the King in chief in Levesham, Neuton, Loketon, Pikeringe, and Scalleby, and which Osbert (it is said) sold to him—made before the Sheriff, Thomas de Stanford, Escheator, and the Coroners of the County, in full county court, by John de Hamerton, Richard de Hoton, knights, Robert de Buleford, Roger Grimet, Stephen *le Westrays* of Aymunderby, William de Percy of Bulemere, William Malecake, Thomas son of Adam of Pikeringe, Roger Haldain, Ralph de Loketon, John de Neuton, Adam de Rouceby, Robert son of Robert of Roston, and John *le Champion*, who, being sworn, say that it would not be to the damage of the King, and that Osbert de Bollebec held of the King in chief, in the town of Levesham, fourteen bovates of land and his capital messuage, by the service of 18s. 8d.

---

a The words between brackets [ ] are filled in from the writ, in place of *etc.* in the inquisition.

b See No. xxxv.

yearly, and by the working of one perch of harrowing[a] *(per operacionem unius perticate hiritini)* at Pikeringe Castle, and in the town of Neuton four bovates, by the service of 5s 3d. yearly, but nothing in the towns of Loketon or Scalleby. He held of the King in chief in the town of Pikeringe four bovates of land by the service of 4s. yearly. Moreover the said Osbert held all the aforesaid lands by the service of doing suit at the Wapen-take [court] of Pikeringe, from three weeks to three weeks, and by the service of two marcs for relief when it shall fall, and by talliage *(talliagium)* when the King's demesnes are talliated.

XLIV. WILLIAM THE ARBLASTER OF GIVENDALE. *Inq. p. m.*

[40 HEN. III. No. 15.]

Writ dated at Bristol, 15 July, 40th year (1256).

INQUISITION made by Thomas de Tanesterne in Hayton, Robert Monstroyle of Bubbewythe, Peter de Hugate, Laurence de Kaldewalde, Peter de Faxeflet, Walter de Mikkel-felde, Roger de Linton in Lathum, Roger de Hugate in Herle-thorpe, Joseph de Hayton, William *le Garge*, John de Esthorpe, Ralph of the same, Robert son of Beatrice of Milington, who say upon their oath that William the Arblaster, *(Arblastarius)*, or cross-bowman, held in two towns which are called Gyveldale[b] four carucates of land, worth by the year 100s., by the service of a cross-bowman *(per servicium arblastr')* and doing ward at York Castle in time of war for forty days at his own charges, if longer at the cost of the King, and to conduct the King's Treasure through the county at the King's charges.

---

a Mr. Vincent has translated *hiritini* "harrowing," as if the genitive case of a possible *hiritinus* or *hiritinum*. Mr. C. Trice Martin suggests that the word may be akin to *hyritius*, a hedgehog, and so signifies the revolving bars with spikes used in fortresses. In some dictionaries the word *eritius* is translated " a fortifica-tion," and there may be some connection with *hyritius* and *hiritini*. It has also been suggested that *hiritini* means ploughing, and has been coined from the Anglo-Saxon *erian*, "to plough," Early English *eryen* and *herien* :

"Quath Perkyn the plouȝmon, 'bi Peter the apostel,
" I haue an half aker to herie, bi the heiȝe weye;
" Weore he wel i-eried, thenne with ou wolde I wende !' "
(Piers Plowman, Clarendon Press Edition, vol. i., p. 193.)
See also instances of *heren* and *herien* (vol. i., p. 203).

b Great and little Givendale, near Pocklington.

The said William had three sisters, to wit, Alice, Eve, and Avice. Of Alice came Walter, her son and heir, now of full age ; of Eve came Cecily, and Alice, and they are of full age ; and of Avice came Alan, who is of full age. These are the heirs of the aforesaid William.[a]

XLV.   EADMUND DE LASCY.[b]   *Inq. p. m.*

[42 HEN. III. No. 27.]

No Writ.

[M. 1.]

SLAYTEBURNE.[c]

ROBERT de Thisteley,[d] Jordan Smith of Braford, Hugh (de) Spectesfold, Hugh son of[1] Arnald, Adam son of Fuke, Adam Forester, Adam *le Bonur* of Rilton, Henry son of Gamel, Roger de Heselheyed, Alan son of Gunilc, Walter de Resholes(?),

[a] On 3 Nov., 1256, the King took the homage of Walter de Donesford, Cecilia daughter of Eve, and Alice her sister, and of Alan son of Avice, the relatives and heirs of William Arblastar' of Geveldale, for all the lands and tenements which the said William held in chief *(Excerpta è Rotulis Finium*, vol. ii., p. 244*)*.
    In a Fine of 15 Hen. III. [No. 40], he is called William de Gevendale son of Richard Balistarius.   In the *Red Book,* " *Serjanteriæ.   Robertus de Geueldale et Thomas de Geueldale totam Geueldale per balisteriam ad castellum Eboracense.*"— W. P. B.
    Testa de Nevill (vol. ii., p. 691) shows that Geoffrey de Geveldale held four bovates of the Honour of Tickhill (besides his serjeanty of York Castle), by ser-jeanty of " *conducere thesaurum Regis extra Comitatum Eborwicsiræ.*" This shows how he helped it along from York Castle, the Depot, to Tickhill, on the borders.
    [b] Son and heir of John de Lascy, Earl of Lincoln, which dignity belonged to his mother, and as she survived her husband and lived till 1279, retaining the title even after her second marriage with William Marshall, Earl of Pembroke, Edmund de Lascy never became Earl, though in the popular eye he was always " the young Earl." He was under age at the time of his father's death, and was still in the royal custody on 26 March, 1249, when the King commanded the Barons of the Exchequer to adjourn, until he came of age, the demand made against Edmund de Lascy for one hundred pounds owing by his father *(Excerpta è Rotulis Finium*, vol. ii., pp. 18, 54*)*.   On 9 Feb., 1256-7, he agreed to pay the King ten marcs of gold for licence to marry his son and heir, Henry, to Margaret, eldest daughter and heir of William Lungespe *(Ibid.,* vol. ii., p. 249*)*.   Dugdale says he died on 21 July, 42 Hen. III. (1258), and was buried at Stanlaw.   He gives the epitaph on his tomb.   From an entry on the *Close Roll* (42 Hen. III., m. 6), it would appear that he was dead before 18 June, 1258, and in Holmes's *Pontefract, its Name, its Lords, and its Castle,* he is said to have died on June 5th.   In this Inquisition (p. 51) it is stated that his son and heir, Henry, was eight years old on Christmas Day, 1257.
    [c] Slaidburn, nine miles north of Clitheroe.   The following guide to the arrangement of this Inquisition will be useful ;—M. 1, Slaidburn, Grindleton, and West Bradford ; M. 1[d], blank ; M. 2, col. 1, Borough of Pontefract ; M. 2, col. 2, Soke of Snaith ; M. 2[d], col. 1, Leeds, Rothwell, Carlton, Woodlesford, etc. ; M. 2[d], col. 2, Barwick in Elmet, Barnbow, Scholes, Morwick, Kippax, Allerton By-water (on these two dorses the heading runs across both membranes) ; M. 3, Lancashire on both sides, in a very bad state.
    [d] Robert de Thisteley is mentioned below, under Bradford.

Alan Scot of Esington, Jurors for making an extent of the lands of Eadmund de Lascy in Boulande, before Peter de Percy, in the 42nd year of the King.

The Jurors say by their oath, that the said Eadmund de Lascy had in demesne thirty acres of arable land and eight acres of meadow in the town of Slayteburne, at 4*d.* an acre.

Sum in money *(denar')* 12*s.* 8*d.*

A mill paying £4 a year, because a moiety of the suit of the said mill was given to Robert Dayvil. Sum, £4.

Free tenants by charter.

Name.	Holding.	Annual rent.
Elias de Knolle . .	30 acres of land .	12 barbed arrows
Walter son of William of Neuton . .	40 acres of land .	12*d.*
Geoffrey de Meneley .	15 acres of land .	5*s.*

Sum, 6*s.* and 12 arrows.

Bovates.

Thirty bovates of land, each bovate containing six acres, and the sum of acres is nine score, at 4*d.* an acre.

Sum in money, 60*s.*

There are men who hold lands of the assarts freely, not by charter, that is, 316 acres, at 4*d.* an acre. Sum, £6 5*s.* 4*d.*

Cottars.

Four cottars, who pay 3*s.* 2*d* a year, to the value of one acre of land. Sum, 3*s.* 2*d.*

Stephen de Hamerton holds all Hamerton[a] by charter, and pays 8*s.* a year for everything. Adam Biry holds forty acres of land in Old Wihekul,[b] and pays 4*s.* a year for everything. Sum, 12*s.*

Sum of Slayteburne with the mill, £20 19*s.* 2*d.*

GRINLINGTON.[c]

A mill worth £6 a year, but it belongs to the rents of Clyderh'.[d] Sum, £6.

Bondmen.

Twenty-four bovates of land in bondage, each bovate containing twelve acres, with meadow. Sum of acres, 248. Each bovate pays 16*d.* a year, and makes three cartings a year to Pontefract, and ought to plough one day, and mow nine days in

---

[a] Hammerton, in the township of Easington and parish of Slaidburn.

[b] Withgill. Mitton cum Wythekill occurs in Kirkby's *Inquest* (p. 17). Henry de Biri contributed to the Poll Tax for 1379 amongst the taxpayers of Mitton.

[c] Grindleton, in the parish of Mitton.

[d] An abbreviation of Clitheroe.

autumn. The service of each bovate of land is worth 2*s.* 8*d.*, and the rent of each bovate is 4*s.* Sum, £4 16*s.* besides the mill. Four score and nineteen acres of land of the assarts with . . . . . . at 4*d.* an acre. There are no cottars. Sum . . . . 8*d.* Sum total of Grinlington, £6 15*s.* 8*d.*

[BRAFFOR]D'.[a]

Nothing in demesne. A mill paying 46*s.* 8*d.* a year.

[*Free tenants by charter.*]

Name.	Holding.	Annual rent.	
		s.	*d.*
Robert de Thisteley .	. 9 acres and one perch .	2	4
Jordan Smith .	. 10 acres . .	2	6
Hugh son of Arnold .	. 12 acres .	3	0
Hugh de Spectesfold .	. 10 acres .	2	0
John de Hori3 .	. 10 acres . .	2	0
Robert de Heri3[b] .	2 acres . .	0	3

Sum, 12*s.* 1*d.*, besides the mill.
Sum of the mill, 46*s.* 8*d.*, and so the sum total [5]8*s.* 9*d.*

Bovates.

Sixteen bovates of land. Jordan Boc holds one bovate of the said sixteen by charter, at an annual rent of one bundle of bows[c] for all. Each of the other bovates contains 15 acres, and pays 5*s.* annual rent. Sum of acres, 11 score and five. Sum in money, 75*s.*, and one bundle of bows.[c] Five score and a half acres of the assarts, at 4*d.* an acre. Sum, 33*s.* 6*d.*

Cottars.

Five cottars, paying 3*s.* a year, and holding to the value of half an acre of land. Sum, 36*s.* 6*d.* There can be seven vaccaries in the forest of Bouland', the herbage of each being worth 5*s.* a year, Sum, 35*s.* All the lands above written are held by knight service. He[nry] de Lascy is the true heir of the said Edmund de Lascy, and is of the age of eight years and a half and one month, at the feast of St. Mary Magdalen in the 42nd year (22 July, 1258). Sum total of Brafford', £11 18*s.* 9*d.*

---

a West Bradford, in the parish of Mitton.
b Does not hold by charter.
c "j ligamen de . . . ub3," " one bundle of . . . ." The parchment is torn in both places. The word is probably *arcubus.*

7

[M. 2, col. I.]

EXTENT of the Borough of Pontefract, made before Sir Peter de Percy, on Sunday next after the feast of St. James the Apostle 42nd year (28 July, 1258), by Ralph Arbet, Richard Seman, Thomas son of . . . , Adam . . . , Peter Touplamb, John de Cnaresburg', Nicholas de Arkesey, Thomas Foxe, Robert de Lund . . . Geoffrey *le Kepur*, and Robert Arlot, sworn.

PONSFRACTUS.[a]

Fourteen score tofts and two parts of a toft in the Borough of Pontefract, of which 18 tofts are standing empty and do no service to the lord, and 13 score and two pay each 12*d.* a year.
Sum of these in money, £13 2*s.*
78 booths *(selde)*, 2*d.* each, but of these six are empty, so that 72 booths pay 12*s.* Sum, 12*s.*
42 booths *(selde)* of cobblers and of those who sell salt, 2*d.* each. Sum, 7*s.*
60 stalls *(stall')*, one penny each. Sum, 5*s.*
70 acres of land called *Plotheland*, at 2*d.* an acre.
Sum, 11*s.* 8*d.*
A fair *(forum)* worth £4 a year. Sum, £4.
The toll of beasts, iron, wool, hides and skins, is worth £30 a year. Sum, £30.
The markets *(nundine)* are worth £12. The toll of Knottinglay is worth 10*s.* A certain custom, called *Ferthepenye*, worth one marc a year. Sum £13 3*s.* 4*d.*
The toll of fish is worth half a marc, of oil half a marc, of linen web 5*s.*, of building material *(mairemii)* five marcs ;[b] pleas one marc ; the toll of woad *(wayde)* half a marc. Sum, 42*s.* 4*d.*
Eleven score and fourteen acres and one rood *(perticata)*, at 4*d.* an acre. Sum, 78*s.* ½*d.*
Ten score and a half acres of land in the assarts of Pontefract, at 2*d.* Sum, 33*s.* 5½*d.*
Rent of Englesher',[c] of the Honour of Pontefract, by the year, £17 5*s.* 10½*d.* Sum, £17 5*s.* 10½*d.*
Rent of Helmeshal, a year, £13 4*s.* 4½*d.* Sum, £13 4*s.* 4½*d.*
Knights' fees of the same Honour, 5 . . . fees.

[a] This extent should be compared with the Compotus of 23 and 24 Edw. I., printed in the *Yorkshire Archæological Journal*, vol. viii., p. 351.

[b] Should be "shillings" to make the total correct.

[c] " De firma Englesher' de Honore de Pontefracto." This rent is thus referred to in the Compotus above mentioned : "De xviij*li.* xij*s.* x*d.* ob. de firma quæ vocatur Englechere termino Martini." In the same document an abatement of 13*s.* is claimed " in decasu firme Englecher de Wridelesforde que in manu domine Alesie."

Eleven score acres of land at Tanesolf in the lord's demesne. And be it remembered that there are 26 acres of land which were in the demesne, which the lord gave to the Borough of Pontefract by charter, in exchange for a certain plot of land, which he gave to the Friars Preachers. Each acre of the eleven score is worth twelve pence. Sum in money, £11.

The garden of Tanesolfe[a] is worth (? 12)*d.* And there are 10 cottars and two curtilages in Tanesolfe worth 10*s.* And . . . . of . . . . for works in autumn 7*d.*

Fifty-six acres of meadow in Castelforde in demesne, at 3*s.* an acre. Sum in money, £8 8*s.*

A pasture called . . . . and Thilloles, which Hugh Clerk holds, and pays 5*s.* a year. A toft at 6*d.* Another toft at 6*d.* Another toft at 2*s.* Sum, 7*s.* 6*d.*

24 bovates of land in Carleton and Herdwyke,[b] held in bondage, each bovate containing 15 acres, and paying for each acre 4*d.* Each bovate ought to work two days a week for forty-seven weeks in the year, each work being worth three farthings; and each bovate during the five weeks of autumn ought to work for six days, each work being worth one penny. And each bovate of twenty bovates pays three fowls at Christmas and forty eggs at Easter. And each of four bovates pays two fowls and fifteen eggs. And each bovate of the twenty-four ought to plough twice a year, with dinner from the lord once a day (*ad prandium domini semel in die*); and if no dinner, the lord shall give 3*d.* Each of which twenty bovates is worth 9*s.* 3½*d.*, and each of the four bovates is worth 9*s.* 2½*d.* Sum of rents and works, £11 2*s.* 8*d.*

A toft in Karleton, 12*d.* a year. Nine bovates of land in Herdewyke are held freely of the lord, of which Simon de Herthewyke holds five bovates at half a marc, and ought to serve summonses of the Court of Pontefract with the serjeant of the same, and ought to testify them (*testificabit illas*). Thomas *le Parmenter* holds three bovates and pays 4*s.* a year. The heir of Robert Lageman holds one bovate of land in Herdewyke, and pays 16*d.* a year for all service. All these are holden of the lord King in chief, but they know not by what service.

The mills of Hast'ford[c] and Cnottingley with the fisheries are worth 40 marcs a year with the windmill. Sum, 40 marcs.

Henry, the first-born son of Eadmund de Lascy, is his next heir, and was of the age of eight years on Christmas Day in the 42nd year (1257).

---

[a] Tanshelf, adjoining Pontefract on the West.

[b] Carlton and East Hardwick, in the parish of Pontefract.

[c] Probably a mistake for Kast'ford, *i.e.*, Castleford. See *Yorkshire Archæological Journal*, vol viii., p. 353.

SOKE OF SNAYT.[a]

E ADMUND de Lacy held two parts of the Soke by the service of one knight; also a certain culture, containing 7 score and 20 acres of land (at 4d.); a pasture of 4 score acres (at 2d.); a wood, worth yearly 40s.; three acres of meadow (at 12d.). He had a market, worth yearly £8; one windmill, 13s.; five cottars and one acre of land, by the year, 11s. 3d.   Sum, £14 7s. 3d.

Villans at great farm.

Name.	Holding.	Annual rent.	
		s.	d.
John Liosl'	Half a bovate	4	o
William de Behale . .	,, ,, . . .	4	o
William de Lincoln . .	,, ,, . . .	4	o
William de Wythelay. .	,, ,, . . .	4	o
Martin	One bovate . . .	6	o
Simon Whyhet . . .	Half a bovate . .	4	o
William Paynoc . .	,, ,, . .	4	o
Roger Paynoc . . .	,, ,, . .	4	o
Ralph Francis . . .	One bovate . .	8	o
William son of Cecily .	,, ,, . . .	8	o
Hugh Little *(parvus)* . .	Half a bovate .	4	o
Robert Armue . . .	,, ,, . . .	4	o
Henry son of Simon . .	Fourth part of a bovate	2	o

Sum of bovates, 7½ and a fourth part.
Sum of the money, 60s.

Villans at little farm.[b]

Name.	Holding.	Annual rent.	
		s.	d.
Richard Smith *(faber)* and Jordan his brother . . }	One bovate . . .	3	3½
Henry Joce . . . Hugh son of Ranulf . . }	,, ,, . . .	3	3½

¶ These do one ploughing *(faciunt unam carucam)*, value 2d., and reap 2 days in August, value 5d.

Simon Jade . . Michael Francis . . }	Three parts of a bovate	1	11¾
a Michael Francis[c] . . *a* Ranulf Godnasse . . }	One bovate . . .	3	3½

[a] This Inquisition has been read with great difficulty. The names, cannot, therefore, be given with certainty.

[b] " Ad parvam firmam."

[c] The names marked *a* do one ploughing (2d.), and reap two days, value 5d. Those marked *b*, the two days' reaping is valued at 7d.; those marked *c*, at 4d.; *d*, at 3d.; and *e*, at 2d. The value of the ploughing remains constant.

Name.	Holding.	Annual rent. s.	d.
a Henry son of Simon	One bovate	3	3½
a William de Behale			
a Hugh son of Alan	„ „	3	3½
b William Amine			
b Roger Godewerdle	„ „	3	3½
b Peter Young *(juvenis)*			
b Peter Short *(bref)*	„ „	3	3½
b James			
b Hugh son of Ranulf	„ „	3	3½
b and Flarde			
b Adam Hill *(de Monte)*	Half a bovate	1	7¾
b Geoffrey son of Ralph			
b Stephen Tippinge			
b John Smith *(faber)*	One bovate	3	3½
b William Hill *(de Monte)*			
b John de Dor	„ „	3	3½
b Ranulf de Saliciis			
a Cecil' Towye	„ „	3	3½
a Thomas Fiz	Half a bovate	1	7¾
a Jordan Fox			
a Ralph de Fraxino	One bovate	3	3½
a Roger his brother			
c William son of Ranulf the Mercer	Half a bovate	1	7¾
c Iveta, widow	One bovate	3	3½
c Adam Orre	„ „	3	3½
c William son of Richard			
d Ralph Maubride	„ „	3	3½
d Robert the Mercer			
d Alexander Rud	Three parts of a bovate	3	4
e Geoffrey de Crofto	One bovate	2	8½
e John Lyolfe	Half a bovate	1	7¾

Sum of bovates, 19.

Sum of the money, 68s. 5¾d.

Free tenants.[a]

Name.	Holding.	Annual rent. s.	d.
Thomas son of Osmund	One and half bovates	4	6
Robert de Belne	Half bovate	1	6
William son of Roger[b]	„ „	1	6
Nicholas son of Herbert	„ „	1	3

[a] All these (down to Alexander son of William) do one ploughing, value 2d., and reap two days, value 2d. and 3d.

[b] This name is repeated a second time.

Name.	Holding.	Annual rent. s.	d.
William son of Anyn .	Half bovate .	1	3
Henry son of Simon .	One and half bovates .	3	$11\frac{1}{4}$
William son of Gamel	Two and half bovates .	10	0
Thomas son of William	One bovate .	2	$4\frac{1}{2}$
Alan son of Beatrice .	,, ,, .	2	$4\frac{1}{2}$
Adam de Mora .	,, ,, .	2	$4\frac{1}{2}$
Thomas son of Alexander .	,, ,, .	5	$2\frac{1}{4}$
Walter Forester .	Half bovate .	1	$2\frac{1}{4}$
John de Baulne .	One bovate .	2	$4\frac{1}{2}$
Alexander son of William .	One and half bovates .	6	$4\frac{1}{2}$

Sum of the bovates, 15.
Sum of the money, 49s. $11\frac{1}{4}d$.

Name.	Holding.	Annual rent. s.	d.
William *de la Wuarderobe* .	Two bovates [a]	5	8
Peter de Mora .	,, ,, .	4	4
William de Pouelington [b]	Thirty-five bovates	48	8
Nicholas de Insula .	Nine bovates .	18	5
Adam de Arnethorpe .	Two and half bovates	4	$10\frac{1}{2}$
Jordan son of Amabil	One bovate	2	4
Hawyse Olfride .	Half bovate	1	6
Gilbert de Crofto .	,, ,, .	3	0
John Laysinge .	Two bovates	5	10
Henry son of Hugh .	,, ,, .	5	6
William Bole .	,, ,, .	4	8
Matilda (or Maud), widow .	Three-quarters bovate .	1	10
Henry de Vermyl .	Three and half bovates.	9	2
Geoffrey Gewyn .	Two and quarter bovates	6	0
Henry de Goldale .	One and quarter bovates	3	0
Margaret de Peningstone .	Five bovates .	10	6
John de Heke .	Nineteen and quarter bovates .	39	3
John de Everingham .	One carucate.	8	0
Ninius de Folkehuardeby [c] .	Half bovate .	0	$9\frac{1}{2}$
William son of Diana .	,, ,, .	1	0
William son of Hugh .	,, ,, .	1	$2\frac{1}{4}$
Roger son of Edus (?) .	Two bovates	4	9
Thomas son of Aleta .	One bovate .	2	$4\frac{1}{2}$
Ralph de Rouhale .	Eleven bovates	24	$9\frac{1}{2}$
Henry Wendilok .	Three and half bovates.	6	3
John Fowler *(auceps)* .	One and half bovates	4	6

[a] And in addition, one assart.
[b] Pollington, in the parish of Snaith.
[c] Fockerby, in the parish of Adlingfleet.

Name.	Holding.	Annual rent. s. d.
Reginald Wace . . .	Half bovate . . .	1 o
John Spenke . . .	Five-sixths bovate .	3 2
Adam de Aula . . .	One bovate . . .	3 6

Sum of the bovates, six-score and one.
Sum of the money, £11 16s. 8¾d.

Nicholas Parker for suit of Court 4 0
Abbot of Seleby for Estofte 38 8
Sum, 42s. 8d.
Sum of the sums, £37 5s. 0¾d.

Henry, son of Eadmund de Lascy, is his next heir, aged eight years and a half, one month, and six days, at the feast of Saint James the Apostle, 42 Hen. 3 (25 July, 1258).

[M. 2ᵈ, col. 1.]

EXTENTᵃ made before Sir P[eter] de Percy in . . . on Sunday after the feast of S. James the Apostle, 42 Hen. (28 July, 1258), of the manors of Lord Eadmund de Lascy, namely; Ledes, Rowelle, Berwyke, Kipex, Allerton, with their appurtenances by sworn men, . . . ftehous (?), Thomas de Lofthus, Peter Dawtrey (de Alta ripa), Richard de [Rey]nevile, Adam de Kipex, Gilbert de Keddel, John de Carleton, Thomas Bywater (juxta aquam), William de Allerton, ... of Berwyke, Thomas of the same, Simon de Rupe, Thomas son of Richard of Lede . .

[LEDES]

[The lord Eadmund de Lascy] held Ledes in chief of the King by the service of barony (per servicium baronie). There are in demesne seven score four acres and a half of land (at 4d.), 20 acres of meadow (at 3s.), and two gardens, value 10s. by the year. Also a mill, £12, profit of wood, 8d., farm of the borough with market and oven (cum foro et furno), £10 by the year.

Free [tenants].

Robert de Wudehus yields by the year, 4s.; Thomas Bywater (juxta aquam) 1s. 4d.; Thomas son of Richard, 2s. 5d.

ᵃ This document at the commencement is all but illegible, and in this, and many other parts of the membranes following, the words are read with the greatest difficulty.

Bondmen.

Name.	Holding.	Annual rent. s.	d.
Paulin de Wudehus	Two bovates	5	8
Thomas Brodheie[a]		12	8
Ralph son of John	Two bovates	5	8
William Pain	,, ,,	5	8
William son of William Cobbler *(sutoris)*	,, ,,	5	8
William Cobbler *(sutor)*	,, ,,	5	8
Peter Ruffus	,, ,,	5	8
Adam son of Paulin	,, ,,	5	8
William Carpenter	,, ,,	6	6
William son of Ralph	,, ,,	5	8
Wife of William son of Thomas	,, ,,	5	8
William son of Alexander	,, ,,	5	8
Robert Moncel	,, ,,	5	8
William Newcomen	,, ,, ,	5	8
William P.[b]	Two and a half bovates	7	6
Robert son of Juliana	Two bovates	6	0
Geoffrey P..	,, ,, and Lyntwait[c]	6	8
Thomas de Buselingtorpe	,, ,,	6	0
Gilbert de Cuntestorpe	Three ,,	7	9
Richard of the same	,, ,,	7	9
Alexander P.	Six ,,	15	6
Robert son of Gilbert	Two ,,	4	7
Wife of Gilbert *del hil*	Two ,, and toft	6	8
Thomas Rochengg'	,, ,,	5	0
Bondmen at Wudehus[d]	One ,,	2	6
Roger Plumer	Toft and croft	3	4
William de Buselingtorpe	,, ,, and parcels of land	8	0

Cottars.

Name.		Annual Rent. s.	d.
William de Holebeke		1	11½
William de Fareburne		2	11½
Margaret de Adelton		1	4
Agnes *(Angn')* Long		0	6
Alexander *del Hil*		1	8

[a] No tenement given.

[b] This " P " or " pp," which occurs several times, probably stands for *prepositus.*

[c] Query Linthwaite, in the parish of Almondbury.

[d] Great Woodhouse, in the parish of Leeds.

Name.	Annual rent.	
	s.	*d.*
Wife of John Banastre	3	0
Roger Shepherd *(bercarius)*	1	6
William Webster *(textor)*	2	4
Wife of William Baldewyn	1	0
Robert son of Adam	0	2
Henry Carpenter	0	4
Richard Taillur	1	2
John son of the Smith	2	0
Simon Forester	2	8
Andrew Taillur	0	4
Reginald Prii	2	8
Robert Plumer and Milner *(molend')*	2	8
John Lister *(tinctor)*	2	2
Thomas Baker *(pistor)*	1	2
For the mill-court	1	4
Alexander de Lede	0	6
From thirty and a half acres of land at 4*d.*	10	2

Sum total of the manor, £38 4*s.* 7*d.*

ROWELLE.[a]

The lord Eadmund de Lascy held Rowelle of the King in chief by the service of barony. In demesne six score and three acres (at 3*d.*); a garden of the court, 12*d.*; a pasture under the wood, 9*s.*; curtilage next the court, 15*d.*; two mills by the year, £18 13*s.* 4*d.*

Free tenants (Liberi).

Name.	Annual rent.	
	s.	*d.*
James de Methel'	5	0
Adam Butalle	6	4
and 2lb. pepper at Martinmas.		
John Beriner	1	1
and 2lb. pepper.		
Richard Forester	19	4
William Tailor *(cissor)*	one pound of pepper.	
Walter Smith *(faber)*	6	0
John Grumet	6	6
Adam Kitchener *(focar')*	5	0

Bondmen.

Name.	Holding.	Annual rent.	
		s.	*d.*
Cile (?)Mauger	One bovate[b]	8	2
John de Methel'	,, ,,	6	8

[a] Rothwell, four and a half miles from Leeds.　　[b] And one assart.

Name.	Holding.	Annual rent. s.	d.
William Snel	One bovate	7	8
William de Farnle	Two bovates[a]	17	6
Richard Po	One bovate[a]	9	0½
Henry de Holt	,, ,, [a]	8	2
Jord[an] Barn	,, ,, [a]	8	2
William Sire	,, ,, [a]	8	2
John son of Nicholas	,, ,,	7	8
Jord[an] in Wro	,, ,,	7	8
Adam de Midleton	,, ,,	7	8
Thomas de Hocht'	,, ,,	7	8
Peter son of Simon	,, ,, [a]	8	8
Peter Everarde	,, ,, [a]	8	6
John Yngeri	,, ,, [a]	8	6
Robert son of Austin	,, ,,	7	8
William Reeve (p'p')	,, ,, [a]	9	0
Robert Walais	,, ,,	6	8

Cottars.

Name.	Annual rent, s.	d.
Thomas Flecher	4	1
David Mower *(falcator)*	2	6
Elewys	0	10
William son of Ralph	0	10
David Parker *(percarius)*	1	0
Wife of Crane	1	4
John Dote	1	0½
Robert Skinner *(peliparius)*	1	0½
Stephen Shepherd *(bercarius)*	1	0½
Juliana Blakeprest	1	4½
Peter Merwin	1	0½
Alexander	1	8
John Winter	1	0½
Simon Merwin	0	6
John de Bradele	1	8

Wife of Peter de Rodes for assart, 10s.; and 12d. for
the alder-bed from William Reeve *(p'p')* . . . 11 0

Sum total of the manor, £32 10s. 4d.,
and 5 lb. pepper.

[HOLTON.]

There are in demesne, 10 acres of land (at 4d.), and herbage
of a pond, 6s. 8d.

ᵃ And one assart. William de Farnle holds in adddition, meadow.

Bondmen.

Name	Holding.	Annual rent. s.	d.
Humphrey de Millers	One bovate	6	5
Hugh son of Nigel	,, ,, ᵃ	10	4
Roger son of Ralph	,, ,, ᵈ	7	1
Adam son of Robert .	,, ,, ᵘ	7	3
Ralph P. . .	,, ,, ᵈ	7	3
Hamery de Midelton .	,, ,, ᵈ	6	10
Adam son of William	,, ,,	6	5
Hobioc . .	,, ,,	6	5
Wife of Walter de Holton . .	,, ,, and bulehil	7	7
Jordan son of Robert	,, ,, ᵈ	8	11
Peter Norais . .	,, ,, ᵈ	10	11
Robert son of Richard	,, ,, ᵃ	7	9½
Peter Swetemilk	,, ,, and one acre	7	3
Adam son of William	for land fflop(?)	6	11
Hugh de Methele	half bovate .	3	11½

Cottars.

Name.		Annual rent. s.	d.
William Messager	. .	2	0
Adam Milner	.	12	0
Henry Waylaunt .	. .	4	0
Agnes *del Grene* .	.	1	0
Robert son of Peter	.	3	8½
Yngramus .	.	1	2½
Juliana . . .	.	1	4½
Roger son of Emma	.	1	4½
Malle Linbetere .		2	2½
Henry Sponere	.	1	0
Evote . . .	.	1	0½
Richard son of Ynger .	.	1	0½

Sum total of the manor, £7 13s. 3½d.

LOFTHUS.

Free tenants.

Name.		Annual rent. s.	d.
Henry son of Henry .	. . .	2	0
Wife of Peter de Assart'	. . .	6	8

ᵃ And one assart

Bondmen.

Name.	Holding.			Annual rent. s.	d.
Adam son of John	Two bovates[a]			9	2½
Robert son of Hugh	One bovate[a]			9	0
William son of William	,,	,,	and toft	6	2½
Alice Underwood *(sub bosco)*	,,	,,	and assart	6	4½
Thomas de Methele	,,	,,	,,	7	9½
Adam de Herteshevede	,,	,,	,,	5	10½
Hugh son of Hugh	,,	,,	and croft	6	4½
Henry son of Peter	,,	,,	and assart	7	4½
Robert son of Laurence	,,	,,	,,	6	6½
Ralph Clerk	,,	,,		5	4½
Martin son of Ivetta	,,	,,		4	0

Cottars.

Name.	Annual rent. s.	d.
Henry son of Roger	1	9
And from land of Edith *(Et de terra Edith)*	9	3½

Sum total, £4 13s. 8½d.

CARLETON.[b]

Free tenants.

Name.	Annual rent. s.	d.
John de Carleton	2	2
Robert son of John	0	8
Peter of the same	6	8
Rose	0	2
William son of Walter	0	5
The vicar of Rowlle	3	0

Bondmen.

Name.	Holding.			Annual rent. s.	d.
Richard Hereward	One bovate and assart			6	11
Ralph son of John	,,	,,	,,	7	1
William de Holebeke	,,	,,	,,	6	8
Richard *Ruffus*	,,	,,		5	9
John Gille	,,	,,	and assart	6	3
Hamery *(Hamericus)*	,,	,,	,,	7	3½
Robert son of Hamery	,,	,,	,,	6	9½
Nicholas son of Richard	,,	,,	,,	6	11
Also a bovate of land yields				3	0

Sum total, 69s. 9d.

[a] And one assart.   [b] Carlton, in the parish of Rothwell.

WRIDLES[FORD].[a]

There are three acres of meadow, every acre 3*s.*; a garden, worth 5s.

Free tenant.

Name.	Annual rent. s.	d.
James de Methel'	o	8

Bondmen.

Name.	Holding.	Annual rent. s.	d.
John de Methel' . . . One bovate . . .	14	5
Roger de Methel' . . ,, ,, . . .	14	5
William at Gate *(ad portam)* ,, ,, . . .	14	11
Hugh de Holgate . . ,, ,, . . .	14	5
Ellen wife of Hugh . . ,, ,, . . .	14	5
Robert Milner . . . A third part of one bovate	3	9¾

Cottars.

	Annual rent. s.	d.
A certain cottage	1	8

Sum total, £4 13*s.* 8¾*d.*

[M. 2ᵈ, col. 2.]

BEREWYKE.[b]

LORD Edmund de Lascy held Berwyke of the King in chief by service of barony. There are in demesne eight score and ten acres of arable land (8*d.* the acre); five acres of meadow (2*s.*); two mills, both £4; herbage of Blakefen by the year, 5*s*; a garden, 10*s.*

Free tenants.

Name.	Annual rent. s.	d.
John de Vesscy	2	2
Alan son of Richard	4	3
Thomas Smith *(faber)*	4	0
Richard Marshal *(marescallus)*	2	0
Robert Forester	2	0
Hugh son of Eustace *(Eustac')* . . .	0	6
Roger Clerk	1	0
Gilbert de Kiddale	1	6

[a] Woodlesford, in the parish of Rothwell.
[b] Barwick-in-Elmet.

Bondmen.

Name.	Holding.	Annual rent.	
		s.	d.
Eight bondmen each		10	3
Paulin P. and Thomas at			
Well *(juxta Fontem)*	Two bovates .	17	4
Robert Glewman . .	One bovate .	8	4
Four bovates, each by the year		18	0

Cottars.

Name.	Annual rent.	
	s.	d.
Adam Kinstan	3	0
Ydda	3	0
Eva	3	0
William Gaure	3	0
William Mason *(cementarius)* . .	3	0
Adam son of Hervey *(Hervic')* .	3	0
Robert Cobbler *(sutor)* . . .	3	6
Muriel	3	3
Adam Lilleman	3	3
Hervey Smith *(faber)* . . .	3	6
Robert Carpenter	4	8
Jordan Here	3	6
John son of Jordan	5	0
Wife of Jordan	3	5
Rose daughter of Humfrey	2	5
Roger Cobbler *(sutor)*	3	0
Hugh Pruderay	2	5
Agnes wife of Gregory	2	5
Thomas Langald	2	5
Alice wife of Richard	2	5
Works of towns adjacent	5	7

Forlande.

Name.	Holding.	Annual rent.	
		s.	d.
	Thirty acres at 10*d.*		
Robert Forester . .	Other three acres .	2	6
Paulin P.	Three acres . .	3	0
Hervey Smith *(faber)*	For Wulueterode	3	0
Adam de Kiddale .	Two acres . .	1	0
Jordan P. . . .	For new land acquired .	0	3
Richard P. . . .	For two acres .	0	10
Robert P. and Roger P.	For two acres . .	1	4
Michael Pindere . .	For three acres .	3	0
Thomas Langalde .	For one acre . .	1	0

Sum total of the said manor, £27 15s. 1d.

BARNEBU.[a]

Free tenants.

	Annual rent.	
Name.	*s.*	*d.*
Peter Dawtrey *(de Alta ripa)*	10	2
Richard de Reynevile	8	2
Nicholas de Barnebu	8	0
Robert Forester	8	0
William Hurttenent	8	0
Henry	10	0
Richard Waleys *(Walens')*	One lb. cumin.	

Sum total, 52*s.* 4*d.*, and 1 lb. cumin.

SCALES.[b]

In demesne four score acres of arable land, at 6*d.* Eight cottars, who all yield by the year 9*s.* 10*d.*

MORWYKE.[c]

There are four bovates of land at 15*s.* the bovate.

RODA.

Also Roda with meadow is worth by the year 20*s.*

Sum total, £6 9*s.* 10*d.*, one lb. of cumin.

KYPEXK.[d]

Eadmund de Lascy held Kipex of the King in chief, and it is of barony *(Et est de baronia).*

There are in demesne seven score fourteen acres of arable land, each yearly 8*d.*

Free tenants.

	Annual rent.	
Name.	*s.*	*d.*
Adam Freman	4	0
and 1 lb. cumin.		
William *de Warderoba* for custody of certain land .	4	0
Jordan Frerman	19	0
and one pair of gloves.		
William Clerkheved, 3½ ac. land	2	6
and 1 lb. pepper.		
Also from Preston-pond[e] *(Item de stangno de Presto', 1d.)*	0	1

[a] Barnbow, in the parish of Barwick in Elmet.
[b] Scholes, in the same parish. See No. LVI.
[c] Morwick, in the same parish.
[d] Kippax, near Pontefract. See No. LVI.
[e] Great and Little Preston, in the parish of Kippax.

Bondmen.

Name.	Holding.	Annual rent. s. d.
Robert Brun . .	One bovate . .	22 0
	and 1d. for one day's work.	
Robert son of Robert of Rowlle . . .	One bovate .	22 1
Roger Newbonde .	,, ,, . .	22 1
Peter son of Hugh .	,, ,, . .	22 1
	And for curtilage . .	1 0
Hugh P. . . .	One bovate . .	22 1
Laurence . .	,, ,, .	22 1
	And for a meadow	0 6
Adam Parcur . .	One bovate	22 1
Adam son of Hugh . .	,, ,, .	22 1
John Harding . . .	,, ,, .	22 1
John son of Roger	,, ,, .	22 1
	And for half an acre .	0 6
Adam Milner . .	One bovate .	22 1
Jordan son of Goda .	,, ,, .	22 1
	And for one rood [a]	0 3
Elias Parcur .	One bovate	22 1
	And for half an acre	0 6
Ralph Parcur . .	One bovate .	22 1
	And one acre one rood [a]	1 6
John son of Martin . .	One bovate .	22 1
Walter *del Grene* . .	,, ,, .	22 1
Richard Rote and Curtehose	,, ,,	22 1
Peter Pindere and Reginald	,, ,, . .	22 1
Reginald	One acre and croft .	2 0
Plough-works *(de operibus carucarum)* of Ledeston .		2 0

Cottars.

Name.	Annual rent. s. d.
Adam *del Grene*	3 1
Robert son of John	3 1
John Cnyvet	3 1
Cecily *(Cecilia)*	3 1
Walter Smith *(faber)*	3 1
Robert . . . dr'	3 1
John Shepherd *(bercarius)*	1 3
Robert Clerk	2 1
Roger de Stretton	2 1
Walter Smith *(faber)*	1 0
Roger Kene	3 6

[a] *Perticata*

Name.						Annual Rent. s. d.
Thomas Johns	.	.	.	.	.	3 1
William Abot	.	.	.	.	.	7 1
Richard de Stretton	.	.	.	.	.	1 7
Also of Tolcestre (*Tolcestra*)	.	.	.	.	2 0
For the hall and barns .	.	.	.	.	15 0

Sum total of the manor, £29 15s. 2d.,
one lb. cumin, one lb. pepper, one pair of white gloves.

ALLERRTON-BY-WATER (*juxta aquam*).

Lord Eadmund de Lascy held Allerton of the King in chief. There are in demesne five score acres of arable land (acre, 4d.) ; also 17½ acres one rood[a] of meadow (acre, 3s.) ; and a garden, 2s.

Free tenants.

Name.					Annual rent. ɔ. d.
Geoffrey	.	.	.	One pair of spurs, price	0 6
Richard Pikeston .	.		.	.	2 0
Robert Pygot	.			.	2 6

Bondmen.

Name.			Holding.	Annual rent. s. d.
William P. .	.	.	One bovate and assart .	12 0
			And for works . .	0 3
Roger son of Richard		.	One bovate .	10 3
Hugh Shepherd (*bercarius*)				
and Walter Long .	.		„ „ . . .	10 3
Warin P. .		.	„ „ and assart .	12 9
Adam Bonde	.		„ „ . . .	11 3
Leysing	.	.	„ „ .	10 3
William Ruter .			„ „ .	11 1
Richard Cobbler (*sutor*)	.		„ „ . . .	10 3
Adam son of Emma .			„ „ and assart .	12 3
Richard Ryot	.		One toft . . .	1 5
John de Rowelle	.	.	. . .	1 7
Adam de Horsford	.		One toft	2 3
Fishery by the year	.	.	. . . .	3 0

How much lord Eadmund de Lascy held of others the jurors know not. Henry, his son, is his next heir, aged eight years and a half, one month and six days, at the feast of Saint James the Apostle, in the 42nd year of the reign of King Henry (25 July, 1258).

Sum total of Allerton, £10 2s. 5d.
Sum of the sums of this roll, £168 0s. 2¾d.,
6 lbs. of pepper, 2 lbs. of cumin, and one pair of gloves.

ᵃ *Perticata.*

9

XLVI. RICHARD AND WILLIAM DE PERCY.[a] *Inq. p. m.*

[43 HEN. III. No. 38.]
No writ.

EXTENT of the manor of Tadecastre made before John Gubaud and the Sheriff of the county, by Sir William de Merstone, Geoffrey de Rufford, Robert de Dunesford, Robert de Hoton, William *de Marisco*, William son of Henry of Whihale, Hugh de Oxtorp, Henry de Grimestone, Robert Langethehit, Robert de Hybernia, Hugh Gernun, and Thomas de Uskelf, who say upon their oath that the demesne, excepting villenage *(preter villenagium)*, contains eight score and ten acres (by the perch of eighteen feet), each worth by the year 2s., and thirty-four acres of meadow (at 4s.). There are held in villenage eight bovates and a half, each extended by the year at 10s. 6d. for all services and demands. There are eight cottages, worth in all by the year 23s. 2d. The court with garden is worth 50s. An oven *(furnus)* is worth yearly one marc. Also the mills with fisheries which appertain to the King, saving 62s. 8d. which the Prior of Park,[b] Robert de Brus, and Thomas *le Lardiner* receive yearly from the mills, and of which the widow *(quondam uxor)* of William de Percy ought to acquit the third part, £11 10s. The underwood in the park with alderbed *(alneto)*, turbary, and pasture, is worth by the year 100s. Rent of free tenants yearly, 12s. 10d.

[M. 2.]

EXTENT of the Manor of Spoforde, made before Sir J. Guboud, and the Sheriff, by William de Plumton, Henry de Ribestayn, Thomas his brother, Robert son of Robert of Timbel, Henry de Dicton, Robert de Stokeld, Walter de Mikelthayd, William de Beugraunt, Luke de Hoperton, Richard Wyting of Wyton, Thomas *le Lardener* of Tatecastre, Nigel son of Thomas of Dicton, and Adam *le Taylur* of Coltorp, who say upon their oath that there are in demesne fifty-four acres of arable land (at 4d.), also 16½ acres one rood of meadow (3s. the acre). Rent of free tenants yearly 44s. 1d. Villenage of the manor by the year for merchet and tallage 103s. 2d. Cottages are worth by the year 15s. 6d., and the court is extended at half a marc; the dovehouse, half a marc; the vivary, 40s.; an oven, 2s. A plot which was taken to make a garden is extended at 3s. Two forges in the foreign wood *(in bosco forinseco)*, yield by the year 16 marcs to the King. The underwood

---

[a] See No. v.   [b] Helagh Park.

of the park with dead wood except greenwood is extended to keep up two forges which yield to the King 24 marcs. Pannage and herbage in the wood are worth by the year 100s. The pasture called Wetecroft and Tidoverker, which used to be enclosed, is worth by the year 8s. 10¾d.; the mill, 50s.; a plot near the mill, 4d. There are due in the manor three pounds of cumin of rent of assize yearly. The parson's men owe to the King 3s. 2d. yearly for four carucates and 26 reaping hooks *(faucibus)*. The villans and cottars ought to mow six acres of meadow and carry to the lord's house, and to make the mill-pond, and they shall have from the lord's purse twelve pence. The work of every acre is worth eight pence, if they do not mow the said meadow.

[M. 2ᵈ.]

EXTENT of the manor of Linton[a] made by the same jurors, who say that there are [of land] five score and 17 acres and two parts of one acre (at 10d. the acre), and of meadow, six acres and two parts of one acre (4s. the acre). There is a mill, whereof the King's portion is extended at six marcs, 4s. 5½d., and a garden (of which the lady demands a third part), worth by the year two marcs. There is a sheep-fold *(bercaria)* which could not be extended at any price. Rent of free tenants, 14s. 8d. and one pound of pepper. Villenage with merchet and tallage is extended by the year at £6 2s. Cottages of the manor are worth by the year 2s. 6d., rent of assize. Labour of six days in autumn from three cottars who have their food, 6d. yearly. The villans of the manor ought to make the mill-pond, and to mow the lord's meadow without food, and they shall not give merchet or tallage, because both are extended with their bovates. The work of every acre of meadow, as to mow, make, and carry, is worth by the year 12d., if the villans do not mow it.[b]

[M. 3.]

INQUISITION of lands which were of Richard and William de Percy, made by Marmaduke de Disford, William de Neuby, William son of Oliver, Robert *le Venur*, William son of Hugh,

---

a Both Linton, in the parish of Spofforth, and Linton, in Staincliffe, belonged to the Percies. The former is probably the manor extended above. The place with the same name in Staincliffe, occurs below.

b "Item memorandum quod vilani ejusdem manerii debent facere stangnum molendini et falcare pratum domini sine cibo, et non dabunt merchetum neque talagium, quia ambo extenduntur cum bovatis suis. Item opus cujuslibet acre prati, ut falcare, facere, et cariare, valet per annum xijd., si predicti vilani illud non falcaverint."

Nigel de Dicton, William Bougraunt, Robert Fattinge, William Fraunkelayn, Thomas *le Lardiner*, Thomas *le Marescall*, Henry son of the Master *(fil' Mag'ri)* and Thomas at the Cross *(ad crucem)*, who say upon their oath that in the manor of Toppeclive there are in demesne 600 acres of land (at 6*d.*), £15; 53 acres of meadow, 53*s.* The capital messuage is not extended because nearly down *(quia fere decidit)*. The garden and curtilage are worth by the year half a marc. There are four watermills, worth 14 marcs; wood and pasture, 10 marcs. Fifteen cottars hold fifteen messuages only, and yield yearly 26*s.* There are 24 bovates of land in bondage (each contains six acres), which twelve bondmen *(bondi)* hold, each bovate worth 6*s.*, £7 4*s.* In Aystanby,[a] which is in the same manor, are eight bovates (each contains ten acres), each bovate worth 10*s.*, which four bondmen *(bondi)* hold, £4. In Carleton[b] one bovate (eight acres) in bondage, held by one man *(bondus)*, 5*s.*

There are seven free tenants :—

Name.	Holding.	Annnal rent.	
		s.	*d.*
Richard son of Hervey	. Two bovates . . .	3	0
Hervey *le Kipper* .	. One bovate . . .	2	0
John of Boroughbridge *(de Ponte Burgi)* .	. Two bovates . .	2	0
Peter *le Sumenur* .	. Five acres . . .	4	0
Walter Scrike (or Strike) .	. Two bovates . . .	1	0
Richard Baker *(pistor)* .	. One toft with croft, half acre . . .	3	2
Robert Cobbler *(sutor)* .	. One toft and one acre .	1	4

Also Robert Forester holds two bovates in Grisethwayth'[c] for 6*s.*; John de Bulemer, the manor of Wilton[d] for £10; the Abbot of Fountains, the grange of Marton[e] for 8*s.*, by the year. There are pleas and perquisites which are worth yearly half a marc. Sum, £58 11*s.* 10*d.*

In the manor of Tatecastre there are seven score acres in demesne (8*d.* the acre), 101*s.* 4*d.*; 20 acres of meadow (4*s.*), £4. A garden is worth by the year 10*s.* There are three watermills, which with the fishing of the same are worth by the year eight marcs. There is a pasture, 2*s.* A wood there which bears no fruit is therefore not extended. There are ten cottars, who hold ten messuages and one acre and a half of land, which are worth by the year 19*s.* 3*d.* Eight bovates (each five acres, and worth 6*s.*) are held in bondage by six men *(bondi)*, 48*s.*

---

[a] Asenby.
[b] Probably Carlton Miniot.
[c] Gristhwaite, in the parish of Topcliffe.
[d] Wilton in Cleveland.
[e] Marton-le-Moor, near Boroughbridge.

There are four free tenants, viz.

Name.	Holding.	Annual rent.	
		s.	d.
Robert de Smahus	One toft and three acres	6	8
Walter Page	,, ,,	0	8
Isabel	,, ,,	5	6
Ralph Fisher *(piscator)*	,, ,, and one acre and a half	6	8

There are no pleas. Sum, £19 6s. 9d.

[M. 3ᵈ.]

A LSO they say that in the manor of Spoford there are in demesne fifty-two acres of land (at 4d.), 17s. 4d., and of meadow, ten acres at 4d., and six acres at 2s., 15s. 4d. Two gardens are worth by the year 11s., one dovehouse, 2s., a vivary worth nothing. Five cottars hold five messuages for 7s. 6d. One watermill is worth by the year 20s. There are eleven bovates (each nine acres, and worth 7s.) in bondage, held by ten bondmen for 77s. There is a dyehouse *(tinctura)*, worth by the year 2s. 8d.

There are five free tenants :—

Name.	Holding.	Annual rent.	
		s.	d.
Thomas de Arches	Manor of Kereby[a]	6	0
William Fraunkelayn	One bovate	1	4
Walter Belle	One toft and one croft	3	0
Robert Fattinge	Two bovates	1 lb. cumin worth 1½d.	
John the Parson (pˢ)	Two bovates	ditto.	

Sum, £8 3s. 5d.

And there is at Spoford the advowson of a church, which is worth by the year 100 marcs.

In the manor of Linton[b] are five score and three acres of land in demesne (at 6d.), 51s. 6d., six acres and two parts of one acre (at 3s.), 20s. A garden, one marc, one watermill, five marcs by the year. Three cottars hold three messuages for 20d. Twelve bovates (each ten acres, and worth 6s.) in bondage are held by ten bondmen, 72s.

---

[a] Kereby, in the parish of Kirkby Overblow, near Wetherby.

[b] Linton, in Staincliffe.

There are three free tenants :—

Name.	Holding.	Annual rent.
		s. d.
William son of Simon	One bovate	5 0
Alexander Fisher *(piscator)*	One bovate	5 0
Robert *le Chaumberlayn*	Four bovates	1 lb. pepper worth 6*d*.

There are pleas and perquisites which are worth by the year half a marc.

Sum, £12 2*s*. 4*d*.

At Langestrothe[a] there are three cottars who hold three messuages, which are worth by the year 6*s*. The herbage of Langestrothe is worth 100*s*. 8*d*.

There are six free tenants :—

Name.	Holding.	Annual rent.
		s. d.
Henry de Percy .	Manor of Setel	50 0
Rayner de Scotthorpe	Pasture called Raheved .	5 0
William Pollard .	Four bovates in Swinden	0 6
Hugh de Halton	Two bovates in the same	0 4
Adam de Westby	Westby .	8 6
Abbot of Fountains .	Malgum	5 0
John de Hamerton	Treskefelde	11 0
Piers *(Petrus)* de Percy	Ilkelay	21 4
The heir of Nigel de Plumton .	Gersington[b] .	. . . .

[Here the document (at the bottom) has been cut, and a portion is missing. On the other side *(recto)*—" Summa summarum hujus rotuli infra et extra, cix*li*. vjs." and in another line— " Summa omnium summarum utriusque rotuli. ciiij*xx* xiij*li*. xiiij*s*. viij*d*. ob.]

[M. 4.]

INQUISITION of the lands which were of Richard de Percy, and William de Percy, made by William fitz Hugh *(f' Hug')*, William de Gunneys, Robert de Neuton, William son of Simon of Wilberfosse, Thomas son of Bertram of the same, Thomas Agilun, Hugh de Tornholme, William son of Laurence, Richard son of Helewise, Henry son of Hugh of Sutton, Richard de Dunington, and John de Catton son of Ilger, who say upon their oath

---

[a] Langstrothdale Chase, in North-West Yorkshire.

[b] Swinden and Westby, in the parish of Gisburn ; Malham, Thresfield, and Grassington, in the parish of Linton ; and Ilkley.

that in the manor of Catton[a] there are in demesne eleven score and seven acres of land (at 9*d.*), £7 0*s.* 3*d.*; also two orchards, one curtilage, one dovehouse, three trenches *(fossata)*, and one pond with a mill sometimes grinding *(aliquando molente)* in winter, and one fishery beneath the court *(subtus cur')* in Derewente; all which are worth by the year in common years, 46*s.* 8*d.* There are also twenty-one acres of meadow (at 3*s.* 6*d.*), and nine acres one rood of meadow (at 2*s.*), £4 12*s.* There are seven mills upon one pond *(super unum stangnum)* in Derewent at Stamford Bridge *(Pontem Belli)*, which are worth by the year in common years, thirty-six marcs. There is a wood of about nine score acres which bears no fruit and is therefore extended at nothing; but there is pasture in the same, worth 10*s.* There is an advowson, and the church is worth by the year four score marcs. Twenty-three cottars hold twenty-three tofts, and six acres one rood of land, worth yearly 67*s.* 3*d.* In bondage fourteen bovates, £6 7*s.* 11*d.*, also thirty-eight bovates and two-thirds *(due partes)* of one bovate of land and two tofts held in socage by free tenants, who yield yearly 56*s.* Pleas and perquisites are worth half a marc, saving ladies' dowers *(exceptis dotibus dominarum).* Sum, £51 6*s.* 6*d.*

NAFFERTON.[b]

There are in Nafferton nineteen cottars who hold nineteen tofts and 15½ acres of land, which are worth by the year 38*s.* 6*d.* In bondage 20 bovates of land, £9 13*s.* 4*d.*, and in bondage seven bovates without tofts, 60*s.* 8*d.*, and five bovates without tofts, 41*s.* 8*d.* There are two-thirds[c] *(due partes)*, of a watermill which are worth by the year eight marcs; forty acres of meadow, 40*s.*; four score acres of pasture, 20*s.* Seven bovates of land which are set *(posite sunt)* to farm for a term, are worth by the year 77*s.* 8*d.* There are free tenants who hold three bovates and one toft, yielding yearly 11*s.*, 4*d.*, and doing foreign service. Laurence Chamberlain *(Camerar')* holds four bovates of land in Nafferton and renders yearly one pound of cumin, which is worth three half-pence (iij. ob.); and he does foreign service. In Wandesford, and Foston, which are members of Nafferton, there are ten cottars who hold ten tofts, worth by the year 36*s.* Two bovates and a half of land are set to farm and are worth 20*s.*, ladies' dowers excepted *(exceptis dotibus dominarum).*

The lands are worth less than they were at the time of the said Richard and William, because they lie uncultivated and the houses, mills and ponds lie overwhelmed *(obruta).*

---

[a] Catton, in the East Riding, between York and Pocklington.
[b] Nafferton, Wansforth, and Foston, in the neighbourhood of Driffield.
[c] The remaining one-third in dower probably.

Be it remembered that in Lekinfeud there are twelve acres one rood of land, worth by the year 42*s.* These are without dowers *(Hec sunt exceptis dotibus).*

Sum, £33 1*s.* 11½*d.*
Sum of the sums of this roll, £84 8*s.* 8½*d.*

XLVII. ON THE STATE OF SCARBOROUGH CASTLE.[a]

[44 HEN. III. No. 28.]

Writ dated at Westminster, 20 May, 44th year (1260).

INQUISITION made at Scardeburg', on Saturday after the feast of the Holy Trinity, 44 Henry (5 June, 1260), before Sir John de Oketon, Sheriff of Yorkshire—in what state the lord Gilbert de Gaunt left the castle of Scardeburg', and in what state the lord H. le Bigot, Justiciar of England, received it by commission from the King—by William de Roston, Ralph son of Peter of the same, William de Everle, Robert de Careby, Richard de Neville, Adam de Rouceby, Ralph de Loketon, Reginald de Haterberg', Roger son of Richard of Aton, Alan son of Martin, John le Campion, and Thomas de Helm, who say upon their oath that the great hall and great chamber with wardrobe, in many places are uncovered, and want great repair, the kitchen and tresonce *(tresoncia)* are nearly uncovered, the stable is wholly uncovered, the mangers broken, and one door *(hostium)* is wanting. The walls of the millhouse are broken, and there is no mill. The granary too is in a poor state *(debile est).* The hall within the enclosure of the tower is wholly uncovered, some of the beams *(tingnis)* are broken, and it threatens to fall. Also two of the castle bridges and the bridge attached to the tower are weak and rotten for a great part. Four leaves of two internal gates *(Quatuor vero walve duarum januarum interiorum)* are entirely wanting, and the walls between the said gates are ready to decay and have begun in great part to decay. In the great tower seven doors *(hostia)* and twenty-nine windows are entirely wanting. The flooring *(planchiatura)* of four turrets at the top of the tower is defective and nearly rotten. The wall flanking the tower is in many places thrown down, and the remainder threatens to fall. The outer gate of the tower is weak. The battlements *(kernelli)* and allours *(alure)* of the castle wall towards the town are in many places deteriorated, and need great repair. One of the turrets laid with lead

[a] See No. xxv.

is uncovered in divers places. The flooring of three turrets in the enceinte of the castle walls is nearly rotten. The battlements and allours *(alure)* of the outer barbican are in many places thrown down and injured, and need great repair. The little gate of the barbican is weak. In the castle there is an entire deficiency of cross-bows, quarrels, and all manner of arms necessary for its defence.[a]

XLVIII. WILLIAM DE FORTIBUS, EARL OF ALBEMARLE.[b]

Inq. p m.

[44 HEN. III. No. 26.]

Writ dated at Westminster, 1 Aug., 44th year (1260).

EXTENT of the manor of Pockeling[ton] made by Thomas son of Bartholomew, Thomas de Fyenes, Robert Puntif, Richard Marshal *(marescall')*, Richard Godard, Richard de Herlethorpe,

[a] The following extracts from the *Close Rolls*, give some information as to the work going on at Scarborough Castle at this time, 29 Nov. (1259). Appointment of overseers of the work of the Castle (44 Hen. III. Part I., m. 19). 6 Nov. (1259), Gilbert de Gaunt to have estovers in the Hay of Scalleby for fuel in Scarborough Castle, whilst it remains in his custody *(Ibid.)*. See also *Close Roll* 40 Hen. III., m. 21[d].

[b] This document is very difficult to read. On 18 Sept., 1241, the King informed Henry de Neketon, Escheator beyond Trent, that he had taken the homage of William de Fortibus, son and heir of William de Fortibus, late Earl of Albemarle, for the lands and tenements the said Earl held in chief. The Escheator, after taking security from the said William for the payment of £100 as his relief, was commanded to give William seisin of all the lands and tenements the Earl held in his bailiwick on the day he commenced his pilgrimage *(die quo iter peregrinationis arripuit)* to the Holy Land *(Excerpta è Rotulis Finium*, vol. i., p. 353). On 24 Oct. following, the King made certain concessions to William de Fortibus, son of William de Fortibus, late Earl of Albemarle, in relation to debts owing by his father to the Crown, and amongst others, £94 10s. 11d., which he owed the King of the debts of J., late Earl of Chester, for the portion which fell to the same W. and Christiana his wife, of the debts of the same Earl *(Ibid.*, vol. i., p. 357). On 29 July, 1246, the Sheriff of Yorkshire was ordered to seize the lands which William de Fortibus, Earl of Albemarle, held of the heritage of Devorgoyl, late his wife *(Ibid.,* vol. i., p. 459). On 12 June, 1260, William de Fortibus, Earl of Albemarle, having died *(viam universe carnis ingressus)*, William de Wendling, the Escheator *citra*, was ordered to seize the lands in his bailiwick held by him in chief *(Ibid.*, vol. ii., p. 327). His mother was Avelina, one of the daughters and heirs of Richard de Munfichet *(Calendarium Genealogicum*, vol. i., p. 127). His widow Isabella, was sister and heir of Baldwin de Insula, Earl of Devon *(Ibid.*, vol. i., p. 106, and *Excerpta è Rotulis Finium*, vol. ii., p. 402). She survived him many years, her *Inq. p. m.* not being taken until 21 Edward I. *(Cal. Gen.*, vol. ii., 764). Thomas, son and heir of the Earl, it is stated in the Holderness Inquisition given below, would be seven years old on 9 Sept., 1260. By an extent (not dated) of the manors of Polhamptune and Wimeringe in the County of Southampton, Thomas, son and heir of the Earl, is said to be seven years old. By an extent of the manor of Clopton, in Suffolk, made on Tuesday after the Translation of St. Benedict (13 July), in the same year (1260), the heir is said to be six or seven. An extent made in Derteforde, Kent, has seven years, "as it is believed." An inquisition, made at

10

Roger son of William of Meltenby, Ralph son of Mariota of Fangefosse, Nicholas of Saint James, William [son of] Thomas of Brunneby, Thomas de Hundegate of the same, and Thomas Young *(juvenem)* of Pockelington.

The capital messuage with the enclosure *(cum toto clauso)* is worth by the year, 2s. There are twenty-four bovates of land in demesne; a bovate with meadow worth half a marc (6s. 8d.), and without meadow, 5s.   Sum, £8.

Remigius de Pockelington holds six bovates of land, paying for each, 2s. 2d.   Sum, 13s.

Sixty-six bovates of land are held by the sokemen of Pocklington, each bovate yielding by the year 20d.   Sum, 110s.

The works of the said sokemen are these :—Each one ought to plough once in winter before Christmas-day, according to the plough which he has. He who has no plough ought to find one for half a carucate of land. He ought also to plough once in spring in the same manner. The ploughmen *(carucatores)* ought to have to eat, wheaten-bread and flesh *(panem frum' et carnem)*, and ale to drink in winter, while they have day *(dum diem habent)*, in spring wheaten-bread and fish to eat, and ale to drink, during their day's work. Every tenant of one bovate of land ought to find one harrow *(herciam)* in winter and another in spring, like one who holds two bovates, except six men who hold twelve bovates, of whom every one ought to find two harrows in winter and two others in spring. The harrowers ought to have to eat, wheaten-bread and flesh or fish once a day. Every horse *(caballus)* shall have one sheaf *(garbam)* of oats in spring while the harrowers are eating, but in winter none. Also every one ought to find a man to hoe for one day, with food like the harrowers. Every tenant of one bovate ought to find a man to reap in autumn for two days, like him who holds two bovates, except six men who hold twelve bovates, each of whom ought to find two men to reap two days, who are to eat once a day, and have wheaten-bread with flesh one day, and fish the other,

Borle, Essex, 8 Sept., 1260, finds him to be seven years of age, and yet in his mother's custody *(est septem annorum et est adhuc in custodia matris sue)*. He and a brother William died without issue, and were succeeded by a sister Avelina, who married Edmund, Earl of Lancaster, second son of Henry III. *(Cal. Gen.*, vol. i., p. 224) On the same file or bundle as the above inquisition is included an inqui-sition, taken after the death of another William de Fortibus in the County of Dorset. He left four daughters and co-heirs, Joan, aged eight years and five weeks; Sibil, aged six; Mabel, aged four; and Cecily, aged two years *(Ibid.*, vol. i., p. 89). His widow was a Matilda or Maud de Kyme to whom dower was assigned on 20 July, 1259 *(Close Rolls*, 43 Hen. III., m. 7). The lands held in dower were restored to her (2 Aug., 1260) on having sworn that Sibil and Mabel, two of her daughters, were in foreign parts and out of her power; and further having given security that she within a month would give up to the King the other two, Joan and Cecily *(Ibid.*, 44 Hen., III., part i., mm. 8, 16, 18, 19).

with pottage *(potagio)*. Every tenant of one bovate ought to give two-pence for mowing meadow, like the tenant of two bovates, except six men holding twelve bovates, each of whom is to give four-pence. Also every one of them ought to find a man to turn the hay *(ad fenum levandum)* in meadows for one day, without food, except six who are each to find two men. Every bovate ought to carry one cart-load of hay and one cart-load of corn, without food.

It should be known that every ploughing is worth in winter, without food, 2*d.*, and in spring 2*d.*; every harrowing without food $\frac{1}{2}d$.; hoeing one day without food, $\frac{1}{2}d$.; mowing without food, $\frac{1}{2}d$.; turning hay in meadow without food, $\frac{1}{2}d$. Every cart carrying hay or corn, is worth $\frac{1}{2}d$.

Sum of the works in money, 27*s.* 6*d.*

Work of one bovate without food, 5*d.*, and so one bovate yields with farms and services, 25*d.*

The aforesaid sokemen hold one culture by itself containing forty acres, called Northmor, which yields yearly half a marc.

Every tenant of land owes suit of court, his relief, 16*s.*, amercement, 5*s.* 4*d.*; and their merchete, 5*s.* 4*d.*

There are eighteen cottars, each of whom yields yearly 12*d.*, and ought to find one man to hoe, which is worth a halfpenny, also one man to reap in autumn two days, with food. The works of two days, without food, are worth one penny. He ought to find one man to turn hay for a day, and one man to make hay in the court, without food, worth one penny. He ought also to go with serjeants in socage to make summonses and distresses, worth a halfpenny; and to keep prisoners in fetters *(et debet custodire captivos in compedibus)*.

Sum of one cottar's work 3*d.*, and so every cottar yields with farms and all services 15*d.*.　　　　Sum, 22*s.* 6*d.*

Moreover there are two more cottars who ought not to go with serjeants in socage, or keep prisoners in fetters, because each does the same works as the tenant of one bovate (except suit), and yields yearly 2*s.*, one cottar's work, without food, being worth 5*d.*.　　　　Sum, 2*s.* 10*d.*

There are four gresmen who hold messuages, each having four acres of land and yielding for farm . . . Each does the same works as the cottars but does not go with serjeants in socage, or keep prisoners. He has to carry his lord's writs within the East Riding *(Haustriding)* but not to go beyond the Great Waters.[a] These four gresmen shall carry . . . . meadow for the lord's use when he stays there, and make the hearth before

---

[a] *Magnas aquas* in the original—Probably the river Humber.

him, having food, the service of one gresman being worth by the year . . . and so he yields with farm and all services 22*d*.

Sum, 7*s.* 4*d.*

The said sokemen ought to grind at the Earl's mill to the sixteenth measure *(ad xvj. vasculum* ª *),* from the feast of S. Peter *ad Vincula* (1 Aug.) to Christmas-day, and from that day to the aforesaid feast (1 Aug.) " *ad vicesimum vasculum.*"

Moreover two acres of wood may be sold every year (at half a marc the acre) for one marc. There are three mills, worth in common years 13 marcs; toll with fairs *(nundinis)* of S. Margaret of Pokelington is worth in common years 100*s.*; and herbage of the wood, 12*d.* Herbage of the field, nothing, because common. One oven *(furnus)* yields yearly 5*s.*

Adam Fuller and Thomas Taylor yield yearly for increments of their tofts 20*d.*

The perquisites of Pockelington are worth by the year 20*s.*

Gilbert Carpenter and William son of Ralph Smith yield for their willows, each one pound of cumin, worth one penny.

The Baron of Craistoke ᵇ holds in Beleby, ᶜ of the Earl, six carucates of land for 8*s.* rent; Sir William fitz Ralph of Crimpthorpe holds 18 carucates for £4 8*s.* 7½*d.*; Ralph de Lascelles, 27 bovates in Brunneby, ᵈ for 20*s.*; and they all do suit.

The Earl had by purchase—in Gevildale ᵉ half a carucate, worth 10*s.*, and in Meltenby ᵉ 2½ bovates, worth 16*s.* He had in Gevildale half a carucate of the land of Sir William the Parson, ᶠ taken into his hand for default of service, and worth yearly 10*s.*

Sir Thomas son of William de Belkerthorpe holds in Ulvestorpe ᵍ four carucates for 19*s.* 4*d.* rent, and does suit. Hugh de Yoltorpe holds in the same two carucates for 3*s.* 6*d.*, and

---

ª The meaning of this phrase "to the sixteenth measure" is that the sokemen had to grind at their lord's mill, paying one measure in sixteen from August 1 to Christmas, and one measure in twenty for the remainder of the year, as a toll or multure as it was called, for having their corn ground. At Ormesby in Cleveland, at about the same date, the charge was one in sixteen as here *(Guisbrough Chartulary*, vol. i., p. 278*)*; and at Hackness, near Scarborough, one in thirteen *(Whitby Chartulary*, vol. ii., p. 367); and the same proportion was payable at Sleights, near Whitby *(Ibid.*, vol. ii., p. 370*).*

ᵇ William fitz Thomas was Baron of Graystoke at this time (No. xxxix).

ᶜ Beilby, in the parish of Hayton, near Pocklington.

ᵈ Burnby, a parish in the same neighbourhood.

ᵉ Givendale and Meltonby.

ᶠ " De terra domini Willelmi P'sone."

ᵍ Owthorpe, in the parish of Pocklington. An account of the descendants of Sir Thomas de Belkerthorpe will be found in Kirkby's *Inquest*, pp. 28, 342. The learned editor observes, " Belthorpe House, where there are some remains of a moat, is one mile east of Gouthorpe, and in the parish of Bishop Wilton." Sir Thomas's son, " Willelmus filius Thomæ de Merston," took his name from the manor of Long Marston in the Ainsty.

does no suit. Sir Thomas son of William de Belkertorpe holds in Fangefosse 18 bovates for 2s. 3d. Remigius de Pockelington holds in Meltenby one carucate for 8s. Robert Tully holds half a bovate for 12d. Roger Haphel one acre for (1d.), James son of William of Meltenby one acre for 1d., Roger Bargayn one acre for (1d.). Sum, £9 6s. 11½d.[a]

Thomas de Fienes for one toft and increment of one toft, 6d.; William son of Auger, one toft for . . . ; Richard son of Everard for increment of his toft, 2d.; Robert Daunsel for one toft, 2s.; Robert Foxe for one toft, 12d.; William son of the Chaplain (f' cap'li) for one toft, 12d.; Beatrice at the Kirk-stile (ad scalar' ecclesie) for one toft, 18d.; Henry Coksauel for one toft, 18d.; Henry de Maghneby for one toft, 12d.; William Chaplain for one toft, 4d.; Remigius for forges, 6d.: Richard Baker (pistor) for two tofts, 2s.; Ralph de Belton for one toft, 18d.; Hervey (Heruisius or Hernisius) Milner for one toft, 12d.; Yvo in the (?) Chamber (Camera) for one toft, 16d.; William Godard for one toft, 2s. 2d.; William Hill (de Monte) for one toft, 14d.; Peter Hill (de Monte) for one toft, 12d.; John son of Richard for one toft, 12d.; Geoffrey Chapman (mercator) for one toft, 9d.; Roger son of Julian (or Juliana) and Richard Baker (pistor) for one toft, 2s. 6d.; Alan Marshal (marescallus) for one toft, 14d.; William de Meltenby for one toft, 12d.; Walter le (Surais?) for one toft, 10d. Sum, 27s. 5d.

Sum of all the sums, £44 2s. 8½d.

The Baron of Craistoke for his land of Beleby, Sir William fitz Ralph (filius Rad'i) of Crimpthorpe, Sir Thomas son of William de Belkerthorpe, Ralph de Lascelles, Hugh de Yolthorpe, and the sokemen of Pockelington ought to be talliated when the King talliates his demesnes, and this by the King's writ.

Neither the King in his time, nor the Earl in his time, had any several pasture.

The Earl held this manor of the King for one mewed hawk (uno niso mutato). Thomas is his son and heir, but his age is not known.

EXTENT[b] made . . . . after the Translation of S. Thomas the Martyr (7 July), 44 Hen. III., of the lands and tenements of (William de) Fortibus, late Earl of Albemarle, in

---

a Written on the margin thus " Sa. ixli. vjs. xjd. ob.," and apparently to come in here.

b This part of the extent has been read with very great difficulty.

Holdernes, by Geoffrey de Melsa, John de Hanthorp, Symon de Preston, ... Stephen de Brusthwick, William de . . . . , William de Wytheton, Stephen de . . . , Anketine de Redmar, and Costantine de Esinton.

(BRUSTWYK)ᵃ

. . . . arable land, of which four are sown every year, price of the acre 6*d.*, and 2 . . . . . price of the acre 12*d.*
Sum, £12 3*s.* 0*d.*
. . . . and one small foreign *(forinsecus)* wood of 10 acres, extent of the pasture of the said two small parks 100*s.*, and they sustain wild beasts *(sustinere feras bestias)* . . . . . pannage when it happens 20*s.*
Fern *(de feuger')* 10*s.*; foreign underwood *(subboscus forinsecus)*.
3*s.* 4*d.*ᵇ
. . . . an aery of herons *(de aera hayronum)* of which they know not the value; herbage of the garden with the fruit thereof, 13*s.* 4*d.*
Sum, £6 12*s.* 8*d.*ᵇ
Fishery (?) of Eumerske £8; a place called Brademire, 40*s.*
Sum, £10.
In Rugeo[monte]ᶜ are twelve score acres of arable land, of which eight score are sown yearly, the acre 4*d.*, and four score lie fallow *(jacent ad warrectam)*.
Sum, 53*s.* 4*d.*
There are there five score and two acres and a half of meadow, at 6*d.*
Sum, 51*s.* 3*d.*
In Bondarruswichᵈ (?) are seven bovates of land at 11*s.* 6*d.* for all services.
Sum, £4 0*s.* 6*d.*
Five cottars, 6*s.* 5½*d.*
Free tenants: William le Carpentar for . . . . bovates of land 12*s.*; . . . . . for 7 bovates of land 5*s.* 6*d.*; Nicholas Gilian for 2 bovates 4*s.*; Peter . . . . by serjeanty . . . . Symon Maupas holds one bovate by serjeanty . . . . William Smith holds 8 (?) bovates by (the service of) making irons for the eight ploughs of Brustwick *(per ferr' viij caruc' de Brustwick faciend')*.
Sum, 40*s.* 3½*d.*
The bondmen of Brustwick living in Pideseburton hold 40 bovates of land, each bovate 10*s.*
Sum, £20.
. . . cottars, 30*s.*; Peter Maledicth (?) for a toft, 6*d.*; sokemen (?), 4*s.*; Symon Bonde . . . . 10*s.* . . . . . Robert de Burton for half a carucate of land, 13*s.* 4*d.*; wife of Andrew for a bovate, . . *s.*; Symon Colin (?) holds a bovate for keeping the

ᵃ Burstwick, four miles from Hedon.
ᵇ These figures are doubtful.
ᶜ Ridgemont, in the township of Burstwick.
ᵈ Perhaps Bond Burstwyk (Kirkby's *Inquest*, p. 376).

south park *(pro custodia p'ci australi)*; William Yocktdoeg (?) 2 bovates of land by serjeanty of Lindesaya; a mill, 20*s.*; of the fishery of eels in Piddese, 5*s.*   Sum, £4 7*s.* 4*d.*

The bondmen of Brustwick, living in Preston, hold 60 bovates of land at 2*s.* 6*d.* the bovate, and they do (works) to the value of 7*s.* 6*d.*, and they owe talliage yearly . . . . the bovate is extended at 10*s.* yearly.   If a bovate shall be demised to . . . it is worth 20*s.* yearly.   Sum, £30 without talliage.

Eleven cottars pay 19*s.* 2*d.*; from the free tenants 72*s.* 5*d.*
                                        Sum, £4 11*s.* 7*d.*

The bondmen of Brustwick living in Lelle[a] and Dick' hold eleven bovates and a half of land, price of each yearly in all 8*s.*; Hugh Long holds a toft for 20*d.*; from free tenants 28*s.* 8*d.*
                                        Sum, 118*s.* 4*d.*

Fishery of eels in the water of Lambwat, with the reeds *(cum coopertorio)* growing in the same, 13*s.* 4*d.*   Sum, 13*s.* 4*d.*
                    Sum of the sums, £116 1*s.* 5½*d.*

HEDON.

Toll of the town of Hedon £23 10*s.*; toll of Pahilisflet,[b] mill and oven of Hedon, £9.; pleas and perquisites of the Court of the town, 40*s.* yearly.
                    Sum, [£34 10*s.*] without talliage.

The burgesses of the town ought to be talliated once a year at the gule (?) of August by the oath of 12 . . . . .

Farm of Pahilsflet, 25*s.* (?); herbage of the park of Hawig, (?) 40*s.*; . . . . 12*d.* yearly.   Sum, ...

WAHENE.[c]

There are 28 acres to be sown yearly, price of the acre, 6*d.*; 20 acres of meadow, price of each 12*d.* (?); 4 (?) acres of meadow, price of each 20*d.*; pasture for four score and ten oxen.
                                        Sum, ...

LITTLE HUMBER.

There are in demesne 23 score acres of arable land of which twelve score are sown yearly, price of each acre 12*d*; also five score and two and a half acres of meadow at 9*d.* the acre.
                                        Sum, ...

Pasture for 30 oxen, price of each 9*d.*   Sum, ...
Also pasture for 5 score sheep, price of each 1*d.* (?) Sum, . .
                    Sum of Little Humber, £19 9*s.* 4½*d.*

[a] Lelley, in the parish of Preston, four miles from Hedon.
[b] Paul, or Paghil, a parish three miles from Hedon.
[c] *Query* Wawne.

KEYNGHAM MERSKE.[a]

There are in demesne 22 score and 19 (?) acres of arable land, of which 15 score and six are sown yearly, at 4d. the acre.
Sum, ...
Eleven score and 6 acres of meadow at 9d.   Sum, ...
Pasture for 22 oxen, at 12d. an ox.   Sum, ...
. . . . pasture for sheep.   Sum, ...
Bondmen hold 31½ bovates of land, price of each bovate in all 10s.   Sum, . . .
Fifteen cottars; each pays yearly 18d.   Three tofts, 5s. . .
. . . . 4s. 8d.; seven acres of meadow, price 7s. . . . .
Free tenants 29s. 6d.; the mill 20s.   Sum, ...
        Sum of the sums of Keyngham, £55 1s. 8d.

SKEFTLING.[b]

There are five bovates and a half of land at 7s. 6d. the bovate.   Sum, 49s. 6d. (sic).
55 acres of meadow at 8d. the acre . . . In usdecrof (?) 25 acres of pasture, at 4d.; a garden 3s.
        Sum, £3 13s. 0d.
Bondmen of the same : Hugh Yoktdogge 14 acres of land, 18s. in all; Alan Periz (?) one bovate, 13s. in all; Stephen Sudhiby half a bovate, 14s. 6d.; Alice Enote (?) ¾ of a bovate, 18s.; Stephen son of Hugh half a bovate, 13s.; Robert Enote (?) ¼ bovate and a toft, 7s. 6d. (?); Robert del Syme (?) ¼ bovate and a toft, 7s. 6d.; Walter Angus ¼ bovate, 6s. 6d.   From a place called noutegange, 12s.   Sum, £5 . . . .
Farm of Ulrame[c] for all.   £1 6s. (?).
        Sum of the Sums of Skefling, £104 5s. 5½d.
KILNESE.

There are 15 bovates . . . . arable land at 5d. the acre, and 2 acres of meadow at 10d., and each bovate is extended at 5s. yearly.   Sum, £3 15s.
Two bovates of meadow (?) and 21 bovates of land, paying each bovate with aid and all services 10s. . . . . seven bovates of land, each with aid and all services 6s.   Sum, ...
Fourteen bondmen (?) yearly for all services 18d. Philip Carpenter holds . . . . . . for 16d. . . . . . and one toft for 14d. Thomas Brun (?) one toft 12d. William Smith for a forge 12d. . . . . and the mill for 30s. (?) . . . . . and his partner 20s.
. . . . .   Sum, ...
        Sum of the sums, ...

[a] Kayingham Marsh, in the parish of Kayingham.
[b] Skeffling, near Patrington.
[c] Ulrome, in the parishes of Barmston and Skipsea.

HESINTON.[a]

In demesne there are of arable land in each year seven score and ten acres, price per acre (5*d*.). Sum, 62*s*. 6*d*.
Fifty-one acres of meadow, price 6*d*. Sum, 25*s*. 6*d*.
A garden 2*s*.; a mill yearly 20*s*. Sum, 22*s*.
In bondage, 18¾ bovates of land, each 10*s*. Sum, £9 7*s*. 6*d*.

In Dimbilton,[b] 8 bovates of land at 6*s*. for all services.
Sum, 48*s*.
Cottars there who render yearly, with *forlant*, for all services 21*s*. 7½*d*. Sum, 21*s*. 7½*d*.

Free tenants.

Robert at Sea *(ad mare)*, 6*s*.; Geoffrey Broton, 8*s*. 4*d*.; Abbot of Thorneton, 10*s*.; John de Redmar, 10*s*. 8*d*.; Emma Chandelers, 4*d*.; Costantine, 1 pound of pepper, price 6*d*.
Sum, 40*s*. 10*d*. *(sic)*.
Sum of the Sums of Hesinton, £20 7*s*. 11½*d*.

EXTENT of RAUENESER HODDE, to wit, the farm of the town yearly 52*s*. The mill yearly 24*s*. Tan house *(domus tanarie)*, 13*s*. 4*d*. Toll with the perquisites of the Court, 40*s*.
Sum, £6 9*s*. 4*d*.
They ought to be talliated when the men of Grymesby[c] are talliated. Sum of Raueneser Hodde, £6 9*s*. 4*d*.

EXTENT[d] of Wytthoren and Wythorense. In demesne 16 bovates of land worth 3*s*. 6*d*.; 8 acres of arable land (at 4*d*.); also 20 acres of meadow (at 8*d*.); a pasture called Heynglant, 16*s*.; herbage of garden of Withoren, and seaweed *(subbang' de la mare)* 13*s*. 4*d*.; from a mill, 20*s*. Sum, ...
In bondage 18 bovates of land, each worth by the year with works, 8*s*.; 21½ cottars, of whom each renders yearly 6*d*., and works with aid which are worth 12*d*., and so every one renders 18*d*. There is a lake called Wythornsemar, from which the take of eels *(avallacio anguillarum)* is worth by the year, 6*s*. 8*d*. Sum, £9 2*s*. 11*d*.

[a] Easington.
[b] Dimlington, in the parish of Easington.
[c] The initial letter of this word is rather doubtful. This sentence is interlined.
[d] Withernsea in Holderness. The place here called " Wytthoren " is spelled " Hutthorn " lower down; it is probably Owthorn, which is close to Withernsea.

Free Tenants.

Gilbert de Munteny, 2s. 4d.; Matilda (or Maud) Blome, 8d.; Richard Baker, 2s. 6d.; William son of Beatrice, 2s. 6d.; Alice daughter of Reginald, 18d.; Richard del Hil, 6s.; Roger son of Beatrice, 6s.; John Reeve, 7s. 8d.; Astin Saloman (?)[a] 3s.; William del Crakes (?), 3s.; . . . frey Briddemun, 3s.; Alice del Grene, 2s.; Thomas Clerk, 6s.; Robert Milner, 16d.; Roger le Wariner, 3s.; Ralph Stauin, 3s.; Adam le Wariner, 3s.; Ami wife of Vale (?), 3s.; Thomas le Wariner, 12d.; Gilian wife of Lumbarde, 18d.; Elemos'[b] ad barram, 6d.; Simon Vast (?), and John son of Stephen of Halaym, 20s. Sum, . . .
Sum of the sums of Hutthorn and Wythorense, £18 6s. . .

In demesne at Cleton 16 . . . acres of arable land (at 4d.); 4 score acres of meadow (at 8d.); a pasture worth yearly 40s.; herbage and fruit of garden, 3s.; one mill, by the year 40s.
Sum, £12 8s. 4d.
Bondmen of Cleton dwelling in Skipse, hold forty bovates of land (at 5s. 6d.). There are 13 cottars each of whom renders yearly 15d. From two tofts, 6s. a year. From Nicholas Lutthe, 2s., from Thora (?), 2s. for a close. There are five acres, one perch of meadow, 5s. 3d.; and half an acre of meadow, 2s. From Ulfe for a close, 6d.; from Ralph Smith (fabro) for a close, 4d.; of the bayl of Skipse, 13s. 4d.; from Stephen man of Alduse (homine Aldus'), 3s. 6d.; from Thomas . . unsele (?), for two bovates 18d.; from . . .[c] for one toft, 2s.; from Lulle Cokeman, 4d.; from Ralph Fuller (fullone) for burgage, 4d.; from Richard Fayring for burgage, 4d.; from Robert de Welleton, for burgage, 4d.; from . . . neuhithe by the year, 20s. for all. Also from take of eels (de avallacione anguillarum) in Skipse mere and from . . . ker, 10s. At Horneseburton[d] from William Wytthe for 2 bovates of land and 3 tofts, 5s. 5d.
Sum, £15 11s. 5d.
Sum of the sums of Cleton and Skipse, £27 19s. 9d.

KILLING[e] FARM.

William the Templars' man (homo Templar') holds half a bovate, 32d.; Alan Daunce, two bovates, 14s.; Thomas Trane, two bovates, 14s.; William Cartar, half a bovate, 4s.; William son of Muriel for one toft, 2s. 6d.; Alan, one toft, 3s.; Thomas

---

[a] Stileman ?

[b] *Query* Elymas at the Bar or Attebar.

[c] Apparently "toftem 'to," but the reading is doubtful.

[d] Hornsea Burton, now depopulated, stood about a mile S.E. of Hornsea.

[e] Nunkeeling.

Trane, one toft, 3*s.*; *Tenny de Pyrii*, one toft, 2*s.*; Robert Scarppe, one toft, 3*s.*; Alan Clitecan, one toft, 2*s.*; also from wood near William Carpenter, 6*d.*; William Tannay for one toft, 2*s.* 6*d.*; William Smot for one toft, 2*s.* 6*d.*; of Forland *(forlantd)* in Killing, 2*s.*; from Alan Daunce, 1½*d.*

Sum, 56*s.* 9½*d.*

Sum of Killing, 56*s.* 1*s.* 3½*d.*

CASTLE-GUARD WITH FOREIGN RENTS *(Wardum_castelli cum forinscecis redditibus).*

Of castle-guard, 40*s.*; from Seer de Sunton,[a] 4,000 eels, price 24*s.*, and for farm, 14*s.* at Saint Andrew's day; Ralph son of Stephen of Sutton, 12*s.*; Peter son of Thomas of Sutton, 2*s.*; William de la Twyer, 25*s.* 4*d.*; Sir *(domino)* Hugh Bigot for Holume in Holderness,[b] 5*s.*; Walter de Etherwick, 6*s.*; Martin Fiske, 6*d.*; Stephen son of John of Hedun, 6*d.*

Sum, £6 9*s.* 4*d.*

The Earl held the Wapentake of Holdernes in fee by ser- jeanty for 60*s.*, and it is worth by the year £10.   Sum, £10.

He held the lands and tenements aforesaid of the King in chief by knight's service, and by the same service two knights' fees of the Archbishop of York. Eight knights' fees in Holder- ness were held of him.

Thomas, son of William de Fortibus, Earl of Albemarle, is his next heir, who on the morrow of the Nativity of the Blessed [Virgin] Mary (Sept. 9, 1260), will be seven years old.

The Earl had a rabbit-warren in Holdernes, but the jurors know not its value.

There are four meres and a half, to wit, Lambwad, Skipse, Fwitthouker and Wythornse meres, and a moiety of Piddese mere with fishery through the whole. The other moiety is of the lord William de Ros with fishery *(et piscare per totum).*

ADVOWSONS OF CHURCHES.

The Earl had the advowsons of three churches, viz.: Esin- ton, Kahingham, and Skipse, each church being of the value of £40; and the Earl ought to present to the Abbot of Albemarle,[c] and he to the Archbishop of York.

The Earl had warren throughout his whole fee in Holdernes, but the jurors cannot estimate its value, because the expenses exceed the revenue coming therefrom *(set nesciunt extendere valorem quia plus capit in sumptibus quam commodum inde pro- veniat).*

[a] Usually called " Saer de Sutton."
[b] Hollym, near Patrington,
[c] Aumale, in Normandy.

OF WARDSHIP.

Geoffrey Berchot, who was in custody of the Earl, has lands worth yearly 26s. 8d.; also Amand de Routh (de Ruda), by reason of the wardship of G. Berchot, worth by the year £10.

Sum, £11 6s. 8d.

ᵃ HOLDERNESSE IN THE COUNTY OF YORK.

Sum of Brustwyk with Hedon, £116 1s. 5½d.

Sum of Preston with Pawelflet, Wawene, Little Humbre, Keyngham, £115 19s. 8½d.

Sum of Skeftling, Kilnese, Esinton, Odrauenser, Withornese, Houthornese, Skipse, Cleton, Killing, Castle guard with foreign rents, and the Wapentake of Holdernens', £129 1s. 4½d.

Sum of the sums, £361 2s. 6½d.

Poklinton £44 5s. 8½d.

Skipton in Crauene, £107 15s. 7d.

Thorenton, £47 16s. 7d.

Sum of the sums, £561 0s. 5d.

Cokermue, in the County of Cumberland, £69 10s. 5d.

Sum total in both counties, £630 10s. 10d.

ᵇ Cokermue and Pokelington; and the second part, to wit, Preston, and more of the second part which is extended at £115 19s. 8d.; and the park which is called North Park; and one third of the issues of the Wapentake of Holdernesse; and one third of the lake called Langwath; and the lake of Wythornese for three residues (pro tribus residuis); and the church of Keyngham; and one third of the rabbit-warren (cuningerie).

And be it known that the above lands exceed the reasonable dower of the lands and tenements north of the Trent by £22 18s. 2½d.ᶜ

ᵃ A small membrane stitched on to the last membrane.

ᵇ The dorse of the small membrane. It appears to refer to the widow's dower.

ᶜ The extents of Skipton in Craven and Thornton, mentioned in this summary, are wanting. Thornton is probably Thornton Dale, near Pickering (Kirkby's Inquest, p. 144).

XLIX. WILLIAM DE KYME.ᵃ *Inq. p. m.*

[44 HEN. III. No. 25.]

Writ dated at Westminster, 13 Oct., 44th year (1260).

INQUISITION of the fees, held of William de Kyme, at the time of his death, in the County of York, made before the Coroners, by Richard de Colton, Richard Prudfot of Katherton, Hugh de Bylburg', Thomas Alle[w]ays of Merstone, Elias de Katherton, Alexander *del Hyl'* of Walton, of Aynesty Wapentake, Matthew de Kelebrocke, Peter de Lofthus, Henry de Fauvelthorp, Gilbert de Wetelay, Geoffrey de Everby, William de Huton, Robert de Haunlith, Richard *le Nunnefrere*, Nicholas de Gergrave, William de Stoke, Matthew *le Palmer* of Braythwelle, and William *le Cordwaner*, of Stayncl[iff] Wapentake, Thomas at the Cross *(ad Crucem)* of Tadecastre, William de Grimestone, John de Mileforde, Hugh de Brinkel, John Broket of Neuton, William de Langetwayt, Robert de Clifforde, Robert de Langetwayt, Hugh Gernun, William son of Alexander of Clifforde, Hugh de Occlesthorp, and Thomas de Barkestone, of Bark[stone] Wapentake, William Tarthkurtays, Mark Dway, William de Graynesby, Geoffrey Mauleverer, Roger son of Hugh, William Clerk *(Clericus)*, Ralph son of Martin, Geoffrey de Mikelfelde, of Hert[hill Wapentake].

They, being sworn, say upon their oath that Mauger *le Vavasur* held immediately of William de Kyme in Wlsington,ᵇ two carucates of land, whereof twelve carucates make one

---

ᵃ On 11 Feb., 1219-20, the Sheriff of Lincolnshire was informed that the King had agreed to accept by instalments the relief of one hundred pounds, payable by Philip de Kyme for the lands belonging to Simon de Kyme his father *(Excerpta è Rotulis Finium*, vol. i., p. 44*)*. On 30 May, 1242, the Sheriffs of Lincolnshire and Yorkshire were ordered to seize into the King's hand, all the lands which were Philip de Kyme's. On 20 July following, the Sheriff of Lincolnshire, having received sufficient security for the relief of one hundred pounds, was commanded to give up the lands to Simon, son and heir of Philip de Kyme *(Ibid.*, vol. i., pp. 380, 382*)*. On 20 Oct., 1248, the King took the homage of William, brother and heir of Simon de Kyme, for the lands and tenements Simon held in chief. The relief the same as before, £100 *(Ibid.*, vol. ii., p. 43*)*. On 10 Oct., 1259, the Escheator of Lincolnshire was commanded to seize into the King's hand, the lands of William de Kyme, and on 7 Nov. following, the King, for a fine of three thousand marcs which Hugh le Bigod made with him, granted him by the counsel of his magnates, who are of his council, the custody of the lands and heirs of William de Kyme, late deceased *(Ibid.*, vol. ii., pp. 312, 318*)*. The council referred to was the one forced on Henry III. by the Provisions of Oxford, in 1258. Lucy, William de Kyme's widow, was living in 1268 (No. LXI.). At the time of Kirkby's *Inquest* 1284-5, the Kyme property was in the possession of Philip de Kyme, probably a son of William de Kyme.

ᵇ Called Wlsyngton in Kirkby's *Inquest* and Ulsitone and Wlsintone in *Domesday*. Afterwards called Wolsington, or Wolston, and now Ouston, which is the name of a farm in the township of Oxton, and parish of Tadcaster (Kirkby's *Inquest*, 25n.). On 29 May, 1280, the King in consideration of a fine of £300, granted to Agnes, widow of Mauger le Vavasour or Vavazur, the custody of the lands and heirs of the said Mauger, with their marriage *(Patent Rolls*, 8 Edward I., m. 17 (19), 49 *Dep. Keeper of Public Records' Reports*. 179*)*.

knight's fee. Hugh de Brinkel held immediately of him in the town of Neuton[a] two bovates and a half of land, whereof fourteen carucates make a fee. John de Oykumbe held immediately of him in the same town, two bovates of the same fee. Elias son of William Clerk *(fil' Will'i Clerici)* held immediately of him in the same town, four bovates of the same fee. John Broket held immediately of him in the same town, one bovate. John Clerk, one bovate and a half. William de Elkenton held immediately of him in Toulestone,[b] one carucate and a half, whereof fourteen carucates make a fee. Ralph de Normanvile, in Coningestone[c] and Smawes[d] three carucates and a half, whereof twelve make a fee. Peter de Percy, in frank marriage in Torneton and Ylkelay,[e] one carucate (twelve to the fee). William *le Rus*, in Torneton, two bovates. Matthew de Kelbroke, in Kellebroke, two bovates. Geoffrey Wyllun, in Everby,[f] one bovatē. Godfrey Dawtry *(de Alta ripa)* in the same, two bovates.

They say also that two carucates and a half of land in Catherton (fourteen make a fee) were held of the same William; of which the Prior of [Helagh] Park holds nine bovates of land, and forty acres of William de Kathertoñ, who held of William de Kyme; the Abbot of Furness holds one toft and 20 acres of land; Adam *le Cerf*, of York, holds three tofts and half a carucate of William de Katherton, and he of William de Kyme; Walter de Grimèstone holds one toft and one bovate of the said William, and he of William de Kyme. The residue was held by William de Katherton immediately of William de Kyme.

Also Thomas de Katherton holds one carucate of land in Touleston (fourteen carucates to the fee) of William de Katherton, and the Prior of [Helagh] Park holds half a carucate there of William de Katherton, and he held of William de Kyme. The said William de Katherton held immediately of William de Kyme in Neuton in Cravene,[g] four carucates of land (fourteen to the fee). Ralph Darel holds in Elleslake in Cravene, two carucates (fourteen to the fee) of William de Catherton, who held of William de Kyme. William de Marton holds in Elleslake mediately of William de Kyme (here *Kymb'*) one carucate, and William Tempeste holds in Thorneton in Cravene,[e] one bovate,

[a] Newton Kyme, near Tadcaster.
[b] Toulston, in the parish of Newton Kyme.
[c] Cold Coniston, in the parish of Gargrave.
[d] *Query* Smaw's Hall, in the parish of Tadcaster.
[e] Thornton in Staincliffe and Ilkley. Sir Peter de Percy's Inquisition occurs afterwards (No. LVIII.).
[f] Kelbrook and Earby (*Domesday* Eurebi), in the parish of Thornton.
[g] Bank Newton, in the parish of Gargrave.

and Robert de Stocke one bovate there, immediately of William de Kyme.

Also they say that five carucates of land with the appurtenances in Wylberfosse, were held of the fee of William de Kyme by foreign service only (whereof 23 carucates make one knight's fee); whereof William son of Simon of Wylberfosse, held of William de Kyme immediately nine bovates of land by foreign service. William *le Rus*,[a] three bovates; of which Thomas de Boulton, in the name of ward *(custod'),* holds two bovates by the gift of W. de Kyme, and the wife of William *le Rus*, one bovate in the name of dower. Robert Burdun holds six bovates of Alan de Katherton, who held of W. de Kyme (here again *Kymb'*). The Prioress of Wylberfosse holds three bovates of Robert Burdun, he of Alan de Katherton, and Alan of W. de Kyme. She holds also of William son of Simon[a] three bovates, and of the heir[a] of the said William *le Rus* one bovate. Peter *le Rus* holds of the said heir[a] two bovates. Thomas son of Rand[olph] holds of William son of Simon[a] one bovate. Peter *le Rus* holds of the said William son of Simon[a] one bovate.

The following hold of Robert Burdun, who holds of Alan de Katherton,[a] namely: Goscelin de Wylberfosse, two bovates; Hugh son of Hugh, two bovates; Laurence son of Thomas, two bovates; Laurence son of Alan, two bovates; Robert son of Simon, two bovates; Nicholas Waldinge, and Agnes daughter of Alexander of Wylberfosse, one bovate.

There were not held of William de Kyme more fees in the County of York.

L. OF SERJEANTY OF THE GATE OF YORK CASTLE.

[45 HEN. III. No. 56.]

Writ dated at Winchester, 10 June, 45th year (1261).

INQUISITION made in full County court before the Sheriff and Keepers of the Pleas of the Crown, by William de Barton, Richard de Torny of Tyverington, Ivo Punjardun, Peter *de Gayola*, Peter de Ross, Geoffrey de Basinggis, Walter de Touthorpe, Robert de Torny of Touthorpe, William son of Robert, William de Torny of Wygentorpe, Michael de Yolton, and Walter de Hemelsaye, as to who is the next heir to hold the serjeanty of the Castle gate of York *(serjantiam porte Castri*

[a] He held immediately of William de Kyme by foreign service.

Ebor.), and how much that serjeanty ought to yield yearly by the new fine of serjeanties, &c. They say that John son of Elienor, is next heir by reason of a certain ancestor of his, named Coleswayn, who had that serjeanty by gift of a King of England from time immemorial. The serjeanty ought to yield by the year eleven marcs 2*s.* 5*d.* The custody of the gate aforesaid is worth yearly one marc. The serjeanty aforesaid was taken into the King's hand by his own will, like all other serjeanties of England, and for no other cause.

LI. RICHARD DE ASLAKEBY. *Inq. p. m.*

[46 HEN. III. No. 14.]

Writ dated at Windsor, 12 Feb., 46th year (1261-2).

INQUISITION made by Richard de Berygh, John de Hagwrthingham, Eudo de Aslakeby, Richard Boye, Richard Erchenbaud, William Cruer, Ralph de Loketon, Roger son of Mart[in], Richard son of William of Wrelton, Alan son of Andrew, Walter Guer, and Eustace de Pert, who say upon their oath that Richard de Aslakeby held of the King in chief, two carucates of land with the appurtenances in Aslakeby,[a] for forty shillings yearly, to be paid to the Exchequer of London at two terms, namely: 20*s.* at Michaelmas, and 20*s.* at Easter, whereof he held in demesne as of fee 2½ bovates of land (each 8*s.*), one toft worth 3*s.*, and one capital messuage, 5*s.* by the year. Sum, 28*s.*

Of the said two carucates the Prior of Malton holds of Sir H. le Bygot, six bovates of land and ten acres of meadow, and he (H.) of the said Richard for 15*s.* yearly.

Likewise of Richard held:

Name.	Holding.	Annual rent. s.	d.
Master Roger de Schardeburge	Half a carucate of land and two tofts . .	14	0
Alan de Schoter . .	One bovate . . .	6	0
William son of Guy (*Wydonis*) . . .	One bovate and one toft	4	0
William Fraunceys . .	,, ,, ,,	2	6
Eustace de Pert . . .	One toft . . .	3	0
The same	Four acres of land .	0	3
Nicholas son of Beatrice .	,, ,, . .	0	3
Thomas Scot . . .	One toft . . .	2	6

ᵃ Aislaby, in the parish of Middleton, near Pickering.

Thomas son of the said Richard, one plot *(placeam)* and one toft for one pound of cumin, with half an acre of land.[a]
Richard, son of the said Richard, is his heir, aged thirty years.[b]

LII. INGRAM DE PERCY. *Inq. p. m.*

[46 HEN. III. No. 2.]

Writ dated at Westminster, 24 Oct., 46th year (1262).

EXTENT of the lands and tenements, formerly of Ingram de Percy, in the County of York, made by William de Pyketon, Richeman Calle, William de Bovington, Alan de Toppeclyve, Henry de Levyngton, Henry Serjeant *(servientem)* of the same, Simon de Gygelswyke, Thomas *le Lardiner* of Thadecastre, Henry *fil' Magistri* of the same, Walter de Levyngton, Elias de Dalton, and Gilbert son of Richard of the same, who say on their oath that the demesnes of the manor of Levyngton[c] are worth £8 10s., the service of villenage £16, and the mill, 30s. by the year. No other services or issues appertain to the manor there.

William de Percy, brother of Ingram, is his next heir, and aged twenty-six years.

LIII. ROBERT DE CLERBEC. *Inq. p. m.*[d]

[47 HEN. III. No. 45.]

No Writ.

EXTENT made on Sunday after the feast of Saint Mark the Evangelist, 47 Hen. 3 (29 April, 1263), of the land late of

---

[a] At the foot before naming the heir is :—Sᵃ. xlvjs. vij*d*. ob., which seems to be wrong, as there is no halfpenny. By the figures given the total is 47s. 6*d*.

[b] The King took the homage of the heir, and commended seisin to be given to him of the lands held by his father, on 15 March following (1261-2). These lands seem to have been in Lincolnshire *(Excerpta è Rotulis Finium,* vol. ii., p. 368*)*.

[c] The manor of Kirk Levington, near Yarm, is said to have been given by Peter de Brus I., who was in possession of the Barony of Skelton between the years 1200 and 1222, to Henry de Percy, son of Agnes de Percy and Joscelin de Louvaine, in frank marriage with his sister Isabel, by the service of coming on Christmas day to the Castle of Skelton, and leading the lady of the same from her chamber to the chapel for mass, and returning afterwards to eat a meal with her, and then departing *(Dodsworth MSS.,* clvi., 151ᵇ*)*. His heir, the above-named William de Percy, was a canon of York. A William Piercy resigned the prebend of Tockerington, in York Minster, in 1295 (Le Neve's *Fasti,* vol. iii., p. 217). William de Percy gave the moiety of Dalton, which accrued to him by the death of his brother Ingelram, to his other brother Walter.

[d] Late 57 Hen. III., No. 1. Wrongly attributed to Yorkshire in the Calendar. It really refers to Acton in the County of Suffolk. See *Hundred Rolls,* vol. ii., pp. 142, 144, 150.

Robert de Clerbec in Aketon, by William Rydel, William Thurgor, John Dering, John *le lung*, Hugh of the Grange, William Brian, William de Brantestone, Nicholas de Medeueyn, Hugh son of Maurice, Nicholas de Bulneye, Geoffrey son of Alan, and Robert Eadward. They say upon their oath that there are eight score acres of arable land (the acre 4*d.*), four marcs ; six acres and one rood of meadow (the acre, 2*s.*), 12*s.* 6*d.*; 13½ acres of pasture (the acre, 6*d.*), 6*s.* 9*d.* ; 20 acres of wood, of which five acres may be sold yearly (the acre 8*d.*), 3*s.* 4*d.* ; annual rent, 67*s.* 8¼*d.* ; three hens, price 3*d.* ; works by the year four score sixteen, which are worth 4*s.* ; also averages, 2*d.*

Sum of the whole, £7 8*s.* 0¼*d.*

They say also that he holds of the King in chief, by the service of half a knight's fee. The heir of Robert is called John, and is four years and a half old. He had in the county of Dorset four marcs of annual rent.

[On the dorse] Memorandum that Robert de Clerbec died on Friday after Palm Sunday (30 March, 1263).

LIV. BALDWIN DE INSULA, EARL OF DEVON.[a] *Inq. p. m.*

[47 HEN. III. No. 32 c.]

Writ dated at the Tower of London, 13 July, 47th year (1263).

HAREW[O]DE.

EXTENT of the manor of Harewde made on Friday after Mid-lent, 48 Henry[b] (28 March, 1264), by William de Alwaldeley, [Ad'] de Thouhus, Richard de Wygedon, Jordan of

[a] The manor of Harewood, near Leeds, came to the Insula family by the marriage of Baldwin's grandfather, another Baldwin de Insula, also Earl of Devon, with Margery, daughter and heiress of Alice de Curzi, wife of Warin Fitzgerold, and granddaughter of Avice, daughter and co-heir of William de Meschines, by Cecily, daughter and heiress of Robert de Romilly, Lord of Skipton and Harewood. This last mentioned Margery married first Baldwin de Ripariis, or Rivers, Earl of Devon, by whom she had a son of the same name, and secondly, about 1218, Faukes de Breauté *(Excerpta è Rotulis Finium*, vol. i., p. 11*)*. On 29 Sept., 1252, the King ordered his Escheator in Oxfordshire to seize the lands in his baili-wick which belonged to Margery de Ripariis *(Ibid.*, vol. ii., p. 140*)*. Her son Baldwin was under age at the time of his father's death. In 1235, Gilbert de Clare, Earl of Gloucester, made a fine with the King, of two thousand marcs, to marry his eldest daughter with Baldwin, son of Baldwin de Rivers, son of William de Rivers, Earl of Devon *(Ibid.*, vol i., p. 151*)*. The Earl of Gloucester's daughter was called Amicia, and is mentioned at the close of this Inquisition. From another entry concerning a fine for the manors of Moreys and Rydeleston, in Devonshire, it appears that Baldwin's grandfather was also called William de Vernun *(Ibid.*, Vol. i., p. 397*)*. The family, as in the Inquisition, also called themselves de Insula or de Lisle. On 15 Feb., 1244-5, the Sheriffs of Southampton, Devon, Somerset, Dorset, and Surrey, were ordered to take into the King's hand all the lands which belonged to B. de Insula, late Earl of Devon *(Ibid.*, vol. i., p. 431*)*. On 4 May,

the same, John de Bramdon, Adam de Arthington in Keswich, Adam de Midleton of the same, Henry son of Gamel of Wymrtheley, Henry son of Robert of the same, John Clerk of the same, Richard de Neuhale, William Attebeck of Hetheruch, William son of Adam of Lofthus, Jod' of the same, William de Stubhus, Henry his brother, William de Hillum, Adam *le Biengrant*, Hugh de Scarthecrofth, Robert son of Walter, John son of Henry of Stubhus, Hugh Segge of Lofthus, Roger de Nafferton, and William *le Biengrant,* who say upon their oath, that the profits of the court of Harewde, together with the curtilage and all issues of the garden are worth by the year, as commonly estimated, eight shillings.

Earl Baldwin last deceased had in demesne in the fields of Wetecrofth, Rugemund,[a] 35 acres of arable land (at 10*d.*), 29*s.* 2*d.* Also in demesne in fields called Pulehale and Fites,[b] 9 score and one acres of arable land (at 8*d*). £6 0*s.* 8*d.*

In other places 63 acres of arable land (at 6*d*.). 31*s.* 6*d.*

Sixteen acres of meadow (at 4*s.*). 64*s.*

Other three acres and a half of meadow by parcels (40*d.* the acre). 10*s.*

Demesne pasture to support three plough-teams of oxen, worth nothing beyond the keep of the oxen. He could have in the common pasture one bull and fifteen cows with their calves *(cum sequela earum iij. annis)* three years, worth by the year half a marc ; in summer time twelve mares with their sequel three years, worth 5*s.* yearly ; sixty goats *(capras),* worth 2*s.* 6*d.* yearly ; one hundred ewes, worth 4*s.* yearly ; five sows with litters *(cum sequela earum)* three years, worth 2*s.* yearly.

Of dovehouse, mill, vivaries, weirs, fisheries, and turbaries, nothing. Sum to this point, £14 4*s.* 6*d.*

1251, the King pardoned Amicia, Countess of Devon, £100 a year of the £400 a year, by which she made a fine for having the custody of the land of her son Baldwin *(Ibid.,* vol. ii., p. 103*).* This is the Baldwin of the Inquisition, who was still under age, and in the King's custody, 22 July, 1254 *(Ibid.,* vol. ii., p. 192*).* On 29 Jan., 1256-7, the King gave him back his lands *(Ibid.,* vol. ii., p. 340*).* He only enjoyed the Earldom for a short time, the Sheriff of Devon being ordered on 13 Sept., 1262, to seize his lands into the King's hand, and on 17 Aug. in the next year, his sister and heiress, Isabella de Fortibus, Countess of Albemarle, had seisin of her brother's lands *(Ibid.,* vol. ii., pp. 383, 402*).*

b The regnal year is torn off ; it was probably 48.

a Rougemont, on the north bank of the Wharfe, near Harewood. In the *Yorkshire Archæological Journal* (vol. iv., p. 107), some account is given of Robert de Insula, or de Lisle, of Rougemont, who was summoned to Parliament in 1312.

b Fitts Lane, close by the Wharfe, lies two miles E.N.E. of Harewood. FITTY. A term applied to lands left by the sea ; Marsh-lands, *Linc.,* (Halliwell). In the *Whitby Chartulary* (vol. i., p. 7, and vol. ii., p. 601), mention is made of a Fittis Mersc, near Middlesborough, and some fyths, low-lying lands by the riverside, near Whitby.

Free tenants.

The Abbot of Fountains holds half a knight's fee,[a] and does foreign service, and suit of Court.

Geoffrey Maude (de Monte alto) holds half a carucate of land and does suit of Court only *(et sequitur curiam tantum).*

The heir of Simon Maude[b] holds half a knight's fee, and does foreign service, and suit of Court.

The prior of Bolton (Boueltona) holds five carucates of land,[c] and does foreign service, and suit of Court.

William Grammaire (Gramaticus) holds one carucate of land, and does foreign service and suit of Court.

The heir of Benedict de Yedon holds two carucates of land, and yields yearly 2*s.* 6*d.*, half at Pentecost, the other half at Martinmas; and he does foreign service and suit of Court.

Adam de Everingham holds one carucate of land, and does foreign service and suit of Court.

John de Goukethorph *(sic)* holds seven bovates of land, and does foreign service and suit of Court.

Katherine, daugher of Richard de Stubhus holds one carucate, and does foreign service and suit of Court.

Robert Frauncke holds four carucates and five bovates of land, and renders yearly 16*s.* 4*d.* at the aforesaid two terms, and does foreign service and suit of Court.

Adam de Wytheton holds eleven bovates, and renders yearly 6*s.* 9½*d.* at the same terms; and he ought to find two boon-works *(precarias)* in winter time with one plough, and two boon-works with one plough in oat seed time, and he will have his food. That service is worth 8*d.* He ought to find nine boon-works in autumn with one man at the lord's food, and the work is worth 9 pence.

The heir of Roger Luvel holds twelve acres of land, and renders yearly 2*s.* 5*d.* only at the said two terms.

The heir of Walter Bruer holds one bovate of land, and renders yearly 3*s.* at the same terms, and does suit of Court.

Gregory de Helthwaith holds three bovates of land, and renders yearly 2*s.* 8*d.* at the same terms, and does suit of Court. He ought to testify summonses *(testificare sumonitiones).*

---

[a] Stainburn, in the parish of Kirkby Overblow (Kirkby's *Inquest,* p. 45), three and a half miles N.E. of Otley.

[b] At the time of Kirkby's *Inquest,* 1284-5, the heirs of Simon de Monte Alto held half a fee of the Countess of Albemarle by military service in East Keswick. In 1197, a fine was levied between Simon de Muhalt and Warin Fitz Gerold and Alice de Curzi his wife, about eight carucates in Wike and East Keswick *(Yorkshire Archæological Journal,* vol. xi., p. 183).

[c] At Wigton, in the parish of Harewood (Kirkby's *Inquest,* p. 42).

William del Bech holds one bovate of land, and renders yearly 6s. only at the said terms. He holds one toft and croft for 12d. at the said terms, and does suit of Court.

William de Alwaldeley holds two carucates of land, and renders yearly 18s. 8d.; paying 6s. at Martinmas, 6s. 8d. at Purification B. M., and 6s. at Pentecost; and he does suit of Court.

The heir of William Espurmi (or Espurun) holds one carucate of land[a] for 6s. at the said three terms, and does suit of Court.

William de Stubhus[b] holds one bovate and a half of land, for 4s. 9d. at the said three terms, and does suit of Court. He will find one plough and a half three times in the year at the lord's food; and that service is worth 9d. He will find nine reapers in autumn *(Et inveniet ix. homines metentes in autumpno ad cibum domini)* at the lord's food, and the work is worth 9d. He does suit of Court *(et sequitur curiam)*.

Robert son of William of Stubhus holds half a bovate of land for 19d. at the said three terms, and he will find half a plough for three days in the year at the lord's food, service worth 3d., and three reapers in autumn at the lord's food, service worth 3d., and does suit of Court.

Adam de Wytheton holds one carucate of land for 3s. at the aforesaid two terms, and does suit of Court.

Jord[an] de Lofthus holds one carucate of land for 6s. 4d. at the said three terms, and does suit of Court. He ought to testify summonses *(et debet testificare sumonitiones)*.

The whole township of Lofthus ought to find three boonworks with three ploughs yearly at the lord's food, and that service is worth 18d.; also thirty-three reapers in autumn for one day at the lord's food, worth 2s. 9d.

Thomas son of Peter of Harewde holds one bovate of land for 16d. at the said two terms. He does suit of Court, and ought to testify summonses.

The heir of William son-in-law *(generis)* of Henry Clerk *(clerici)* holds eight acres of land, and renders yearly 3s. 3d. only at the said two terms.

Adam le Biengrant holds two bovates of land, and renders one pound of pepper at the feast of S. Peter *ad Vincula* worth 8d. He does suit of Court by the brother of William de Tarent *(per vim fratris Will'i de Tarent)*.

---

[a] In Alwoodley, where the Countess of Albemarle had three carucates in 1284-5, at which time this carucate was held by William de Brandon (Kirkby's *Inquest*, p. 42).
[b] The Stubusen of *Domesday*. Stub House, the name of a farm nearly two miles S.W. of Harewood, stands, probably, on the site of this lost vill *(Ibid.)*. Wytheton, now Weeton, and Lofthouse, mentioned below, are both in Harewood parish.

William Folbarun holds one toft for 3*d.* at Martinmas.

The Prior of Bolton (Boueltona) holds one croft, and yields yearly one pound of pepper only at Pentecost, worth 8*d.*

Henry son of William holds half a carucate of land for 3*s.* 4*d.* at the said two terms; and he does foreign service and suit of Court.

The Master of S. Leonard's Hospital holds one toft for 4*d.* at the said two terms.

Richard de Neuhale holds one bovate of land for 2*s.* at the said two terms, and one penny at Christmas. He does suit of Court and ought to testify summonses.

Agnes de Stoketon holds one bovate of land for 2*s.* at the said two terms.

The heir of Roger Luvel holds one carucate of land in Neuhale for 8*s.* 4*d.* at the said three terms. He ought to find three ploughs for three days in the year at the lord's food, service worth 18*d.*; and twenty-one reapers in autumn for one day at the lord's food, service worth 21*d.*

Hosbert de Arch[es] yields yearly 6*s.* 8*d.* for attachment of the mill-pond of Kerbi[a] *(pro atachiamento stagni molendini de Kerbi)* at the said two terms.

Hugh de Langwath holds four bovates of land, and renders yearly one pound of cumin only at Easter, worth three half-pence.   Sum of rent of Free tenants, £6 1*s.* 0*d.*

Tenants-at-will (De illis qui tenent ad voluntatem domini).

Hugh de Langwath holds one bovate of land worth 3*s.* 4*d.*; also one acre, worth 12*d.*, payable at two terms.

Hugh de Scarthecrofth holds 3 acres, worth 2*s.*, at two terms.

William Toller holds 2½ bovates, worth 15*s.*, at two terms.

Ralph Rudde holds one bovate, worth 6*s.* 8*d.*, at two terms.

Sum, 28*s.*

	s.	*d.*
Fines and perquisites of courts	40	0
Surplus of fine of county and wapentake . . .	2	1
Pannage of Swindene[b] wood yearly ,. . .	13	4
Wind-falls of the same . ,, . .	4	0
An alderbed there . . ,, ...	10	0

Sum, 69*s.* 5*d.*

Tenants in bondage (De illis qui tenent in bondagio).

Jordan de Helthwaith[c] holds two bovates of land, and yields yearly 12*s.*, half at Pentecost and half at Martinmas. He will find

[a] Kereby, two miles N. W. of Harewood.

[b] Swindon, in the parish of Kirkby Overblow, about two miles north of Harewood.

[c] Healthwaite Hill just north of Weeton.

two ploughs for two days in the year at the lord's food, service worth 4*d.* He ought to harrow *(herciare)* for two days at the lord's food, work worth one penny. He ought to cut wood in Swindene two days, and carry five cart loads of wood to Harewde Court at the lord's food, work worth 4*d.* He ought to carry corn, or whatever the lord may wish, for one day, so that he can return the next day, having a half-penny for food; and the carriage is worth three half-pence. He ought to hoe two days at the lord's food, worth one penny; and mow two days and turn hay two days at the lord's food, worth 5*d.* He ought to carry hay one day, and corn another day, at the lord's food, worth 4*d.* He ought to find two mowers in autumn for six days at the lord's food, worth 12*d.* He ought to give two hens at Christmas, worth 2*d.*, and ten eggs at Easter, worth a farthing.

Sum, 14*s.* 10¾*d.*

Henry son of Robert and Adam Ded	Two bovates	by the same service.
Henry de Stainburne . . . . ,,	,,	
William Neucume and Robert Postel . ,,	,,	
William Clerk . . . . . ,,	,,	
Richard Fox and Walter son of Paulin ,,	,,	
Jordan de Stoketon . . . . ,,	,,	
Agnes de Askeham	Two bovates	
John Bandi and Walter Wade . . .	,, ,,	
Laurence de Stiveton and William at Gate *(ad portam)*	,, ,,	
Ralph Derlingh and Henry son of Paulin .	,, ,,	
Walter at Bridge *(ad pontem)* and Stephen the Fool *(stultus)*	,, ,,	
Henry son of Maud *(Matild')* . . .	,, ,,	
Roger at Gate and John Gildanher . .	,, ,,	
William son of Agnes	,, ,,	
Robert Pintel	,, ,,	
Robert Mel and William son of John . .	,, ,,	
Roger de Stoketon	,, ,,	
Richard Hicke	,, ,,	
William son of John and Durant de Stoketon	,, ,,	
Nicholas de Stoketon	,, ,,	
William Faukes	,, ,,	
Agnes relict of Gilbert	,, ,,	
Petronilla and William Puselin . . .	,, ,,	
Jordan son of Agnes	,, ,,	
The same Jordan and William Penke . .	,, ,,	
Robert son of Peter and Stephen de Kyrkebi	,, ,,	
Adam le Westrais and William son of Peter .	,, ,,	
Thomas son of Peter	,, ,,	

William son of John and Robert son of Hugh	Two bovates
Alan Campiun	,, ,,
William Cocke and Ralph son of Robert .	,, ,,
John Slawe	,, ,,
Robert Bere and Robert de Hetherich . .	,, ,,
Cecily Godith	,, ,,
Gilbert Goye	,, ,,
Robert de Harewde and Henry For' . .	,, ,,

Sum total (bondmen), £26 11s. 1¼d.

Ralph Nogge helds one bovate for 4s. 6d., and does the aforesaid service, so much as appertains to one bovate.

Alan de Casteley holds one toft and seven acres of land for 5s., and does all the works which appertain to half a carucate of land. Sum, 11s. 8½d.

Alan de Wygedon holds two bovates for 4s., without services.

Cottars.

Name.	Holding.	Annual Rent.	
		s.	d.
Tilla de Stiveton . .	One toft .	1	0
Robert Postel . . .	,, ,, .	1	4
John Smith *(faber)* . .	,, ,, .	1	4

He finds three day-works *(precarias)* in autumn, and makes hay one day, worth 3½d.

Robert Weltecarte . .	One toft .	2	0

(works as above)

William Milner . . .	,, ,, .	1	4

and 3 day-works in autumn, worth 3d.

Walter at Bridge *(ad pontem)*	One toft .	2	1
Robert Frauncais . .	,, ,, .	1	4

(works as John Smith)

[Here the document is torn and the two last entries cannot be read further than :—]

. . . .	One toft .	1	0

(works as John Smith and besides) to take distresses and to keep prisoners *(capere namios et custodire prisoncs)*.

[Isabel[a] de Fortibus, wife of the Earl of Albemarle, and his (Baldwin) sister and heir, is aged 25 years].[b]

[a] The finding as to the name and age of the heir is supplied from the Inquisitions taken in the Counties of Southampton and Surrey. It appears from the extent of Plympton Castle, co. Devon, that the Countess Amicia, the Earl's mother, was yet alive in February, 1262-3.

[b] There are other extents and inquisitions, put up in four separate files distinguished by the letters *a, b, c, d*. These are taken in the Counties of Devon, Hertford, Oxford, Southampton (including the Isle of Wight), Surrey and Wilts. The extents are written in a symmetrical manner, and give the names of tenants with their holdings and rents in great detail.

LV. ROGER DE QUENCY, EARL OF WINCHESTER.[a] *Inq. p. m.*

[48 HEN. III. No. 27.]

Writ dated at Canterbury, 7 Oct., 48th year (1264).

EXTENT OF THE MANOR OF ELMESALE.[b]

EXTENT made on Tuesday, the morrow of the Nativity of the Blessed Virgin, 48 Hen. 3 (9 Sept. 1264), before Sir Henry Waley (*domino Henrico Walens'*), then Steward of

[a] On the death of Saer de Quency, Earl of Winchester, who died in the Holy Land in 1219, he was succeeded by his second son, the above named Roger. In 1253 Roger paid a fine of three hundred marcs for marrying Alienora, widow of William de Vallibus, without the King's leave. This lady was daughter of William de Ferrers, and one of the heirs of William Marshal, Earl of Pembroke (*Excerpta è Rotulis Finium*, vol. ii., pp. 15, 149). According to two other inquisitions taken at the same time in Bedfordshire, his heirs were the two daughters of Roger de Quency (his younger brother, a second of the name), Joan wife of Sir Humphrey de Bohun the younger, and Hawise, the latter under age (*Cal. Gen.*, vol. i., p. 111). Joan died without issue on 25 Nov., 1283, and was succeeded by her sister, then the wife of Baldwin Wake (*Ibid.* vol. i., p. 346). The connection between the families of Lascy and Quency arose from the marriage of John de Lascy with Margaret, daughter and heir of Robert de Quency, by Hawise, fourth sister and coheir of Ranulph de Meschines, Earl of Chester and Lincoln (*Excerpta è Rotulis Finium*, vol. i., p. 396). The heir apparent of the Earldom of Winchester had been Robert, but he died before his father. The above Roger, the second son, inherited, though he did not receive the Earldom till the death of his mother in 1235.

Hugh, Earl of Chester=Bertreia, daur. of Simon Earl of
Montfort and Evreux.

Ranulph, Earl of Chester and Lincoln, ob. 1232, left the latter dignity to his sister Hawise.

Hawise, 4th daur., and coheir of her brother.

Robert, eldest son and heir of Saer de Quincy, Earl of Winchester.

Margaret.=John de Lacy, Earl of Lincoln *jure uxoris.*

The following shows the short course of the Earldom of Winchester (extinct at the death of the second Earl) :—

Saer, 1st Earl, created 1207,=Margaret d. and coh. of Robert, Earl of Leicester.
died 1219. Held the Earldom till her death in 1235.

Robert, heir to his father, but predeceased him.=Hawise. Roger, 2nd son. Ob. 1264.

A second Robert, who also predeceased Roger.

It is not clear why the Earldom, which was conferred upon the first Earl, was retained by his wife for life, nor why the arms of the first Earl, Or, a fess gules, a label of seven points, azure, did not descend to this Roger, who bore, Gules, seven lozenges or. The label of Saer, Earl of Winchester, is the earliest example known of that bearing. Till Roger received the Earldom in Feb., 1235-6, he was known only by his name, Roger de Quency. For instance, in No. 52 of the Pontefract Chartulary, is a missive under date 19 Oct., 1233, from Archbishop Gray, notifying his institution of Milo, the presentee of the Prior and Convent of Pontefract, to the church of Kippax, and recording that he had done so, as a consequence of the decision in a suit at law between the Prior and Convent on the one part, and "nobilem virum Robertum de Quenci, ex altera," which had been terminated in favour of the Convent. Only a rough undated draft of this communication has been published, in the Surtees Soc. vol. L., No. 276. In the *Dodsworth MSS.*, vol. cxxii., fo. 85, is an extract taken from "a great book in the Duchy Office,

Pontefract, assigned thereto by order of Sir Richard de Hemmigton, and before William de Burton, Bailiff of the place, with many others, by the oath of good and lawful men, viz.: Iwain de Fryckelay, Adam son of Adam of Stobis,[a] William son of Robert of Stobis, Hervey Lovecok of Stobis, William son of Adam of Stobis, Robert Belle of Moirhus, Richard son of William of Moirhus, Hugh Paynel of Moirhus, John Chese of Clayton, William de Kirkeby in Hoton Paynel, William Trilleman of Hoton Paynel, and Thomas de Pickeburne in Hoton Paynel; who say upon their oath as follows:—

	Annual value.		
	£	s.	d.
The capital messuage with granges . .	0	6	8
In demesne nine score and 16 acres of land, at 8d. the acre	6	10	8
In demesne five acres of meadow, at 4s. .	1	0	0
In villenage eleven bovates and a half, at 10s. the bovate	5	15	0
William Smith (faber) holds one toft and one acre of land, worth	0	2	6
Also six score seven acres and a half and one rood of assart land, every acre 4d., but one acre, worth 8d.	2	3	3

Sum total, £15 18s. 1d.

Henry de Lascy is the next heir, and he will be fourteen years old on the day of the Epiphany next (6 January 1264-5).[b]

Richard son of Robert, Reeve of the manor, has received the farms and other perquisites from the day of decease of the Earl of Winchester; for which he will answer from the feast-day of S. Mark the Evangelist (25 April).

divided into 10 parts sub titulo, County of York," "I Roger de Quency, Earl of Winton, constable of Scotland, have given to Edmund Lacy, my cousin, my manors of Kippax and Scales. Witness, Richard, E. of Cornwall" (fo. 247), which throws some light on an expression at the conclusion of the inquisition. How De Quency became possessed of Kippax and Scholes in the first place, does not so readily appear.

[b] Elmsall, in the parish of South Kirkby, near Pontefract.

[a] The Stubbs which furnished so many of these jurors was Stubbs Walden, in the parish of Womersley, which took its second name from one Walding, who held it in the time of King Stephen, and of whom this Richard, son of Robert, the reeve, was the grandson's grandson, the reeveship having been hereditary during the intervening generations. Moorhouse, like Elmsall, is in the parish of South Kirkby. All these places, with Frickley and Hooton Paynell, are a few miles between south and east of Pontefract.

[b] This does not quite tally with the age of the heir (eight years and a half, and a month, and six days, on 25 July, 1258), as given on p. 65; which would give his birth, 19 Dec., 34 Hen. III., 1249. The present document says fourteen on Epiphany, 49 Hen. III., born i.e. on Epiphany, 35 Hen. III., that is, 6 Jan., 1250-1, a difference of a year and three weeks.

INQUISITION as to the value of the manor of Elmesale, late of R[oger] de Quency, Earl of Winchester, made on the day of S. Edmund the Confessor 49 Hen. 3 (20 Nov., 1264) by William de Preston, John of the same, Alan son of Josian, Peter de Arches, William de Sayvile, John de Thorpe, Alexander de Wyttelay, Herbert de Arches, Henry de Goyce of Skelhale, William de Sainpol, Thomas de Reynell, William son of the Rector of the church of Camesale, and Roger de Birum, who say on their oath that there are in demesne nine score and two acres, each worth 9*d.* by the year, also in demesne five acres of meadow (at 4*s.*). There are fourteen acres of several pasture (in the place of one bovate), worth 10*s.* yearly. In vilenage there are eleven bovates and a half of land held by 18 bond-men *(bondi)* who yield 115*s.* and do no works. There is a smith who makes plough-shares *(ferra carucarum)*, or gives 2*s.* 6*d.*, for one toft and one acre of land, but does no other service. Of assarts there are six score eight acres and a half and one rood, every acre worth 4*d.* except one which gives 8*d.*; and the sum is 43*s.* 3*d.* The capital messuage is worth yearly 3*s.*

Of knight's fees and advowsons of churches there are none ; and as to the conditions made on the exchange of the said manor (with Edmund de Lascy, late deceased, *writ*), the said Earl held it for term of his life for the manors of Kypes' and Scales'.[a]

The lady Aleysia de Lascy[b] received the farm at Whitsuntide, viz., 32*s.*

Total of the parcels, £16 10*s.* 1*d.*

No one holds the said manor, but it is in the custody of the reeve until otherwise commanded by the King.

LVI.   ROGER DE MERLAY *or* MERLEY.[c]   *Inq. p. m.*

[50 HEN. III. No. 39.]

Writ dated at Westminster 4 Dec., 50th year (1265).

EXTENT of the lands and tenements, which were of Roger de Merlay, made by Richard de Midelton, assigned *ad hoc*, at Threske on Tuesday before the Conversion of S. Paul, 50 Henry

----

a Scholes, in the parish of Barwick in Elmet, and Kippax, near Pontefract.

b Alesia, the widow of Edmund de Lascy, who received the rents of this manor as the guardian of the infant heir named in the inquisition, was one of the " foreign damsels " brought over in 1247, for marriage to English heirs, by Peter of Savoy, the maternal uncle of the Queen. Alesia was a daughter of Manfred, Marquis of Saluzzo.

c The family of Merlay, whose chief possessions lay in Northumberland, where Morpeth· was their principal seat, were great benefactors to the Abbey of New-minster, in that county. On 10 April, 1239, the King took the homage of Roger,

(19 Jan., 1265-6), by the oath of William son of Theobald of Brigham, Richard son of Martin of Roston, Thomas *le Bret* of Brumpton, Henry de Wykam, John de Burton, Robert *le Provost* of Burton, Peter son of Richard of the same, Walter son of Oda *(Ode)*, Robert *le Clerk* of Burton, John Dyard, William Raas, and John de Kyllum, who say that at Burton[a] there are in demesne 29 bovates of land (the bovate 12s.) with 29 acres of meadow adjoining, and 76 acres of meadow, £4 2s. In bondage 38 bovates (each one marc); also six bovates held in drengage by three drenges *(quas tres Drengy tenent)*, each yielding by the year 5s. Every of them shall mow in autumn for fourteen days, being fed by the lord *(ad cibum domini)*, and each day's work is worth a penny. Every of them shall carry the lord's corn in autumn with two carts for one day, the carriage of a cart worth 3d. Every of them owes the lord one ploughing *(aruram)* without food, worth 4d., and another ploughing with food, which is not reckoned, because it costs as much as it is worth. Every of them owes three harrowings, each worth a penny, and two fat fowls *(altilia)* at Christmas, each worth a penny. Every of them owes the lord annual aid, which is taxed in all at 4s. 6d.

There is one watermill worth by the year one marc. Forty-eight cottars pay in all 76s. 3½d. Also a brewery *(bracinum)* yields yearly one marc. One croft called Cumbeland is worth yearly 6s., one plot called C . . , 3½d. There is one *cultura* in the field of Thyrnum[b] which contains 16 acres, and is worth by the year 9s., and one in the fields of Burton, called Elyesflat which contains ten acres, and is worth 5s. One watermill at Thyrnum, whereof the lord received a fourth part of farm, which fourth part is worth yearly 5s. One William *le Fuler* holds at

son and heir of Roger de Merlay, who undertook to give security for the payment of one hundred pounds for his relief *(Excerpta è Rotulis Finium*, vol. i., p. 322). He died in 50 Hen. III., and was buried in the cloister at Newminster, near his father. He had three daughters, who became his coheirs. Mary, the oldest, aged 24 at her father's death, married William de Graystoke. The second, Isabella, then aged ten, and unmarried, became the wife of Robert de Eure, and in 1274-5 of Robert de Somerville *(Patent Rolls*, 3 Edw. I., m. 25 (2), 44 *Dep. Keeper Public Records' Reports*, p. 60). The youngest, Alice, aged eight at her father's death, was then already married to the son and heir of Marmaduke de Thweng. She was dead before 25 Feb., 1267-8, when the King took the homage of William de Crai-stoke, who had married Mary, sister and one of the heirs of Alice de Merlay, late deceased, for the moiety of her lands. Isabella de Merlay, the other sister, was still unmarried *(Excerpta è Rotulis Finium*, vol. ii., p. 467). All Isabella de Somerville's children, six in number, five sons aud a daughter, died without issue, so that all the Merlay property became vested in the Graystokes *(Newminster Chartulary*, p. 281).

    [a] Burton Agnes (Kirkby's *Inquest*, p. 312).

    [b] Thornholme, in the parish of Burton Agnes. Thirnon, Tirnum in *Domesday*, and Thirnom, Thirnum in Kirkby's *Inquest*

will of the lord six acres, and John *le Clerke* also six acres, each
paying 9*s*. Ranulf Smith holds 12 acres and yields yearly 14*s*.
8*d*. There is a remnant of demesne land by a former partition,
and they call it "*avantagium patrimonii*," which yields by the
year 5*s*.

All the under-written are free tenants, namely:

	Annual rent.
	s. *d.*
Peter *de la Chaumpayne*, who holds by inheritance a fourth part of the town of Drenghou[a]	5 11
Constance de Meus, her tenement there	5 11
Joan who was wife of Hugh *de Capella*, her tenement in Burton	8 0
John son of William, 2 bovates of land in Burton	6 8
The same for another tenement	0 1
Anselm *le Engleys*, tenement in Thyrnum	1 pound pepper
Ralph de Enesneue, for his tenement there	4 3
William *le Oyseleir*, for his tenement there	2 2½
Anselm Dreng, for his tenement there	44 0
William de Hasthorpe	0 1
Richard de Harpam, for the site of a windmill	0 1
Leuedy Bece, for a tenement in Burton	3 0
Thomas son of Oda *(fil' Ode)*, for a tenement in Burton	2 0½
Robert *le Clerke* . . . ,, ,,	1 0
Thomas Clervaus . . . ,, ,,	1 0
John *le Engleys* for Cnalcroft	1 0
Alan Romund, for one toft in Thyrnon	0 6
Hugh Hyrning, for a tenement in Burton	0 8
Of issues of the market there	10 0
From a turbary in common years	10 0
A garden worth in common years	3 0

Sum, £59 19*s*. 1*d*.

These are the knights' fees appurtenant to the same manor,
viz:

Knights' fees.

Herbert de Saint Quintin holds his tenement in Harpam,
Burton, Thyrnom, Mapelton, Rollestone, and Grance-
more,[b] by the service of 2⅓
Hugh Gubyon holds in Jetengham, Brentingham, Clif,
and Cave,[c] by the service of 1
The same in Burton, five bovates of land, by the service of 1/20

---

[a] Dringhoe, in the parish of Skipsea in Holderness, near Hornsea.

[b] Harpham, Burton Agnes, Thornholme, Mappleton, Rowlston, and Grans-
moor, in the parish of Burton Agnes.

[c] Jetengham not identified, Brantingham, Cliff, and Cave.

Knights' fees.

William de Rodestayn holds in Rodestayn, Benton, and
Buketon,[a] by the service of   I
William de Hasthorpe holds in Hasthorpe,[b] by the ser-
vice of   .   .   .   . $\frac{1}{6}$.
Alan Romund holds in Thyrnom and Grancemor, by the
service of   .   .   .   . $\frac{1}{12}$
Anselm *le Engleys* holds in Thyrnome, by the service of . $\frac{1}{40}$
John *le Engleys* holds in Thyrnome, by the service of   . $\frac{1}{40}$
Thomas de Louthorpe holds in Harpham, by the service of $\frac{1}{16}$

The said manor was held by Roger of Peter de Brus. He
had three daughters[c] and heirs; of whom the eldest is twenty-·
four years old, and married to William de Graystoke; the
second, ten years old, and not married; the third, eight years
old, and she was married before the death of Roger, to the son
and heir of Marmaduke de Tuenge (Thweng).[d]

LVII. LANDS OF JOHN DE SOTHILL AND JOHN DE HETON.

[51 HEN. III. No. 33.]

Writ dated at Kenilworth, 30 Nov., 51st year (1266).

EXTENT of the lands and tenements which were of John de
Sothill and John de Heton, made by the oath of Richard
de Hiperum, Thomas at Well of the same, William de
Nortlande, Thomas son of Adam of Erdeslawe, William de
Trimigham, Adam son of Arnald of Erdeslawe, William de
Roulay, Henry de Emmelay, Robert *le Ragget* of Emmelay,
Robert de Wolewra, Michael de Langlay, and John *de Mora*,

---

[a] Rudston, Bempton, and Buckton.

[b] Haisthorpe, in the parish of Burton Agnes.

[c] Roberts *(Cal. Gen.,* vol. i., p. 120*)* reads here—"habuit tres suas hæredes,"
but I should read rather—"habuit tres filias heredes," for "suas" first written
seems to me altered to "filias." (J. A. C. V.)

[d] A writ of the King, dated at Reading, 6 Nov., 55th year (1270), and directed
to John de Reygate, his Escheator beyond Trent, refers to an order previously
given for an extent to be made of lands and tenements which formerly belonged to
Roger de Merlay, in which extent the Escheator omitted to include the woods and
parks in the County of Northumberland, into which Robert de Eure, who married
Isabel, the second daughter and coheir of Roger, had intruded, and would not
permit them to be divided between himself and William de Graystoke or Craystoke,
who had married Mary, eldest daughter of Roger, Alice, the third and youngest
daughter having in the meantime deceased. Another writ dated at Westminster,
20 July, 55th year (1271), alludes to partition having been made before that date
between the two daughters and coheirs. This partition relates to the County of
Northumberland *(Inq. p. m.,* 55 Hen. III., No. 35*)*.

who say upon their oath that John de Sothill had at Sothill,[a] a capital messuage worth by the year with garden half a marc; in demesne fifty acres of arable land (at 4*d.*), meadow worth one marc yearly, pannage and herbage, half a marc. He had there one water-mill, worth by the year 24*s.*, and in service of free men yearly, 4*s.* 4*d.*; and there are in villenage seven bovates of land, at 9*s.* the bovate. In Ovendene[b] he had from free tenants by the year 13*s.* 7½*d.*, and from his share of one water-mill, 4*s.* In Stanesfelde[c] and Routonstale[d] he had from free men yearly £4 6*s.*; in meadow and pasture one marc; from one small meadow in Stanesfelde 12*d.*; and from one water-mill there, half a marc. In Derton[e] a capital messuage and a meadow, worth by the year one marc; from one water-mill 20*s.*, and from one toft there, 12*d.*; also 8*s.* rent of assize yearly in Holandeswayn.[f] He had in villenage fifteen bovates of land, at 6*s.* the bovate; but of the said tenement of Derton, Robert de Stuteville has seisin by the King. The said John rendered yearly to Richard de Thorenhill his lord, for the land of Ovendene, Routunstale, Sothill, and Stanesfelde, 6s. 7*d.*

John de Heton had in Westheton[g] a capital messuage worth by the year 2*s.*, from a pasture 12*d.*, beside forty acres of arable land in demesne, at 3*d.* the acre, and three acres of meadow, at 2*s.*; from his share of one water-mill yearly, 10*s.*; and from service of free men and cottars, two marcs. He had in Northlande[h] from a certain tenement yearly four-pence with relief, and in Hingandeheton[i] sixteen bovates of land, at 4*s.* the bovate; from a watermill there yearly 5*s.*; but Hugh his (John's) brother is enfeoffed of the said tenement for life, yielding yearly to the Earl of Warrenne[k] 17*s.* 2*d.*, and doing suit at the Earl's court. John de Heton held Westheton of Thomas de Burgh, but it is not known by what service.

John de Sothill took yearly from free tenants in Scholekroft[l] 40*d.* with reliefs, and rendered for the said rent to Jollan de Neville 40*d.* He had yearly for attachment of a pond (*pro attachiamento unius stangni*) in Hage[m] six-pence.

a Soothill, near Dewsbury.
b Ovenden, near Halifax.
c Stansfeld, near the same place.
d Rawtenstall, near Hebden Bridge, parish of Halifax.
e Darton, near Barnsley.
f Hoyland Swain, near the same place.
g Kirkheaton.
h Norland, near Halifax.
i Hanging Heaton.
k *Com' War'.* The Earl of Warrenne at this time was John Plantagenet, Earl of Surrey. He was lord of the manor of Wakefield. The Court referred to was the Wakefield Court.
l Scholecroft, in Morley.
m Haigh, near Barnsley.

LVIII.   SIR PETER DE PERCY.[a]   *Inq. p. m.*

[51 HEN. III.   No. 27.]

Writ dated at Cambridge, 23 March, 51st year (1266-7).

INQUISITION made at York on the morrow of Easter in the
51st year of the reign (18 April, 1267), before Master
Richard de Clifforde, Escheator beyond Trent, by Richard Tros-
sebote, William de Rodestan, Anketin Malure, Thomas *de la
More*, knights; Richard de Clif, William de Holm, Robert *le
Veyl* of Scopton, Robert de Breddale, William de Graynesby,
Robert *de la More*, Geoffrey de Meningthorp, John Broun of
Aclom, William Croc, Henry de Pokethorp, Thomas Agilon of
Sotton, John *le Walays*, Elias de Burelle, Richard son of Odard
of Boulton, Richard Knict of Hornington, and Peter de Hornington; who say upon their oath that Sir *(dominus)* Peter de
Percy held the town of Warru[m],[b] with the advowson of the
church and other appurtenances of the King in chief, for the
fourth part of one knight's fee; and it is worth by the year in
all issues £21 12s. 2d.   He held also in chief of Maulay fee by
knight's service a moiety of the town of Sotton upon Derwent,
worth by the year £7 7[s.] 10d.; and of Percy fee by knight's
service the other moiety, worth yearly £13 12s. 2d.   He held
also in chief by knight's service of Percy fee eight carucates of
land in Kerneteby,[c] worth £37 11s. 4d., and seven carucates in
Boulton,[d] worth £38 11s. 4d. by the year.   He held of Eufem[ia]
de Queldale in chief by knight's service, two parts [*i.e.* thirds]
of one carucate of land in Poles,[e] worth yearly 43s. 9d.

Robert de Percy,[f] who was aged twenty-one years [on the
feast] of St. Dunstan in the 50th year of the reign, [*i.e.* 19 May,
1266] is his next heir.

[a] Sheriff of Yorkshire for the last half of 45 Hen. III., and for the following
year.   His son and heir, Robert de Percy, held the office on his behalf as farmer,
for the first three quarters of 47 Hen. III.   Peter de Percy bore as his arms, Or a
fess engrailed azure *(Nicolas's Roll of Arms, temp. Hen. III. p.* 11*)*.   Held Thornton in Staincliffe & Ilkley in frank marriage.

[b] Wharrom Percy, near Sledmere.

[c] Carnaby, near Bridlington.   *Domesday*, Cherendebi.

[d] Bolton Percy, near Tadcaster.

[e] Pool, in the parish of Brotherton, near Ferrybridge.

[f] The homage of Robert de Percy, son and heir of Peter de Percy, was taken on
30 April, 1267, when the Escheator was ordered, after taking security for a reasonable relief, to give him full seisin of the lands his father died seised of in chief
(Excerpta è Rotulis Finium, vol. ii., p. 456*)*.

LIX. JOHN DE KAUWODE.[a]

[52 HEN. III. No. 5.]

No Writ.

INQUISITION made at York, on Monday after the feast of S. Hilary [52] Henry (16 Jan., 1267-8), concerning the lands and tenements which John de Kauwode held of the King in chief—whether Robert his son took his father's lands, whether he of malice detained his nephew, named David, the son of his eldest brother, whether the custody of the lands and tenements belongs to the King by reason of the said David's minority, and whether David is the next heir of John de Kauwode—by William Freman of Wikestowe, Gilbert de Hodelstone, Richard Freman of the same, Henry Erle of Fenton, Robert de Wodehouse, Master William de Kirkeby, Thomas of the Grene of Bretton, William de Lotrington, Henry Freman of Ledestone, ... de Sotton, William Stirchut of Fenton, Robert son of Gilbert of Fenton, and John de Wridelford of Ha[t]helsay. They say by their oath that the said John held his land in Kauwode of the King in chief, by the service of sufficiently keeping the King's wood of Langwathe, and that he was vested and seised of the lands on the day of his death. Robert son of John of malice eloigned *(maliciose prolongavit)* David son of John, his (Robert's) eldest brother, during the life-time of the said John, and yet detains him; but they know not how or where. And David is next heir of the said John, aged eleven years.

LX. ROBERT DE CHANCY.[b] *Inq. p. m.*

[52 HEN. III. No. 4.]

No Writ.

INQUISITION made at York before J. de Reygate, Escheator beyond Trent, on Monday before the feast of S. Michael 52 Henry (24 Sept., 1268), by the oath of Richard *le Waleys* of Aclom, Walter de Barkthorpe, Thomas Chancy of Skekinby, William de Toroldeby, Walter Clerk *(clerici)* of Berthorp,

---

[a] Cawood. In No. LXV., it is stated, that the keeper of the King's Hay of Langewath, which lay between Ouse and Derwent, had a carucate of land in the town of Kawode, as his fee for that office. Langwathe may be Langwith, in the parish of Wheldrake.

[b] See No. VII. On 24 Sept., 1268, the King took the homage of Thomas de Chauncy, son and heir of Robert de Chauncy late deceased, for all the lands of which his father died seised in chief. Thomas de Raygate, the Escheator, was ordered to give Thomas full seisin of these lands (*Excerpta è Rotulis Finium*, vol. ii., p. 478).

William son of Jordan of the same, Robert son of Alice of the
same, William de Kenerthorp, Thomas *le Paumer* of Barkthorpe,
John *le Noreys* of Skerkenby, Roger Basil of the same, Ralph
Vernon of Boogethorp, Robert de Grymmestone of Leymynge,
and Willliam Wyt of Breydishale, who say that Robert de
Chancy held of the King in Skirkenbec a manor with garden,
worth by the year 40s. He held also in demesne three carucates
of land and six bovates, worth by the year with meadow and
pasture (the bovate with meadow and pasture, one marc), thirty
marcs; and also six acres of land, 6s. There are free tenants who
yield yearly 17s. 3d. The perquisites of Court are worth by the
year, one marc. Twenty-two bovates of land are held in bondage, and are worth by the year with meadow and pasture, 22
marcs. There are sixteen cottages, 46s. 8d., and two mills in
demesne, 6 marcs by the year.

Thomas de Chancy is son and next heir of Robert, and of
full age, namely, 23 years.

Sum, £44 16s. 7d.

The said Robert held in barony of the King *(Et tenuit in
Baronia de dicto domino Rege).*

LXI.   LUCY DE KYME.[a]

[53 HEN. III. No. 28.]

Writ directed to John de Raygate, Escheator this side Trent,[b] referring to
the complaint made by the Prioress and Nuns of Apelton, that whereas
William de Kyme (long deceased) by his charter gave to them 40s. rent
from the mill of Neuton upon 'Querffe' to be received yearly in perpetual
almoign, Lucy, who was his wife, to whom that mill after her husband's
death was assigned in dower, had withdrawn the rent, although the
Prioress and Nuns had been in seisin of the same before the death of
William de Kyme.   Inquiry to be made.   Dated at York 24 September,
52nd year (1268).

INQUISITION at York, before J. de Reygate, Escheator beyond
Trent, on Tuesday after the feast of All Saints, 53 Henry
(6 Nov., 1268), made by John de Milforde, Thomas de Grymmestone, Robert de Clifford, Henry son of the Master *(fil'
Mag'ri)* of Tatecastir, Robert Marshal *(Mareschallum)* of the
same, Alan Calle of Smawes, John de Merstone, Guy *(Wydon')*

---

[a] See No. XLIX.   Her husband, William de Kyme, by his deed *(Monasticon
Angl.,* vol. ii., p. 795, *n* 10*),* bearing date at Lincoln, upon the day of St. Katherine
the Virgin (25 Nov.), anno 1258 (40 Hen. III.), for the health of his soul and the
soul of Lucy (de Roos) his wife, ratified unto the Canons and Nuns of Bolington,
whatsoever they had of his fee.   The date here is wrong, either it must be 1255, or
42 Hen. III., if 1258.

[b] This is correct, as the King was at this time staying at York.

de Appilton, Hilary *(Yllarium)* of the same, William Marshal *(Marescallum)* of Oxton, Thomas *le Mason* of the same, Walter the Chaplain's brother *(fratrem Capellani)* of the same, and William de Ribbestane, who say upon their oath that William de Kyme gave and granted to the Prioress and Nuns of Appilton by his charter, in pure and perpetual almoign, forty shillings of annual rent to be received from the mill of Neuton upon "Querffe" (Wharfe), and they had the forty shillings during the whole life of William de Kyme. After his decease the then Escheator took into the King's hand all his (William) lands and tenements, and detained 20*s*. for Martimmas term in the 44th year (1259). Afterwards the King having assigned to Lucy de Kyme the said mill of Neuton in dower, she held it entirely by that assignment, and for that reason withdrew the forty shillings of rent now eight years past, from the said Prioress and Nuns.

LXII. JOHN DE BALLIOL.[a] *Inq. p. m.*

[53 HEN. III. No. 43.]

Writ dated at Westminster, 27 Oct., 52nd year (1268), and directed to the Escheator beyond Trent.

EXTENT and Inquisition of the lands and tenements which were of John de Balliol, as well of his own inheritance and purchase, as of his wife's inheritance, made before J. de Reygate, Escheator beyond Trent, on Monday the morrow of S. Katherine, at York, 53 Henry (26 Nov., 1268), by the oath of William son of Robert of Holm, Robert *le Frankelyn* of Wytone, William Tart Corteys of Catton, Elias de Brunneby, Richard de Cokerynton, Robert *de la More* of the same, Peter Hosbonde of the same, William de Grenesby of the same, Geoffrey de Hayton in

[a] In 1229, John de Baillol, son and heir of Hugh de Baillol, made a fine with the King of £150, for his relief for thirty knights' fees, which Hugh de Baillol, his father, held in chief, that is 100*s*. from each knight's fee *(Excerpta è Rotulis Finium*, vol. i., p. 183). He was buried at New Abbey, in Galloway, also called Sweetheart Abbey, from his widow having buried his heart there. He and his wife founded Balliol College, Oxford. The King took the homage of his son and heir, Hugh de Balliol, 26 Dec., 1268, and John le Moyne was commanded to give him full seisin of all the lands and tenements held by his deceased father, reserving to Deverguill, late wife of John de Balliol, her own inheritance, and reasonable dower out of the lands of her deceased husband *(Ibid.*, vol. ii., p. 482). Devorgill was daughter and heiress of Alan, Lord of Galloway, by his second wife Margaret, eldest daughter and coheir of David, Earl of Huntingdon (brother to William and Malcolm, Kings of Scotland), and sister and coheir of John, Earl of Chester and Huntingdon. She married in 1223 *(Chronicon de Mailros)*. Settled the foundation and ordained the statutes of Balliol College, Oxford, under her seal, at Botel, in Galloway, 1282, when she styled herself "Devorgilla de Galvidia, Domina de Balliolo. See Walbran's *History of Gainford*, for an account of this family.

Skipton, Robert son of Peter of Brunneby, Adam son of Walter Cook *(Coci)*, and Richard de Warplington; who say that the capital messuage with herbage of the park is worth by the year 24 shillings. There are in demesne twelve bovates of land (at 10*s.*), £6; also pasture worth 20*s.* Two mills are worth yearly six marcs. Forty-two bovates of land (at 10*s.*) held in villenage, £21. One bovate held by charter yields 8*s.*, and another, 3*s.* Four bovates, held by charter, yield one penny by the year. There are two tofts and one bovate held by charter, which yield 8*s.* Cottars pay yearly 4*s.* The advowson of the church appertains to the lord of Everingham, and the church is worth by the year 24 marcs.

The capital messuage of Kibbelinton is worth by the year 2*s.* In demesne 22 bovates of land (at 5*s.*), 110*s.*

The capital messuage of Clenyng is worth by the year 2*s.* In demesne four bovates (at 10*s.*), 40*s.*

HAYTON.

The capital messuage is worth 4*s.*; and there are in demesne nine bovates (at 10*s.*), £4 10*s.*

The lord Hugh de Balliol is the next heir of John, and of full age; and the said lands are by purchase. Sir Adam de Everingham bought back *(redemit)* the said lands from the said lord John, but had not seisin of them before his (John) death.

EXTENT and inquisition &c. (as before) made before the same Escheator at Driffeud on Saturday the eve of S. Katherine Virgin, 53 Henry (24 Nov., 1268), by the oath of Peter Scharfe of Driffeud, Robert upon the hill *(super montem)* of the same, William Young *(juvenis,)* William le Tonnour, Simon de Hugate, Ralph de Mifranceys, Henry Young *(juvenis)* of the same, Thomas Noys, Thomas son of Everard, Simon Gymelin, Adam son of Stephen, and Robert de Spileman; who say that the capital messuage of Driffeud is worth by the year 20*s.* There are free tenants who hold at will of the lord 28 bovates of land, each worth 25*s.* by the year with all services, as in ploughs, harrows, and other things.   Sum, £35.

Other free tenants hold in socage 16 carucates (at 16*s.* 10*d.*), £13 9*s.* 4*d.* Eighteen bovates of land, which are held by charter, are worth by the year 20*s.* Stephen Hamond holds by charter six bovates which yield yearly 12*s.* There are four watermills with market *(cum foro)* and they yield £33. There are small farms which are worth yearly, 15½*d.*

Sum total of Driffeud, £103 2*s.* 7½*d.*

In the town of Kelithorpe,[a] there are 5 carucates and 6 bovates (each bovate, 16s. 10d.), £4 4s.

In Brigham[b] one carucate with meadow and pasture, yields yearly 5½ marcs, and half a carucate yields 5s. 3d.

In Besewike[c] there are 3 carucates which are held in socage and yield by the year 40s. In Killum one bovate yields 10s. of demesne, and 5 carucates and 7 bovates in socage; of which every bovate is worth yearly 2s. 1¼d. Sum, 102s. 8d.

There are no advowsons or knights' fees.

Hugh de Balliol is next heir of John, and of full age. John de Balliol did not die vested or seised of the above said lands, because they were of the inheritance of Dervorgill his wife; and they were given to Hugh de Balliol before his father's death.[d]

LXIII. ROGER LE PEYTEVIN.

[53 HEN. III. No. 41.]

Writ dated 8 June, 53rd year (1269), on the back of which is a note that all the persons named in the Inquisition dwell within the liberty of the lady Alesia de Lacy[e] of Osg[oldcross], where the bailiffs of the Sheriff dare not and cannot enter, unless it be by force and arms.

WHEREAS the King lately ordered the Sheriff of Yorkshire, that he should cause all moneys coming to him by summons of the King's Exchequer, as well debts of Jews as otherwise, to be levied with all haste and brought to the Exchequer aforesaid, whereby the Sheriff, as the custom is in the realm, sent his bailiffs for the purpose of levying the King's dues in which Roger *le Peytevin* is bound, to the said Roger's lands and tenements which are within the liberty of Alesia de Lascy of Pontefract, the bailiffs and men of the said Alesia from Pontéfract and those parts assaulted the King's bailiffs, coming

---

[a] Kellythorpe, in the parish of Emswell.

[b] Brigham, in the parish of Foston.

[c] Beswick, in the parish of Kilnwick.

[d] A further inquisition (at great length) was taken at Bywell, on Monday the morrow of St. Martin, 53 Hen. III. (12 Nov., 1268), by John de Reygate, of lands in Northumberland. By this, Hugh de Balliol, son and heir of John, is found to be thirty years old and more; but by an inquisition concerning the manor of Hich' (Hitchin in Hertfordshire), made before the attornies of John le Moyne, the King's Escheator this side Trent, his age is said to be twenty-eight and more. Though without date, this last inquiry was doubtless taken in pursuance of the writ (before alluded to) dated 13 Dec., 1268.

[e] Widow of Edmund de Lascy, who died in 1258, and whose Inq. p. m. appears above (No. XLV.). She is mentioned in No. LV. and, as guardian of her infant son, retained throughout the disturbed reign of Henry III. a position almost regal.

to levy for the dues aforesaid, wounded, beat, and illtreated them, taking Thomas *le Porter*, the King's bailiff, and carrying him to Pontefract Castle and detaining him there in prison with the King's money in his possession, to the most grievous damage and manifest contempt of the King.

INQUISITION is made in full County Court by Richard Derling of Fenton,[a] Richard son of William of the same, Richard son of Maud *(fil' Matild')* of the same, John de Lede,[b] clerk, Gilbert de Heselwode, Richard son of Roger of Levenaton, John son of Richard of the same, Robert son of Serlo of Bretton,[c] Alan Calle of Smawes,[d] John de Essekmue of Neuton,[e] Richard Malleson, Elias Clerk *(Elyam clericum)* of Neuton,[e] and Robert de Clifforde; who say that William serjeant of Alesia de Lascy at Saxton, Richard serjeant of Ralph de Rye, Robert Skinner *(pelliparius)* of Saxton, Robert son of Brun of the same, Gregory son of the Reeve, Simon son of Benjamin of Saxton, Robert Erodin of the same, William son of John, William son of Margaret of Toueton, John *le Den* the younger *(le Jovene)*, Robert Plochewrychte, Robert son-in-law of Walter de Toueton, Walter husband *(vir)* of Eggledina, John *le Messer* of Toueton, together with the whole commonalty of the towns of Saxton and Toueton (except William, Reeve of Saxton, and William Bateman of the same, and other men, old and young, not able to go, or walk, or carry arms), going to the lands and tenements of the aforesaid Roger on the occasion aforesaid, assaulted the King's bailiffs, beat, wounded, and illtreated them (as abovesaid), and took Thomas *le Porter* and kept him in prison in Pontefract Castle.

They say also that the trespass was done in the said Roger's land which is geldable to the King, and not within the liberty of Alesia de Pontefract.

[a] Kirk Fenton, or Church Fenton.
[b] Lede in Ryther, near Saxton.
[c] Now Burton Salmon.
[d] Smaw's Hall, near Tadcaster.
[e] Newton Kyme. All these places are in the immediate neighbourhood of Saxton, where the offence was committed concerning which the inquisition was made.

LXIV. ISABEL ELDEST DAUGHTER AND ONE OF THE HEIRS OF ROBERT DE VIPONT.[a]

[53 Hen. III. No. 44.]

THE answer of Robert Wallerond (or Waleraund) to the King's writ, dated at Windsor, 28 April, in the 53rd year (1269), and commanding inquiry to be made concerning the age of Isabel (wife of Roger, son and heir of Roger de Clifford) the eldest daughter and one of the heirs of Robert de Vipont, long time deceased, who held of the King in chief.

I signify to your Excellence that I lately went to Erdes-leye, where I saw the said Isabel, and diligently examined her as to her age; whereby I have adjudged her to be of full age. Dated at Erdesley 15 June, in the year aforesaid (1269).

LXV. EDWARD SON OF HENRY III. *Inq. ad. q. d.*

[54 Hen. III. No. 59.]

Writ of the King, as directed to Roger de Leyburne, Justice of his forest beyond Trent, is recited by Roger in writing to his friend and kinsman Roger de Lancaster, who is desired to execute the King's command with all haste.

INQUISITION made at Langewath[b] before lord Roger de Lancaster, Steward of the King's forests this side of Trent, on Thursday in the first week of Lent, 54 Henry (27 Feb., 1269-70), by Robert de Kawode, keeper of the said hay *(custodem dicte haye)*, Conan de Kelkefeld, and Walter de Hemelsey, verderers of the same, William de Thorp, agister of the same, and twelve knights and free dwellers around the hay aforesaid *(milites et libere manentes circa hayam predictam)*, namely; Sir *(Dominum)* Nicholas de Paumes, Hugh de Morers, William Darell, Geoffrey Mordagge, Philip de Morers, Adam Mordagge, Robert de Menthorp, Roger de Arnest, Ralph Freman, Adam Amy, Walter son of Hugh of Osegoteby, and Hugh son of Peter of the same, jurors, and by the foresters, verderers, and regarders of the forest of Gautres, whether it would be to the damage of the King, or to the annoyance of his forest of Gautres, or to the annoyance of his forests in the County of

[a] Great grand daughter of Idonea de Vipont, whose inquisition is given in No. XIII. Her father, Robert de Vipont, Lord of Appleby, in Westmoreland, died of wounds received whilst fighting on the side of Simon de Montfort. He left two daughters, the abovenamed Isabel, and Idonea, wife of Roger de Leyburne *(Cal. Gen.*, vol. i., p. 331*)*.

[b] See No. LIX.

York, if the King should grant to Edward his eldest son the forest and hay of Langewath to have for ever, or not. They say upon oath that it would not be to the damage of the King, if he were to grant to the lord Edward his eldest son the aforesaid hay, so that he should retain it to his own use; but if he were to alien it then it would be to the damage of the King, for he would lose every year in herbage one marc; in pannage, 40s. one year; another, 20s.; a third, half a marc; a fourth, nothing; according to the mast of acorns. What vert and venison ought to be worth by the year, they cannot estimate, because the King takes ransoms and amercements in the Eyre of the Forest, for trespasses made of vert and venison.

They also say that it would be to the annoyance of the forest of Gautres, because the hay aforesaid is between Ouse and Derwent where the King's forest was de-afforested by the King, and nothing remained there but the hay, and when the King's game *(fere Domini Regis)* cross from the forest of Gautres they have refuge in it because it is not more than a league distant.

The hay contains by estimation, by the perch of the King's forest, in covert, 400 acres, and in plain, 100 acres. They estimate within the covert, 4,000 oaks, the price of each 3s. Every acre of underwood is worth 5s. They say also that if the hay were reduced to cultivation, every acre would be worth yearly, 6d. They have estimated the number of acres because they were unable to measure the hay on account of inundation. The hay is kept by one forester of fee, who holds in considera- tion of that keeping one carucate of land in the town of Kawode.[a]

LXVI. INQUIRY CONCERNING THE MILLS OF THE
TEMPLARS AT YORK.

[54 HEN. III. No. 36.]

Writ dated at Westminster, 29 March, 54th year (1270).

INQUISITION at York, before J. de Reygate, on Tuesday after the close of Easter, 54 Henry (22 April, 1270), as to how much the mills of the Templars beneath the King's Castle of York are worth by the year in all issues, save costs and charges

---

[a] The names, sixteen, of those sworn are repeated at the foot of the inquisition in column, but present no variation in spelling except in one case, Roger de Aren- nest, more usually "Arnenest," *i.e.*, eagle's nest. Each name has the tag to which the seal was formerly appended.

which it will be necessary to set for their keeping and repair, made by twenty-four free and lawful men, that is to say, by twelve men of the City of York and twelve men without the City, namely: by Arnald Clerk of York, Henry Baker, Alan Crokebayn, John de Sutton, all of the same, Stephen de Hundemandby, John Gerrocke, Richard de Wykestowe, Geoffrey de Pykeringe, Ralph the Marshal *(le Ferrur)*, Richard de Ryther, Ralph *le Long*, Simon Scraggy, Peter de Ros of Barton, William de Wyginthorpe, Adam de Hoby in Crambum, Robert son of William of Barneby, Richard son of Osbert of the same, William de Touthorpe, William Darel of Quelderyke, Geoffrey Murdoke of the same, Hugh Mureres of Elvington, William de Thorpe of Heselington, Robert de Henlay (?) in Stivelingflet, and Robert *le Long* of Kelkefeud, who say by their oath that the mills aforesaid are worth by the year in all issues, save costs and charges which ought to be set for their keeping and repair, and save tithes of the same, twelve marcs.

LXVII. PARTITION OF THE LANDS AND TENEMENTS OF
RALPH FITZ RANULF.[a]

[54 HEN. III. No. 24.]

Writ directed to John de Reygate, Escheator, and dated at Westminster, 12 May, 54th year (1270).

PARTITION of the lands and tenements of Ralph fitz Ranulf, made on Thursday in the week of Pentecost, 54 Henry (5 June, 1270), by the oath of Robert de Lasceles, Richer de Wadsant, knights: Alan de Eskelby, Gilbert de Rugemond, Peter de Rand, Thomas de Thorneton, Richard de Burton, Ralph de Baudeseye, Ralph de Seyreby, Henry de Rokeby, Reginald de Ridmere, and William de Leyborne, clerk.

PART OF ROBERT DE NEUVILLE.

The manor of Middilham with the appurtenances except dower, is extended at £34 19s. 11½d. Also Carleton[b] with its

---

[a] Ralph, son and heir of Ranulf fitz Robert, paid his homage to the King at Winchester, on 25 Dec., 1252 *(Excerpta è Rotulis Finium*, vol. ii., p. 147). On 14 April, 1270, John de Raygate, the Escheator beyond Trent, was commanded, after taking security for the payment of the debts due to the King, to hand over the goods of Ralph fitz Ranulf to his executors for the execution of his will *(Ibid.*, vol. ii., p. 508). He left three daughters, Mary, wife of Robert de Neville, Joan, wife of Robert de Tatershale, and Anastasia, at this time under age and in the king's custody. She died shortly afterwards, when her share fell to her two sisters *(Ibid.*, vol. ii., pp. 514, 563).

[b] Carlton in Coverdale, Bradley, Woodale, Hindleythwaite, and Arkelside, in the parish of Coverham. Thoralby, Aysgarth, and Thornton Rust. Doveskar, and Walden, in Bishopdale. West Layton. Whitaside.

appurtenances, the forest of Coverdale (save dower) and vaccary, that is to say, Bradeleie, Wlvedale, Hyndeletheyt, and Arkelsat, £44 6s. 2½d. Two parts of corn-mills of Thoroldeby, Aykesgard [here Arkesgard], and Thorneton, £10 7s. 3d. Of yearly rent from Stephen Messenger *(nuncio)* in York, 2s. 8d.; also Douuesker, and Waldene, with their meadows and pastures, 30s.; 20s. yearly rent in Richemond; 10s. 8d. in Latun; from the lodge *(loga)* of Wytey in Waldene, 20d. In this part are allowed to the other two parts, £4 10s., for lordship *(dominio)* of the house of Middleham, chace of the forest of Coverdale and lordship of the same forest.   Sum, £97 8s. 4d.

Fees appertaining thereto.

William de Preston holds in Snape, Texton,[a] and Westbolton, seven carucates of land; Stephen de Coverham, in Coverham, Scrafton, and Caldeberg,[b] six carucates; Geoffrey Picot, in Melmorby,[c] two carucates; the Abbot of Coverham, in pure and perpetual almoigne in Scrafton, Ridemere, and Texton, seven carucates with the advowson of the abbey; Elias of the Gyle *(de le Gyle)* holds in Aykesgard, half a carucate; the heir of Ralph Brekedore in Carleton, half a carucate; William son of Richard, and Alan son of Walter in the same, half a carucate; Henry de Rokeby in Mortham,[d] one carucate; Richard de Preston in Ridmere, one carucate.

Sum, 25½ carucates.

PART OF ROBERT DE TATESALE.

The manor of Welle with the appurtenances, with a moiety of the whole wood of Welle and of Snape (save dower), is extended at £48 0s. 7d.; in Neubieging[e] with scales[f] *(cum scales de Hilton)* of Hilton, £28 6s. 10d.; in Burton[g] and Waldene, £19 5s. 1d. Also the vaccary of Flemmeshope[h] in Coverdale, with pasture in the whole forest, and with its meadows and estovers of wood, 40s.

Sum, £97 8s. 4d.

[a] Theakston, in the parish of Burneston, near Bedale.
[b] Scrafton and Caldbergh, in Coverdale.
[c] Melmerby, in Coverdale.
[d] Mortham, near Rokeby, on the Tees.
[e] Newbigging, in Bishopdale.
[f] Scales, *i.e.* ladders. For an instance of ladders, or stiles, placed on a hill for public use, see *Yorkshire Archæological Journal*, vol. x., p. 69.
[g] West Burton.
[h] Fleensop, in Coverdale.

Fees appertaining thereto.

William de Lasceles holds in Texton and Arlathorp,[a] six carucates of land; Reginald (?) de Clifton in Clifton,[b] three carucates; Ran[ulf] de Pikehale in Thorneton Watlous, five carucates and two bovates; Roger de Yngoldeby in Yarnewike,[c] one carucate; Robert de Yarnewike in the same, one bovate; Richard de Thyrne in Thirne,[d] half a carucate; Gilbert Ruchemond, Hugh de Aske, and Stephen Malovel, hold in Geytenby,[e] four carucates; William de Ebor. in Aclethorpe,[f] two carucates; Simon de Aclethorpe in the same, two carucates; John son of William of Westlaton, one carucate; Adam Litillouerd in Westbolton, one bovate.   Sum, 25 carucates of land.

PART IN THE KING'S CUSTODY.

The manor of Snape with the appurtenances with a moiety of the whole wood of Welle and of Snape[g] (save dower), £54 8s. 3d.; the manor of Crakehale,[h] with appurtenances (save dower), £38 2s. 9d., the vaccary of Swinesate in Coverdale,[i] with pasture in the whole forest and estovers of wood, £4 13s. 4d.; also 16d. from Robert de Catton in Rypon; from the lodge *(loga)* of Wytey in Waldene, 2s. 8d.   Sum, £97 8s. 4d.

Fees appertaining thereto.

Brian fitzAlan holds in Thorneton Collinge,[j] four carucates; Robert Tortemeyns in Neuton,[k] three carucates and a half; John de Grafton in the same, one carucate; Peter de Rand, two carucates; Robert de Wytclife in Thorp,[l] one carucate; the Abbot of Saint Agatha in Barton,[m] three carucates, and renders foreign

---

[a] Allerthorpe, in the parish of Burneston. In *Domesday*, Erleuestorp, Herleuestorp; in Kirkby's *Inquest*, Arthethorp.

[b] In Thornton Watlas.

[c] Yarnwick, now depopulated, stood a little to the north of Kirklington (Kirkby's *Inquest*, p. 183 n).

[d] Thirn, in the parish of Thornton Watlas.

[e] Gatenby, in the parish of Burneston

[f] Agglethorp, near Coverham. In *Domesday* Aculestorp, and in Kirkby's *Inquest*, Akelthorpe.

[g] Snape, in the parish of Well.

[h] Great Crakehall, in the parish of Bedale.

[i] Swineside, in Coverdale on the right bank of the river.

[j] Now Cowling only,—a hamlet in the township of Burrill-cum-Cowling, and parish of Bedale (Kirkby's *Inquest*, p. 162 n).

[k] Newton-le-Willows, in the parish of Patrick Brompton.

[l] Thorpe, in the parish of Wycliffe.

[m] Barton, a parish between Richmond and Darlington.

service *(et r' forincecum);* John de Roald Burton in Little Bolton,[a] three carucates; the heir of Richard de Rybef in Leyborne, Haukeswelle, and Walbron,[b] three carucates, two bovates; Richard de Burton in Burton upon Yor,[c] four carucates; Robert son of Henry in Great Crakehale, half a carucate; William son of Amicia, two bovates.   Sum, 25½ carucates of land. Besides the advowson of the church of Aygesgard,[d] with presentation of the same, remains to every heir successively.[e]

LXVIII.   NIGEL DE PLUMPTON.   *Inq. p. m.*

[55 HEN. III. No. 8.]

Writ wanting.

INQUISITION made by John de Hamerton, William de Plumton, Robert de Middelton, Henry de Ribbestayn, Reyner de Goldeburg', Thomas de Ribbestayn, Robert *le Beuuor,* Henry de Dicton, Alan de Colethorpe, Peter de Moneketon, Nigel de Dicton, Thomas de Moneketon, Matthew de Bram, Robert de Staynburn, and William Waleman, who say on their oath that the land which Nigel de Plumton held there of the fee of lord William de Wescy in demesnes, rents, villenages, and other issues of land, is of the annual value of ten marcs 2s. 3d., without the three dowers of three ladies; of the fee of lord William de Percy in demesnes, &c., to the annual value of ten marcs 3s., without the three dowers aforesaid.[f] He held in Nessefelde[g] of Peter (or Piers) de Percy land to the annual value of 108s. 8d. (excluding the three dowers), yielding yearly for the same 42s. He held Gersinton[h] of lord William de Percy, páying yearly one marc of silver, and it is worth in issues of land yearly 10 marcs 4s. 1d., without the dowers aforesaid.

[a] Bolton Castle, in the parish of Wensley.

[b] Leyburn, Hauxwell, and Walburn, in the parish of Downholme.

[c] High Burton, in the parish of Masham.

[d] Aysgarth. Called *ante* Arkesgard and Aykesgard.

[e] Extents are also made of manors and lands in Norfolk, with partition in three parts or shares.

[f] These two rents of ten marcs each probably arose from the manor of Plumpton, in the parish of Spofforth, which was held by the Plumptons in moieties of the Vescies and Percies (Kirkby's *Inquest,* p. 45).   They also held the manor of Hornington, in the Ainsty, of the Percies, as of their manor of Spofforth (*Ibid.,* p. 24).

[g] Nesfield, in the parish of Ilkley.

[h] Grassington, in the parish of Linton.

Robert son of Nigel, is his next heir, now aged four years and a half; and the wardship and marriage of the heir appertain of right to lord William de Percy.

Also the jurors say that the same Nigel held Idel[a] of the Earl of Lincoln, and afterwards of the King, by reason of the Earl's heir; Idel is worth by the year in demesnes, rents, &c., of the land, five marcs, without the three dowers of the three ladies.[b]

LXIX.   DAVID LARDINER.[c]   *Inq. p. m.*

[55 HEN. III. No. 11.]

Writ dated at Westminster, 25 Oct., 55th year (1271).

EXTENT made on Monday after the feast of S. Leonard, 56 Henry (9 Nov. 1271), at York, before John de Reygate, by Thomas Bustard, Thomas de Routheclive, William de Cotele, Thomas de Monkegate, Robert Frend, Robert de Cravene, Stephen de Schipton, John de Beverle, William Mawe, Alan de Thweyt, Roger de Heselle, and Robert Russell of Angram, who say upon their oath, that David *le Lardiner* held a certain messuage in York, of £7 12s. 1d. yearly rent, which he received by the hands of the bailiffs of York. He received 2s. yearly rent by the hands of John *le Especer*, and in York from John de Beverle, 4s. Thomas Bustard paid him 7s. for his land in Bustardthorp.[d] He held land called Cortteburne, worth by the year 6s. 8d. All

---

[a] Idle near Bradford. The heir of the Earl of Lincoln was Henry, son of Edmund de Lascy, who was aged eight on Christmas Day, 1257 (p. 51.)

[b] No date appears in the inquisition, but on the back in a very much later hand, "A° Regis Henrici quinquagesimo quinto." Peter de Percy, who is spoken of as alive at the time of this inquisition, was dead defore 23 March, 1266-7, the date of the writ ordering his *Inq. p. m.* to be taken (No. LVIII). On 10 Nov., 1244, the King granted to Earl Richard (of Cornwall) for 60 marcs, the custody of the land Nigel de Plumton held in Hydel, to the full age of his heir *(Excerpta è Rotulis Finium*, vol. i., p. 426). The heir was still a minor in 1256, when William de Ireby, his guardian, paid 20s. to have an assize about the church of Corthorpe, in Yorkshire *(Ibid.* vol. ii., p. 240).

[c] See No. XIV.

[d] All traces of the village of Bustardthorpe have long since disappeared. It stood, I believe, a little to the north of Middlethorpe, and near the road leading to York. In 1484, the manor of Bustardthorpe is described as extending in length from the village of Drynghouses on the west, as far as the river Use on the east, the common pastures of Knasemyer and Middilthorp forming, respectively, portions of its northern and southern boundaries *(City Records,* lib. A., p. 368). See Kirkby's *Inquest,* p. 23 *n.*

the aforesaid he held of the King[a] in chief for keeping the King's gaol of the forest, and for making and keeping the King's larder and finding salt at his own cost. For this he shall have the upper legs and *loynes*, and shall make sales for the King's debt by summons of the Exchequer, and for every sale shall have 2s. 8d.

He held of Sir Robert de Neuville in Skelton,[b] a messuage with dovehouse and garden, worth yearly one marc. He held of the same in demesne five bovates of land, each 10s., doing foreign service for the said Robert; also a windmill, worth yearly one marc; and in Morton,[c] in demesne one carucate of land worth £4, yielding to the altar of S. Mary's Monastery at York 5s. by the year.

David, son of this David, is his next heir and of full age.

LXX. JOHN DE HOLTEBY. *Suit of County Court.*

[56 HEN. III. No. 46.]

Writ dated at Tower of London, 16 Jan., 56th year (1271-2), ordering the Sheriff to enquire whether John de Holteby ought to do suit, and whether he or his ancestors have been wont to do suit, at County Court of York, and at Wapentake of Bolmere, for lands and tenements in Holteby.[d] If he be quit, how and for what reason.

INQUISITION made before the Sheriff and the keepers of the Pleas of the Crown, in full County Court—whether or not John de Holteby ought to do, and whether or not he or his ancestors have been used to do suit at the County Court of York, and at the Wapentake Court of Bulmere, for their lands and tenements in Holteby, &c.—by William de Thorney of Tiverington, John de Stockton, Richard of the same, Walter *le Bret*, Thomas *le Norreis*, Richard de Touthorp, Ralph de Hoton, Michael de Hew[ort]h, William de Galmethorp, Thomas de Meningthorp, Thomas de Dunstaple, and Richard Maunsell of Tiverington : who say, that John de Holteby ought not to do suit at either Court ; and that his ancestors did not, because the lands and tenements are of the Honour of Eye, and heretofore an inquisition was taken which found for his ancestors.

---

a The terms, in which the tenure is expressed, are as follows :—"Omnia predicta tenuit de domino Rege in capite ad gaolam domini Regis de foresta custodiendam, et ad lardariam domini Regis faciendam et custodiendam, et ad sal custibus suis inveniendum ; et pro hoc habebit crura superiora et *loynes*, et faciet vendiciones pro debito domini Regis per summonicionem de Scaccario, et ad quamlibet vendicionem habebit ijs. viijd."

b Skelton, near York.

c Murton, in the parish of Osbaldwick.

d Holtby, five miles N.E. of York.

LXXI. JOHN DE GREY.[a] *Inq. p. m.*

[56 HEN. III. No. 34 B., m. 7]

Writ, directed to John de Reygate Escheator beyond Trent, and dated at
Winchester, 5 Jan., 56th year (1271-2).

EXTENT of Barton, made on Sunday before the Purification of
the B.V.M., 56 Henry (31 Jan., 1271-2), by John de Butter-
wike, Henry Young *(le Jovene)* of Appulton, William de
Wadtht ,John son of Roger of Lengeby, Philip de Barton, John
de Watht, Nicholas de Aymunderby, Roger Drenge, Richard de
Skakeldene, John Abraam, William Yol, and Gervase de Barton,
who say that there is a capital messuage with garden and dovehouse. There are in demesne three carucates of land which
contain twenty-four bovates, each of which with easement of
the capital messuage, and dovehouse, and with meadow, is worth
by the year 10s. Sum, £12. One free tenant holds one bovate
of land, and yields on the day of the Nativity S. John Baptist,
a seat of rushes *(unum sessum juncorum),*[b] value one half-penny.
Thirty bondmen *(bondi)* hold in bondage fifty-one bovates of
land, each worth yearly 10s. Sum, £25 10s. There are nine
cottars, each of whom with works yields 2s. yearly, half at
Martinmas and half at Pentecost. Sum, 18s. One more cottar
pays one penny yearly, half at Martinmas and half at Pentecost.
There is no court there. This land of Barton is held of the
King in chief by doing foreign service *(faciendo forinsecum).*
     Henry de Grey, son of John de Grey, is his next heir, and
at Lent coming will be aged fifteen years ; but one Thomas de
Codenouere came to Barton, bringing a writ of Sir *(D'ni)* John
de Grey, and he took seisin of Barton to the use of Joan,
daughter of the said John, and received fealty and acknowledg-
ment from the men there. As this was after the date of the

---

[a] Son of Richard de Grey, Lord of Codnor, co. Derby, married Lucia, daughter
of John de Humet, and died in 1271. His son, Henry de Grey, was summoned to
Parliament, and according to Dugdale, gave his second son Nicholas, Barton in
Ryedale, from whom descended the family of Grey of Barton, whose pedigree is
in Glover's *Visitation* (p. 70, Foster's Ed.). It is a curious coincidence, that a
William de Grey who had property in North Yorkshire, should have married a
member of the Humet family, Agnes by name. They were both alive in 1246
(Rievaulx Chartulary, pp. 249 and 394). This William de Grey bore on his seal
two bars and in chief three fleur-de-lys *(Ibid.)* John de Grey bore barry of six
argent and azure *(Archæologia*, vol. xxxix., p. 406), which the Greys of Barton
differenced by adding a bend gobony or and gules.

[b] This word *sessum* may be meant for *cessum,* for-*cessionem.* *Sessus* seems to
equal *sedes,* Ducange; but it is difficult to see how a rush seat could exist apart.

King's writ directed to him, the Escheator took the land into the King's hand. And they add that the said Joan is sixteen years old.[a]   Sum total, £38 8s. 1½d.

LXXII.   NICHOLAS DE BOLTEBY.[b]   *Inq. p. m.*

[57 HEN. III. No. 3.]

Writ dated at Westminster, 31 Oct., 57th year (1272).

INQUISITION and Extent made at York before Sir John de Reygate, 57 Henry, on the morrow of Saint Andrew (1 Dec., 1272), by Peter Franceis, Jurdan Berner, Robert Wigothe, Henry de Hastinges, Richard son of Hugh of Trilleby, Hugh de Thorneton, Simon de Blenkeneshope, Elias de Carleton, Roger de Kirkeby, Ralph de Stitnom, Thomas son of Thomas of Ravenesthorpe, and Hugh de Upsal, who, being sworn, say that Nicholas de Bolteby held no land of the King in chief in

[a] There are inquisitions for other counties, viz.: Southampton, Norfolk, Essex, Kent, Nottingham, and Leicester. By these the age of Henry de Grey is variously stated, as follow:—Southampton—16 years. Norfolk—17 years old at the feast of St. Edmund King and Martyr, 56th year (20 Nov., 1271). Essex—14 years old at the feast of All Saints (1 Nov., 1271). Inquisition dated Friday, 5 Feb., 1271-2. Kent—14 years old on All Saints' Day last past (1 Nov., 1271), the extent of Eyllesforde being dated on the morrow of Pur. B.V.M. (3 Feb., 1271-2); the same age by a second (relating to Hoo, here " Ho ") taken on the same day by another jury. Nottingham—15 years; another, he will be 14 years old in the coming Lent *(in ista instanti Quadragesima proximo futura)*, the inquisition being taken at Radeclyve on the morrow of St. Valentine, 56th year (15 Feb., 1271-2); a third, 14 years old at Lent next in the year abovesaid, the inquisition (for Newbotil manor) made on the morrow of the Octave of Pur. B.V.M. (10 Feb., 1271-2). Leicester—14 years in the coming Lent *(in ista instanti Quadragesima)*, the inquisition being made on Saturday before the feast of St Valentine (13 Feb., 1271-2.

By the mandate of R. de Cliff[ord], Escheator this side Trent, directed to Thomas Peverell, his sub-Escheator in the County of Southampton, it is shown that Lucy *(Lucya)*, who was wife of John de Grey, had complained that, although she was jointly enfeoffed with her late husband of the manor of Upton, the Escheator had taken it into the King's hand. Dated at London, on Saturday after the feast of the Pur. B.V.M., 56th year (6 Feb., 1271-2). 4 July, 1281. The King, in consideration of £200, pardoned Arnald Murdake his transgression in marrying without licence Lucy, widow of John de Gray *(Rot. Finium,* 9 Edw. I., m. 7*)*.

[b] Members of the family of Boltby occur as benefactors to the Abbey of Rievaulx. They were descended from a certain Odo de Boltebia, who gave land in Boltby to that Abbey between the years 1131 and 1145 *(Rievaulx Chartulary,* pp. 45, 260). On 13 Dec., 1 Edward I. (1272) the fealty of Adam de Bolteby, brother *(sic)* and heir of Nicholas de Bolteby, was taken, and John de Reygate, the Escheator beyond Trent, was ordered to restore to him the lands held in chief. At the same time was taken the fealty of Adam de Bolteby, son and heir of Nicholas de Bolteby and Philippa his wife, one of the heiresses of Adam de Tindale deceased. The King restored to him the lands and tenements, on condition that at the arrival of the King in England, he should appear before him and pay homage for them *(tali condicione quod in adventu suo in Angliam coram Rege veniat inde homagium suum facturus) (Rotuli Finium,* 1 Edw. I., m. 26 *bis)*. This proviso was added in consequence of the King's absence in the Holy Land.

the County of York, but by the fee of Haubercke he held of Joan de Estoteville one knight's fee, made by ten carucates of land, and Adam de Bolteby his son is his next heir, and of full age. The extent of lands and tenements is this :—In Ravenesthorpe ᵃ and Trilleby ᵇ he held in demesne 300 acres of land (6d.), 60 acres of meadow (18d.) ; in Bolteby ᶜ thirty-two bovates of land, of which ten acres of land and meadow make one bovate, which is worth yearly 6s. Six cotters *(coterii)* in Bolteby hold six tofts, for which they yield by the year 9s. 4d. One garden in Bolteby yields yearly 5s. The capital messuage of Ravenesthorpe with garden yields yearly half a marc. In Trilleby he held 22 bovates of land *(value and content as before)*, and eleven cotters there for seventeen tofts pay yearly 30s. 6d. Six cotters in Ravenesthorpe for six tofts pay 10s. One watermill in Ravenesthorpe yields by the year eight marcs. He received also from the town of Kereby (?)ᵈ for herbage yearly 10s. Also ploughing, harrowing, and autumn works are worth by the year half a marc. Sum total, £38 12s. 2d.ᵉ

LXXIII. OF SERJEANTY IN THE COUNTY OF YORK.

[Incert. temp. HEN. III. No. 19.]

SIXTEEN bovates of land held by John *le Chamberlenge,* formerly of Walter *le Poer,* in Yappum, Barneby, and Waplington,ᶠ worth by the year, £4. Six bovates held by Simon the Archer in Yappum, worth by the year 30s. Two bovates held by the Prioress of Wylberfosse in the same, worth by the year 10s. One bovate held by William Gunnesse in the same, worth by the year 5s. Fourteen bovates held by the Prior of Drax in Wapplington, worth by the year 56s. Six bovates held by the Templars in the same, worth by the year

ᵃ Ravensthorpe, in the township of Boltby and parish of Feliskirk. " The vill of Ravensthorpe has disappeared, but the moat which once nearly surrounded its ancient manor house may still be traced in a field near to Ravensthorpe Mill, about one mile south of Boltby " (Kirkby's *Inquest,* p. 97 *n*).

ᵇ Thirlby, in the parish of Feliskirk.

ᶜ Boltby, five miles N.E. of Thirsk, in the parish of Feliskirk.

ᵈ A mistake for Bereby, now Borrowby, in the parish of Leake (Kirkby's *Inquest,* p. 97). It appears as Bergebi in *Domesday,* and in Kirkby's *Inquest* as Bergeby, Bereby, Berekeby, Berheby, and once as above, Kereby.

ᵉ There is also an extent of lands in the County of Northumberland, made at Morpathe, on Thursday after the feast of St. Clement, 57th year (24 Nov., 1272). Observe that Henry III. died on the 16th of November, and that Edward his son, then in the Holy Land, was proclaimed King on the 20th of November, 1272. It follows, therefore, that the extent here referred to, as well as that for Yorkshire (abstracted above), ought to be placed in the first year of Edward.

ᶠ Yapham, Barmby-on-the-Moor, and Waplington.

34s. One toft held by Remigius de Poclington in Barneby, worth by the year 3s. One toft held by William Balle in Yappum, worth by the year 2s. One toft held by Robert Belle in the same, worth by the year 2s. One bovate of land held by Thomas de Wylton in the same, worth by the year 5s. All these to be taken into [the King's] hand.

LXXIV. COMPLAINT OF THE BURGESSES OF SCARBOROUGH.

[Incert. temp. HEN. III. No. 152.]

THE Burgesses of Scarborough[a] *(here throughout written Scartheb')* complain of Simon de Hal, Sheriff of Yorkshire,[b] and his servants.

Firstly of wine, corn, salt and all other merchandize which come into the King's harbour of Scarborough they take, as well from foreigners as those who dwell in the town, by tally at half the selling price, without the consent of the merchants; and when the term comes they pay to some persons something or a little, and to others nothing; on which account merchants so avoid the harbour that they cannot fulfil the King's farm or keep up the town.

Also they take in harbour from foreign and other fishermen, herring without market, by four, three, and two lasts out of the ship; and, when a last is sold for twenty shillings, they pay ten, and sometimes less.

Also the Sheriff in person has come into harbour and wished to take all the herring from the fishermen of Scarborough and others, without market; and, if any one says to the contrary, he is threatened with imprisonment and to have his house burnt. Afterwards he takes the man's herring by force; and, when they sell for eighteen shillings, he pays nine shillings only, and sometimes less. Within hearing of all, he forbids any carter or trader to bring merchandize into the King's town or to carry it out, and threatens to imprison any one bringing merchandize through his bailiwick, and to take away his chattels. Therefore no trader dares to return to the town, whereby we lose the farm and the town remains destroyed.

[a] In the first year of King Edward II., Emery Gregg and Robert Wawayn, for themselves and the rest of the middling and poor burgesses of Scardeburgh, brought an action in the Exchequer, against Roger at Cross and others the rich burgesses of that town, for divers trespasses done by the latter to the former (Madox, *Firma Burgi,* p. 96).

[b] Simon de Hal acted as Deputy Sheriff for Geoffrey de Neville, 5—7 Hen. III., that is, 28 Oct., 1220, to 27 Oct., 1223. In 8 Hen. III. he was himself Sheriff. This Geoffrey de Neville, called below Geoffrey de Noville, was Chamberlain of England. He is mentioned p. 9 *ante.*

Also when the butchers of Scarborough go through his bailiwick to slaughter cattle, the Sheriff's servants take the cattle away from them; part they kill, and part they retain by force, until they are ransomed.

Also the garrison of the Castle *(castellani)* together with the Sheriff have taken from the Burgesses of Scarborough, as was shown to the King's Justices last in eyre, in bread, flesh, ale, fish, corn, salt, cloths, and other chattels, £300 6s. 4d. of which they have returned and will return nothing, whereby those in easy circumstances have become poor, and have afterwards vacated the town, whereby it is reduced to such poverty that they fear the King may lose aid from the town and his men, when need shall arise, because they cannot give to the King that which others by force and unjustly have extorted.

Also it is to be shown to the King and his Council that, when the Sheriff wishes to have any wares in the town, and any one will not give them at his pleasure, he threatens to set fire to the town. And at the coming of G[eoffrey] de Noville, Chamberlain, he will seize the better inhabitants of the town, imprison them in the Castle, and deprive them of all their lands and property, wherefore we pray most diligently the King and his Council in these things abovesaid to bestow aid and advice.

Also the Sheriff gives his servants such mastery as was never known in our harbour. A servant of his forbids all traders to sell their merchandize before the Sheriff takes what he wants for himself, which is against the customs of the realm and our liberties.

Also ships and traders, when they come to Scarborough with their merchandize, ask leave from the King's bailiffs to enter the harbour with their cargo in safety; and, when in harbour, the Sheriff's servant comes and takes their merchandize, at his own pleasure. Whereas the bailiffs give them leave to enter, and neither the Sheriff nor his servant will acquit the things taken, the ships of Scarborough and men on their arrival in harbour are distrained to discharge the Sheriff's debt, wherefore we pray counsel and aid for the love of God.

LXXV. EXTENT OF THE RENTS OF THE MANOR OF DRAX.[a]

[Incert. temp. HEN. III. No. 155.]

EXTENT of all the rents of the manor of Drax, made by twelve lawful men of the same manor, sworn for this before the Sheriff of Yorkshire, namely: Thomas Clerk, Walter

---

a Drax, near Snaith.

de Faleyse, Adam de Faleyse, Robert Oliver, Adam Marshall, Walter son of Silvester, Robert son of John, Richard son of Eva, Thomas son of Alice, William son of Iveta, Nigel de Suwelle, Geoffrey son of Ralph. Profit *(gaynagio)* of the court and garden of the same, that is, in fruits and other things growing in it, 8*s.* They were wont to give 10*s.*, but afterwards 2*s.* were taken away on account of the pinfold *(pondfald)* in the said court, whereby they now pay only 8*s.* Fourteen acres of land of the demesne held by the Prior of Drax, 8*s.* 4*d.* Ferry *(passagium)* and fishery, which were wont to give only two marcs, now give three marcs by the increase of the bailiff *(per incrementum ball')*. Two mills of the lord, by the old extent two marcs, but now by the increase of the bailiff, 37*s.* 8*d.* Herbage of the park, 1*s.* 4*d.* A certain fishery at Newland[a] *(apud Novam terram)*, 6*d.*

Sum, £4 15*s.* 10*d.*

The Prior of Drax for land held of the lord, 14*s.*; John Dringe, 2*s.*; Walter de Faleyse, 13*s.* 6*d.*; land of Nicholas Bechemin, 4*s.* 8*d.*; Richard de Ropholm, 12*d.*; David Black, 12*d.* Alan *le Despenser*, 9*d.*; Robert Oliver, 3*d.*; Henry son of Richard Clerk *(Clerici)*, 4*s.* 8*d.*; Hugh de Haldanby, 5*s.* 6*d.*; Nodde Wisman, 4*s.*; Geoffrey Deacon, 1*s.* 3*d.*; William son of John, 3*s.* 8*d.*

Sum, 56*s.* 3*d.*

Rents from the borough *(Redditus de burgo)*. Robert Oliver, 10*s.*; Alan son of Robert Woods *(de silvis)*, 7*s.*; Alan *le Despenser*, 5*s.* 5*d.*; Richard King, 4*s.* 4*d.*; John son of Die, 7*s.* 5½*d.*; Walter son of Jordan, 4*d.*; Stephen Fibry, 5*s.* 4*d.*; John de Seleby, 12*d.*; Thomas son of Eva, 12*d.*; Alan Wastehese,[b] 4*s.* 10*d.*; Annisia Blowehorn, 6*d.*; Thomas Stalkere, 2*s.* 10*d.*; Thomas Large *(largo)*, 6*d.*; Osebert Clerk, 2*s.* 11*d.*; Roger Oliver 4*s.* 8*d.*; Adam de Faleyse, 6*s.* 4*d.*; Lece Cade, 12*d.*; Walter Wyce, 7*s.* 1*d.*; Davi *de Burgo*, 1*s.* 6*d.*; Henry Smith, 12*d.*; Roger *del Calgarth*, 12*d.*; Thomas Russel, 8*d.*; Roger Bonum, 1*s.* 7*d.*; Alice Fleming, 2*s.*; Robert de Bayeus, 4*s.*; Thomas Clerk, 16*s.* 6*d.*; John Macon, 4*s.* 2*d.*; Bron Keling, 2*s.* 1*d.*; Ralph Kippehalde, 12*d.*; Astin, 12*d.*; William son of Iveta, 2*s.* 2*d.*; Annis' wife of Eustace, 3*s.* 9*d.*; John Sp's, 12*d.*; Walter Haggebayn, 3*s.*; Thomas son of Alice, 3*s.* 5*d.*; Walter Hikedon, 2*s.*; Adam Marshal, 2*s.* 10*d.*; Thomas Blowehorn, 7*d.*; Emma daughter of Nodde, 2*s.* 2*d.*; William son of John, 2*s.*; Henry son of Walter, 2½*d.*; Annisia

---

[a] Newland, in the parish of Drax. Called in every instance but one in this and the following inquisition, *Nova terra*.

[b] Called Wasthose in No. XXVII., which is the *Inq. p. m.* of his daughter Emma, taken 13 Feb., 1250-1, so that the date must be prior to that time, but probably not much, as the next inquisition, which is very close to this one in date, must have been taken about the middle of the thirteenth century.

Moddry, 3*d.*; Eon de Hales, 1*s.* 6*d.*; Geoffrey Large *(largo)*, 3*s.* 10*d.*; William Priest *(presbitero)*, 4*d.*; Robert Bollok, 4*s.* 4*d.*; Eva de Rocclive, 4*d.*; Henry Cobbler *(sutore)*, 1*s.* 7*d.* All these are so free that they pay nothing else than the rents abovesaid.
Sum, £7 4*s.* 4*d.*

The manor of Drax receives annually from Appelton[a] for everything £13 5*s.*, but they of Drax do not know *(set nescitur ab eis de Drax)*, who of Appelton is free, who a serf, or who are the tenants. Sum, £13 5*s.*

The manor of Drax receives from York these rents :— Annisia de Seleby, one marc; John de Hul, 2*s.*; Oter Viniter, 4*s.*; Hugh Hosere, 4*s.*; Alice de Donwik, 2*s.*; Geoffrey de Stokton, 2*s.* These pay nothing but the aforesaid rents.
Sum, 27*s.* 4*d.*

Now of those who give a certain tallage *(dant tall' certum)*, and first of Newland. Richard son of Eva, 7*s.*; Walter son of John, 8*s.* 6½*d.*; John son of William, half a marc; William son of Geoffrey, 8*s.* 8*d.*; Adam son of William, 9*s.* 3*d.*; Thomas son of Milisent, and Adam his brother, 9½*d.*; John son of Richard, 9*s.*; Adam son of John, 2*s.* 11½*d.*; Walter son of Wynsy, 4*s.* 8*d.*; Nigel son of Thomas, 3*s.*; Jordan his son, 12*d.*; Hugh son of Walter, 4*s.* 10¼*d.*; Thomas son of Sevola, 2*s.* 3½*d.*; Robert de Eyreminne, 8*d.*; Robert de Cowik, 3*s.* 5½*d.*; Ralph de Huk, 2*d.*; Henry Paumer, 4*d.*; Reginald Mogge, 2*s.*; Geoffrey Catelove, 2*s.*; Geoffrey son of Ralph, 6*s.* 1*d.*; William son of Ralph, 2*s.* 10*d.*; Fulk son of Ralph, 4*d.*; Thomas Baker, 3½*d.*; Hugh son of William, 3*s.* 1*d.*; Nigel *Ruffus*, 5*s.*; William son of Henry, half a marc; William *Ruffus*, 8*s.* 4*d.*; William son of Iveta, 2*s.* 4*d.*; John son of Hawise, 5*s.* 4*d.*; William Tayllur, 2*s.* 2*d.*; John son of Geoffrey, 8*d.*; Henry Smith, 2*s.* 4*d.*; Juliana Good *(bona)*, 2*s.* 2*d.*; John son of James, 4*s.* 9*d.*; Simon son of Roger, 4*s.* 8*d.*; Amfrid de Suwelle, 3*s.*; John son of Peter, 10*s.* 2*d.*; Nigel de Suwelle, 3*s.* 4*d.*; John de Roeclive, 1*s.* 8*d.*; John Belle, 8*d.*; Amfrid de Nes, 2*d.*; William Canon *(canonicus)*, 5*s.*; Cecilia wife of Thomas son of Eva, 2*s.* 8*d.* These said men of Newland *(de Nova terra)* do for their lord each year nothing, except a certain tallage, fixed and below a fixed sum,[b] except William son of Ralph, and John son of James of the same vill, who were proved *(deraynati)* villains before the Justices of the Lord King. The others are not villains. Sum, £8 0*s.* 12¼*d.*

Now of those who give cocks, hens, and eggs, and first of Kirkedrax. Walter Sp's, 1*s.* 8*d.*; John son of Thomas, 9*d.*;

---

a Appleton-le-Street.

b " Nichil aliud facient domino nisi quolibet anno quoddam tall' certum et sub certa summa."

Wife of Osebert Sp's, 1s. 8d.; Richard Peper, 12d.; Annisia de Riseby, 6d.; Osebert de Gren', 2s. 10½d.; William Little *(parvus)*, 2s. ½d.; Ralph Wip, 7s. 6d.; Ralph son of Geoffrey, 4s. 1½d.; Robert Ayrik, 10s.; Adam son of Laurence, 4s. 8d.; Henry son of John, 4s. 2d.; Wymark 11d.; William Winter, 12d.; William son of William, 2s.; Wife of Thomas son of Vivian, 1s. 4½d.; Hugh son of Vivian, 4s. 1½d.; Robert de Goukwelle, 2s.; Henry son of Gerard, 2s 7d.; Laurence son of Goda, 2s.; William son of Roger, 1s. 6d.; William son of Peter, 2s. 3d.; John son of Astin, 2s. 9d.; Roger son of Fulk, 12d.; Geoffrey son of Reginald, 4s. 8d.; Geoffrey de Hales, 11d.; Henry Witfot, 1s. 9d.; Wimpe, 10½d.; William Wip, 4s. 11d.; John son of Richard, 5s. 1d.; Maurice son of Wimpe, 1s. 9d.; John Megre, 1s. 4d.; Laurence son of Astin, 2s. 2d.; William Godsib, 8s. 4d.; Arnald Chapman *(mercator)*, 8d.; Silvester, 6d.; Robert Clerk, 8d.; Nigel Spellere, 4s. 2d.; John Siwrit, 8d.; John Litelred, 12d.; Annisia Bel, 2d., and is a cotter *(cotiere)*; William Crak, 2d.; Geoffrey Purdev, 8d.; Nigel Shepherd *(bercator)*, 2½d.; Robert New, 4d.; Annisia Scertelthorp, 10d.; Roays Bollok, 4d.; Richard Priest *(presbiter)*, 4d.; William son of Margaret, 3s. 8d.; German, 1s. 5d.; Walter de Hales, 1s. 4d.; Roger de Hales, 1s. 8d.; Eudo de Hales, 1s. 2d.; Thomas de Hales, 3s. 10d.; Hugh son of William, 1s. 11d.; Fulk, 2s.; Thomas son of John, 8d.; John son of Maud *(Matildis)*, 2s.; Geoffrey Deacon, 1s. 6d.; Geoffrey Marshal, 3s. 11d.; John son of Geoffrey, 3s. 8½d.; John de Helawe, 4d.; Thomas son of Walter, 4s.; Walter son of Adam, 1s. 10d.; Annisia de Scertelthorp, 6d.; Alice Wimpe, 12d.; Edusa wife of Reginald Stote, 4d.; Henry Wodenot, 8d.; Robert son of Walter son of Silvester, 6d.; Increase, 5s.

Sum, £7 10s 11d.

Now of Langerak.[a] William son of Goda, 2s. 7d.; William Pogge, 2s. 4½d.; Edusa wife of Adam, 1s. 7d.; Geoffrey Serjeant *(serviens)*, 6s. 2d.; William Redhod, 6½d.; Maud *(Matildis)* Pye, 10d.; Hugh Ruce, 2s. 3d.; Walter Vavasur, 12½d.; Hugh son of William, 4s. 5½d.; Albredus de Beverle, 2s.; Thomas Matefray, 1s. 8d.; Simon Skat, 1d.; John Passur, 3s.; John Bakon, 9s. 5d.; John son of Jordan, 3s.; William son of John, 4s. 5d; Jordan his brother, 5s. 7d.; William son of Horm, 9s. 2d.; Edusa Widow, 2s.; Cecilia Charbocle, 2s.; William de Wresel, 1s. 8d.; Annisia Crake, 3s. 1d.; John Clok, 3s. 3d.; Walter son of Jordan, 4s. 2d.; Thomas son of Osebert, 6s. 2d.; Lecelin Gomme, 4d.; Walter Pelle, 2s. 11½d.; Thomas son of Jordan, 4s. 8½d.; Henry son of Thomas, half a marc and a halfpenny; Nicholas de Newbald, 10d.; Goda Cannere, 1s. 8d.; William

---

a Langrick, or Long Drax.

Priest *(presbiter)*, 1*s.* 8*d.* ; of the store *(de instauramento)*, 1*s.* 7*d.*; Wynterflote, 4*d.*; William son of Adam, 2*s.* 9½*d.*; William son of Robert, 4*s.* 2½*d.*   Sum, 110*s.* 3½*d.*

The men of Newland *(Nova terra)*, Drax, and Langerak giving tallage, all give the lord yearly 20*s.* 5*d.*, to be able to go to whatever mill they like, freely without molestation *(sine occasione)*.   Sum, 20*s.* 5*d.*

The tallage set in Newland *(Nova terra)*, Kirkedrax, and Langerak is £10, to which £10 all must give who are placed in this roll after those who only give rents.   Sum, £10.

The men of the Lady Letitia de Katenis[a] of Eyreminne pay 60*s.* for four score quarters of oats, of granary (? corn) measure *(de mensura de granar')*, which measure of the said four score quarters only makes three score quarters of right measure.   Sum, 60*s.*

For fowls and eggs, paid by the men of Kirkedrax and Langerak, 8*s.* a year.   Sum, 8*s.*

It is to be known that all the rents are to be paid at the feast of St. Michael and Easter, except the rents of York, which are to be paid at Martinmas and Whitsunday.

Sum of sums, £65 6*s.* 1¾*d.*

Endorsed.   Extent of the lands of Drax.

LXXVI.   EXTENT OF THE MANOR OF DRAX.

[Incert. temp. HEN. III.   No. 212].

EXTENT of the manor of Drax, made before Thomas de Stanforde,[b] by a writ of the lord King, on Thursday before the feast of St. Thomas the Apostle, ... below-named, namely : Walter Clerk of Schurd, Hugh de Haldaneby, Walter Falays, Adam Falays, Richard de . . . . Clerk, Adam son of William of Neulande, John Drenge of Routheclive, Thomas son of Henry, William son of Adam of Neulande, Walter (?) son of Geoffrey of the same, and Adam Marshal, who say on their oath that there are in demesne in Drax, 16 acres and one rood, at 6*d.* an acre.   Sum, 8*s.* 1½*d.*   From the rent of assise *(de redditu assis')* in bondage, £8 2*s.* 8*d.*   Rent of an old mill, 11*s.*   Rent of a windmill, 26*s.* 8*d.*   The Prior of

---

a See Inquisition CVII. on the death of a lady of the same name. Letitia, widow of William de Kaaynes, had dower assigned to her in Wiltshire, in 1222 *(Excerpta è Rotulis Finium,* vol. i., p. 86*)*. She is called Letitia de Shenes in No. LXXVI. Airmyn is in the parish of Snaith.

b Thomas de Stanforde was Escheator between 1247 and 1255 (Nos. XII. and XLIII.).

Drax for rent of land called Brocholes, 14s. 11d. Rent of the Town *(burgi)* of Drax, £7 9s. 11½d. Capital messuage, 10s. Rent of assise of hens, 60 hens at ¾d. a hen Sum, 3s. 9d. Rent of assise of 270 eggs (3d. a hundred). Sum, 7¾d. Rent in the City of York, 27s. 4d. Rent of assise of Langerake in bondage, £6 5s. 7d. The old mill there, 3s. 4d. The ferry there, 20s. Rent of assise there 20½ hens, ¾d. a hen. Sum, 1s. 3d. Rent of assise there of nine score and 6 eggs, 3d. the hundred. Sum, 4½d. Rent of the free tenants of Newland *(Nova terra)*, £8 17s. 6d. Hugh de Angervile for himself, 12d. Walter Falays, 13s. 6d. David Black *(Nigro)*, 12d. William de Horkes-touwe, 5s. 2d. Alan Steward *(Dispensatore)*, 9d. Oliver, 3d. Sum of these parcels, 21s 8d. Rent of assise of the tenants of Ayreminne, 60 quarters of oats, 12d. a quarter. Sum, 60s. Rent of assise of the tenants of Apelton in Ridale, £12 10s. The tenants of the manor of Drax were wont to pay annually for their tallage, £10, but afterwards a marc a year was remitted to them on account of poverty in the time of the Count of Bigorre [a] *(tempore Com' Bigorn')*, and now they pay annually, only £9 6s. 8d. Of pleas and perquisites of court, the jurors desire to say no fixed sum, because they are sometimes more and sometimes less. Sum total of the manor of Drax, except pleas and perquisites of court which are not extended, and except the third part of the Lady Letitia de Shenes, who is dowered very liberally *(valde large)* of a third part of the said manor, £63 17s. 0¾d.

There is besides in the manor of Drax, a Priory [b] worth £300 a year and more, besides the advowsons of five churches belonging to the Priory. The advowson of the Priory belongs to the lord of the said manor.

The Priory of the Holy Trinity of York was founded by Fulk Painell, [c] lord of the said manor, the advowson of which belongs to the lord of the said manor, whoever he be. Of the

---

[a] The County of Bigorre, in Gascony, is now included in the Department of the Hautes Pyrénées. It formed part of the dowry of Eleanor of Poitou, wife of Henry II. of England, and remained in the possession of the English Crown until the year 1451, when the whole of Gascony was surrendered to the French.

[b] A house of Austin Canons was founded at Drax in the reign of Henry I. by William Paynell, instigated to that devotion by Archbishop Thurstan, who died in 1140. The advowsons of seven churches were given by William Paynell at the foundation, namely Drax and Bingley in Yorkshire; Roxby, Middle Rasen, and Irnham in Lincolnshire; and Saltby in Leicestershire. The house was dedicated to St. Nicholas.

[c] This is a mistake. The Priory of the Holy Trinity, in Micklegate, was founded in the reign of William II., by Ralph Paynell, a Domesday Baron. A very full account of the founder and his descendants, is given in the York Volume of the Archæological Institute. It was a Benedictine House, subject to the Abbey of St. Martin, near Tours.

value of the Priory or of the advowsons appurtenant to it, they cannot say any fixed sum, but it is worth twice as much as the Priory of Drax *(set in duplo valet predictum Prioratum de Drax)*. The whole manor of Drax is warren, but of the value of the warren they can say nothing. The perquisites of the said warren belong to the court of Drax.

Seven and a half knights' fees belong to the manor of Drax, of which Geoffrey de Beningworthe holds three, and Simon de Steynegreve four and a half. Carleton and Camelesforde [a] are members of the manor of Drax. Peter de Brus holds them, but the jurors do not know by what warrant. They are worth £100 a year or more.

(Endorsed). Extent of the manor of Drax, made by Thomas de Stanford.

LXXVII. OF THE LAND OF AGENOIS [b] GIVEN IN EXCHANGE FOR RICHMONDSHIRE.

[Incert. temp. Hen. III. No. 175].

KNOW all those who shall see or hear these present letters that whereas the noble baron, John, Count of Britany, required from Henry, King of England, Richmondshire *(la Conte de Richemunt)* and the appurtenances, which his ancestors had formerly held, as his inheritance, which county the king had given to Peter of Savoy, his uncle, [c] and from which gift he

---

[a] Peter de Brus held Carlton and Camblesforth by right of descent from Robert de Brus, to whom they were given some time after the date of the Domesday Survey; that is to say, either in the last few months of the Conqueror's reign, or in that of his son. The Peter who held these manors at the time of this extent was Peter de Brus II., son of Peter I., son of Adam II., son of Adam I., son of Robert de Brus, the original grantee. These manors are still held by his descendants, having never been sold since the time of the original grant.

[b] The district around Agen, a town on the Garonne, N.W. of Toulouse.

[c] This grant is entered on the Charter Roll, 25 Hen. III., m. 4. On 2 July, 1261, the King, then in the Tower of London, after reciting that he had granted to Peter of Savoy, that his executors might retain possession of the Honour and Earldom of Richmond for a period of seven years after his death, for fulfilling the trusts of his will, further granted that if Peter's heirs should be out of England at the time of his death, he would, without making any difficulty, receive their homage, provided the heirs made proper provisions for the executors receiving the rents and profits during the period of seven years abovementioned *(Patent Roll*, 45 Hen. III., m. 9). Dugdale *(Baronage,* vol. i., p. 50) says his testament was dated 53 Hen. III.; even if this be correct, he lived for many years after, as it is not until 3 June, 1268, that Henry III. granted to Edward, his eldest son, the custody of the Honour of Richmond, and of all the lands and tenements in England which belonged to Peter of Savoy, late Earl of Savoy, the King's uncle, to hold during the royal pleasure *(Excerpta è Rotulis Finium,* vol. ii., p. 472). Dugdale *(Baronage,* vol. i., p. 51)* says—In 46 Hen. III., Prince Edward releasing and quit-claiming to the

cannot withdraw, the said King gives in exchange for that county to the said Count, to have and to hold to him and to his heirs, in the name of inheritance, the land of Agenois, or the money which Louis, King of France,[a] ought to give for Agenois, up to the value of Richmondshire with its appurtenances, which the ancestors of the said Count held, and will be well and lawfully appraised at its just annual value by two knights elected for that purpose; one to be nominated by the King of England, the other by the Count.[b] If one or both these knights die after election, and before the valuation be made, then the King and the Count shall put others in their stead; each his own as above said. And if it happen that such two knights cannot agree as to the value of that county, then a third shall be chosen by the noble lady Marguerite, Queen of France; so that the value agreed upon by the last with one of the others shall be taken. The King of England binds himself to distrain those whom the last-named knight shall call to make the valuation, and to aid and advise loyally upon their oaths. This valuation is to be made within the year that John, eldest son and heir of the said Count, and the lady Beatrice, daughter of the King of England, shall be espoused and married.[c] And the said Count of Britany shall have the land of Agenois aforesaid, or the money rendered

King *(Cart.,* 46 Hen. III., m. 3*)* all his interest to the Honor and Rape of Hastings, the King thereupon granted *(Pat.,* 53 *(sic)* Hen. III., m. 27*)* the said Honor, Castle, and Rape to this John (son of Peter de Dreux), in lieu of the lands belonging to the Honor of Richmond; which lands Peter de Savoy passed to the King in exchange for the Honor of Hastings. After which, viz., in 50 Hen. III., this John had livery of the said Earldom of Richmond from Guiscard de Charron, a servant to the same Peter de Savoy *(Pat.,* 50 Hen. III., m. 17 and m. 15 *in dorso).*

[a] St. Louis, King of France, 1226—1270, married Margaret of Savoy, who is mentioned below.

[b] On 17 June, 1261, the King granted to his beloved son, John, eldest son of the Duke of Brittany, £1,200 for the extent and value of the Earldom of Richmond, and two hundred marcs as a gift, so that he should receive 2,000 marcs a year at the Exchequer, that is, 1,000 marcs on Ascension Day, and 1,000 marcs on All Saints' Day, until the said extent should be fully made, as in the agreement between the King and Duke was more fully contained. Provision for adjusting accounts between the King and Duke, in case the extent should exceed, or be less than the said sum of £1,200. This grant not to derogate from an agreement made before about making an exchange for the Earldom, or from anything else touching the said agreement *(Patent Rolls,* 59 Hen. III., m. 9*).* Dugdale *(Baronage,* vol. i., p. 51), gives references to *Patent Roll,* 45 Hen. III., mm. 26, 27, 28, for a quitclaim by John de Dreux to the King, of all right and title to the Earldom of Agenois, in France. The date of the treaty with St. Louis about the Agenois was "le Mardy apres la quensene de Penthecost," that is, 27 May, 1258 *(Forty-first Report of Dep. Keeper of Public Records,* p. 285).

[c] Beatrice, daughter of Henry III. and Eleanor, second daughter and coheir of Raymond Berengar, Count of Provence, born at Bordeaux, 25 June, 1242; died 1272, having been married 1260, to John de Dreux, Duke of Brittany and Earl of Richmond; he died 1305, having had two sons and three daughters (Foster's *Peerage* p. lxxviii).

for it every year by the King of France to the King of England,
in such manner, that if the land of Agenois or the money be
more than the value of the county of Richmond, found by the
knights aforesaid, the King of France shall render to the King
of England the overplus; if less, the King of England shall
make up to the Count the value of that county in his lands
nearest to Agenois.   And this exchange the King of England
wills and grants to the Count in such wise, that he may take and
hold all these things well and in peace, as his inheritance, of the
King of France, and do homage to him, until the King of
England has appointed to him the value of the county of Richmond, as aforesaid, either in the kingdom of France, or in the
kingdom of England.   And this appointment shall be made
and completed by the King of England, within six years after
the date of these letters by the award of the two knights, or of
the third with one of the two if the two cannot agree; and also
the King of England will assure all these things according to
the award of those knights.

LXXVIII.   WAPENTAKE OF HANG.

[Incert. temp. Hen. III.   No. 264].

JURORS:—Sir Elias de Bellirby, Hervey de Clifton, John de
Thorneton, William de Thorisby, John de Burton, Robert
de Sutton, Thomas de Horneby, Roger de Wuendislay, Wimer
de Laiburne, Matthew de Rand, John de Hellirton, Robert Scot
(de Scocia).
They say that a certain Earl Richard, gave three carucates
of land in Offbolton,[a] to the ancestors of Ymania, daughter of
Richard,[b] in drengage, that is to say, to carry the Earl's wine
from the castle to the forest, and to feed the Earl's dogs and
birds, but they know not the number.   This service was withdrawn to a certain fixed farm (ad quandam certam firmam), of
9s. by the year; by what warrant they know not.   Of the said
land Peter and Ymania hold one carucate and a half, which are

----

a The form Offbolton, does not occur in Domesday or Kirkby.   There is
nothing to show which of the Boltons is meant, whether Castle, Low, or West
Bolton.   Off, probably for Ost=East.

b This lady appears in the Rievaulx Chartulary (p. 92), as Ymagina, Wymania,
Ymena, Ymenia, or Ymenea, daughter of Richard de Tunstal.   She married Peter,
son of William de Boeltona, alias Peter de Est Bouilton.   Her second husband,
Reginald de Bodelton, also rejoiced in an alias, appearing as Reginald Chubbe
(Ibid., pp. 92-97).   Helyas de Bellerby, and William de Thuresby, are witnesses
to a charter by Ymena and her first husband (Ibid., p. 94).   Unluckily none of
these charters are dated.

worth 30*s.* Of them the heirs of William the Clerk, hold one
carucate aliened, worth 20*s.*, and the heirs of William, son of
Ulfy, hold half a carucate of land aliened, and worth 10*s.* Of
the carucate held by the heirs of William the Clerk, seven acres
are given to the house of Jervaulx *(domui de Jore vallibus)*,
which are worth 3*s.*

Also they say that a certain Earl Richard, gave to the
ancestors of Peter Boterel, the town of Hestwitton,[a] which is
worth £40, with the donation of the church, which is worth £20;
and Peter sold the said town with the donation of the church to
the house of Jervaulx, when the Honour of Richmond was in
the King's hand, reserving to himself a yearly payment of £20.
This farm the lord Peter of Savoy received after his coming
thither.

In the same Witton, Alan fitzBrian holds one carucate of
land by charter, as they understand.

Also they say that the lord Ranulf fitzRobert ought to be
forester of Wuendislandal in fee, which forest the lord Peter has
in his own hand.

Of the officers, called Steward, Puturer, and Chamberlain,
(Senescallus, Putuarius, Camerarius) de feodo, it is said that all
were enfeoffed of their lands, before they received serjeanties,
and they hold their lands by knight's service.

LXXIX. CONCERNING TRESPASSES COMMITTED BY WILLIAM
DE HORSEDENE[b] WHILE SHERIFF.

[Incert. temp. Hen. III. No. 276.]

INQUISITION as to what manner of trespasses were done to
the King and the men of Yorkshire by William de Hors-
[edene], his clerks, bailiffs, or ministers, while he was Sheriff of
the County, made by Richard de Colton, Elias Burel, Robert de
Saxeby, William *del Hil'* in Bilton, Martin of the same town,
Thurstan de Heton, Adam of the same, Henry de Thorpe,
Adam de Stiveton, Robert the *Masun*, John de Oxton, and
Lambert de Bilburge, before the Sheriff and his fellows. They

---

ᵃ In 1284-5, there were six carucates in East Witton, of which the Abbot of
Jervaulx held five, paying £20 a year to the King, and Brian fitzAlan one (Kirkby's
Inquest, p. 155).

ᵇ William de Horsedene or Horsedene held the office of Sheriff for Yorkshire
for the last half of 37 Hen. III., and the first three-quarters of the following, being
preceded by Robert de Crepping' and succeeded by William le Latimer *(Thirty-
first Report of Deputy Keeper of Public Records*, p. 364).

say upon their oath that, of the . . . . extortions and plunders *(rapinis)* which William de Horsedene and his bailiffs, clerks, or ministers did, while he was Sheriff, they are wholly ignorant; save only that Stephen *de Eya*, his bailiff in the Westrithinge, put Sir Richard de Stiveton in pledge against the said William de Horsedene concerning seven score . . while he (Sir Richard) was in the King's service in parts beyond sea, and set one . . . . to the charter under the name of the said Sir Richard. They have nothing further to say of him *(Aliud de eo nesciunt dicere)*. This they know by the relation and presentment of the said Richard, and thereof he complains.

LXXX. GEORGE DE CANTILUPE.[a] *Proof of age and Inq. p. m.*.

[1 EDW. I. No. 16, m. 22.]

WITNESSES brought to prove the age of George de Cantilupe, before the King's Council at Westminster, on Sunday, three weeks from Easter-day, viz. the eve of the Apostles, Philip and James, in the first of the reign of Edward (30 April, 1273). Peter, Prior of Henton, of the Carthusian order, sworn and examined, says, that the said George was born at Bergeveny, on

---

[a] Son and heir of William, son of William de Cantilupe. He was a minor and in the King's custody at the time of his father's death in 1254 *(Excerpta è Rotulis Finium*, vol. ii., pp. 100, 195, 209). His mother was Eva, daughter and coheir of William de Braose, who brought as her portion the Lordship of Brecknock and the Castle of Abergavenny. On 4 Nov., 1273, Master R. de Cliff, Escheator *citra*, was ordered to seize into the King's hand the lands of George de Cantilupe which he held in chief; and at the same time similar orders were given to Geoffrey de Geneville, Justiciar of Ireland, to seize the lands held in that country in chief by barony *(in capite per baroniam)* by George de Cantilupe, who had gone the way of all flesh *(viam carnis universe ingrediebatur)* on Wednesday the feast of St. Luke (18 Oct., 1273) *(Rot. Fin., 1* Edw. I., m. 3). On 1 March, 1273-4, the King took the fealty of Eudo la Zusche, who had married Milisent, one of the sisters and heirs of George de Cantilupe, and of John de Hastinges, son and heir of Joan de Hastinges, the elder sister *(eynescie sororis)*. A partition of the estates was made, but it does not refer to the Yorkshire portion *(Ibid.,* 2 Edw. I., m. 30). 12 Nov., 1275. The King to the Sheriff of Somersetshire. The manors of Evesham and Ottescumb, which Joan la Bruere held in dower of the inheritance of William Bruere, have fallen into purparty of Roger de Mortimer *(Mortuo mari)* and Maude his wife, John de Hasting', Eudo la Zuche and Milisent his wife, sister and one of the heirs of George de Cantilupe, and Humfrey de Bohun, of the inheritance of the said William Bruwere, which manors Roger seized after the Battle of Evesham, and which he has now given back to us to be partitioned between him and his coheirs and parceners of the said inheritance. The Sheriff is directed to give seisin to the said Roger and Maude, Eudo and Milisent, John, and Humfrey, the heirs of the said William. John de Hasting', who is a minor and in ward to the King, ought to have together with Eudo and Milisent one third of the said manors, and John's half of the said third to be taken into the King's hand *(Ibid.,* 3 Edw. I., m. 2).

Good Friday *(die Parasceve)*, 35 or 36 Henry, father of the now King ;[a] and this he knows because he was some time chaplain of William de Cantilupe, grandfather of George ; and, at the time George was born, he attended to the execution of the testament of the said William, in the place of W. de Cantilupe, Bishop of Worcester, and William father of George, executors of the testament aforesaid. And he says that William, grandfather of George, died in the year of George's birth,[b] or in that immediately preceding, and that the report of the country *(fama patrie)* is that George was twenty-one years old on Easter-eve last past.

John, Prior of Saint Mark's Hospital, Billeswyke, outside Bristol, says, that he understands for certain according to country report, and by the testimony of trustworthy persons, that George was twenty-one years old on Easter-eve last ; and this he knows because he was ordained priest twenty-five years ago, and the father of George died at Calvestone,[c] now eighteen years ago, and three years before his death, George was born at Bergeveny. And he is confident of the premises, because he (witness) was a native of the parts of Calvestone *(quia traxit originem in partibus de Calvestone)*, where the said William died and had land.

Alan de Wauton, knight, sworn, says, that he agrees with the Priors, and this he understands by common report of the country, and by knights and other trustworthy persons, who have related the same to him in good faith.

Peter de Bruges, sworn, says, that on Easter-eve last, twenty-one years had past since George was born ; and he knows this, because he was then at Bridgewater *(Bruges Walteri)*, with the Constable of the Castle, who on the morrow of the Close of Easter next following, held the Hundred-court there, and the rumour came to them of the birth of George, at Bergeveny. And he adds that about one or two years after the birth, he crossed with King Henry to Gascony.[d]

Robert de Trilleke, sworn, says, like the aforesaid, and adds that he knows this by inspecting the chronicles in Bergeveny

[a] Easter, 35 Hen. III., fell on 16 April, 1251, and in the following year on 31 March.

[b] William, son of William de Cantilupe, paid homage for his father's lands on 3 March, 1250-1 *(Excerpta è Rotulis Finium*, vol. ii., p. 100). This evidence, which is contemporary, contradicts some of the above statements. George would seem to have been born at Easter, 1252.

[c] The Abbot of Pershore, and James Fres' (Fresell), the King's Escheator, were commanded on 10 Oct., 1254, to seize the lands of which William de Cantilupe died seised in their bailiwick, and keep the same until the King should otherwise order *(Excerpta è Rotulis Finium*, vol. ii., p. 195).

[d] Henry left England, 6 Aug., 1253, reached Bordeaux, 15 Aug., and did not return to England until 27 Dec. in the following year.

Priory. He heard the men of Bergeveny disputing together as to the age of George, who finally agreed that he was twenty-one years old on Easter-eve this year.

Thomas Creyke, sworn, says as before, and he knows this because Anastasia, his wife, was first married to Richard Wason, who had by her a son, now a Canon at Briweton, born in the same year as George, namely, on the feast of all Saints, now twenty-one years ago (1 Nov.), and George was born at Bergeveny, on Easter-eve next following.

Robert Blundel, knight,[a] sworn, says, that he knows well that George was twenty-one years old on Easter-eve last, because he was sent to Bergeveny, as a messenger by Sir Thomas Corbet to William, father of George, to ask for his lord's land in Lydeham, who came on Wednesday in Easter-week, to Bergeveny, where he found the wife of William lying in childbed with George.

John de Baskerville, knight, agrees with the others, and adds that he knows this by the relation of knights, and other trustworthy persons of the County of Bergeveny, where George was born.

Henry Murdake, knight, says the same, and adds that he knows this by the relation of knights, &c., as above.

John Faukes, of Dertemuthe, sworn, agrees with the aforesaid, and says, that he knows that George was born at Bergeveny, on Easter-eve, 36 Henry (30 March, 1252), by inspecting the chronicles of Totnes Priory, in Devon.

William de Merle,[b] knight, agrees &c., and adds, that he knows this by the oath of Sir Adam de Gurdun, and other trustworthy persons, who were of the household (familia) of William de Cantilupe, father of George.

John de Pycheforde, knight, agrees with William de Herle, adding that he married a cousin of the said George, viz., the daughter of William de Evreux (ipse desponsavit consanguineam predicti G. scilicet filiam Will'i de Ebroicis), and so more diligently inquired as to the age of the said George, from Sirs Adam de Gurdun and Robert de Tregoz, and others, who were of the household of W. de Cantilupe, his father.[c]

---

[a] Opposite some names of the witnesses is the word "miles" on the margin. This addition is in the text, put after the name of the person sworn.

[b] Afterwards, Herle.

[c] There were other inquisitions, and extents of lands in the counties of Wilts, Bedford, Northampton, Devon, Leicester, Somerset, Nottingham, Dorset, Hereford, Salop, and Warwick.

[M. 17.]

Writ dated at Saint Martin-le-Grand *(Sanctum Martinum Magnum)*, London, 17 Dec., 2nd year (1273), and tested by W. de Merton, Chancellor.

BINGELE.

EXTENT of the land, etc., of George de Cantilupe *(Cantilupo)*, made by Robert Vileyn, Hugh de Hannewrthe, Simon Vileyn, Hugh de Ledes, John de Kihele, John son of Walter of the same, John de Martherle, Hugh de Leyes, Richard de Martherle, Walter de Hannewrthe, Lovetot de Bingele, John Vileyn, William de Helewike, and John de Gildestede, who say that there is no capital messuage; there is a watermill worth yearly £8. Formerly there were 30 acres of land in demesne let to farm which yield with meadow by the year 36s. A certain meadow there is worth by the year 10s. Toll with the oven *(tollonium cum furno)*[a] is worth yearly 15s.

There are twenty-one free tenants who pay yearly £4 0s. 3d., of whom eight do suit at the Court of Bingele from three weeks to three weeks. Richard de Kihele holds two carucates of land in Kihele,[b] at 8d. rent, and owes suit to the Court.

There are in Bingele, inhabitants[c] who pay yearly 36s. 5d. at Martinmas and Whitsuntide, and bondmen *(bondi)* who hold 27 bovates of land with nine assarts, and they pay yearly at the said terms, £4 18s. 9d. The Court of Bingele is worth in common years one marc. Pannage, with wood thrown down by the wind, is worth in common years one marc.

Milisand, wife of Ivo[d] la Suche, and John, son of Henry de Hastinges, are heirs of George de Cantilupe, Milisand of full age, and John aged 15 years.

There is no advowson because the Prior of Drax[e] has the church in his own use, and there is not a knight's fee. The jurors know not of whom the said tenements are held.

Sum total, £23 2s. 9d.

(Endorsed). "Extenta de Bingele et de Baseford que fuerunt Georgii de Cantilupo."

---

[a] *Tollonium cum furno.* The income from tolls and from the public oven or bakehouse was 15s. See Glossary—*Tollonium, Furnum.*

[b] Keighley.

[c] The original is "bugenses," evidently a clerical error for "burgenses," as to which see Glossary.

[d] Name defaced, apparently "Ivo," but no doubt "Eudo." "Ivo" and "Eudo" seem to have been used indifferently.

[e] The church of Bingley was given to the Priory of Drax with one carucate of land, being the whole town of Presthorpe, by William Paynell (Lawton, p. 247.)

LXXXI. GILBERT DE GAUNT.[a] *Inq. p. m.*

[2 EDW. I. No. 31.]

Writ dated at Westminster, 26 Jan., 2 Edw. I. (1273-4).

EXTENT and Inquisition as to how much land Gilbert de Gaunt held of the King in ¢hief, in the county of York, on the day he died, and how much of others, and by what service, and how much those lands might be worth a year, and who might be his nearest heir, and of what age, taken before the Escheator on Wednesday after the Purification of the Blessed Mary, in the 2nd year (7 Feb., 1273-4), by William de Fleynburge, Richard de Lascy, Thomas de Plumstede, Nicholas de Karthorpe, clerk, Nicholas de Grendale in Garton, Peter *le Ferur* of the same, Hugh *le Norays* of the same, William de Besingby, John *del Hay*, Stephen de Killom, Geoffrey Modypas, Peter de Munceus, Peter Paytefyn, Henry *le Porter*, John de Fryboys, Richard Aylward, John son of Isabella (*Ys'*) of Hundemanby, and Stephen of the Meadows *(de pratis)* of the same—who say upon their oath, that Gilbert de Gaunt, who is dead, held of the King in chief and barony, the town *(villatam)* of Hundemanby,[b] but that he granted the same town *(villam)* with its appurtenances without any exception, to Gilbert, his son and heir, in marriage with Lora de Balliol *(de Balyolo)*,[c] and gave her dower of it, and placed them a long time before his decease in full seisin.

He held the manor of Helage, in Swaldale,[d] of the grant of John of Brittany, Earl of Richmond *(Richemund)*, by the service of one pair of gilt spurs. There is in demesne there, a capital messuage, worth 4*s.* One hundred acres of arable land

---

[a] The family of Gaunt is said to have acquired Swaledale by the marriage of Gilbert de Gauht, Lord of Folkingham, in Lincolnshire, with Matilda, daughter of Stephen, Earl of Richmond. He died in 1138. His great grandson and namesake was the Gilbert de Gaunt whose inquisition is given above (Plantagenet Harrison's *History of Yorkshire*, vol. i., p. 229). He paid homage to the King on 23 Feb., 1241-2, for the lands of his father, another Gilbert de Gaunt (*Excerpta è Rotulis Finium*, vol. i., p. 370). On his death, which was probably shortly before the date of this inquisition, he was succeeded by his son Gilbert, who after paying fealty, had his father's lands given back to him on condition, that when the King should come into England he should then pay homage (*Rot. Fin.* 2 Edw. I., m. 31). The Fine Roll, whilst Edward I. was still on his way home from Palestine, is headed thus:—"Fines for the first year of the reign of King Edward, son of King Henry, namely, for the time in which he was in the parts beyond the seas in returning from the Holy Land." This last named Gilbert died without issue, and in 26 Edw. I., his heirs were Roger de Gertheston, or Kerdiston, Peter son of Peter de Mauley, and Julia de Gaunt, his sister *(Cal. Gen.*, vol. ii., p. 556*)*.

[b] Hunmanby, in the East Riding, near Bridlington.

[c] She survived her husband *(Cal. Gen.*, vol. ii., p. 556*)*.

[d] Healaugh, in Swaledale, about one mile west of Reeth.

18

worth 100s. A meadow in a place called Fytun[a] and Skaleflat, containing 27½ acres, at 3s. the acre. Sum, £4 2s. 6d. Another meadow of the sheep-fold (pratum berkarie), containing six acres, at 16d. Sum, 8s. A watermill, £4. In bondage 24 bovates of land, each bovate, with services, being worth 5s. 9d. Sum, £6 18s. Nine cottars paying 22s. 9d. with services. In Helage 32 cottars holding 51 acres of arable land, and one rood with tofts, and paying £4 3s. 3d.

Vaccaries and pastures of the forest belonging to the manor of Helage, £47 0s. 12d. Tenants at will of the lord, holding 12 acres of arable land, and three roods of meadow, paying 11s. 10d. Four tenants in Ruckcroft,[b] holding 23½ acres with four tofts, paying 21s. 8d. Nine tenants in Arkelgarth,[c] holding nine tofts and 29 acres of meadow, and paying 42s. 6d. Free tenants (liberi tenentes). Hugh, son of Henry holds the village (villam) of Fremyngton, by the service of the fourth part of one knight's fee, and pays yearly one sporting dog (brachettum). William over Swale (ultra Swale),[d] holds one carucate of land and one assart in Rythe,[e] by military service. . . . . holds a bovate and a half of land in the same by the same service, and pays yearly . . . . John de Rythe holds a bovate and a half of land in the same by the same service, and pays yearly 6d. John Ode holds one bovate of land in the same, and pays yearly 4s. William de Dalton holds one bovate of land in the same, by military service, and pays yearly one pound of cumin. John . . . . . . holds three acres of land in the same, and pays yearly 2d. The Prior of Bridelington holds the town (villatam) of . . . . . . of which the church of the said town (ville), is dowered in pure almoign (dotata est in pura elemosina). Also the Abbot of Ryevalle holds . . . . called Menhaker, and pays yearly, 66s. 8d. He has no church in his gift (in advocacione sua).

Sum total of the manor of Helage in Swaldale, £87 7s. 7d.

Gilbert, his nearest heir, is of full age. [f]

(N.B. The lower part of this document has been much injured with galls, and is almost illegible.)

[a] Perhaps Feetham on the Swale, a little above Healaugh.

[b] Called Ruckroft in 1563 (Yorkshire Fines, Tudor, vol. i., p. 272); and Ruccrofte in 1575 (Ibid., vol. ii., p. 70). Probably Rawcroft, near Reeth, on the road to Arkengarthdale.

[c] Arkengarth, near Reeth.

[d] In 1284-5, William Overswale held a carucate in Reeth (Kirkby's Inquest, p. 172).

[e] Reeth.

[f] There are two Lincolnshire inquisitions, one says he was twenty-four, the other twenty-five.

LXXXII. PETER DE BRUS.[a] *Extent of Lands.*

[1 EDW. I. No. 31.]

Writ directed to William de Boyville, Escheator beyond Trent, and tested by Walter de Merton,[b] Chancellor, at Westminster, 20 April, in the second year of Edward (1274). Reference is made to a command lately given to John de Reygate, late Escheator beyond Trent, that he should give seisin of their several shares to the parceners of the inheritance of Peter de Brus, deceased, according to the partition recently made, but partition of the knight's fees is not yet made: as appears by the petition of John de Bellew, who has taken to wife Laderina, sister and one of the heirs of Peter. The Escheator is now commanded to take into the King's hand all fees which were of Peter in his bailiwick, and keep them until otherwise ordered,[c] giving in the mean time notice to the heirs and parceners to be before the King, or those holding his place in England, in eight days from the feast of S. John Baptist (1 July, 1274), to receive their respective shares of the said fees, according to the partition then to be made in the Court of Chancery.

By the endorsement the Escheator returns that he has done as the writ commanded, but that he is not clearly satisfied as to the full number of fees. The heirs have had notice to appear on the day named, and Hugh de Coloum, sub-escheator in the County of York, has had a precept on Monday the morrow of Pentecost (19 May).

.[d] . . . . Richard de Heton seven carucates of land in the same manner . . for half a fee. Anselm de Harpam three carucates

[a] On 27 Sept., 1237, the King, then at York, was pleased to approve of a marriage which had been contracted between Peter, son and heir of Peter de Brus, and Hillary, eldest daughter of Peter de Mauley *(de Malo Lacu)*; and also of one between Peter, son and heir of the said Peter de Mauley, and Joan, eldest daughter of the said Peter de Brus *(Patent Roll, No. 46, 21 Hen. III., m. 2)*. On 15 Nov., 1240, Peter de Brus, usually called Peter de Brus III., paid a fine of 200 marcs for his relief on succeeding to the lands of his father, Peter, son of Peter de Brus, who had gone on a pilgrimage to the Holy Land *(Excerpta è Rotulis Finium, vol. i., p. 332)*. At his death, as is mentioned in the above inquisition, his four sisters, Agnes, wife of Walter de Faucumberge, Lucy, wife of Marmaduke de Twenge, Margaret, wife of Robert de Ros of Wark, and Ladereyna, wife of John de Bellew, were his coheirs. His sister, Joan de Mauley, it is clear from this, have died without issue. Walter de Hemingburgh (vol. i., p. 341), who was a Canon of Guisborough, a priory of which Peter de Brus was patron, and who lived within a few miles of Skelton Castle, states that he died on 18 Sept. *(xiv. Kalendas Octobris)*, 1272, which is confirmed as to the day by an entry in a calendar formerly belonging to that priory *(Coll. Top. et Gen.*, vol. iv., p. 261, quoted in Atkinson's *History of Cleveland*, vol. ii., p. 25*)*. The year is no doubt correct, although it has been alleged he died in 1271. He certainly was alive as late as 25 Nov., 1271, when there is a memorandum entered on the *Close Roll* (56 Hen. III., m. 13[d]), that the King had granted to Peter de Brus the custody of the land and heir of Walter de Lindeseye, together with his marriage. He was dead before 28 Sept., 1272, when the King ordered John de Reygate, Escheator beyond Trent, to seize Peter de Brus's lands into the King's hand *(Excerpta è Rotulis Finium, vol. ii., p. 582)*.

[b] Edward had not then returned to England from the Holy Land, where he was at the time of his father's death. During his prolonged absence from the kingdom writs were issued with the *teste* of the Chancellor. Edward landed at Dover on Thursday, 2nd Aug., 1274.

[c] The extent of knights' fees is given later on (No. cxiv.).

[d] The inquisition is much mutilated in the upper part. Here and there a word or two are visible, but with no sort of intelligible connection, until the following sentences, much disjointed and fragmentary, appear.

of land . .   , Anselm de . . . . three carucates and a half of
land, whereof eight carucates make one fee. . . . . . holds one
fee . . . . . renders to P. de Brus 20s., of which the said P. de
Brus renders .   . . . Maucovenaunt holds one fee. Robért de
Nevile one fee. William de Boivile holds one fee. Conan de
Lyverton holds half a fee . . . . William de . . . eby holds half
a fee. And it is to be known that all those who hold of the
fee of Henry de Lacy, hold at foreign service *(ad forinsecum
servicium)*. Matthew de Glaphou . . . . . Henry de Merley
holds   . . And the said P. holds of the Earl of Albemarle
. . . .   . [Here several words wanting] chief, with all adjacent
buildings outside the castle,[a] and with the little park round the
castle, and with liberty of taking from every salt pan *(salina)* in
the marsh of Cotum, by the year one skep *(unam skeppam sa.)*
of salt. .   . . . prises of boats of . . . . . in the beach *(marina)*
of Redker, of which how many soever the lord shall have, he
can have from every boat 12s. So the castle with the appurtenances above written is worth by the year, £14.   Also P. de
. . . . . a vivary at Scelton, worth . . . . . from Jarum as far as
Reneswike,[b] and it is so uncertain that it cannot be extended.
                                        Sum, £14 8s. 8d.
    Burgh *(burgum)* of Scelton with farm of the same, and
with pleas of Court of the burgh, and with toll to be taken
there and at Cotum and with the marsh of Cotum, and for the
berth *(situ)* of every ship landing there except the ships of the
Prior of Giseburn,[c] and with toll of Redker Mersk, Bro[cton],
Grenerige,[d] and with all other demesne lands there appertaining,
is worth by the year, £10 4s. 4d. There are five mills, worth
with the suit due and accustomed, £21 8s., and five score
quarters of oats (at 12d.), 100s., ... five score hens or 5s., and
24 geese or 4s.   Sum, £38 2s. 4d.
    There are at Scelton in demesne, 567[e] acres of arable land
(at 5d.), £13 15s 10d. Of demesne meadow 84 acres (at 12d.),
£4 4s. In villenage *(villenagiis)*, 21 bovates of land without
tofts (the bovate, 4s. 6d.) Sum, ... Of cottages, 16½ ; of
which 8½ are worth 17s., and the other 8 are worth 8s. Sum,

---

    [a] No doubt the Castle of Skelton.

    [b] Runswick, in the parish of Hinderwell. The inquisition is speaking of the
right to wreck from Yarm to that place.

    [c] By a fine dated 1246, Peter de Brus III. agreed with the Prior of Guis-
borough that all ships, whether the Prior's or hired, bringing goods belonging to
him or his household to the port of Coatham, for their own use and not for sale,
should be free from all payment of toll and claim for ship's berth *(Guisborough
Chartulary*, vol. i., p. 119).

    [d] Gerrick, in the parish of Skelton.

    [e] The figures are so but the calculation is not correct.

25*s.* John Play holds one bovate by charter, yielding 4*s.*; William de Bellingham holds one toft by charter, yielding 6*s.*; Henry the Porter holds one assart by charter, ... The same holds one toft by charter, yielding 1*d.*; Hugh de Giseburn and Odinel hold by charter one assart, yielding 2*s.*; the same Hugh holds one toft by charter, yielding 12*d.*; the same Odinel holds half a carucate of land by charter, yielding 1*d.*; Peter de Kethou holds by charter six bovates of land; Nicholas Hau. . . . berg holds 12 bovates, yielding 6*d.* and six horse-shoes; William Capun holds one assart and the pasture of Holm by charter, yielding 4*d.*; Godfrey Peper holds by charter two tofts, yielding 6*d.*; Peter Marshal holds one toft by charter, yielding 1*d.*; Walter . . . . . . holds one toft for 1*d.*; the same holds for life four acres of land and half an acre of meadow for 1*d.*; William Levedyman holds by charter two bovates and one toft for 1*d.*; William Usser holds by charter one bovate without toft for 1*d.*; Peter son of Bertram holds half a carucate with two tofts . . . . holds by charter one toft and croft for 1*d.*; Robert son of William the Brasur holds by charter one toft and croft for 1*d.*; Thomas de Burgate holds by charter one toft and croft for 1*d.*; Roger Tapet holds by charter one toft and croft for 6*d.*; John the Barbur holds by charter one toft and croft for 1*d.*; Thomas son of Ralph holds by charter one toft and croft for four hens and one cock; . . . . holds by charter one bovate for one capon; Alexander the Palfreur holds by charter two tofts for 1*d.*; William de Kendale holds by charter one toft and croft for 1*d.*; Stephen . . . . holds by charter 10 bovates, for one pound of cumin; Michael de Thoccotes holds from year to year four acres of land and half an acre of meadow, for 2*s.*; Joan Gurney holds two assarts in the same manner, for 16*d.*; Adam de Thorpe holds one assart in the same manner, for 18*d.*; Adam Ney holds one assart in the same manner, for 4*d.*; William Tynnur (?) holds half . . of land in the same manner, for 2*d.* And they hold at the full value. The dales *(valles)* towards the sea are worth 6*s.* The herbage in the Hay *(Haya)*, with the great park and with Hasdale,[a] is worth 50*s.* The profit of dead wood in the Hay *(Haia)* and Hasdale, without waste, is worth 20*s.* . . . . woods worth 4*s.* The herbage of the Green is worth 3*s.*

Sum, £29 5*s.* 8*d.*

Stanehou[b] appertains to Scelton, and there are in villenage *(villenagiis)*, 10 bovates with 10 tofts (the bovate 5*s.* 3*d.*). Sum, 52*s.* 6*d.* Of cottages, six tofts are worth 12*s.* William Carpenter

[a] Aysdale Gate in the S.W. of Skelton parish. In the foundation charter of Guisborough, Asadala.

[b] Stanghow, in the south of the parish of Skelton.

holds by charter three bovates with three tofts, for 4s. Simon Gide (?) holds by charter one toft and croft for . . barbed arrows. Roger de Aunou holds by charter one assart, called Kateriding,[a] for 1d. Morsum[b] appertains to Scelton, and there are in villenage six bovates with six tofts (the bovate 6s.) Sum, 36s. In cottages, five tofts are worth 10s. Alan de Giseburne holds . . . . . and two assarts by charter for one pound of pepper. Hugh de Tormodeby holds by charter four bovates for four barbed arrows; Adam de Thoccotes holds by charter 14 bovates for four barbed arrows. Pannage there is worth 8d.   Sum, £5 14s. 3d.

GRENERIGE.

Grenerige appertains to Scelton. There are in villenage 10 bovates with 10 tofts (the bovate 5s.). Sum, 50s. Of meadow, seven acres (at 10d.), 5s. 10d. One assart is worth 12s. William de Giseburne holds four bovates for life for 4s.; Michael de Thoccotes holds 24 acres for life for 1d.; Thomas de Wlvedale holds one assart for life for 14s.

MERSKE.[c]

There are in demesne six hundred acres five score and ten of arable land (at 8d.). Sum, £27 6s. 8d. In demesne 69 acres of Percy fee (at 4d.), 23s. Of demesne meadow, four score acres (at 14d.), £4 13s. 4d. In villenage 76 bovates with as many tofts (the bovate 8s.), £30 8s. In cottages, 32 tofts (at 16d.), 42s. 4d. In drengage two bovates, yielding 11s. Adam son of Reyner holds by charter two bovates for 21s.; Roger de Aunou holds by charter six bovates for 6s. 8d.; Richard D . . . holds by charter one croft and . . . . . for 3s.; Richard Young (juvenis) holds by charter one toft and croft for 12d., also one toft and croft and four and a half acres of land for half a pound of cumin; Hugh de Thorneton holds one carucate of land by serjeanty, and a pasture called Dunesdale . . . half a carucate of land and three assarts called Pyleflat, Wudeflat, and Cornegreve,[d] with 12 acres of land lying in Uplithume, for 14d.; John de Thoccotes for heather (bruerio) and for having common in Scelton pasture, eight boonworks (precarias) in autumn . . In cottages, 45 tofts with crofts (at 16d.), 60s.

---

[a] Kate Ridding, near Stanghow Moor. The ridding or clearing (cf. West Riding royd) of Kate or Kade, a very common Teutonic name, which appears in Cadeby and Catton, and in a softened form in Chatton and Chadwick.

[b] Moorsholme to the south and east of Stanghow.

[c] Marske-by-the-Sea.

[d] Corngrave is in Upleatham parish, about a mile N.W. of Skelton Castle. The two preceding places are most likely in the same parish.

BROCTON.[a]

There are in demesne 382 acres of arable land (at 6*d.*), £11 12*d.*; of meadow, 42 acres (at 18*d.*), 63*s.* In villenage 40 . . . (6*s.* 8*d.*), £15. In cottages, six tofts are worth 6*s.*, and for 18 acres of land held by the cottars (at 6*d.*), 15*s.* Eleven tofts with crofts are worth 11*s.* John de Thoccotes holds half a carucate of land with one plot *(placea)* of wood in Cam . . . . . John de Brocton holds half a carucate of land by serjeanty; Peter de Thormodeby holds two bovates for four barbed arrows; Thomas *de Camera* holds for life, two bovates for 1*d.*; William son of Alan holds by charter six acres for 6*d.* . . . . at foreign service.

SCINERGREVE.[b]

There are tofts with crofts and assarts, which are worth 55*s.* 8*d.* In Playgreve there are three assarts, worth 2*s.* 1*d.* The fishery of S[cin]ergreve, is worth 4*s.* For boats, as many as are there, 10*s.* each, and now . . . . Scelton, 30*s.*

Sum, £110 6*s.* 6*d.*

Peter de Brus held the wapentake of Langeberghe to farm and in fee *(ad firmam et in feodo)*, by charter of King Henry, yielding yearly 40 marcs at the Exchequer of London. As to advowsons of churches, the Priory of Giseburne has all the churches in the barony to its own use,[c] and the same priory has the advowson . . . . in pure almoigne. The Abbot of Wyteby has the church of Middelburg with a moiety of the same town in pure almoigne.[d] No extent is made of Courts Baron, because there is no suit due or accustomed from any free tenants, according to custom *(de tenore)* of the whole barony.

DANEBI.[e]

The capital messuage with little park is worth 6*s.* 8*d.* Six acres of land yield six quarters of oats (at 12*d.*), 6*s.* Six acres of meadow are worth 6*s.* In villenage 56 bovates (at 6*s.*), £16 16*s.* In cottages, 32 tofts . . tofts waste (6*d.* each). There are five small forges worth 10*s.*, and two other forges in the

---

[a] Brotton, near Saltburn.

[b] Skinningrove, in the parish of Brotton. Playgreve, which seems to be lost, was no doubt like Skinningrove, a deep narrow glen or valley. Cf. Cornegreve just above, also Mulgrave, and Griff Farm, near Helmsley.

[c] Robert de Brus gave all his churches to Guisborough when he founded the Priory.

[d] Robert de Brus (the founder of Guisborough), and Agnes his wife, and their son Adam de Brus, for the health of their lord Henry, King of England, and for the benefit of their own souls and those of their heirs, gave to Whitby Abbey the church of St. Hilda the Abbess, of Middlesburcd, and two carucates and two bovates in Nehuham (Newham) *(Whitby Chartulary*, vol. i., p. 95*)*.

[e] Danby-in-Cleveland.

forest are worth £4, without destruction of the forest. Two watermills there are worth £10, of which Roger de Burton has by charter 100s., but Ambrose de Camera . . . 66s. 8d. . . s. 4d. Robert Forester holds 35 acres for 30s.; Roger de Middleheved holds two plots (placeas) for 6s.; Roger de Thornhille holds 30 acres for 18s.; John son of Robert holds two tofts and 22 acres of land for 16s. 1½d. The wife of William son of Thomas . . . . Robert the Reeve (p'p's) holds four bovates of land with one plot (placea) of meadow for 30s.; William son of William holds three bovates for 9s.; Richard de Aula holds one bovate for 9s.; John Lucan holds one toft for 12d; Walter de Forgate (?) holds one bovate and a half for 10s.; Alan . . . de Thorpe holds three bovates for 14s.; Matthew de Glaphou holds one carucate for 4s.; Hugh son of Nicholas holds one plot (plac') as contained within certain bounds for 6s. 8d. Roger de Bo . . holds four bovates for 16s. . . . . acres of land for 10s.; Matthew son of Robert holds one bovate for 4s.; the heir of Robert Stormy holds one carucate for 4s. 2d; Simon son of Alan holds two bovates for 10s.; Roger . . . holds two bovates . . . John . . . holds one bovate for six barbed arrows; Kempe holds nine acres of land for two barbed arrows; G. de Johan holds one bovate and a half for 6s.; Laurence de Burton holds one bovate for 1d. . . one acre for 12d. All these free men afore-written hold by charter. The shepherds of the Prior of Giseburne yield yearly for having herbage in the pasture of Danebi for their own cattle (ad averia sua propria) 4s. Sum, £37 14s. 2d.

LELUME.[a]

The capital messuage, which Hugh de Lelume holds with the whole close by chirograph, yields four score and 12 quarters of oats (at 12d.), £4 12s. Lyolf and R . . . . . . quarter 12d., 41s. In villenage—William Carpenter holds six acres of land (at 10d.), 5s.; Roger son of John holds one toft and one nook (angulum) of meadow for 3s. . . Matilda de Thornethevit and Alan . . 25s.; Roger de Hulmes holds 12 acres of land (at 12d.), 12s.; Matthew le Gilur holds one toft and one nook (angulum) of meadow for . . s. Of cottages in the forest, six tofts are worth 11s. . . to which appertain 150 acres of meadow (at 8d.), 113s. 3d. There are in the forest of demesne meadow, five score 14 acres (at 8d.), 76s. 4d.; also herbage of the forest of Heckedale . . . . forest, 40s.; pannage, 3s. The quarry of Clitherbec is worth 3s. Sum, £27 7s. 7d.

---

[a] Lealholme, in the parish of Danby.

FREEMEN IN THE FOREST *(Liberi in forest')*.

William Harkel holds nine acres of land and eight acres of meadow for 12*s*. 2*d*. The wife of William de Lelum' holds 21½ acres of land for 21*s*. 6*d*.; Hugh de Lelum' holds one acre of land under Lelum, and 21½ acres of meadow for 38*s*. . . . . 22 acres of land and four acres of meadow for 23*s*.; Roger de Middelheved holds 19 acres of land and four acres of meadow for 12*s*. 4*d*.; Lyolph *del Dale* holds four acres of meadow and one waste place of a certain bercary for 8*s*. 6*d*.; . . . . 22 acres of land for 14*s*.; Walter son of William holds 26 acres of land for 26*s*.; William *del Dale* holds 12 acres of land for 12*s*.; Geoffrey Bere holds 16½ acres of land for 16*s*. 6*d*.; Thomas son of B . . one toft and two acres of meadow at the will of the lord, yielding 5*s*. Sum, £10 12*s*.

JARUM.[a]

Jarum appertains to the lordship of Scelton, and yields for tofts by year, 15*s*.; from a windmill, 30*s*.; perquisites of court, and toll of brewers, fisheries, and all other profits by the year, £17 6*s*. . . . . land in demesne, whereof Jordan de Lestre held 14 bovates of land by foreign service; Robert de Muncheus holds one carucate of land by foreign service, and Peter de Brus has given that service to the Prior of Park,[b] in pure almoigne; William de L . . . . one pound of cumin, and the same William holds one carucate of land which was formerly of Gerard Thewode, and yields yearly 8*s*. He also holds four bovates with one waldcroft by foreign service. The nuns of Handale[c] hold . . . . half a carucate of land by foreign service. The heir of Ralph de Marton holds three bovates by foreign service. So all the lands there are alienated from the demesne.

Sum, £19 19*s*. 8*d*.

KIRKEBRUNE.[d]

The capital messuage with garden and dovehouse is worth 20*s*. In demesne there are 24 bovates of land with as many tofts (the bovate 13*s*. 4*d*.), £16; in villenage 26 bovates with as many tofts (the bovate 13*s*. [4*d*.]), ... are worth 51*s*. 10*d*.

Sum, £56 18*s*. 6*d*.

In Estbrunne there are in villenage 47 bovates of land (at 13*s*. 4*d*.), £31 6*s*. 8*d*. Richard de Thymelby holds by charter . . . . . 23*s*. 4*d*. Sum, £52 2*s*.

---

[a] Yarm. *Domesday* Jarun.

[b] Helagh Park.

[c] Or possibly Basedale.

[d] Kirkburn, a small village about three miles W. S. W. of Driffield, includes in its parish the townships of Tibthorpe, Southburn, and Eastburn. In *Domesday*, Kirkburn appears as Westburne and Burnous.

In Sutbrunne there are in villenage 35 bovates (at 13*s.* 4*d.*), £23 6*s.* 8*d.* In cottages 18 tofts worth 21*s.* 8*d.* . . . are worth £8. Sum, £52 15*s.* 2*d.* Adam de Setone holds there two carucates of land by foreign service.

All these townships of Br[unne] are held of the King in chief.

In Tibethorpe there are in demesne forty . . . in villenage, 83 bovates (at 13*s.* 4*d.*), £55 6*s.* 8*d.* In cottages, five tofts are worth 11*s.* 6*d.* William de Berton holds by charter one toft for 18*d.* Lands rented *(de arrentag')* . . . . . 4*d.* And it is to be known that William de Hasthorpe holds half a carucate of land of Brus . . And the township of Tipetofte is of the fee of . . ᵃ

KARLETON IN BALNE.ᵇ

The capital messuage with garden is worth 10*s.* In demesne two and a half bovates (at 4*s.* 4*d.*). In Fortkere are 45 ᶜ acres of land (at 4*d.*). In one assart near the manor are six . . . . of land (acre 4*d.*). Of pasture, 40 acres (at 4*d.*) Sum of the whole, 41*s.* 4*d.* Of annual rent for eight tofts, for assarts and for wastes, 116*s.* 3*d.* Of old meadow, 10 acres . . . worth 36*s.* Peter son of Henry holds 40 acres of land for one pound of pepper; Alan de Kawode holds six and a half acres for one pound of cumin; Thomas de Heitone for having common in the moors yields . . . . . the lord shall find timber for keeping them up. Of pasture, 16*s.* In villenage are seven bovates of land (at 4*s.* 4*d.*), 30*s.* 4*d.* From aid of villains according to ancient custom *(de auxilio villanorum)* . . . . and the same H. renders the said 40*s.* to John de Helt . . for life. On the death of H. and J. the 40*s.* revert to the heirs of Brus. William de Winhindering holds for life five acres , . .

THORPE DE ARCHIS. ᵈ

The capital messuage with garden is worth 6*s.* 8*d.* In demesne there are 200 acres of land (at 12*d.*), £12. In demesne meadow 17 acres (at 12*d.*), 17*s.* In villenage . . 12 tofts, worth 19*s.* The herbage of Walton Parkᵉ is worth 13*s.* 4*d.* Roger Holbeghe holds three bovates for 1*d.* In villenage are eight acres of waste, and they yield 4*s.* . . . . . 15*s.* Richard Tailor *(cissor)* holds one bovate and one toft for 15*s.*; Thomas son of Jowet holds one bovate for 15*s.*; Peter *de Groua* holds one

---

ᵃ According to Kirkby's *Inquest* (p. 90), Kirkburn and Tibthorpe formed part of the fee of Brus, being held by the heirs of Brus direct from the King.

ᵇ Carlton, in the parish of Snaith.

ᶜ Or 55, written XLXV.

ᵈ Thorparch, in the Ainsty, near Wetherby.

ᵉ Walton, a parish in the Ainsty, two miles from Wetherby.

bovate for 15s.; Thomas . . . . for 2s. 6d.; William de Walton
holds half a bovate for 20d.; Elias *le Sauf* holds one toft and
four acres of land for 2s.; the Prioress of Munketon[a] holds of
the waste 10 acres . . . . acres of waste for 2s. 6d.; Adam son
of John holds four acres of waste for 2s.; Thomas Milde holds
four acres of waste for . . . . . William Scot holds six acres of
waste . . . . waste for 3s.; William son of Alan holds six
acres of waste for 3s.; Thomas son of Jowet holds four acres of
waste for 2s. These free men afore-written hold by charter one
mill . . . charter 66s. 8d. And Henry de Leirton has for life
66s. 8d.   Sum, £30 0s. 10d.

The heirs of Peter de Brus are—Agnes, wife of Walter de
Faucunberge; Lucy, wife of Marmaduke de Twenge; Margaret,
wife of Robert de Ros of Werke; Ladereyne, wife of John [de
Bellew].

[*The indorsement shows a few words too fragmentary to be
rendered into a complete sentence.*]

¶ *On separate pieces of parchment are set out the shares of
the coheirs. These shares are entered on the Close Roll,* 1 *Edw. I.,
mm.* 10, 11.

SHARE *(pars)* of lord Robert de Ros and Margaret his wife.
The castle of Kirkeby in Kendale with all Kendale,[b]
whatsoever appertained to the lord Peter de Brus in demesnes,
villenages, rents and services of free men and of others (except
the dale *(valle)* of Kentemere, which is assigned to lord John de
Bellew *(Bella aqua)* and *la Dereyne* his wife), together with the
advowson of the Priory of Konigesheved,[c] and fourth part of
wreck of the sea in Cliveland, that is to say, from Renneswys,[d]
as far as Jarum.

SHARE of John de Bellew *(Bella aqua)* and *la Dereyne* his wife.
The manor of Karleton in Baune with demesnes and all
rents, as well of free men as of others, and[e] the marriage of *la
Dereyne*, wife of lord John de Belewe; the manor of Thorpe de
Arches and Waleton, with park and all demesnes, [and] rents
within the town of Torp and Waleton with the appurtenances;

<hr />

[a] Nun Monkton.

[b] The Westmoreland property came into the Brus family by the marriage of
Peter de Brus II. and Helewisa de Lancaster, one of the sisters and coheirs of
William de Lancaster III. *(Furness Coucher,* Chetham Soc., p. 368).

[c] Conishead Priory.

[d] Runswick.

[e] At first written " et cum mariag' d'ne Margarete de Ros et cum omnibus
pertinenciis." These words are struck through, and " et Maritag' la Dereyne vxor
d'ni Joh' de Belewe " written over.

the manor of Tibetorp with all appurtenances; in Suthbrune 14 bovates of land with tofts, and 70s. in the mill of the same town; in Estbrune four and a half bovates of land and four tofts; the dale *(cum valle)* of Kentemere in Kendale with all appurtenances; the advowson of Moneketon Priory[a] and a fourth part of wreck in Cliveland, that is to say, from Renneswyc as far as Jarum, together with all lands and tenements assigned in marriage, as well to Robert de Ros and Margaret his wife as to the other sisters and heirs of Peter, to be in parcenery between them, as the manner is in this kingdom *(participandis inter ipsos ut moris est in regno nostro).*

SHARE of Marmaduke de Tuenge and Lucy his wife.

The manor of Daneby with forest and all appurtenances, together with Lelhom, Wolvedale,[b] and Manselinges[c]; the farm of Thomas de Wolvedale, the manor of Brocton and Skinergrive, the boats *(batell')* of Skinnergrive; rents and demesnes as well of free men as of others with all appurtenances; the town of Jarum with services of free men there; the fishery and town of Great Morsom, and rents and services of free men and others; the forest of the chace of the dales *(vallibus)*,[d] that is to say, Swindale and Lehauenes, and other dales, as the high way stretches from Lardethorn as far as Scelton, by Skaytebec, between Katerige and Stango, and so as far as Liverton wood; the manor of Kirkebrune and Suthbrune; with mills and suit of the same—except 14 bovates of land with tofts and 70s. *(lx. et x. s.)* annual rent in the mills, which land and rent are assigned to John de Bellew and Ladereyne, his wife—a fourth part of the wreck of the sea, that is to say, from Renneswyc as far as Jarum; a moiety of the advowson of Giseburne Priory; and a moiety of the bailiwick of Langeberewe.[e]

[a] Nun Monkton, near York.

[b] Wood Dale House, in the parish of Egton, just across the Stonegate Beck, which divides Egton from Danby. No doubt originally the name applied to the entire dale, though now it is confined to a single farm. Only the west or Danby side belonged to the Brus fee.

[c] This place seems lost.

[d] These dales can still be identified. They are all in the south of Skelton parish. Swinedale House, a mile west of Great Moorsholme, marks the site of Swindale. Avens House and Avens Wood, to the south and south west of the same place, enable us to identify Lehavenes. Lardethorn is perhaps Harlow or Harlott Thorns, Skate Beck close to Avens House, Kate Ridding and Stanghow, these two last in the S.W. of Skelton, are certainly the modern representatives of Skaytebec, Katerige, and Stangho. Katerige is called Kateriding earlier in the inquisition. Liverton is a chapelry of Easington, from which it is detached, the parish of Loftus lying between.

[e] Langbaurgh. This Wapentake corresponds with the modern Cleveland.

Memorandum. Concerning the advowson of Giseburne Priory, it is agreed that, in the first vacancy the Prior shall be presented by lord W. de Facunberge or his heirs, and in the next vacancy by lord Marmaduke; and so, from one to the other, alternately, up to the end of the world.

SHARE of Walter de Facunberge and Agnes his wife.

Scelton Castle with the park round it, and profits of the boats of Cotum and of Rideker, the demesnes of Scelton meadows and dales *(vallibus)*, the rents as well of freemen as of others in the town of Scelton, all mills and toll; the manor of Merske with all appurtenances, Rideker, Plyom,[a] the town of Stangho, the town of Grenerige with appurtenances; the forest of Scelton, that is to say, the Hay and Great Park, with Hasdale and the chace of Westwyc,[b] with the forest, as the high-way stretches *(sicut iter altum se extendit)* between Stangho and Kadriding, and so along the road to Lardegate, then by Sketebek as far as Larthorn, next up to the boundary *(divisam)* of Daneby forest; thence as far as Colemandale.[c] So that all chases within those limits *(divisas)*, that is to say, Locwyt, Wornelesco, Hardale, and Hache,[d] with herbage of the Grene, herbage of the Dynant,[e] with the whole town of Estbronne— except four and a half bovates of land and four tofts, which are assigned to the lord John de Bellew, and *La Dereine* his wife— the fourth part of wreck of the sea, that is to say, from Rennewyc as far as Jarum; a moiety of the advowson of Giseburne Priory, and a moiety of the bailiwick of Langeberewe.

Memorandum. Concerning the advowson of Giseburne Priory, it is agreed that, in the first vacancy the Prior shall be presented to lord Walter de Facunberge, or his heirs, and in the next vacancy to lord Marmaduke; and so, from one to the other, alternately, up to the end of the world.

[*On the dorse.*] It is thus agreed between Walter de Faucunberge and Agnes his wife, Marmaduke de Tweng and Lucy his wife, Robert de Ros and Margaret his wife, John de Bellew and Laderina *(Laderinam)* his wife, the aforesaid co-heirs and parceners of the inheritance of P. de Brus, THAT all lands and tenements which were of the said Peter shall be re-extended,

---

[a] Upleatham.

[b] Aysdale Gate in Skelton, and Westworth Farm, two miles S.W. of Guisborough.

[c] Commondale, in S.E. of Guisborough.

[d] Lockwood and Hardale. Wornelesco or Worvelsco and Hache are lost.

[e] Two stones on the northern boundary of Danby, the Great and the Lesser Dinnond, still preserve this name.

and if to any of them more than his reasonable portion shall be
assigned, he who has more [shall yield] to him who has less by
three or two of the said heirs, according to the consideration
and discretion of four honest men, knights or others, to be
chosen by them: and this every of them for himself and his
heirs hath acknowledged in Chancery and granted. And if any
of them shall presume to contravene this, he hath granted for
himself and his heirs that all the lands and tenements aforesaid
shall be extended yet again by the King, and that the King
shall (as is just) assign and make up in this behalf any deficiency
to him who has less than appertains to him.

In the same manner it is granted by the aforesaid concerning the fees belonging to the aforesaid inheritance.

Saving to the said Marmaduke and Lucy, and to the townships, common of pasture for their cattle and animals, as the
aforesaid Peter and the townships have been used to have it.[a]

LXXXIII. CONCERNING BOLTON PRIORY AND THE RIGHT
OF ELECTING A PRIOR DURING VACANCY.

[3 EDW. I. No. 67.]

[M. 1.]
Writ[b] of *certiorari* on the petition of the Canons of Bolton Priory, directed
to Philip de Wilheby, Escheator beyond Trent, and dated at Kavers-
ham, 4 Feb., 3rd year (1274-5).

[M. 2.]

INQUISITION made at Scipton in Cravene, on the morrow of
Ash-Wednesday *(in crastino Cinerum)*, 3 Edw. (28 Feb.,
1274-5), at the time the Priory of Boulton was void, upon the
right of electing a Prior, before Philip de Wylegeby, Escheator
beyond Trent, by Sir Thomas *de Alta ripa*, John de Fernhil,
John Gilot, Thomas de Malghun, Everard Fauvel, Elias de

---

[a] [*In dorso.*] Ita convenit inter Walterum de Faucunberge et Agnetem
uxorem ejus, Marmeducum de Twenge et Luciam uxorem ejus, Robertum de
Ros et Margaretam uxorem ejus, Johannem de Bella aqua et Laderinam uxorem
ejus, predictos coheredes et participes hereditatis P. de Brus, quod omnes terre et
ten. que fuerunt predicti Petri reextendantur, et si qua alicui ipsorum plus inde
quam racionabilis porcio sua fuerit assignatum, ille qui plus habuerit illi qui minus
habuerit, per tres vel duos ipsorum heredum, juxta consideracionem et discrecionem
quatuor proborum hominum militum vel aliorum per ipsos ad hoc eligendorum,
et hoc unusquisque pro se et her. suis recognovit in Cancellaria Regis et concessit.
Et si aliquis ipsorum contra hoc venire presumpserit, concessit pro se et her. suis,
quod omnes terre et ten. predicta iterato reextendantur per Regem, et quod Rex
illud sibi qui minus habuerit quam ad ipsum pertinet habendum assignet, et
defectum prout justum fuerit supleat in hac parte.   Eodem modo concessum
est per predictos de feodis ad predictam hereditatem spectantibus. Salva predictis
Marmeduco et Lucie et villatis communa pasture ad pecudes et animalia sua,
sicut prefatus P. et villate predicte eam habere consueverunt.

[b] On the back of the writ—"Venit istud breve apud Novum locum (Newstead)
die Veneris proxima ante festum Sancte Scolastice Virginis" (8 Feb., 1274-5).

Kyhelaye, Richard Clerk *(clericum)*, William Revel, Adam de Plumlond, Elias de Hoterburne, Robert de Scothorp, and John son of Robert, who, being sworn, say that from the time of the foundation of the Priory, the lords of Albemarle in time of vacancy had only one man as warden at the gates of the Priory, to defend the house from any coming and injuring the same; and that the Canons by their own will, without asking leave from their patrons of Albemarle, could freely elect as Prior whomsoever they would, and, the election made, they were used only to present their elect to the said patrons, who at such time of vacancy challenged no other right; but whereas the Priory held of their patrons in chief six carucates and a half of land, in the mean time they were seized, though they received nothing else therefrom; and when the Prior is installed he pays the accustomed relief for the said carucates.

[M. 3.]

LETTER from Philip de Wylegeby to R. Burnel, Bishop-elect of Bath, Chancellor. Whereas by the King's letter I lately received in command, that by honest and lawful men of my bailiwick, I should cause inquiry to be made concerning the state of custody and mode of electing a Prior of Boulton in Cravene, at time of vacancy, and in the time of their patrons, formerly lords of Albemarle, the tenor of which I have executed in full, as by the inquisition sealed with the seals of the jurors directed to you hereupon more fully is contained, who say by their oath that the lords of Albemarle at the time of vacancy of the Priory, neither challenged nor ought to challenge any right, save that they sent their man to guard the gates of the Priory, as their warden or janitor, and to defend them against those coming, and from enemies. Of other articles contained in the King's writ, by the inquisition thereof transmitted to you, you may be fully certified. Farewell in the Lord.

[M. 4.]

AND whereas certain things seemed to need inquiry beyond the tenor of the King's letter, I inquired by my office, namely: Whereas it is the custom of every lordship that the tenants in their several changes have seisin of their fee, until it appears who is the next heir and has a better right in that tenement, what did they do in their surrenders for the tenement which they held of the lords of Albemarle, and how much did they hold.

The jury said that they held six carucates of the said lords, and only paid relief out of them as was fitting, the lords receiving nothing else from them.

Asked[a] also whether they were in the habit of giving anything to the said lords at their admission, for according to what
I heard related, five had given; whether such payment was
made by way of amends for any offence committed, such as
coming, to election without asking leave, or that they might as a
benefit obtain greater grace in conducting their own affairs
before the lords of Albemarle, the answer was—that they were
unable to inquire whether they should give any money to the
lords. If they did so, this was rather by way of obtaining the
benevolence of the lords, than any thing which they had of right
so to pay to them.

What will appear upon these points and others in the sealed
inquisition transmitted to you, let your circumspect judgment
discern.   Farewell in the Lord.

LXXXIV., JOHN DE BOULTON. *Land given by his father to
Malton Priory.*

[3 EDW. I. No. 79.]

Writ directed to Philip de Wylegeby, Escheator beyond Trent, that John de
Boulton[b] had shown to the King, that when Thomas de Boulton, his
father, was on the point of death and his mind unsound *(dum laboraret
in extremis non sane mentis)*, he gave to the Prior and Convent of
Malton, in perpetual almoyne, certain land in Swynton[c] which
he held of John Paynel, who held of the King in chief; and the
Escheator had taken that land into the King's hand; but the Prior, by
colour of a letter for again having seisin, had regained it. If Thomas
had aliened the land in the manner stated, the land to be again taken
into the King's hand and safely kept. Dated at Windsor, 8 Feb., 3rd
year (1274-5).

INQUISITION made at York, on Wednesday after the feast of
the Annunciation of the B.V.M., 3rd year[d] (27 March, 1275),

---

[a] The original of this part of the inquisition reads as follows:—"Requisiti
eciam utrum aliquid consueverunt conferre dominis predictis in sua admissione,
secundum quod audivi referre, quod quinque contulerant; utrum talis collacio
facta fuit propter emendacionem delicti quod commiserant, scilicet ad eleccionem
veniendo licencia non petita, an ut majorem graciam in suis agendis coram dictis
dominis Albemarlie ut feod' optinerent.   Responsum fuit quod inquirere non
potuerunt, quod aliquam pecuniam (pec'ciam) predictis dominis conferrent.   Et si
aliquam conferrent, hoc pocius fuit benivolenciam dominorum captando, quam
aliquid pro jure quod habebant eisdem conferendo.   Quid super hiis et aliis in
inquisicione consignata vobis transmissa videbitur, vestra circumspecta descernat
discrecio. Valeat in Domino.

[b] On 7 Jan., 1274-5, Philip de Wyleby, Escheator beyond Trent, was ordered
to seize into the King's hand the lands of which Thomas de Boulton died seised in
chief.   His son and heir paid homage for them on 15 Feb. following *(Rot. Fin.,* 3
Edw. I., mm. 37, 34).

[c] Swinton, two and a quarter miles from Malton, in the parish of Appleton-le-
Street.

[d] The year of the reign is omitted.

before Adam de Agmodesham, sub-escheator in the County of York, by Sir Robert de Bulford, Robert Gillinge, John de Besingeby, Bernard de Appelton, Richard de Saint Oswald, John de Charpenville in Ampelford, Robert de Helmesleye in Stytun,[a] Peter de Thadecastre, Hugh son of Gilbert of Eymunderby, Bernard de Stoketon, Richard Marshall *(Marescall')*, and Walter Brut, sworn, who say that when Thomas de Boulton was labouring at Yarpesthorp[b] with some infirmity from which he did not recover *(qua non evaluit ante mortem)*, and in want of money, he sold his manor of Swynton for eleven score marcs[c] and ten [shillings], to the Prior of Malton, who received seisin thereof. And they say that although the said Thomas was at the point of death, he was nevertheless of sound mind.[d] He held the manor of John Paynel, and John Paynel held of the King in chief.

LXXXV.   JOHN DE NUTTLE (NUTTEL).   *Inq. p. m.*

[3 EDW. I. No. 18.]

Writ dated at Westminster, 27 April, 3rd year (1275).

INQUISITION made at Humbleton, on Monday after the Invention of the Holy Cross, 3 Edward (6 May, 1275), before Sir Simon Constable *(d'no Simon' Constabular')*, in place of Sir Philip de Wilgeby, Escheator beyond Trent, by Stephen son of John of Hedon, Henry de Preston, Stephen de Oustwike, Simon de Lund, Geoffrey de Sprothele, William de Grimestone, Thomas de Neuton, Henry de Wryneton, Roger of the same, Nicholas Warde, Thomas de Humbelton, and Alan *le Oyselyur*, who say that John de Nuttel held of the Honour of Heudrenesse in chief, on the day of his death, two carucates of land in the town and territory of Nuttel,[e] whereof forty-eight carucates make a knight's fee. They are worth by the year £10, do suit[f]

---

[a] Steeton, or perhaps Stittenham.

[b] Easthorpe, in the township and parish of Appleton-le-Street. Called in Kirkby's *Inquest*, Yarpesthorp.

[c] " Pro xj marcis ;" "x" visible over the "xj," but apparently first corrected and then some words erased.

[d] " Et dicunt per sacramentum suum, quod, etsi predictus Thomas in extremis laboraret, tamen compos mentis fuit."

[e] Nuthill, three miles from Hedon, in the township of Burstwick and parish of Skeckling.

[f] The original of this is as follows :—" Et faciunt sectam ad Wapentag' de Heudrenesse de tribus septimanis in tres septimanas, et reddunt liberum forinsecum servicium per preceptum domini Regis quando accidit."

at the Wapentake-court of Heudrenessé from three weeks to
three weeks, and by the King's command render free foreign
service when it falls due.

He held no other lands in chief, either of the King or any
other person ; and Peter,[a] his son, is his next heir, aged twenty-
one years and more.

LXXXVI.   ANDREW LE GRAMMARE, *a Jewry Debtor.*

[3 EDW. I. No. 38.]

Writ dated at Westminster, 24 May, 3rd year (1275).

INQUISITION made as to what lands and tenements Andrew
le Grammare has in the County of York, by Elias Burel,
Thomas Aleways of Merstone, Richard son of William of the
same, Robert Page of Tockewythe, William de Hull in Bilton,
Adam Turpyn in Tockewythe, Henry Sakespey, John de Per-
lington in Aberford, John *le Marescall,* and Richard son of Moy,
who say upon their oath that the said Andrew has in the town
of Bykerton [b] his capital messuage, worth by the year 10s. ; 37
acres of arable land in demesne (12d. the acre); a plot of
meadow *(quamdam placeam prati),* 4s. 6d. ; 18 acres of meadow
in demesne, two marcs 40d. ; pasture in Northeberre, half a
marc ; meadow in a certain croft, 3s. ; pasture of wood half a
marc by the year.   He has also in the same town rent of six
marcs which Henry de Normanton holds for the term of 20
years; and other rent, viz., 2s from Thomas at Town-head *(ad
capud ville) ;* one pair of gloves or a halfpenny ; 12d. from
Thomas de Bykerton yearly; in Abberford 2½d., and a plot
(placeam) of meadow there, worth by the year 4s. ; also in
Beckehathe [c] a messuage with croft worth by the year 4s. ; also
63 acres now lying untilled (3d. the acre), pasture half a marc
and herbage of wood 12d. by the year.   Sum, £10 12s. 6d.

---

[a] In the early spring of 1274-5, Peter de Nuttle, son and heir of John de Nuttle,
paid fealty for the lands his father died seised of in chief, and Philip de Wilgheby,
the Escheator *ultra,* was ordered, on getting security for payment of a reasonable
sum, to give up the lands to the heir *(Rot Fin.,* 3 Edw. I., m. 27).

[b] Bickerton (Ainsty), four miles N.E. of Wetherby, in the parish of Bilton.

[c] Aberford and Becca, about eleven miles N.E. of Leeds, Mr. Scaife (Kirkby's
Inquest, p. 36 n) gives the following note about these two places.   "About 1270,
' Andreas filius dom. Ricardi le Gramarie ' granted to John, son of Alan Sampson
of York, the sites of certain wind and water mills at ' Abberford et Beckhawe '
(MSS. Dodsworth, CLIX., 205).   His widow, Elizabeth, was living in 1292 " *(Ibid.,*
206).

[On another small membrane to this effect.]
YORKSHIRE.
The land of Andrew Gramary with capital messuage is extended by command of the King at £10 12s. 6d., as appears by the particulars of the inquisition in Chancery, in which sum the capital messuage is extended at 10s.; whereof, according to the King's statutes,[a] they assign to the Jew who demands his debt from him, 101s. 3d. out of his land.[a]

LXXXVII. HOSPITAL OF S. NICHOLAS YORK.

[3 Edw. I. No. 55.]

Writ dated at Windsor, 17 July, 3rd year (1275), recited in the preamble to the inquisition annexed.

THE King sent to Gwychard de Charrum and William de Northburgh, that whereas it was shown on behalf of the Master and Brethren of the Hospital of S. Nicholas, York, that one carucate of land and one acre and a half of meadow in the suburb of the City of York, were provided for the support of lepers coming to the Hospital by the ancestors of the King, and confirmed by them, and that they and their predecessors had peacefully held the land and meadow from the time when they were first enfeoffed, until Robert de Creppinge, sometime Sheriff of Yorkshire[b] in the late King Henry's time, ejected them unjustly and without judgment, so that that meadow had been withheld by him and other Sheriffs of Yorkshire for twenty years, to the no mean damage of the said Master and Brethren and their manifest disinherison.—Now Robert de Creppinge, called by the said Gwychard and William, says that while he was Sheriff of Yorkshire, he saw that the acre and a half of meadow abutted upon the King's vivary of Fosse, so that at every inundation of the water the meadow was covered; and because he saw that if the King should wish to move his mills, then beneath the Castle, and to raise the head of his vivary, that meadow would be under water every hour of the year. He believed, as some of the Wapentake of Bulmere gave him to understand, that the meadow appertained to the King, and for

[a] " Unde secundum statutum domini Regis, Judeo qui debitum exigit ab eodem, competunt cjs. et iijd. terre ejusdem." No. xci., is another inquisition under the same statute.
[b] Robert de Creppinge was Sheriff from the last half of 34 Hen. III. up to and including the first half of 38 Hen. III., that is from the spring of 1250 to the same season in 1253.

that reason he seized it into the King's hand and held it so long
as he was Sheriff of the County, and all the Sheriffs up to now
have done the same.

INQUISITION is made by men as well of the City as of the
suburb *(surburbio)* of the same, namely, by the oath of
Walter de Grymeston, John Verdenel, William de Malton,
William de Roston, Peter Walding, Alexander Tailor *(cissoris)*,
Nicholas son of Hugh, Thomas de Nafferton, Simon Everard,
John de Dalton, William Long *(le lung)*, and Thomas Clerk
(clerici), who say upon their oath that the said carucate of land
and the meadow are not, and never were, of ancient demesne of
the crown ; nor were they ever farmed at the King's Exchequer.
They say that the Empress Maud, formerly Queen of England,
bought the carucate of land and the meadow, and gave them
to the said Hospital and Brethren on this condition—that they
would for ever find for all lepers coming to that Hospital, on
the eve of SS. Peter and Paul (28th June), the victuals under-
written, that is to say : bread and ale, mullet *(muluellum)* with
butter, salmon when it could be had, and cheese. By this
service and by no other do they hold that land and meadow.
    Asked whether the meadow appertains to the carucate of
land, they say it is so. They say also that the carucate of land
is worth every year six marcs and a half, and the meadow every
year one marc.

LXXXVIII.   HOSPITAL OF ST. NICHOLAS, YORK.

[3 EDW. I.   No. 76.]

No writ.

INQUISITION made between the King of the one part, and the
Master and·Brethren of the Hospital of S. Nicholas, York,
of the other part, by Walter [de Gryme]ston of York, William
de Melton of the same, Alexander Tailor *(cissorem)* of the same,
William Long *(longum)* of the same, Thomas de Nafferton of the
same, William de Roston of the same, Robert son of Benedict
of Hewrde, Thomas de Hoton of the same, Michael de Hewrde,
John Neubonde of the same, Peter de Dicton of the same, and
William de Wyuestowe.   They say that the good Queen of
England, Maud, gave to the Master and Brethren of the said
Hospital, one carucate of land with one acre and a half of
meadow in the fields of the suburb of the City of York—which
gift was confirmed by King Stephen—to feed all the lepers of

the County of York, coming thither by custom on the eve of the Apostles Peter and Paul, for the souls of all their ancestors and successors; and they were in seisin of the meadow aforesaid from the time of the said good Queen Maud, up to the second time that Robert de Creppinge was Sheriff of Yorkshire, when he disseised them thereof, and held it for the use of his own horses; and so every Sheriff, one after the other, has withheld it. The meadow is worth by the year half a marc; and the disseisin has continued for twenty years and more.

LXXXIX. ALAN DE KYNTHORP.

[3 EDW. I. No. 11.]

Writ dated at Oxford, 6 Aug., 3rd year (1275).

INQUISITION[a] made before Sir Philip de Willeby, Escheator, by Peter de Gayola, ... de Adbriston, William Malcake, Robert *del le Clif*, Ralph de Loketon, Richard Erchebaud, Nicholas de Levesham, Alan de Sandesby, John son of Oda (?), Philip de Adbristan, John son of Robert, and John Campiun, who say upon their oath that Alan de Kynthorp and *Petronilla* (Parnell) his wife, held one messuage and four bovates of land, with the appurtenances, and one windmill in the town of Folcardby,[b] and rents of freemen and bondmen *(bondorum)*, 20s. 9d., by the gift of John de Crachalle, father of said Parnell, in marriage, which land was of the serjeanty of Emma, daughter of Alan Wasthose[c] of Snaythte; and whereas the land of Folkardby was aliened by Emma, who sold it to John de Crakehale, therefore it was farmed to the King at 40s. by the year, and he died no otherwise in homage of the King: which land Parnell holds because it was given to Alan with her in marriage. The messuage, four bovates, and mill are worth by the year £6 8s., of which Alan paid to Sir John de Eyvile 6s. 8d. yearly for suit of his men of Athelyngflet at Alan's mill of Folcardby.

---

a This inquisition is very difficult to read on account of being discoloured with a wash now turned brown. On 17 July, 1275, Philip de Wileby, the Escheator beyond Trent, was ordered to seize the lands of which Alan de Kinthorp died seised in chief *(Rot. Fin.,* 3 Edw. I., m. 17). See also No. xcviii.

b Fockerby, in the parish of Adlingfleet.

c See No. xxvii., where it appears that Emma Wasthose was dead before 13 Feb., 1250-1. The serjeanty by which Emma Wastehose (the ancestress of Alice, daughter of John de Cunthorpe) held twelve bovates of land in chief in Folkardeby, was by carrying the King's breakfast through the country *(cariandi jentaculum domini Regis per patriam)* which was commuted at 40s., payable at the Exchequer *(Yorkshire Assize Rolls,* Hilary, 21 Edw. I. (1292-3), No. 1101, m. 78).

Also the said Alan held of the lord Edmund [the King's brother][a] three carucates of land, with the appurtenances, in Kynthorp,[b] after that the lord Henry, King of England, father of Edmund, gave to him the manor of Pyk', with the appurtenances, and [Alan] held the land by the service of keeping the forest of Pykering *(per servicium faciendi custodiam foreste de Pyk'),* and it is worth with the mill 12*s.* and three pounds of cumin *(cymini)* and one pound of pepper, and he yielded to the lord Edmund 20*s.* yearly for his bailiwick.

Also Alan held in Ellerburne[c] 20 . . . . . one watermill, and six bovates of land of the Hospital of Saint Leonard at York, yielding yearly 10*s.*, and they are worth by the year £ . . 10*s.* 10*d.* and one pound of cumin.

He held in Ellerburne, of the Knights Templars, for 13*d.*, one toft worth yearly 3*s.* ; and in Thornton,[d] of Acilia Mauraunt, by knight service, eight bovates, eight acres of land, worth yearly £6 2*s.*

Petronilla (or Parnell), daughter of Geoffrey, son of Alan de Kynthorp, is his next heir, and aged eight years.

XC. THOMAS BUSTARD. *Inq. p. m.*

[3 EDW. I. No. 22.]

Writ dated at Achestone, 22 Sept., 3rd year (1275).[e]

INQUISITION made at York, on Wednesday after the feast of S. Michael, 3 Edward (2 Oct., 1275), by Richard son of Hugh of Akastre, William son of Ingelram of Torp, Henry Clerk *(clericum),* Alexander son of William of Torp, Alexander son of John of the same, Henry son of Roger of the same, Henry White *(album),* William Hill *(de monte),* Robert Wisman, Adam de Pole, Robert Cusin, Hugh Hill *(de monte),* who say upon their oath that Thomas Bustard[f] held on the day of his

---

[a] Edmund Crouchback, Earl of Chester, Lancaster, and Leicester.

[b] Kinthorpe, in the parish of Pickering.

[c] Ellerburn, near Pickering. According to No. xcviii., he held the capital messuage here.

[d] Thornton Dale.

[e] Note on dorse that the writ came to York, 30 Sept. "Venit breve Ebor. in crastino S. Michaelis." Achestone, where it was tested, is between La Launde and Geytinton.

[f] No doubt descended from Osbert Bustard, who was living at Thorp by York, as it was then called, about 1180, when he had six bovates granted to him there, by Richard, Abbot of Whitby *(Whitby Chartulary,* vol. i., pp. 6, 227). "Osbertus de Torp, pater Roberti Bustard," gave land in Littlegate, York, to the Canons of

death one messuage fifteen bovates of land in Biscupthorp, for four marcs yearly, to be paid to the King ; four bovates of land in Ingramthorp,[a] of the Abbot of Witeby, for 20s. yearly ; and one messuage with eight bovates of land in Bustardthorp,[b] of Davit Lardiner (*Lard'*), for 7s. The lands of the said Thomas are worth in all issues, 100s.

Robert son of Thomas is his heir, aged twenty-four years.[c]

XCI. JOHN DE EYVILLE.[d] *A Jewry debtor.*

[3 EDW. I. No. 63.]

Writ dated at Westminster, 27 May, 3rd year (1275), ordering the Justices assigned for the custody of the Jews, that after searching their rolls and chirographers' chests of Jewry, in the presence of Paytefain, son of Benedict the Jew, if he wish to be present, they should cause to be shown *(purari)* all the debts in which John de Eyvylle is bound to the said Jew ; also in the presence of Master Elias and Salomon son of Salomon, Jews of London, all debts in which the same John is bound to Elyas Blunt, late a Jew of London, which, after his death, came (as it is said) to us and the said Master Elyas and Salomon, namely, as well net as of penalties *(tam de claro quam de penis)*, and usury appertaining to those debts, and that they should send the return made under seal, and return the writ.

Another writ dated at Westminster, 15 June, 3rd year (1275).

EXTENT of the lands and tenements of John de Eyville, in the County of York, made on Wednesday before the feast of S. Wilfrid, 3 Edw. (9 Oct., 1275), before Alexander de Kirketon, Sheriff of the County, by William de Buscy, Marmaduke Darel, knights, John de Neuby, Nicholas de Cneton, Gilbert de Iselbec, Ranulf de Dalton, William son of the Clerk *(fil' clerici)*, Hugh Ke, Michael de Boske (?),[e] Robert Wygot, Adam de Hoton, and John Oliver.

----

[a] Ingramthorpe, which seems to have been a small place in the neighbourhood of Bishopthorpe, no longer exists.

[b] All traces of this place have disappeared. See note to No. LXIX.

[c] He paid fealty for his father's lands on 22 Oct., 1275. They had been ordered to be seized on 23 Sept. previous (*Rot. Fin.*, 3 Edw. I., mm. 9, 12).

[d] No doubt the same person as the John de Eyville who was one of the last amongst the adherents of Simon de Montfort to yield to the royal authority. After the disastrous battle of Evesham, he set up a fortified camp at Ely, and issuing forth thence, plundered Lincoln and Norwich, carrying off the Jews and rich citizens for the sake of their ransoms.~ He was driven out of the Isle of Ely in July, 1267, by Prince Edward, and managed to escape and join the Earl of Gloucester, who was holding London against the King. He shared in the general pacification of the kingdom, which was shortly afterwards brought about by the enactment of the Provisions of Westminster. Some of the above-named debts very possibly arose from expenses and fines imposed in relation to this rebellion.

[e] Probably a form of Boscar Grange, a farm about a mile N.E. of Raskelfe village.

THORENTON ON SWALE.[a]

	Annual value. £	s.	d.
Demesne messuage	0	2	0
Demesne land, 104 acres (at 6d.)	2	12	0
Meadow, 30½ acres (at 2s. 6d.)	3	16	3
Mill and fishery	6	13	4
Services of freemen	1	4	4
Bondmen and cottars	9	19	0½
Underwood half a marc	0	6	8
	£24	13	7½

THORENTON ON THE HILL.[b]

	£	s.	d.
Demesne messuage	0	10	0
Demesne land, 74 acres (at 6d.)	1	17	0
Meadow, 3 acres (at 3s.)	0	9	0
Service of freemen	0	12	0
Mill, 13 marcs	8	13	4
Bondmen and cottars	5	0	0
	£17	1	4

KILBURNE.

	£	s.	d.
Demesne messuage	0	6	8
Demesne land, 57 acres (at 4d.)	0	19	0
Meadow, 14 acres (at 2s.)	1	8	0
Mill, 20s.	1	0	0
Services of freemen	0	1	6
Bondmen and cottars	4	12	0
Parks and vivaries	0	6	8
	£7	5	8 [c]

ATHELINGFLET.

	£	s.	d.
Demesne messuage	0	6	8
Demesne land, four carucates	15	0	0
Services of freemen	0	15	0
Bondmen and cottars	10	0	0
Meadow, 16 acres (at 2s. 6d.)	2	0	0
	£28	1	8
Sum total,	£77	2	3½

[a] Thornton Bridge, on the Swale, in the parish of Brafferton.

[b] Thornton-on-the-Hill, in the township of Thornton-with-Baxby and parish of Coxwold.

[c] The sum of items comes to £8 13s. 10d.; however, the £7 5s. 8d. given in the inquisition agrees with the sum total at the end.

XCII. NICHOLAS, SON OF SIR ANKETIN MALORE.[a] *Inq. p. m.*

[3 EDW. I. No. 12.]

No writ.

INQUISITION made of the lands and tenements formerly of Nicholas, son of Sir Anketin Malore, deceased, on the morrow of S. Leonard the Abbot, 3 Edward (7 Nov., 1275), before Philip de Wyllecheby, Escheator, at York, by twelve freemen, namely : by William Thorny of Tyverington,[b] Patrick de Stytelu[m],[c] Robert Hamelake of the same, Richard Thorny of Wygenthorpe, Robert de Maners of Stytelum, Ralph de Hoton, dwelling in Stytelum, Robert de Clifforde, William de Langetwayte, Robert *Marescall* of Thadcastre, Hugh de Brenkel of Neuton Kyme, John de Oscum of the same, Richard Maunsel of Tyverington, who say that the said Nicholas held in demesne on the day of his death, six bovates of land in North Dalton[d] of the King in chief by serjeanty, worth by the year six marcs, out of which 20s. are paid yearly to the King.

He held also in demesne :—

In Multhorpe[e] three carucates of land of the heirs of Sir Andrew Luttrell by free service, worth by the year £17 10s. 10d.

In Tyverington, of the same fee and for the same service, eleven bovates of land and one watermill, worth by the year £7 6s.; and the advowson of the church of Tyverington, which when void, is worth 40s.

---

[a] On 19 Sept., 1275, the Escheator beyond Trent was commanded to seize the lands of Anketin Malore, his son and heir, Nicholas, having died whilst in the custody of Peter de Chauvente, to whom his guardianship had been granted by the King *(Rot. Fin.,* 3 Edw. I., m. 12). The King, on 23 Nov., 1275, being then at the Tower of London, took the homage of Ralph Salveyn and Margery, his wife, of William Burdun and Avice his wife, of Nicholas de Wolkesthorpe (called above Oclestorpe) and Nicholaa, his wife, and William de Clenton (called above Glenton) and Sarra, his wife, the wives being the sisters and heiresses of Nicholas Malore. A partition was made at the same time between the heiresses *(Ibid.,* 4 Edw. I., m. 32). On 8 Oct., 1287, Thomas de Normanville, Escheator beyond Trent, was ordered to seize into the King's hand the lands of Anketin Salveyn, son and heir of Margery, wife of Ralph Salveyn, deceased *(Ibid.,* 15 Edw. I., m. 3). On 10 June, 1288, the same Escheator was ordered to seize into the King's hand the lands of Sarra, daughter of Anketin Malore, deceased *(Ibid.,* 16 Edw. I., m. 10). From an entry on a *De Banco Roll (Mich.* 6 Edw. II. (1312), m. 105), about the advowson of the church of Terrington, there called Deverington, which William, son of William le Latimer, claimed against Milo de Stapelton, it appears that Nicholas Malore had an elder brother, Anketin, who died without issue, and that William le Latimer, the father, had been enfeoffed in the advowson by William Burdon and Avice his wife *(The Antiquary,* vol. xxi., p. 22).

[b] Terrington.

[c] Stittenham. *Domesday,* Stidnun. In Kirkby's *Inquest,* Stytenom, Stytnam.

[d] North Dalton, seven and a quarter miles S.W. of Driffield.

[e] Mowthorpe and Wigginthorpe, in the parish of Terrington.

In Wygenthorpe, of the same fee and for the same service, two marcs annual rent.

In Huntington,[a] of the same fee and for the same service, 2s. 6d. annual rent.

In Clifforde,[b] of the fee of the lord Peter de Mauley (de Malo lacu), three carucates of land by free service, worth by the year £10 17s. 4d.

Marjory, wife of Ralph Salvayn, Avice, wife of William Burdon, Nicholaa, wife of Nicholas de Oclestorpe, and Sarra, wife of William de Glenton, are his next heirs and of full age.

XCIII. JOHN DE BOSSALE. *Common of Pasture.*

[3 EDW. I. No. 58.]

Writ dated 28 October, 3rd year (1275), and addressed to Geoffrey de Neville, Justice of the King's forest beyond Trent.

INQUISITION made on S. Martin's Day, 3 Edw. (11 Nov., 1275), by the verderers, regarders (*rewardatores*), and other ministers of the forest of Gautris—whether John de Bozhale (Bossale in writ) ought to have, or his predecessors were wont to have, common of pasture in Sandeburne,[c] which is within the metes of the pasture (forest in writ) of Gautris, yielding yearly to the Justice (*Justiciar'*) of the said forest for the time being 3s., from the time of Brian de Insula—who say by their oath that the predecessors of the said John have been always used to have from the time of the said Brian, and the said John yet ought to have common in the pasture of Sandburne, except Land',[d] namely, from Palm Sunday to the feast of S. Michael, every year; and from the feast of S. Michael to Palm Sunday, as well in Land' as without, for 3s. paid yearly to the Justice of the forest in the name of herbage (*nomine erbag'*).

[a] Huntington, near York.

[b] Clifford, in the parish of Bramham.

[c] Sandburn Wood and Sandburn House, in the parish of Stockton-on-the Forest, about two miles east of Sand Hutton Hall.

[d] Probably the Launds or Lawns, clear spaces in a forest.

XCIV. THE BURGESSES OF SCARBOROUGH.
Rents of Houses and Mills.

[3 EDW. I. No. 94.]

Writ dated at Westminster 8 Nov., 1275, and addressed to Robert de Neville, Gwychard de Charrum, William de Northburgh, Ranulf de Dacre, and Alexander de Kyrketon. Reciting that it had been shown to the King on behalf of his men of Scarborough (Scardeburg'), that they have of their own moneys built certain houses and mills there, and that they have, with the common consent and assent of the commonalty of the same, spent a great part of the rents of the same, and of other rents paid for drying nets on their grounds *(fundis)* and for common of pasture (of which they had been accustomed to receive the profit for their own use), towards the keeping up of the quay *(kayi)* of the port of the same town, and have expended the residue of the same rents sometimes in satisfying the farm rents due from the said town to the King, which were not sufficient in themselves, and sometimes by assigning them to other objects for the good of the town ; and that the Sheriff of Yorkshire, by reason of having seised the same town into the King's hand, seised all the aforesaid rents, together with the true and ancient farm of the same town, whereby the quay of the same port had utterly fallen down, and many houses of the same town, through the quay not being repaired, had been destroyed and thrown down by the raging of the sea *(per maris intemperiem)*, and persons arriving at the same port were in great danger, to the ruin and impoverishment of the whole of the same town. The King, wishing to be informed as to whether the said rents belonged to the farm of the town or to the demesne of the said men, assigned Robert de Neville and the others to inquire by the oaths of honest and lawful men of the County of York, by whom the truth of the matter may be the better known, whether the said rents belong to the said farm or to the demesne of the men of Scarborough ; and if to the said farm, how and by what reason ; and if to the demesne of the said men, from what cause, how, in what manner, and by what warrant. Therefore they (the Commissioners), or three of them, were commanded to make the said inquisition on a certain day and place, to be fixed on beforehand, and to send it sealed with their seals and with the seals of those making the inquisition, together with this writ, to the King. The Sheriff, on being informed of the day and place, is commanded to collect together a sufficient number of honest and lawful men for making the inquisition.

INQUISITION made before Sirs *(d'nis)*, Robert de Neville, William de Northburgh, and Alexander de Kyrketon, at York, on the morrow of S. Benedict the Abbot, 4th year (March 22, 1275-6), by the oath of William de S. Quintin, Geoffrey Agwylon, William de Brigham, James Moor *(de Mora)*, James de Friville, Robert de Fritheby, knights, Thomas de Odbreston,[a] Bartholomew de Scalleby, Matthew de Claphov,[b] Robert de Kayton, William de Schireburne, Robert de Wyerne, Geoffrey de Menythorpe, William de Yedingham, Roger de Morpathe, William *de la Chymene*, Peter *de la Gayole*, and John de Friboys, as to whether the rents of certain houses and mills built with the moneys of the Burgesses of Scarborough, as they

[a] Usually written Edbriston, now Ebberston.
[b] More commonly Glaphou.

say, and the rents for drying nets on the grounds *(fundis)*, and common of pasture of the same Burgesses, belong to the farm of Scarborough (Scardeburgh') due to the King, or to the demesne of the said Burgesses ; they say that the rents of certain houses newly placed between the quay *(le Kay)* and the wall of the Borough of Scarborough ; and the rents of two water-mills . . . . nnesdale newly built, and constructed out of the moneys of the said Burgesses ; and the rent of a wind-mill . . . . Wallesgrave[a] and Scarborough, newly built out of the moneys of the said Burgesses ; and also the rent of a house the said Burgesses bought of William, son of Thomas of Lindeberge, belong, and ought to belong, to the demesne of the said Burgesses (the profits whereof they have been accustomed, and ought to take for their own use), and not to the farm of the said town ; saving to the King the ancient gabelage *(gabulagio)* from the tenements on which the three mills are placed, that is for the site of each, 4*d.* ; and saving to the King 6*d.* a year from the house bought from the said William ; saving also to the King the rent for drying nets on the moat and on the rear-mound[b] of the Castle of Scarborough. As to how, and in what manner, and by what warrant, they say that King Henry III. granted by a charter to the said Burgesses the Borough of Scarborough for ever, on paying £66 of silver at the Exchequer in London, every year at Michaelmas. He also granted to the said Burgesses by another charter, that they might lawfully build and approve the waste places within the bounds of the said Borough, belonging to the said Burgesses and their tenements, as they should think best for themselves and their Borough. The same King also gave and granted to the said Burgesses his manor of Wallesgrave, with its appurtenances, to the enlargement of their Borough, to be approved as should seem to them best, as appears by the charter of the said King which they have about it, by paying annually £25 sterling to the said Exchequer on the said feast.

[a] Falsgrave.

[b] *Retrodunam*, a word of doubtful meaning and form. The *dun* or *duna* may be the L. Lat. *dunjo, dunho, dungo,* a donjon or dungeon, the words being etymologically the same. It may however be, and probably is, connected with the word *dun,* a hill, which is so often met with in place names.

XCV. JOHN DE WARENNE, EARL OF SURREY. *Toll of Tenants of the Archbishop of Canterbury.*

[4 EDW. I. No. 90.]

No writ.

INQUISITION made at Thikehull, Co. York, on Thursday the morrow of the Annunciation of Our Lady, 4 Edward (26 March, 1276), before J. de Lovetot, and associated with him Master Reymund de Nolmeriis,[a] and William Clarel, by William Russel, Simon Eshiuet, William de Erdeslowe, Peter de Waleton, Henry de Emmelye, John de Kirkeby, Hugh Marmion, Adam de Thofteclive, Robert de Storthes, Adam de Waddesworthe, Henry de Rissheworthe, John de Miggelye, Adam de Miggelye, James *(Jakob')* de Metelay, Roger son of Malger of Wytewode, Gilbert Rouland, Robert Binny, John Belle, Michael Clerk *(clericum)*, Simon de Ramenesfelde,[b] William de Keueton, John Bernard, Alexander de Clifton, Richard Gervase, William Gervase, Hugh Malet, William de Mondider, William de Endale, William son of Robert, John Jordan', and Adam de Crawell, jurors, upon the value of the toll of men and tenants of the venerable father R., Archbishop of Canterbury,[c] and also of men and tenants of the same men, and of all others frequenting *(conversancium in)* the lands of the Archbishop, and coming yearly to markets or fairs whatsoever of the King's beloved and faithful John de Warenne, Earl of Surrey, in the County of York, and plying any merchandize whatsoever therein *(et in eisdem mercandisas qualitercunque exercencium)* ; and besides concerning toll of men and tenants, &c. (as before) in the fees and lands of the Prior and Convent of Christ Church, Canterbury, coming yearly to the same markets or fairs, and plying merchandize therein. They say upon their oath that the toll of all the men aforesaid, coming to the markets and fairs of Wakefelde yearly, is worth every year five marcs.[d]

---

[a] Nolm'iis.

[b] Query, for Ravenesfelde.

[c] Robert Kilwardby, Archbishop, 1273-1279.

[d] In the same file are like inquiries concerning toll of markets or fairs of the same Earl, in the Counties of Lincoln, Norfolk, Sussex, and Surrey, and in London.

XCVI. ROGER LE BYGOD, EARL OF NORFOLK AND

MARSHAL OF ENGLAND.[a] *Suit to the Court of Thornton in Pickering Lythe.*

[4 EDW. I. No. 85.]

Writ directed to Thomas de Normanvyle, the King's Steward, and dated at Merleberg', 7 Feb., 4th year (1275-6).

INQUISITION made at Thorneton, before the King's bailiff there, on Tuesday after Palm Sunday, 4 Edw. (31 March, 1276), by Thomas de Pokthorpe, Bartholomew de Skalleby, Gilbert de Rillington, Robert de Cliffe, William de Yrton, Roger de Morpathe, Roger de Aton, John de Cayton, Alan son of Andrew, Alan son of John, Hugh Brun (or Brown) and Roger de Wrelleton—if Roger le Bygot, Earl of Norfolk and Marshal of England, or his ancestors, tenants of the manor of Levescam,[b] used at any time to do suit at the Court of Thorneton in Pykeringlithe (formerly of William, Earl of Albemarle, and his heirs, and now in the King's hand), for the said manor or not. They say that neither Roger le Bygot nor his ancestors ever did suit at the Court of Thorneton, for the manor of Levescam, but one Osebert de Bolebeke[c] who formerly held the manor in the time of William de Fortibus, Earl of Albemarle, last deceased, did suit at the said court, until Hugh de *(sic)* Bygot, father of the said Earl, was enfeoffed of the manor, but how and by what warrant the suit for the manor was afterwards withdrawn, the jurors know not.

[*By endorsement.*] Inquisicio ad mandatum domini Regis in Curia de Thornton facta super sectam domini Rogeri Bigot Comitis Norfolch' exigita *(sic)* in eadem Curia de Thornton pro manerio de Levesham in comitatu Ebor' per breve.[d]

---

[a] Son of Sir Hugh le Bigot, and nephew and heir of Roger le Bigot, Earl of Norfolk. Aged about 25, in 54 Hen. III., when the *Inq. p. m.* of his uncle was taken (*Cal. Gen.*, vol. i., p. 143). Paid homage to the King for his uncle's lands, on 25 July, 1270 (*Excerpta è Rotulis Finium*, vol. ii., p. 519). Married Alyna, daughter and heiress of Philip Basset (*Ibid.*, vol. ii., p. 554).

[b] Levesham, near Pickering.

[c] See No. XLIII.

[d] Two other writs, relating to customs and services in the County of Norfolk. On the back of the second is a list of persons, who are plaintiffs in one suit and defendants in another, with the same Earl.

XCVII. JOAN DE STUTEVILE.[a] *Inq. p. m.*

[4 EDW. I. No. 49.]

Writ dated at Lincoln, 6 April, 4th year (1276).

[M. 3.]

EXTENT made of the manor of Kirkeby Moresheved,[b] on Wednesday next after the close of Easter *(post clausum Pasch')*, 4th year (15 April, 1276), by Sir John de Bulford, John Abraham', Nicholas de Fadmore, Richard son of Ysaund, Robert his brother, William Monk *(monacum)* of Heddestone,[c] John son of Roger of the same, Nicholas Gi . . . y of Fadmore, Robert *le Norais* of Kirkeby, William Laundaille of Holme, William *in le Wra* of Kirkeby, and Nicholas Boulay, who say upon their oath that the said manor, with the garden and herbage in the park, is worth 20s. a year without the arable land and sale of wood. There are nineteen score acres of of arable land in demesne belonging to the manor (at 6d. an acre). Sum, £9 11s. Seven score acres of meadow (at 12d.). Sum, £7. A certain piece *(placea)* of pasture in demesne, worth 10s. a year. Herbage in the moor half a marc. Wood may be sold annually to the amount of 15s. A dove-cote *(columbarium)* by estimation 3s. a year. Sum of sums, £19 5s. 8d.

Freeholders *(liberi tenentes)*, pay 17s., two pounds of cumin, worth 2d., and a pound of pepper, worth 6d. Sum, 17s. 8d., from freemen. Fifty-one bovates in bondage (at half a marc a bovate). Sum, £17. Tenants in Brauncedale[d] hold land in the

---

[a] Daughter and heiress of Nicholas de Stuteville. On 19 Oct., 1233, the King ordered P. de Rivall' to give seisin of all the lands of Nicholas de Stuteville, to Hugh Wake, who had married one of his daughters and heiresses, and to William de Mastac, a relative of the King, to whom the King had given the other daughter and heiress *(Excerpta è Rotulis Finium,* vol. i., p. 249*)*. This second daughter, as we hear nothing more of her, must have died young. On 2 Jan., 1241-2, the King, in consideration of a fine of nine thousand marcs paid to himself, of a thousand marcs paid for the Queen's gold *(pro auro Regine)*, granted to Joan, widow of Hugh Wake, the custody of her husband's lands to the full age of his heirs with their marriage, and licence to marry whom she would, provided he were of the King's allegiance. At the same time she obtained some concessions in regard to £20 a year her husband had been in the habit of paying to the Exchequer, for the debt of her father Nicholas de Stuteville *(Ibid.,* vol. i., p. 364*)*. She married not long after this, Hugh le Bigod, whose wife she was on 18 Feb., 1247-8 *(Ibid.,* vol. ii., p. 28*)*. Hugh, as is mentioned in the note to the last inquisition, was himself never Earl of Norfolk, though his brother and son were. Her son and heir, Baldwin Wake, was thirty-eight at the date of this inquisition. The King took the homage of Baldwin Wake, son and heir of Joan de Stuteville, on 1 May, 1276 *(Rot. Fin.,* 4 Edw. I., m. 21*)*. During her widowhood she was called Joan de Stuteville, and not by the name of either husband.

[b] Kirkby Moorside.

[c] Edston, a small village S.S.E. of Kirkby Moorside.

[d] Bransdale.

same dale *(in eodem vallo)* in bondage, that is seven score and one acres of land by cultures, paying yearly 70s. 6d. In the same dale there are cottars paying 6s. 8d. Sum of this schedule *(panelli)*, £21 14s. 10d. Tenants in bondage in Farnedale, holding by acres,[a] who pay £27 5s., that is, at 12d. an acre. Seven cottars in Farnedale, 15s. 8d. Tenants in Duthethwayt,[b] in a certain plot *(placia)* in the moor, holding by plots,[c] 32s. a year. Cottars in Kirkeby for customs, 30s. Other cottars there for their cottages, 4s. 8d. Small cottars *(parvi cotarii)* there, 43s. 6d. A water mill, £18, of which Sir John Denias was enfeoffed of £10 a year of the feoffment (of the said Joan) de Stutivile, after the death of Hugh le Bigot, formerly her husband. And the Prioress of Keldholme, and the Vicar of the same,[d] 40s. Perquisites of the court and market *(forum)*, 40s. a year. Four score hens of *lac*,[e] half a marc. Four score men paying 6d. a piece for nuts, 40s. . . . . . of the Canons[f] 12s. 4d. . . . . . in the moor, 20s., where were the sheepfolds of Hugh Bigot.

Sum of the sums of the whole manor, £98 11s. 4d.

[Baldewin] de Wak is of full age, and is the nearest heir *(eres)* of Lady J. de Stutevile. The said Joan enfeoffed the said Baldewin (in the manor) of Kirkeby two years ago by her charter, and he has been using his seisin up to the present, and ought to hold the said manor.[g]

[M. 4.]

INQUISITION made by Hugh de Collom of the advowsons of churches, services, and customs, belonging *(tangentibus)* to lady Joan de Stoteville, lately deceased, and which are not mentioned in the extent made before Sir Alexander de Kirketon, at Cotingham.[h] The said Joan was seised on the day of her

---

[a] *Per acras* corrected below to *placeas* in another item.

[b] Dowthwaite, four miles north of Kirkby Moorside.

[c] Written first *acras* and struck out.

[d] That is, of Kirkby Moorside. There was only the Priory and no Vicarage at Keldholme.

[e] In an account roll of Whitby Abbey *(Whitby Chartulary*, vol. ii., p. 596) for 1394-5 amongst other items, is "seven fowls called *lakis (gallinis vocatis lakis)*, 7s.," on which the Editor has the following note. "A.—S., *lac*', laec', a gift, offering. Compare *boon*, in *boon-day*, *boon-work*, etc. An enforced offering in either case."

[f] . . . . . *icorum*.

[g] "Et quod dicta Johanna feoffavit dictum Balde . . . . . de Kirkeby duobus annis elapsis per cartam suam, et utebatur saisina sua hucusque, et debet teneri *(sic)* dictum manerium."

[h] See the next membrane.

death of the advowsons of the church of Cotingham, worth two hundred marcs a year; of the church of Roule,[a] worth one hundred marcs a year; of the church of Etton, worth sixty marcs a year; of the church of Skraingham, worth four score marcs a year; of the church of Midelton,[b] worth £ . . . a year. The same Joan had besides 27 bondmen in Cotingham, doing many works, the work of each being worth 10s. a year. Sum, £13 10s. At Hule,[c] 44 bondmen doing works, the work of each being worth 5s. a year. Sum, £11. At Newland,[d] 16 bondmen doing works, the work of each being worth 3s. a year. Sum, 48s. At Cotingham, one boon-work in autumn *(j precaria in autompno)*, owed by the freemen, bondmen, and cottars for one day, worth 8s. 4d. At Wolfreton and Neuton,[e] for beasts *(pro avariis)* in the pasture, four hens and four score eggs. Price of the whole, 7d. From the freeholders *(libere tenentibus)* in Cotingham and elsewhere, four pounds of pepper, a moiety payable at the feast of S. John the Baptist, and a moiety at Christmas. Five pounds of cumin payable at Christmas. A pound of pepper 10d., and a pound of cumin 2d. Sum, 4s. 2d. Of rent of assise, two pair of gloves worth 2d., and 22 horseshoes *(feruras aferorum)*, worth 7½d. Sum of the whole, £27 11s. 10½d.[f]

[M. 5.]

EXTENT of the manor of Cotingham, made by Richard *del Clif*, Nigel de Waldeby, Thomas de Kent, Elias Hardy of Cotingham, John Takel of the same, John de Anlanby of the same, Nigel *le Parker* of the same, Reginald Prat of Bentele, Gilbert de Theford in Hesyl, William *le Monye* of the same, Laurence de Etton, and Roger Russel, sworn, who say on their oath, that lady Joan de Stutteville held in demesne on the day of her death, the capital messuage in Cotingham, with the moat round the court, and a garden, worth 40s. Sum, 40s. Also 1455 acres and half a rood of arable land (at 6d.). Sum of acres, 1455 and half a rood. Sum in money, £38 7s. 10½d. Also in demesne 433 acres of meadow (at 18d.). Sum of the acres of meadow, 433. Sum in money £32 9s. 6d. Also in demesne a separate *(separabilem)* pasture, containing 364 acres of pasture, at 12d. Sum in money, £18 4s. In demesne of

ᵃ Rowley, five and a half miles S.W. of Beverley.

ᵇ Middleton, near Kirkby Moorside.

ᶜ Hull-Bank, in the township of Cottingham.

ᵈ Newland, in the township of Cottingham.

ᵉ Wolfreton, in the parish of Kirkella, and Newton which stood a short distance south of Cottingham, afterwards the site of Hawtemprice Priory.

ᶠ Endorsed "Vicecomit' Eboracenc'."

rent of assise *(de redditu assiso)*, £95 11*s.* 8*d.* Herbage of the Park, Suthwode, Northwode, Bentele Wode, and Westwode, £4 a year. Sum, £4. Underwood of Suthwode, Northwode, and Westwode, £18.

The same Joan held in chief of the King the manors of Cotingham, Buttercram, Skreingham, and Langeton, by the service of three knights' fees. Of these Baldewyn Wake held of her Buttercram and Skreingham, and John de Vesey the manor of Langeton,[a] so that the said Joan on the day of her death, only held in demesne the manor of Cotingham. She held in demesne of the King Cropton and Middelton,[b] which Nicholas Wake held of her, but they do not know by what service, because those lands are of the tenure *(tenura)* of Lidel, which is in the County of Cumberland.[c] She held the manor of Kirkeby Morisheved of the heir of Mounbray, by the service of ten knights, of which manor Baldewyn Wake was seised before the death of his mother, two years past.

Sum of sums in money, together with the schedule,[d] . . . .
£236 4*s.* 11*d.*

Baldewyn Wake is her nearest heir, and is of the age of 38 years.[e]

XCVIII. ALAN DE KYNTHORPE.[f] *Custody of land.*

[4 Edw. I. No. 58.]

Writ that, whereas Philip de Wyleby, late Escheator beyond Trent, immediately after the death of Alan de Kyntorpe took into the King's hand all his lands and tenements, understanding that they were held of the King in chief, and by the complaint of Ascilia Moraunt of Thorinton, it is alleged that Alan held of her the capital messuage of the manor of Ellerburne, together with seven bovates of land in Thorinton, whereby the custody of the land ought to be hers until the lawful age of the heir; inquiry is to be made into the truth of the matter. Dated at Keninton, 25 April, 4th year (1276).

INQUISITION, whether or not Alan de Kynthorpe held anything of Ascilia Morant of Thorneton on the day of his death, made by Peter of the Gaol *(de Gaolya)*, Ralph de

---

[a] Langton, in the East Riding, near Malton.

[b] Both to the west of Pickering.

[c] At a later period the Wakes were summoned to Parliament under the title of Lord Wake of Lidel.

[d] *Una cum cedula.* These three words with a *caret.*

[e] On the dorse, "Domino Regi per Eschaettorem Ebor." In the inquisition for Cumberland (m. 2.) taken at Carlisle *(Karl'm)*, on Saturday after the octave of Easter, 4 Edw. I. (18 April, 1276), the finding is, "Item dicunt, quod dominus Baldwynus de Wake, filius dicte domine Johanne, est propinquior heres ejus, et plene etatis et ultra."

[f] See No. LXXXIX.

Loketon, Nicholas de Dale, William son of Thomas, Richard Archebaud, Philip de Alvestayn, William son of Robert, John son of Oda, Roger Kockerel, John son of Robert, Alan son of Andrew, John Campyun, and Adam de Rouceby, who say that Alan de Kynthorpe held the capital messuage of the manor of Ellerburne, situate in the territory of Thorneton, and seven bovates and eight acres of land in Thorneton, by knight's service—nine carucates making one knight's fee—of the said Ascilia Morant.

XCIX. GEOFFREY BERCHAUD,[a] *Inq. p. m.*

[4 Edw. I. No. 15.]

Writ dated at Westminster, 17 May, 4th year (1276).

INQUISITION made at Neuton on the morrow of Saint Augustine, 4 Edw. (27 May, 1276), before Thomas de Normanville, the King's Steward beyond Trent, by the oath of John *de la Tuyere*, Peter de Meaux *(Mels')*, William de Fronigham,[b] Nicholas de Thorne, Laurence Clerk *(clericum)*, John de Fronigham,[b] Stephen Buke, William Davilers, Eustace Brun, Stephen Gerveys, John de Freboys, John de Redmar, who say that Geoffrey Berchaud held of the King in chief at Neuton in Holdern[ess],[c] on the day of his death, twelve bovates and three acres of land (every bovate containing twelve acres, and worth by the year 10*s.*), one close of meadow (10*s.*), one several pasture (41*s.*), one mill (20*s.*), 29*s.* 8*d.* from free tenants yearly, three cottages (10*s.*), and one capital messuage (5*s.*), by foreign service.

John, son of Geoffrey, is his next heir, aged eleven years.

They say also that he held nothing of others so far as they know.

---

[a] In 1260, Geoffrey Berchot, called Berchoud in the writ, was a minor in the custody of William de Fortibus, Earl of Albemarle (See p. 84). His widow Alice, is mentioned in No. cvi.

[b] A mistake for Frothingham or Frotingham, now Frodingham.

[c] Out Newton, five miles from Patrington, in the parish of Easington. In 10 Edw. I., the Escheator, Thomas de Normanville, accounted to the King for £8, being the rent of Neuton, and spent £4 of it for victuals for the support of John, son and heir of Geoffrey Berchaud, in the King's custody, inasmuch as he was of unsound mind *(eo quod non est compos mentis)*, and of one brother and two sisters *(Escheators' Accounts beyond Trent ³⁄₂.)*

C. WILLIAM DE ARDERNE.[a] *Extent of Lands.*

[4 EDW. I. No. 53.]

Writ dated at Westminster, 6 June, 4th year (1276).[b]

EXTENT of the lands of Sir William de Arden, made at Hundeburton[c] on the day of the Apostles Peter and Paul (29 June), in the year of grace 1276, by Thomas Marmeduc of Disford, Robert Bonet of the same, Andrew Ferthing, John de Burton, Roger de Mildeby, Richard de Hou, Richard son of Alan of Disford, Richard son of Robert of the same, John son of Peter Carpenter of the same, Thomas son of Elias of Cundall, William Wynemer, and Robert son of John of Mildeby.

Annual rent of freeholders by charter—John de Burton holds two bovates of land for 18d., paid at two terms, Michaelmas and "*Pascha Floridum.*"[d] The Abbot of Byland *(Belelanda)*, one bovate in Baggeby,[e] for 12d. Thomas de Helperby pays yearly 6d., "pro quadam haya piscarya atincta super terram dicti d'ni Will'i."[f] Also, the fishery of the water of Swalle yields 2s., and two messuages in Threske, 3s. 6d. The oven *(fornax)* of Burton answers yearly for 2s., at the same two terms.

Sum, 10s.

In demesne land ten bovates of the fee of lord Roger *le Mubray*,[g] in which five score and eleven acres of arable land are contained (10d. the acre) ; nine acres of meadow (at 3s.). Also

[a] Allusion is made in two writs of *certiorari*, to a brother and heir of William de Arderne deceased, but neither inquisition hereupon taken mentions his name. That for the County of Warwick, taken at Hampton, in Arden, on Tuesday after the feast of the Apostles Peter and Paul. in the 4th year (30 June, 1276), has the name William de "Arden." Dower in the manor of La Knolle, and in Grafton, both in Warwickshire, was assigned (18 July, 1276) to Agatha, late wife of William de Arderne *(Rot. Fin.*, 4 Edw. I., m. 13). The brother and heir was Richard, but he being an idiot *(fatuus)*, his lands were in the King's hand, as seen by the *Fine Roll* (m. 3), and from the tenor of the King's writ dated 28 Oct., 1279. Richard was then dead *(Ibid.*, 7 Edw. I., m. 3). See also *Cal. Gen.* vol. ii., p. 544.

[b] Note on the back of the writ, that the execution was entrusted to the Bailiff of the Liberty of Richmondshire, who sent the extent thereto annexed.

[c] Humberton, near Boroughbridge.

[d] Palm Sunday.

[e] Bagby, in the parish of Kirkby Knowle.

[f] The meaning of this passage is not clear. *Piscarya* should probably be regarded as an adjective, the *haya piscarya* will be then some kind of enclosure for fishing purposes. *Atincta* is another crux. Mr. Skeat *(Etymological Dictionary)* *s.v. attaint* quotes Palsgrave, "'*I atteynt*, I hyt or touche a thing,' *i. e. attain* it." To attain a thing it is necessary to reach it, may not the meaning of the passage be "a fishing hay which reached over the land of the said Sir William?" See the verb *attaint*, to touch, to get at, in the *New English Dictionary*, and the examples there given.

[g] Son and heir of Roger de Moubray, at this time in the King's custody.

30 acres of land of the fee of the Earl of Cornwall[a] (at 9*d.*). The capital messuage is not extended because it barely suffices to keep up the houses. Sum of the demesne yearly, £7 2*s.* Bond-land *(terra bondorum).* Also twelve bovates of land in service of Mubray's fee *(de feodo le Mubray),* in which are contained six score and twelve acres (at 10*d.*), seven and a half acres of meadow (at 3*s.*) ; also two bovates in service, of the Earl of Cornwall's fee, containing 22 acres of arable land. Sum of the bond-farm, £7 16*s.* 10*d.*
There are ten cottars *(cotar')* in Burton, each of whom pays 9*d.* at the above said terms.
Sum of the cottars' farm, 7*s.* 6*d.*
Sum total, £15 16*s.* 10*d.*

CI. JOAN, DAUGHTER OF WILLIAM DE DUFTON.[b] *Inq. p. m.*

[4 Edw. I. No. 24.]

Two writs dated at Westminster, 28 Oct., 4th year (1276).

INQUISITION made before the Sheriff and Escheator of Yorkshire, by Alexander de Kirkeby, Walter *de la Bruere* of the same, H . . . de Wytheton, William son of Beatrice of Farnley, Henry son of Ralph of the same, Adam de Elstanbotheme, Richard Atte Becke of Askewyth, John son of Thurstan of Denton, Walter son of William of the same, James Woderove of Methelay, Peter Coleman of the same, and William son of Helot of Ayketon, who say by their oath that Joan *(Johanna),* daughter of William de Dufton, on the day of her death held no lands in fee or of the King in chief, or of any other. One

---

ᵃ Edmund Plantagenet, Earl of Cornwall, second son of Richard, Earl of Cornwall and King of the Romans, brother of Henry III. Richard is called King of Almain or Germany, in No. cxx.

ᵇ By the writs (addressed to the Escheators of the Counties of York and Northampton), it is stated that this Joan held of the late King Henry III. in·chief *(que tenuit de domino H. Rege patre nostro)* at the time of her death. The inquisition for Northamptonshire finds that she held in this county of the King in chief the manor of Wycle, with the exception of three and a half virgates of land held by Isabel de Grey. Mauger le Vavasur, her son and heir, was aged twenty-six years. Mauger le Vavasur, his father, was at this time dead, as stated in the inquisition for Yorkshire, and the above extent of his lands is made, but the respective counties are not named.

There is a pedigree of the Vavasours of Weston in Whitaker's *Leeds,* and Foster's *Yorkshire Families.* They continued at that place in the male line till 1833. There is, however, no mention of Joan de Dufton. Mr. Roberts *(Cal. Gen.,* vol. i., p. 235*)* reads the name, Duston. On 7 Dec. 1277, the King, then at Windsor, took the homage of Mauger, son of Mauger le Vavasour *(Rot. Fin.,* 5 Edw. I., m. 23*)*; and on 29 May, 1280, in consideration of £300, the King granted to Agnes, late wife of Mauger le Vavasour, the custody of the lands and heirs of the said Mauger, with their marriage *(Ibid.,* 8 Edw. I., m. 10*)*.

Mauger, son of Mauger *le Wavasur*, is her next heir, aged thirty years and more ; and his lands, which ought to fall to him as his heritage after the death of his father, were taken into the King's hand because his father held of. the King in chief a manor in the County of Northampton, named Wyclive, of the inheritance of the said Joan by the law of England, and because all lands which ought to fall to him after the death of his father have been taken into the King's hand.

E XTENT of the lands held by Mauger *le Wavesur*.

	Annual value.		
	£	*s.*	*d.*
Manor of Denton,[a] held of the Archbishop of York for the fourth part of a knight's fee . .	6	8	5
Manor of Drachton [b]	2	5	5
Manor of Scharnestone[c]	9	0	4
He held these two manors of John *le Wavesur* for half a fee.			
Moiety of the manor of Ascwyht,[d] held of John son and heir of Henry de Percy for the ninth part of one knight's fee	4	0	0
Land at Wolsington,[e] held of Philip de Kyme for the fourteenth part of a knight's fee, five marcs, 7*s.* 4*d.*[f]	3	14	0

[a] Denton, in the parish of Otley.

[b] Draughton, in the parish of Skipton.

[c] Sharleston, in the parish of Warmfield, near Wakefield.

[d] Askwith, in the parish of Weston, near Otley.

[e] Ouston, in the parish of Tadcaster.

[f] The following is an abstract of the Northamptonshire inquisition (*Inq p. m.*, 8 Edw. I., No. 22), Writ dated at Winchester, 4 Jan., 8th year (1279-80). Extent of Wykele or Wycle Manor, which was of Mauger le Vavasour, on Wednesday before the Annunciation of Our Lady (20 March, 1279-80). Held of the King in chief, for one knight's fee. Malger is son of Sir Malger, deceased, and his nearest heir, and will be fifteen years old on the Nativity of the Blessed John the Baptist next coming in the 8th year (24 June, 1280). The writ refers to Agnes, who was wife of Mauger le Vavasour, lately deceased, who held of us in chief, she made oath that she would not marry (without the King's leave). It is torn at the end.

CII. MARGARET DE STAINTON.[a] *Inq. p. m.*

[5 EDW. I. No. 22.]

Writ of the King, dated at Brehull, 12 June, 5th year (1277), and directed to Thomas de Normanville, is sent by him for execution to the Sheriff of York, and quoted at length.

INQUISITION made by Richard *del Scoles*, William de Hoton, Ingram de Culcothes, Thomas de Stirape, John de Buggethorpe, Peter Leminge of Waddeworde, Peter de Lowedher of the same, Robert de Selton in Waddeworde, Oliver de Wykerslay, Thomas de Helthweby, William de Winteworde, and *Mawaysmum* de Cateby, who say that Margaret de Staynton held in chief of the Castle of Tykehill one knight's fee by doing homage, 10s. for castle-guard yearly, and 8d. for food of the warders yearly, ploughing for ten days with one plough upon the demesne of Tyk[ehill] and the service of every plough is worth 3d., making one perch upon the causeway *(calcetum)* of Tykehill, suit at the Court there every three weeks, wards, reliefs, marriages, and scutages when they happen. She held in demesne at Staynton a manor worth by the year half a marc, nine score acres of arable land and 100 acres of wood (every acre whether of land or wood, 6d.), and six acres of meadow (at 3s.) ; which manor with land, wood, and meadow, the said Margaret delivered to John de Stayngrewe, knt., by a certain writing, for four years in consideration of a certain sum of money, so that if she or her heirs should pay to him the said sum, the manor at the end of the four years should revert to them ; and if they should not pay, the said John[b] should remain enfeoffed of the aforesaid for term of his life paying yearly to Margaret or her heirs twenty marcs. Hereupon when peaceful seisin ought to have been taken, the bailiff of Tykehill hindered because held of the Castle in chief, whereby he did not have seisin.

She also held one watermill and one wind mill, worth yearly 20s., and also 40s. annual rent, homage of free tenants, suits of Court, and other services. The Court is worth by the year half a marc. Of all which she was seised at the time of her death, and her heir is John le Boteler, her son, who is of full age. She held nothing of the King in chief.

[a] Hunter refers to this inquisition in his *South Yorkshire*, (vol. i., p. 255), and presumes Margaret de Stainton had married a Boteler and retained her name. On 21 July, 1277, the King, then at Chester, took the homage of John le Botiller, son and heir of Margaret de Steynton, for his mother's lands *(Rot. Fin.*, 5. Edw. I., m. 9). Stainton is a parish near Tickhill.

[b] " Et si non solverent dictus Johannes [*here a word cut out at the time the inquisition was written*] remaneret, etc."

Another writ, dated at Wodestoke, 6 Feb., 5th year (1276-7), directed to
Nicholas de Stapelton, Constable of the King's Castle of Tykehull,
commanding him to let John de Steyngryve have again until the next
Parliament his seisin, such as before they were taken into the King's
hand of lands and tenements with appurtenances in Steynton, of which
Margaret, daughter and heir of John de Steynton, by charter enfeoffed
him, and which are held of the Honour of the said Castle; and the
King would then certify in such next Parliament whether those lands
and tenements are held of himself, or of another, and how.

EXTENT of the manor of Steynton. There is a hall with
chamber, granges and other houses with a garden, and they
are worth by the year half a marc. Eleven score acres of land
in demesne (the acre 6*d.*), ten score acres of wood (6*d.*), seven
acres and a half of meadow (at 3*s.*), one windmill and one watermill, which are worth by the year 20*s.* Also eleven bovates and
a half in bondage, which pay in all 67*s.* 2*d.* yearly, some bovates
giving more, some less;[a] in cottages 12*s.* 8*d.*; rent of free
tenants, 114*s.* 4*d.* The profit of the court yearly is half a marc.
Also from the Abbot of Roche *(de Rupe)* for the grange of
Lambecotes,[b] 2*s.*　　　　　　　　　　　Sum total, £23 2*s.*

The manor is held of the Castle of Tyk[ehill] for homage,
ward, and relief (when they happen), for one knight's fee. It
pays to the castle 10*s.* for guard yearly, and 8*d.* for food of the
warders. It shall make one perch upon the causeway towards
Thornewode,[c] and shall plough upon the demesne lands of the
Castle with one plough for ten days; all which services the
tenants, as well free as others, shall do, except the 8*d.* for
the warder's food. It owes suit at the Court of Tyk[ehill] from
three weeks to three weeks.

And be it remembered that the lady, who now is, enfeoffed
the Abbot of Roche *(de Rupe)* of 22 acres of wood and 2*s.*
yearly rent, Thomas de Stirap in free marriage with her daughter
of 17*s.* 2½*d.* annual rent and 28 acres of wood, her two sons of
five marcs and 10*s.*, and her two daughters of 42 acres of land
from two bovates of bondage which used to yield yearly 14*s.* 2*d.*,
and 16 acres of wood. The same lady demised to Nicholas de
Meleburne four marcs of yearly rent, to be received from the
tenants for the term of ten years, of which one has passed, and
to John, Parson of Hokerton,[d] . . . . . . watermill worth by the
year half a marc.　　　　　　　　　　Sum, £13 4*s.* 8½*d.*

She demised to Sir John de Steingreve for the term of four
years the manor with all buildings, nine score acres of land,

---

[a] " Et memorandum quedam bovate dant plus, quedam minus."

[b] Lambcote Grange, in the parish of Braithwell, five miles from Tickhill.

[c] " Et solvit castro x*s.* proward' per annum, et viij*d.* pro cibo vig[ilancium], et
faciet unam perticatam super calcetum versus Thornewode."

[d] Hockerton, near Southwell.

seven and a half acres of meadow, six score and fourteen acres of wood, for £100 which he gave to her, so that if she should pay to him at the end of four years the said sum, then the manor with land, etc., should revert to her; if not, he should remain enfeoffed for term of his life of the manor, lands, meadows, wood, rent, homages, wards, reliefs, and all escheats, paying yearly to the lady and her heirs twenty marcs. After his death the manor with its appurtenances to revert to the lady or her heirs.

CIII. ALAN DE ALDEFELDE. *Inq. p. m.*

[6 EDW. I. No. 13.]

Writ tested at Shrewsbury *(Salop')*, by Robert, Bishop of Bath and Wells, Chancellor, 3 December,[a] 6th year (1272).

EXTENT made at Aldefelde[b] on Wednesday before the Nativity of our Lord *(ante Natale Domini)*, 6 Edward (22 Dec., 1277), by John de Seleby, sub-escheator of the West Riding, of the lands and tenements of Alan [de Aldefelde], knt., formerly lord of Aldefelde, by William de Stodlay, Jocelyn *(Gocelinum)* de Brathwayt, Roger de Fegerby, William de Brunby, Elias de Grantelay, Adam Russel, Robert Noel, Alan de Gykelswyke, Walter Bruer, Henry son of David of Aldefelde, Thomas Frauncheays, Hugh Nasmith, who say upon their oath that the manor of Aldefelde as enclosed *(infra clausum)*, is worth by the year one marc, but cannot be kept up for less *(sed idem manerium non potest sustineri minus quam de una marca)*. There are in demesne four score and ten acres (the acre 6*d.*), and 13 acres of meadow (at 2*s.* 6*d.*). There is a certain pasture called Oxeleyes, worth by the year half a marc, and Crakefal and Nicholfal, 2*s.*   Sum of the whole, £4 6*s.* 2*d.*

BONDMEN *(Bondi)*.

	Annual rent.		Precariæ.		Other dues.
	s.	*d.*	*s.*	*d.*	
Maurice Scot, for one toft and one bovate . . .	4	4	1	7	1 cock, 2 hens at Christmas
Maud *(Matild')*, wife of Reginald, for one toft and half a bovate . . .	3	2	1	7	2 hens at Christmas
Humfrey for one toft and eight acres . . .	3	2½	1	7	2 hens

a Edward's itinerary shows that the King was there on that day.

b Aldfield, in the parish of Ripon, S. W. of that town.

23

	Annual rent. s. d.	Precariæ.. s. d.	Other dues.
Henry Brewer *(braciatore)*, for one toft and one bovate .	6 0	1 9	
Richard, son of Reginald, for one toft and half a bovate	4 3	1 7	2 hens
Hugh Colthirde, for one toft and ten acres . . .	4 0	1 7	2 hens
Richard de Coppegrave, for one toft and half a bovate	3 0	1 7	2 hens
Henry de Malur, for one toft and seven acres . .	5 7	1 7	1 cock, 2 hens
Symon Buldbch', for one toft and one bovate . .	4 0	1 7	2 hens

Sum, 53s. 5½d.

FARMERS *(Firmarii)*.

	Annual rent. s. d.	Precariæ. s. d.
William Skinner *(pellipar')*, for one toft and six acres	3 0	
William, son of Humfrey, for one toft and one bovate	6 0	
Parcel of meadow	0 6	0 7
Richard Forester *(forestar')*, for one toft and one bovate	6 1	0 6
William Wryde, for one toft and half a bovate	3 4	
John Heselheved,. for one toft and six acres .	3 0	1 0
Roger Nodde, for one toft and nine acres .	6 1	0 6
Robert de Neuton, for one toft and half a rood	1 10½	
For one forge	0 8	

Sum, 34s. 1½d.

FREE TENANTS.

	Annual rent. s. d.	
Henry son of David . . .	7 3	Foreign service and a pair of gloves
John Carpenter *(carpentario)* .	6 0	„ „
Henry Tailor *(cyssore)* . .	2 0	„ „
Robert Smith *(fabro)* . .	6 0	„ „
Hugh Nasmith . . .	2 4	„ „
Alan Brunbayn . . .	2 7	„ „

Sum, 26s. 2d.

COTTARS *(Cotterr').*

	Annual Rent.		Precariæ.		Other dues.
	s.	*d.*	*s.*	*d.*	
Robert Lister *(tixtore)*, for one toft and two acres	2	0	0	2	
Thomas son of Walter, for one toft and croft	2	1	0	1	
Tylle Curtays, for one toft . .	1	0	0	3	
Robert Grenhode, for one toft and one acre	0	10	0	4	
Beatrice Washer *(lotrice)* for one toft	0	6	.		
Geoffrey Burel, for one toft and one acre and a half	1	2	1	1	2 hens
Richard Cobbler *(sutore)*, for one toft and half an acre . .	1	9	0	1	
Robert Miller *(molendinario)*for one toft and four acres . .	1	4	1	1	2 hens
Geoffrey Leaunder, for one toft, one acre, and three roods . .	1	4	1	1	2 hens
Osbert Tanner *(tanatore)*, for one toft and two acres	3	1			
Ralph, son of Austin, *(Ag'tini)* for one toft, two acres and half a rood .	1	6	1	1	2 hens
Lang usd', for one toft and half a rood	0	10	0	1	
Adam son of Thomas, for one toft and one rood . . .	1	8	0	1	
Alan Brunbayn . .			0	1	
William Mower *(messore)*, for one toft and one acre . . .	1	0	0	2	
Agnes Tuppur, for one toft and one acre	1	8	0	2	
Juliana, wife of Godmund, for one toft and one acre.	0	11	0	1	2 hens
William de Durem, for one toft and two acres	3	2			
Agnes de Stokeslay, for one toft and one rood	2	0	0	1	
William de Scabelton (?) for one toft and one acre and a half . .	0	11	1	1	2 hens
William of the Forge *(de forgia)* for one toft and three roods . .	2	3½	0	1	
Thomas de Sleforde, for one toft and one acre and a half . . .	2	0	0	2	

	Annual rent.	Precariæ.	Other dues.
	s. d.	s. d.	
Jollan, son of Sir Alan, holds by charter the land of Stodlay,[a] and pays at Christmas . .	0 1		
Nicholas, his brother, for land and mill of Aldefelde (by gift of the lord) at Christmas	0 1		

Sum, 42s. 6½d.

	Annual rent.	Precariæ.	Other dues.
	s. d.	s. d.	
Also Symon Clungen of Longelay[b]	4 0		
Walter Cnollan	5 0		
Peter Havermele for one toft and one bovate	4 0	0 1	
William Potter, for one toft . .	2 0		
The aforesaid Jollan, for land of Longelay, renders at Nat. S. John Bapt. . . .	one rose		
Richard son of Norman of Stodlay, holds freely, and renders . .	1 0	Sum, 16s 1d.	

John de Draycotes holds freely of the lord of Aldefelde by charter land there, and renders yearly 2s. or one sparrow-hawk (*spervarium*).   Sum, 2s.

The lord of Aldefelde owes for the land of Langelay to the heirs of Robert de Stiveton, 3s. yearly; to the heirs of Sir Roger de Mubray for, the lands of Aldefelde, Stodlay, Longelay, ward, relief, and foreign service when it shall happen, and, besides, suit of Court at Kyrkeby[c] from three weeks to three weeks.

William, son of Nigel de Aldefelde, is next heir to the aforesaid lands, and at Pentecost last past (16 May) he was aged thirteen years.   Sum total, £13 0s. 6½d.

Another writ directed to the Sheriff, and dated at Dover, 1 Feb., 6th year (1277-8). It had been shown on behalf of Hugh de Beltoft and Egidia his wife, that whereas Nigel, son and heir of Alan de Aldefelde, lately deceased (whose lands and tenements are in the King's custody), dowered the said Egidia on the day he espoused her, at the church door, with a third part of the lands and tenements which were of his father, with the will and assent of the said Alan, and from that time she continuously for sixteen years and more dwelt with Alan and Nigel her husband in those lands and tenements; after the death of her husband Alan refused to assign the said dower to her, whereby the said Hugh and his wife have besought the King to assign dower.

[a] Studley Roger, in the parish of Ripon.
[b] Lungley, a farm about two miles W.N.W. of Aldfield.
[c] Kirkby Malzeard.

INQUISITION made before the Sheriff of Yorkshire, the King's Escheator in that County, by William de Stodlay, Jocelyn *(Gocelin)* de Brathwayt, Roger de Cressewelle, Geoffrey Dagon, John de Stockelde, Richard de Kereby, Robert Noel of Azerlay, John de Beverley, Richard de Lethelay, Thomas de Linc[oln], Robert son of Walter of Mickelthwayt, and Walter de Bruere, who say that Nigel, son of Alan de Aldefeud, with the assent and good will of his father, endowed at the church door of Pennesthorn[a] Egidia his wife with a third part of all the lands and tenements whereof the said Alan was in seisin on the day on which he wedded her, without charter or writing. From the church door Alan received the same Nigel and Egidia at his manor of Aldefelde, and there found them all necessaries continuously for sixteen years, within which time they had six sons and daughters. After sixteen years were past they removed to Egidia's manor of Azerlay,[b] by the council and assent of Alan, and dwelt there up to Nigel's death. Then Alan took William, Nigel's son and heir, and married him to the daughter of Sir Elias de Knol, taking for his marriage forty marcs; and whereas Alan retained with him her children at his own cost, she would not solicit him, but allowed her dower to remain in the lifetime of Alan, as well as of certain lands with which he endowed her.

Alan had on the day on which she was dowered the manor of Aldefelde, extended at £13 0s. 4½d., of Mubray's fee; also in Stodlay seven bovates of land, worth by the year £3 3s., of Moubray's fee; also in Horselay[c] in the field[d] of Aldefelde, 24 acres of land (12s.) and one watermill, worth by the year four and a half marcs, of the same fee. He had also in the field of Notton[e] 22 bovates of land, five acres of meadow, and 3s. 6d. rent from cottars, which are extended at £6 8s. 6d., of the Abbot of Saint Alban's fee; in Rybbestan 30s. rent of assise of the fee . . . . ; of the Prior of Newburgh for a certain pasture in Cundale,[f] 15s. rent of assise, Mubrai's fee.

Richard Huberd for one messuage in Rypon, 3s.; rent of assise of the fee of the Archbishop of York; and in Longelay one bovate, worth 6s. by the year.

[a] The only parish with a similar name seems to be Pensthorpe, in the diocese of Norwich, which is too far away. It is more likely a clerical error for Penistone, which is not far distant from Aldfield.

[b] Azerlay, in the parish of Kirkby Malzeard, five miles from Ripon.

[c] Horsley Gate, a farm a mile north of Aldfield.

[d] That is the common field.

[e] In the parish of Royston, near Barnsley. Here again the common field is meant.

[f] Cundall, six miles south of Thirsk.

Of the aforesaid lands and rents, Alan gave to Jollan, his son, seven bovates of land in Stodlay, worth yearly £3 3*s.*; and in Longelay one bovate, worth yearly 6*s.*; to Nicholas, his son, the mill of Aldefelde, worth yearly four and a half marcs, and 24 acres of land in Horselay in the field of Aldefelde, worth yearly 12*s.*, and 30*s.* rent of assise in Ribbestayn.[a]

CIV.   GILBERT DE BERNEVAL.[b]   *Inq. p. m.*

[5 Edw. I. No. 4.]

Writ directed to Thomas de Normanville, the King's Steward, and dated at Canterbury, 18 Feb., 6th year (1277-8). Gilbert de Neville and Cecily *(Cecilia)* his wife, aunt and co-heir of Gilbert le Cundy (under age and in ward to the King) have shown that, whereas Gilbert de Berneval, father of Cecily and grandfather of Gilbert le Cundy, was on the day of his death seised in fee of nine messuages and nine bovates of land in Aberford and Luterington,[c] which the King's bailiffs ought to have taken and did not, John, son of Alan Sampson of York, asserting that he was enfeoffed by the said Gilbert de Berneval of the said messuages and land, fraudulently intruded into the same, and yet detains them in occupation, in prejudice of the King's right and wardship, and to the manifest damage and disherison of the said Cecily and Gilbert le Cundy, inquiry is therefore to be made.

INQUISITION made before Thomas de Normanville, at York, on Thursday after the feast of S. Matthias the Apostle, 6 Edw. (3 March, 1277-8), by Richard son of Maud *(Matild')* of Fenton, William Styrthup, Nicholas de Okelestorp, William de Langewheyt, Robert de Mikilfelde, John son of Philip of Milforde, Elias de Neuton, clerk, Robert Marshal *(marescallum)* of Tatecastre, Henry de Rithere, Hugh de Brinkil of Neuton, John de Oscombe of the same, and Walter de Barkestone, who say by their oath that Gilbert de Bernevale was not seised in fee of nine

---

[a] The lower part of the inquisition is rather difficult to read.

[b] By an inquisition taken in the County of Southampton (upon a writ dated 25 Oct., 5th year, 1277), it is found that Gilbert had two daughters, Albreda and Cecily; and that Gilbert de Cundy, son of Albreda, aged seventeen years at Pentecost last past, and the said Cecily, who is of full age, are his next heirs. Nov. 21, 1277. The King to Ralph de Sandwyco, his Steward in Co. Southampton. Whereas Gilbert de Berneval, deceased, held in chief the manor of Fernham, and Cecily, daughter of Gilbert (whom Gilbert de Neville married), and Gilbert de Cundy, son of Albreda, Cecily's sister, are the next heirs of the said Gilbert, and parceners of his inheritance, and we have taken the homage of Gilbert de Neville for Cecily's share, the Steward is directed to take from him security for his reasonable relief, saving to Sarra, widow of Gilbert de Berneval, her reasonable dower, etc. The share of Gilbert de Cundy to remain in our hand until further order. Given by the hand of the venerable father R. Bishop of Bath and Wells, Chancellor, at Shrewsbury *(Rot. Fin.,* 6 Edw. I., m. 29).

[c] Lotherton *(Domesday* Lodresdene) and Aberford, near Tadcaster.

messuages and nine bovates of land with the appurtenances in Aberford and Luterington at the time of his death, but John, son of Alan Sampson of York, was enfeoffed of the said messuages and land by Gilbert in his life time, and had full and peaceful seisin thereof for one day and one night before Gilbert died; he taking the esplees *(explecia)* as in rents and acknowledgements half a marc and more.

They say also that John Sampson had no seisin of the aforesaid lands and tenements by any other or others, than by the said Gilbert as aforesaid.

A further writ, directed to the same Thomas de Normanville, and dated at Westminster, 18 May, 6th year (1278), recites the foregoing inquisition; and, after pointing out its unsatisfactory nature, by reason of the shortness of the seisin had, and the debility of the said Gilbert, orders that further inquiry be made, and that all lands and tenements be taken into the King's hand and safely kept, until further order be given therein.

INQUISITION made at Tadechaster, on S. Denis's *(Dyonysii)* day, 6 Edward (25 May, 1278), before Sir *(d'no)* Thomas de Normanville, the King's Steward, and in presence of the Sheriff of Yorkshire, by Nicholas de Okelstorpe, William de Langethwait, John de Lede, Robert Marshal *(marescall')*, Richard M . . . ouer, Simon de . . . . , Thomas de Barkeston, Richard son of William of Fenton, William Styrthupe of the same, *Batheman* de Saxton, Thomas Lardiner *(lardinarium)*, and Hugh de Brinkil of Neuton, who say by their oath that John Sampson of York was seised of nine bovates of land and nine messuages in Aberforth and Luteryngton, by Gilbert de Bernivalle in his lifetime, and had full and peaceful seisin thereof on S. Batholomew's day, taking the esplees to the value of half a marc and more, Gilbert being on that day of sound mind 'and good memory, though he was weak and died on the morrow. They say also that John Sampson of York was put in seisin by Gilbert de Rugemonde, Steward of the said Sir Gilbert, and this by his command and good will, in presence of John de Eyton, who came to put him in seisin of the said tenement on behalf of the Archbishop, who is chief lord of the fee, and had impeded John Sampson for fifteen day before he had seisin by Sir Gilbert.

CV.   CONCERNING THE RIGHT TO A WHALE STRANDED
IN FILEY BAY.

[6 EDW. I.   No. 81.]

Writ dated at Westminster, 27 May, 6th year (1278), referring to Gilbert
de Gaunt and Richard Malebysse, who, alleging that they and their
ancestors had been used to have a sea-whale wheresoever stranded on
their lands adjoining the sea, now complained that the Sheriff would not
permit them to have a whale lately stranded in their port of Fyvele.

INQUISITION made at Fiweley, on Monday after the feast of
S. Botulph (20 June, 1278), before Alexander de Kirketon,
Sheriff of the County, by eighteen free and lawful men of
three Wapentakes, namely: Dekeringe, Buccros, and Hertehille.
Dekeringe—Roger *le Dispenser*, John de Fenton, Richard Martin,
Jolan de Horkestou, Anselm Dreng', Azo de Flickeston.
Buccros—Robert de Heslerton, William de Edingham, John de
Friboys, Robert de Cayton, Robert de Crohom, Geoffrey son
of Peter de Ledemer.   Hertehille—William de Norththorpe,
Richard de [B]aynton, William Fossarde of the same, Thomas
Walran, Ralph de Halton, Robert Baty.   They say upon their
oath that Gilbert de Gaunt and Richard de Malebisse and
their ancestors, have been up to now used to have of right a
whale when it came on shore in their port of Fiweley, and such
appertains to them of right, as contained in the writ; saving
nevertheless to the King the head and tail.

CVI.   ALICE, WHO WAS WIFE OF GEOFFREY BERCHAUD.[a]
Dower.

[6 EDW. I.   No. 31.]

Writ directed to Thomas de Normanville, the King's Steward.   Whereas
Alice, who was wife of Geoffrey Berchaud, demands against the Prior
of Bridelington, before the King's Justices of the Bench, reasonable
dower out of one messuage, four tofts, one mill, one carucate of land,
and ten shillings rent, with the appurtenances, in Burton Flamming;[b]
and the Prior vouched to warrant John de Carleton, who further
vouched John, son and heir of the said Geoffrey, under age and in ward
to the King, whereby the assignment of dower was delayed; the King,
wishing to be fully certified thereof and that justice be done to the said
Alice, commands an extent of the lands and tenements to be made, and
inquiry to be made if anything prevents her from having a third part of
the same.   Dated at Westminster, 20 June, 6th year (1278).

EXTENT made at Burton Flammynge, on Sunday before the
feast of the Beheading of S. John Baptist, 6 Edward

[a] See No. XCIX.

[b] Burton Fleming or North Burton, seven and a half miles N.W. of Bridlington.

(28 Aug., 1278), before Thomas de Normanville, of the lands and tenements which were of Geoffrey Berchou in Burton Flammynge, by Ralph de Cotegrave, John son of Isabel, John son of John, Simon Thorald of Hundmanby, Henry *le Porter* of Burton, Henry de Wykham of the same, Richard Aylewarde of the same, John Rudde of the same, Robert son of Henry *le Porter* of the same, Simon Avenel of Swathorpe, Walter de Hunkelby of Twenge, and John de Fenton, who say upon their oath that there are :—

	Annual value.	
	s.	*d.*
A capital messuage with fruit of garden	10	0
Four tofts, held by Martin Den, Hervey Mose, Geoffrey son of Gilbert, and Adam son of Wytha *(fil' Wythe)*, each at 2*s.*	8	0
Rent of free tenants	2	0

In demesne eight bovates of land, at 10*s.*, £4.

There is no mill, but only the site of one, which is valued among the demesne lands.

They say that they know of nothing to prevent Alice, who was wife of Geoffrey Berchoud, from having dower, and she, ought to have a third part of the tenements aforesaid.

Sum total, 100*s.*

CVII. LETITIA DE KAYNES.[a] *Inq. p. m.*

[7 EDW. I No. 28.]

Writ directed to Thomas de Normanville, the King's Steward, and dated at Westminster, 25 Jan., 7th year (1278-9).

EXTENT of lands which Letitia de Keines held in Drax of the inheritance of John Paynel, made at York, 10 March, 7 Edward (1278-9), by Richard de Rosholm, Henry son of

---

[a] See No. LXXVI. By an inquisition taken in the County of Dorset, it is found that Leticia de Caynes held of Robert de Kayngnes in dower a moiety of the manor of Cumbe; and that the same Robert is next heir of William de Kayngnes, son of the said Letitia, and of full age. On 28 April, 1279, Richard de Holebroke was ordered to hand over to John de Lolleworth the lands and tenements which Letitia de Kaynes held in dower in the vill of Rasne, which are of the heritage of John, son and heir of John de Paynel deceased, who held of the King in chief, being under age and in the King's custody; to hold to the full age of the said John de Lolleworth, to answer to the King's exchequer for all claims by the hand of the Sheriff of Lincoln *(Rot. Fin.,* 7 Edw. I. m. 15). According to Dugdale, Letitia, widow of Ralph de Kaynes, re-married John Paynel. From the *Inq. p. m.* (26 Edw. I. No. 48) of William de Vescy, taken in 1298, it appears that Letitia, there called Letitia de Kenys, was the daughter and co-heir of Adam de Perinton, and that she had two sisters, Isabel, wife of William de Vescy, who died without issue, and Katherine Paynell *(Cal. Gen.,* vol. ii., p. 558).

Walter of Newland *(de Nova terra)*, Walter *le Rus*, Thomas son of Sewall of the same, William Hubert *(Huberti)* of the same, Alan *de Bosco*, Richard Clerk *(clericum)*, Peter *de Aula*, James de Berel, William *del Holme*, John de Wyxton, and John Cook *(coc')* of the same town, who say upon their oath that the said Letitia held nothing of the King in chief, or of any other, save only of the inheritance of John Paynel, and this in the name of dower; namely, in Drax, a garden on the site *(loco)* of the capital messuage (4*s.* by the year), one croft containing one acre and rather more (5*s.*), eight acres one rood of arable land in demesne (8*s.* 3*d.*), one fishery in the river Use (12*s.*).

Sum, 29s. 3d.

There are free tenants in fee who held of her 486 acres three roods of land, yielding yearly at Easter and Michaelmas, £9 8*s.* 11*d.*; and they do suit at court from three weeks to three weeks. <div style="text-align:right">Sum, £9 8<i>s.</i> 6<i>d.</i></div>

Also certain sokemen *(sokemanni)* holding of her 281½ acres half a rood of land in socage, yielding for every acre 5¼*d.*, that is to say, at the feast of the Purification 1¼*d.*, at Easter 2*d.*, at Michaelmas 2*d.*; and they do suit at court as above.

Sum of the rent, £6 5s. 8d.

And the same sokemen of the said lady held 26 bovates of land in bondage, yielding for every bovate 2*s.* 7½*d.* yearly at the three aforesaid terms. <div style="text-align:right">Sum, 56<i>s.</i> 6½<i>d.</i></div>

And the same sokemen yield at Christmas 47½ hens, worth 3*s.* 11½*d.*; at Easter thirteen score eggs, worth 6½*d*; from a certain custom called mill rent *(firma molendina)*, 4*s.* 4½*d.*; forty quarters of oats by the small measure, valued at 33*s.* 4*d.*

Sum, 42s. 2½d.

Perquisites of Court, with merchete and legerwyte from the daughters of the said sokemen, are valued at one marc by the year. <div style="text-align:right">Sum, 13<i>s.</i> 4<i>d.</i></div>

Roger de Mortimer[a] *(de Mortuo mari)*, dwelling in Lindeseye, held one knight's fee of the said lady in Billeburg, Munketon and Sandewathe[b] in this county, and he owes homage, relief, and scutage when it shall fall.

John Paynell, son of John Paynel is next heir of the said Letitia; and he will be eighteen years old at the feast of S. Peter *ad vincula* next (1 Aug., 1279).

[a] Roger de Mortimer is named amongst the tenants of the Archbishop of York in a list made about this time. He held lands to the amount of £200 a year in the Ainsty, which was the amount required for one Knight's fee (Kirkby's *Inquest*, p. 434).

[b] Sandwath, near Bilburgh, occurs in 1528 *(Tudor Fines Yorkshire*, vol. i., p. 51); and Oxton (in the parish of Tadcaster) and Sandwith are coupled together in 1552 *(Ibid.* vol. i., p. 160).

CVIII. ABBOT OF MEAUX. *Ad. q. d.*

[6 EDW. I. No. 82.]

Writ of *ad quod damnum* directed to Thomas de Normanville, the King's Steward, and referring to the petition of the Abbot of Meaux, that he and his successors may have a weekly market on Thursday, at Wyke, near Mitton-on-the-Hulle, and an annual fair there on the eve, day, and morrow of the Holy Trinity, and twelve following days. Dated at Westminster, 12 Nov., 6th year (1278).

INQUISITION taken at York, in eight days of Easter 7 Edw (9 April, 1279), before Thomas de Normanville, to inquire whether—if the King should grant to the Abbot of Meaux, that he and his successors might have for ever a market on Thursday in every week at Wyke, near Mitton-on-the-Hulle, and a fair there every year, on the eve, day, and morrow of the Holy Trinity, and for twelve days following—it would be to the damage of the King and his heirs and to the annoyance of neighbouring markets and fairs or not, by Sir John de Bilton, Sir Thomas de Gunneby, Sir German Hay, Sir James de Nevile, William son of Robert of Sutton, Peter de Rue, Henry de Skardeburg', Robert Young *(le jovene)* of Ulram, Stephen son of John of Hedon, William de Thikton, Robert son of Baldwin, William de Mountbray, John de Withornewyke, John' Lobyas, Robert *le Veil*, Thomas de Hundegate of Witton, William *de la Gerge* of Hugate, Henry Clerk *(clericum)* of the same, John de Rydale, Stephen de Etton, William de Graymsby, Richard de Cokerington, and Robert *de la More*, who say by their oath that the said Abbot and his successors may have the market and fair at the Wyke *(apud le Wyke)*, as is aforesaid, without damage of the King and his heirs, and without annoyance of neighbouring markets and fairs.

CIX. JOHN DE GARTON.

[7 EDW. I. No. 70.]

Writ of *certiorari* directed to Thomas de Normanville, whether John de Garton has twenty pounds in land, or one knight's fee; and whether, being worth £20 by the year, he ought to be a knight. Dated at Westminster, 28 April, 7th year (1279).

INQUISITION made at York, on Wednesday after the feast of Holy Trinity, 7 Edward (31 May, 1279), before Geoffrey Aguyllun, and John de Stayngrive, by Azo de Flixton, Peter de Mounceus, Thomas de Plumstede, John son of Isabel, William de Haulay, Jollan de Horkestowe, Peter de Thornholme, Adam son of Walter of Garton, Hugh Noreis, Peter *le Ferur* of the

same, John Birninge, and John de Windosene, who say upon
their oath that John de Garton has in the town of Garton,[a]
21½ bovates of land, every bovate worth by the year one mark,
and two acres, worth by the year 4s., beside in rent of cottars,
two marcs; out of which land and rent he pays to the Master
of the Templars, 6s., and to the Prior of Kirkeham, 12d.

Also he has in Wartre four bovates of land and two tofts,
worth yearly 40s., and in Neusum and Aynderby,[b] of the inheritance of Avelina his wife, £20 in land at least.

The said John has not, and never had a son or daughter by
his said wife. He has not a knight's fee worth £20 by the year.
If he had £20 in land he ought to be a knight.

CX. WALTER GIFFARD, ARCHBISHOP OF YORK. *Inq. p. m.*

[7 EDW. I. No. 22.]

[M. 11.]

> Writ directed to Thomas de Normanvylle, the King's Steward, by the hand
> of Master Thomas Beke, at Westminster, 16 May, 7th year (1279).

[M. 12.]

INQUISITION taken at York, on Monday after the Octave of
Holy Trinity, 7 Edward (5 June, 1279), before R[anulf] de
Dakere, Sheriff of Yorkshire, by Robert Vilayn of Bi[n]gelay,
William Gentil, William de Midilton, William de Hillum, Robert
de Bretteby, William de Alwaldelay, Richard de Wigton, Richard
de Muhout, Thomas de Ulskelf, John de Saint Nicholas, Peter
de Alta ripa, and William de Ledes, who say upon their oath
that Walter Giffard held in fee at the time of his death a manor
called Burlay,[c] in the Wapentake of Skireocke, which he bought
of Sir Ralph Maunsel, to hold to him and his heirs of the
Archbishop of York for the time being, by doing the service of
half a knight's fee, and suit of the Archbishop's court of Ottelay
from three weeks to three weeks. The manor is worth entirely
in all issues, £26. He held also in fee 50s. annual rent in the
manor of Pole,[d] from mills and other things therein. And the
said lord is bound by his charter to defend them before whom-
so ever it be.[e]

---

[a] Probably Garton-on-the-Wolds, near Driffield, where in 1315-6, Peter le
Ferour occurs as a tenant of the Archbishop (Kirkby's *Inquest*, p. 318).

[b] Ainderby Steeple, by Northallerton, and Newsham, in the parish of Kirkby
Wiske.

[c] Burley-in-Wharfedale.

[d] Poole, in the parish of Otley.

[e] " Et predictus dominus tenetur eos defendere per cartam suam penes quos-
cumque."

Godfrey Giffard, Bishop of Worcester, brother of the said
Walter Giffard, is his next heir and of full age.[a]

[M. 13.]

INQUISITION taken at York, on Monday after the Octave of
Holy Trinity, 7 Edward (5 June, 1279), before R[anulf] de
Dakere, Sheriff of Yorkshire, by Robert de Pavely, John de
Sutton, Richard de Rosholm, John de Mileforthe, Richard de
Kente, Richard Derli[n]g of Fenton, John de Lede, Robert son of
Nicholas of Mikelfeude, Henry de Ledisham, Ralph de Mileforthe, David de Cauwode, and Henry de Neulande, who say
upon their oath that Walter Giffard, on the day of his death,
held and had in fee a manor, called Abholm,[b] in the Wapentake
of Barkeston, which he bought of Sir William de Hamelton,
to hold to him and his heirs. It ought to be held of the Archbishop for the time being, and ought to be defended against him
by the lords of Steweton[c] in all services for so much land (pro
tanto terre). He had in the said manor only 60 acres of land
and meadow, which are worth by the year, 60s.

Godfrey Giffard, Bishop of Worcester, brother of Walter
Giffard, is his next heir and of full age.

[M. 2.]

INQUISITION taken at Molescroft, before the Bailiff of the
liberty of Beverley, on Wednesday before the feast of S
Barnabas the Apostle, 7 Edward (7 June, 1279), by Richard le
Caretter, Gilbert de Snaythe, Geoffrey de Lounde, Simon de
Lounde, Geoffrey de Killum, Roger de la Wudhalle, John de
Garton, Ekuard Gem'an, Robert Saloman, Robert de Osgoteby,
John son of James, Henry de Hoveninge, and Geoffrey son of
Henry, who say upon their oath that Walter, Archbishop of
York, died vested and seised in fee of five bovates of land in
the territory of Molescroft by his own purchase; but no
messuage appertains to that land. He held these bovates,

---

[a] By the inquisition taken in the County of Oxford, ths age of Godfrey Giffard
is said to be forty-four years. On 14 June, 1279, the King, then at Canterbury,
took the homage of Godfrey, brother and heir of the late Archbishop, for all lands
and tenements which were held of himself in chief, and ordered full seisin to be
given, under date 21 June following (Rot. Fin., 7 Edw. I., m. 12).

[b] Called in Kirkby's Inquest (pp. 213, 384n) Albeholm and Abholm. Mr. Scaife
gives the following note on this place: "The site of Albeholme is probably indicated
by Albeholme Dike, a small stream running into Hambleton Dike, about one mile
west of the village of Hambleton."

[c] Steeton, in the parish of Sherburn.

worth 40s. by the year (the bovate, 8s.), not of the King in chief, but of the Archbishop and his successors for foreign service only.

Godfrey Giffard, Bishop of Worcester, is his next heir and of full age.[a]

CXI. THOMAS DE HEDON. *Prebend of Tange.*

[7 EDW. I. No. 61.]

Writ of *certiorari* directed to Thomas de Normanville, the King's Steward beyond Trent, and given by the hand of Master Thomas Beke, at Westminster, 13 May, 7th year, (1279). Recites that Master Thomas de Hedon, Canon of York, complained that, whereas five acres of meadow between Layrthorpe and Tange[b] appertain to his prebend in Tange, and all his predecessors, Canons of that prebend, were in possession of the same as of right, Robert de Creppinge, formerly Sheriff of Yorkshire, by taking that meadow into the late King's hand, unjustly, disseised John de Gayteham his (Thomas) immediate predecessor, and the now Sheriff still detains it. The King to be certified of the truth of the matter.

INQUISITION made at York, before Thomas de Normanville, on the morrow of the Apostles Peter and Paul, 7 Edward (30 June, 1279), concerning five acres of meadow with the appurtenances between Leyrthorpe and Tange, belonging to the prebend of Master Thomas de Hedon, Canon of York, by the jurors under-written, viz: by William de Holteby, Robert de Bulforde, Richard de Waxande, Nicholas de Rivers *(de Riper'),* Paulin de Lyllinge, William Burdoun, knights, Thomas de Vespount, Peter de Evercewyke,[c] Robert de Yolton, William de Touthorpe, John de Stoketon, and Richard son of Hugh of the same, who say by their oath that all the predecessors of the said Thomas, Canons of the said prebend, as in right thereof, were in possession of the meadow until Robert de Creppenge, formerly Sheriff of the County, took it into the hand of the late King Henry, and unjustly disseised John de Geytham, the last predecessor of Thomas; and so that disseisin has continued since then from Sheriff to Sheriff until now. The said Robert took the meadow into the hand of King Henry for his own convenience in order to feed his own horses, and for that reason he appropriated to the King as much soil as was flooded yearly by the Fosse. When during the year the Fosse rises, then a boat

---

[a] There are other inquisitions, taken in the counties of Wilts., Somerset, Hereford, Gloucester, Southampton, Nottingham, and Oxford.

[b] Tang Hall is about a mile east of Layerthorpe.

[c] Name doubtful.

of York Castle and the men of the Sheriff for the time being can come and go by water, and at will mow grass, one foot of the mower being in the boat and the other upon the land. When the water goes down, the soil remains to the prebend, and that meadow is worth in all issues by the year, ten shillings.[a]

CXII. PETER DE MAULEY.[b] *Inq. p. m.*

[7 EDW. I. No. 11.]

Writ[c] dated at Windsor, 16 July, 7th year (1279).

EXTENT of all the lands of the lord Peter de Mauley *(Malo-lacu)* the second in demesnes and services, on the day of

[a] Qua racione predictus Robertus cepit predictum pratum in manum domini H. regis dicunt quod racione proprie utilitatis ipsius Roberti ad pascendum equos suos proprios, et ea racione appropriavit totum solum domino Regi quantum aqua de Fosse per annum altius superhabundaverit. Et quid juris dominus Rex habet in prato illo et qualiter et quo modo dicunt quod cum aqua de Fosse in anno altius habundat, tunc batellus Castri Ebor. et homines Vicecomitis, qui pro tempore fuerit, per aquam de Fosse ultra solum predicti prati possunt ire et redire et herbam pro voluntate sua metere, uno pede metentis existente in batello et alio super terram, et cum decrescerit aqua, remaneat solum predicti prati prebende predicte, et valet pratum illud in omnibus exitibus per annum xs.

[b] Peter de Mauley II., son and heir of Peter de Mauley, a Poitevin, by Isabella, daughter and heiress of Robert de Turnham and Joan, daughter and heiress of William Fossard of Mulgrave and Doncaster. If Walter of Hemingburgh (vol. i., p. 232) can be trusted, the first Peter got his wife, with her great inheritance, as a reward for having murdered John's nephew, Arthur of Brittany. "Loco mercedis iniquiæ" are his words. But the fact that he agreed to pay the large sum of 7,000 marcs for marrying this heiress throws considerable doubt on this statement *(Excerpta è Rotulis Finium*, vol. i., p. 54). It was not until 1221 that he managed to get the debt paid *(Rot. Litt. Claus.*, vol. i., p. 466 *b).* He was a man very much connected with King John, and held many official positions then and in the next reign. In 1202 John gave him land in Normandy *(Rot. Normanniæ*, 66 *).* Under the year 1211, Matthew Paris *(Chronica Majora*, vol. ii., p. 533 *)* enumerates him amongst the King's evil counsellors. He was Sheriff of Dorset and Somerset, 2—5 Hen. III., and of Northants, 20 Hen. III. In 1220 he had the custody of the important Castle of Corfe confided to him, and in 1226 that of Shirburn as well *(Excerpta è Rotulis Finium*, vol. i., pp. 52, 143 *).* In 1240 he had a grant of the marriage of Beatrix, widow of John de Basingeham, for the benefit of his kinsman, Gerard de St. Flouer *(Close Rolls*, 24 Hen. III., m. 18 *).* He was dead before 22 Dec., 1241, when the Sheriff of Yorkshire was ordered to take into the King's hand the lands which were Peter de Mauley's, his son being a minor *(Excerpta è Rotulis Finium*, vol. i., pp. 364, 379, 409, and No. XIII.*)* On 15 Oct., 1247, the King took the homage of Peter, son of Peter de Mauley, for all his father's lands, of which the Sheriff of Yorkshire was commanded to give him seisin *(Close Roll*, 31 Hen. III., m. 2 *).* He had been already married, when not much more than eleven years of age, to Hillaria, eldest daughter of Peter de Brus II. *(See* p. 139 *n).* There was no issue by this marriage, for if there had been they would have appeared amongst the heirs of Peter de Brus III. As he left a son and heir he must have married a second time, but the name of this wife does not appear. On 9 Feb., 1253-4, he had a grant of free warren in his demesne lands of Sandeshende, Lithe, Great Barneby, Little Barneby, Mikélby, Eluuerdeby, Slethholme, Westingeby, Egeton, Cukewald, Hoton, Briddeshale, Baynton, Nessingwike, Lokinton, Clif, Danecastre,

his death, in the Wapentake of Langeberg.[a]   At Coldeburgh[b]
. . . . . . acres of cultivated land (the acre 6*d.*),£7 13*s.* 6*d.*; 64½
acres of uncultivated land (2*d.*) . . . . meadow, which are worth
by the year 5*s.* At the Grange of Lyth, 256 acres of cultivated
land (6*d.*), £7 8*s.*; also . . (2*d.*), 19*s.* 11*d.*; 27 acres of meadow
(8*d.*), 18*s.* At Cukewalde[e] eight score acres . . . £4; 57½ acres
of uncultivated land (2*d.*), 9*s.* 7*d.*; 14 acres of meadow . . 4*d.*;
from other profits, 6*s.* 8*d.* In Bircschoke[d] 30 acres of meadow,
15*s.*   Sum of this extent, £23 14*s.* 9*d.*

EGGETON.[e]

At Eggeton, in bondage, 31 bovates of land, which yield
yearly £12 8*s.* Also there, 24 cottars who pay, 33*s.*, . . . Free
farm from free tenants enfeoffed, 22*s.* 2*d.* William Alchorn
holds one carucate, 52*s.* . . . . At Lecerige, 32½ acres of land,
yielding 32*s.* 6*d.* In the east wood, 52½ acres of land, yielding
52*s.* 6*d.* In le . . . . 150½ acres of land, worth £7 10*s.* 6*d.*
In Wlvedale,[f] 65 acres of land, yearly 65*s.* At Sletholm,[g] . .
with a croft, worth yearly 73*s.* 4*d.* Stephen de Mauley holds
within the forest and without 20 librates of land, so that, . . .
                              Sum of this extent, £34 4*s.* . .

Sandalle, Wheteley, Heythorp (*sic*, read Hexthorp), Balleby, Rossington, and
Bramham (*Charter Roll*, 37 and 38 Hen. III., m. 9, No. 49). At the same time he
had a grant of a market on Wednesdays at his manor of Lithe, and a fair there to
last eight days, on the vigil and day of St. Oswald (Aug. 5) and the six days
following (*Ibid.*, and *Cartæ Antiquæ* II., No. 8). He was dead, as appears from
the writ mentioned above, before 16 July, 1279. On 21 Aug. following, the King,
then at Lydington, took the homage of Peter de Mauley (son and heir of Peter)
for all the lands held of himself in chief; and Thomas de Normanville was ordered
to give him seisin (*Rot. Fin.*, 7 Edw. I., m. 8, and *Pipe Roll*, 8 Edw. I., *Ebor*).

  [c] On the dorse of the writ return to the following effect :—Sum of the whole
extent of his lands, £321 1*s.* 1½*d.* Sum of fees held of him, 33½ fees, a fourth part
and a fifth part of one fee. He had the advowsons of four churches. All the aforesaid lands with fees and advowsons the said Peter held of the King in chief by the
service of two knights' fees. The same Peter held of the Bishop of Durham in
chief the manor of Clif, worth £20 18*s.* 11*d.*, by the service of half a knight's fee.

  [a] The Wapentake of Langbargh is coextensive with Cleveland. It comprises
the N.E. corner of Yorkshire.

  [b] Goldsbrough, in the parish of Lythe.

  [c] Cocket Nook, a mile and a half south of Ugthorpe.

  [d] Briscoe, about a mile S.E. of Ugthorpe. Called more correctly in the Guisborough Chartulary (ff. 326, 329) Birkescov and Birkscough, *i.e.* Birchwood.

  [e] Egton, a station on the Cleveland line.

  [f] Wood Dale House, on the east bank of the Stonegate Beck, the stream
dividing Ugthorpe and Lealholm.

  [g] Identified by Mr. Scaife (Kirkby's *Inquest*, p. 125), with Lealholm, but no
doubt erroneously, as Lealholm is in the Brus fee. "If a mere surmise is at all
admissible, I should be more inclined to connect the name with the Sleights in
'Barnby Sleights,' the name of a tenement lying about three quarters of a mile
south of East Barnby (Atkinson's *History of Cleveland*, vol. i., p. 165).

WESTINGBY.[a]

Robert de Schelton holds one carucate of land in the town of Westingby, and renders yearly one pair of white gloves at Christmas, . . . The same holds 37 acres of land, and renders yearly 3 pounds of cumin. And be it known that the aforesaid Robert is enfeoffed of all the land, ... The same holds a vaccary, worth by the year 13s. 4d.

Sum of this extent, 110s. 4d.

MICCHELBY.[b]

In town of Micchelby, 15 bovates and five acres, which yield by the year £4 1s. 10d., also free farm from free tenants . . . thirteen bovates of land by knight's service, doing suit at the Court of the lord. Sum of this extent, £4 12s. 2d.

BERGBY.

Robert de Bergby holds four carucates of land by knight's service, without doing suit.

NEUTON.

Robert de Acclum holds in Neuton four carucates of land by knight's service, doing suit at the lord's court.

ELVERDEBY.

In town of Elverdeby, two acres of meadow, which yield by the year 3s. 4d. Also Robert, son of Nicholas, holds in the same one carucate by knight's service, doing suit at lord's court . . . holds two carucates by the same service.

Sum of this extent, 3s. 4d.

BARNEBY.

In town of Barneby, 15 bovates in bondage, which yield by the year £4 13s. 6d. Five cottars, who yield by the year 8s.; free farm from free tenants enfeoffed, 6s. 5d. Sir John de Ferlington holds ten bovates by knight's service, doing suit of Court . . . . by same service. Alice Breton holds six bovates by same service. William le Botiller holds eight . . . . . Also Robert de Mauley[c] holds one carucate and renders yearly a rose.

Sum, 107s. 11d.

[a] Westonby Moor, a mile and a half N.W. of Egton.

[b] Mickleby, Borrowby (*Domesday*, Bergebi, Bergesbi), Newton Mulgrave, Ellerby (*Domesday*, Aluuardebi, Elwordebi), East and West Barnby, Lythe, Sandsend, and Hutton Mulgrave.

[c] In all probability a younger son of Peter de Mauley II., to whom this inquisition relates. He differenced the golden bend which the Mauleys had inherited from the Fossards, by placing three white eagles on it (Nicolas' *Roll of Arms, temp. Edward II*). His brother Stephen is mentioned before and afterwards.

LYTH.

In town of Lyth, 24 bovates in bondage, which yield by the year £7 6s. 8d., . . . also free farm (from free tenants) enfeoffed, 6d. yearly. Alice Sturmy holds ten bovates by knight's service.

Sum of this extent, £9 6s. 6d.

SANDESHEND.

In town of Sandeshend, 53½ tofts, which yield by the year 53s. 6d. Also sea fishery, worth yearly 13s. . . . his land when it shall happen, but we know not how much it is worth by the year. Sum, 66s. 10d.

In town of Hoton, 23 bovates in bondage, which yield by the year £8 16s. 4d. Also in the same, eight carucates . . . . Also Emma. . . . . enfeoffed, holds one bovate, and renders by the year one pound of pepper.

Sum, £9 . . s. 4d. and one pound of pepper.

Also the same had there four mills, which yield by the year £20; also advowson of a church worth by the year . . herbage worth by the year 6s. 8d. Perquisites of Court, worth by the year 20s. Also . . . . worth yearly 24s.

Sum of this extent, £ . . . .

Also Sir Nicholas de Menille held of said lord Peter one knight's fee in towns of Grenhou, Thunstalle, and Aton, where 12 carucates [make one knight's fee].

Sir Peter de Mauley, son of the said Sir Peter, is aged thirty years old or more, and is his true heir.

Sir Peter was bound to the King for all his lands which he held of the King ª . . . . Sum total, ...

EXTENT of lands in Wapentakes of Herthille, Bucros, Dyker', and Bolemer.

INQUISITION taken at Pokelington, on Sunday after the feast of S. Peter *ad vincula*, 7 Edward (6 Aug., 1279), before Ranulph de Daker, Sheriff of Yorkshire, and Geoffrey Agoylun, of the lands and tenements which were of Peter de Mauley, in the Wapentake of Herthille, by William son of Gamel, Ralph de Halton, Richard de Wymthorpe, William *de la Garde* of Hugate,

---

ª On a small slip of parchment 3⅜ by 4⅝ in. high. " Names of those by whom was made the extent of the lands and tenements of Sir Peter de Mauley in the Wapentake of Lang':—William de Camera of Esington (Easington), Robert de Berghby, William de Camera of Lofthus', Robert Wiles, William Haxthorne, Geoffrey de Thocotes, Adam de Lyth, Nicholas de Barnby, John de Mikelby, Thomas Forester *(le forester)*, Richard Clerk of Lith, Adam de Warthul."

Henry Clerk *(clericum)* of the same, John de Hake, Laurence de Oketon, William Fossard, Walter Fraunceys, Roger *le Somuner*, and William de Nortthorpe, who say that in Baynton and Nessingwyk,[a] which are held of the King in chief, there are in demesne 24 bovates of land (at 15*s.*), £18; and 24 acres of meadow (at 2*s.* 6*d.*), 60*s.* A windmill is worth by the year £4. Forty-eight bondmen *(bondi)* hold 95½ bovates of land and yield yearly £71 12*s.* 6*d.* There are cottars, holding cottages and small parcels *(particulas)* of land by the acre, and they pay by the year 72*s.* 6*d.* Sum total, £100 5*s.* Of which John de Houton held thirty librates of land for term of his life and that of his wife (whichsoever of them shall survive), by the gift of the lord Peter de Mauley, deceased, whereof the said John has not satisfied the King for entering the King's fee *(eo quod intravit feodum domini regis)*; and so there remains, £70 5*s.*

LOKENTON.[b]

At Lokenton there are in demesne 14 bovates of land (at 7*s.*), £4 18*s.*, and 20 acres of meadow (at 2*s.*), 40*s.* There is a several pasture *(pastura separabilis)* worth by the year 4*s.* There are 19 bondmen *(bondi)* holding 19 bovates in bondage, for £19, and 11 cottars holding cottages, for 30*s.* 6*d.* by the year. There are free tenants in fee who yield yearly 35*s.* 8*d.*

Sum total, £29 18*s.* 2*d.*

Sum of the whole value of Baynton and Lokenton (except the portion of John de Houton), £100 3*s.* 2*d.*

The advowson of the church of Baynton was in the gift of the said Peter, and the church is worth by the year 100 marcs. The church of Lokenton likewise, which is worth by the year 30 marcs.

Peter de Mauley, who is now, is next heir of Peter deceased; and he was aged thirty years on the feast of S. Mary Magdalen last past (22 July, 1279).

BRIDESHALE.[c]

INQUISITION of Briddeshale taken by William de Thoraldeby, Walter Wascelin, Thomas Wascel[in], Richard de Thorgrin-thorp, William de Kenerthorpe, William Croc, Adam de F . . . William Clerk *(clericum)*, Roger Basille, Henry de Ryspale, William Slegh of Wharrum, and Richard Almote of the same,

---

[a] Bainton, S.W. of Driffield. Neswick, in the parish of Bainton.
[b] Lockington, near Beverley.
[c] Birdsall near Malton, now the seat of Lord Middleton.

who say upon their oath that Peter de Mauley held in chief of the King the manor of Briddeshale. There are in demesne 48 bovates (at 5*s.*), £12. Six bondmen *(bondi)* hold in bondage 22 bovates, and yield by the year for rents and services £13 19*s.* There are free tenants in fee, who yield yearly 40*s.*

Sum total, £27 19*s.*

Of which Stephen de Mauley,[a] brother of the said Peter, deceased, holds ten librates of land for life by the gift of his said brother: and so there remain, £17 19*s.*

Sum total, £118 2*s.* 2*d.*,[b] except the portion of John de Houton, as above.

Knight's fees in the Wapentakes of Herthille, Bucros, Dyk', and Bolemer.

Knights' fees.

Robert de Ros in Middelton, Kiblingecotes and Etton[c]	I
Robert de Percy in Sutton upon Derewent	½
German Hay[d] in Achton	I½
Ralph de Rypplingham and parceners in Rypplingham and Elvele[e]	I
James de Fryvyle in Etton	I
The heirs of Ravenesthorpe in the same[f]	I
John de Hothum in the same, Esthorp and Craunzwyk[g] .	2
William Daniel in Lokenton and Wynthorp[h] .	¼
Geoffrey Aguyllon in Besewyk[i]	⅕
John Salvain in Kilnewyk	⅕
Hugh de Langethwait in Appelgard[j] . . .	½

[a] Stephen de Mauley occurs as Archdeacon of Cleveland in 1289 and 1306.

[b] On the dorse the sum total is £118 4*s.*

[c] Middleton-on-the-Wolds, Kipling Cotes, and Etton.

[d] Achton is now Aughton. *Domesday,* Actun, and Acton and Aghton in Kirkby.

[e] Riplingham and Kirk Ella.

[f] The vill of Ravensthorpe has disappeared. It stood about one mile south of Leckonfield.

[g] Easthorpe, in the parish of Londesborough, and Cranswick, in Hutton Cranswick, near Driffield.

[h] Wynthorp not identified, but probably in or near Beswick, where William Daniel held land in 1302 of the fee of Mauley (Kirkby's *Inquest,* p. 259). Licence was granted in 1308 to Sir William Danyel, knt., worn out with illness and old age *(tam egritudine quam senio confractus),* to hear divine service in his manor of Besewyke *(Reg. Greenfield,* vol. i., fo. 110*).*

[i] Beswick, in the parish of Kilnwick, between Beverley and Driffield.

[j] In 1302 William de Langewath held in Langewath and Bramley the fourth part of one fee of Peter de Mauley (Kirkby's *Inquest,* p. 231). Langewath, now Langthwaite, is the name of a farm about three miles N.W. of Doncaster, and Bramley is in the parish of Braithwell, near Rotherham. Appelgard is probably near one of these places. In 1545, an Appilholme is mentioned somewhere in the neighbourhood of Adwick, Bentley, or Arksey *(Test. Ebor.,* vol. v., p. 295 *n).*

Knights' fees.

William Fossard and parceners in Baynton	$\frac{1}{5}$
John de Vescy in Watton	2
The heirs of Peter de Bruys in Brunne[a]	1
John de Bolemer in the same and Welleburne[b]	1
John de Vescy in Stitnum[c]	1
Robert de Neville in Schyrrevehoton[d] and its members	6
Anketin Malure in Huntington and Clyfford[e]	$\frac{1}{2}$
John de Oketon in the same[f]	1
Ralph fitzWilliam *(fil' Will'i)* in Butterwyk[g]	1
Geoffrey Aguyllon in Ky[llingwyk][h]	$\frac{1}{2}$
William de Barkthorpe in Warr'[i]	$\frac{1}{2}$

Sum of fees, $23\frac{1}{2}$ fees and a fourth part.[j]
Peter de Mauley held all his lands of the King in chief, by the service of two knights when the King goes in his army, except the manor of Clyf which is held of the Bishop of Durham. Of the value of that and by what service the jurors know not.

INQUISITION in the Wapentake of Ouse and Derewent. The lord Peter de Mauley was seised of a manor in Cliff,[k] with its appurtenances, which he held of the Bishop of Durham in chief by the service of half a knight's fee. Appertaining to the manor—which by itself is worth half a marc—are eight score and 12 acres (12*d*.) of land. An alderbed the pasture of which is worth 40*s*. yearly. In bondage and cottage *(cotagio)* five bovates, worth by the year £10 0*s*. 3*d*.

Sum of the value, £20 18*s*. 11*d*.
Peter de Mauley is the next heir of the said Peter, and he was aged thirty years and more on the day of his father's death.

[a] Eastburn, Kirkburn, Southburn, and Westburn, were all held by the heirs of Brus, but there is no mention in Kirkby's *Inquest* of Peter de Mauley intervening between them and the King.

[b] Bulmer, a parish six miles S.W. of Malton. Welburn is in the parish of Bulmer.

[c] Stittenham, in the parish of Sheriff Hutton.

[d] Sheriff Hutton.

[e] Huntington, near York, and Clifford, in the parish of Bramham.

[f] Octon, in the parish of Thwing.

[g] Butterwick, in the parish of Foxholes.

[h] In 1284-5 Geoffrey Aguillon held lands in Beswick, in the parish of Kilnwick, of the Mauley fee (Kirkby's *Inquest*, p. 83).

[i] Wharram-le-Street.

[j] On the dorse a further fifth part is mentioned in the total, as well as the advowsons of the churches of Lokenton and Baynton.

[k] Long Cliff, in the parish of Hemingborough.

The names of the inquisitors are these :—Robert de Men-
thorpe, John de Averenges, Robert de Hacthorpe, William de
Midilton, Thomas de Rusceby, Gamel de Duffelde, Richard *le
Venur*, John son of Julian *de la Wdhalle*, Henry *de Nova haya*,
Hugh son of Peter of Osgotby, John son of Nicholas of the
same, and John *de Castello*.

[E XTENT of] Donecastre and Rosington, made by Thomas
Framfr', Roger *de Aula*, Henry Stirchouer, Hugh de
Kannewick, Adam . . . . . Thomas *del Brom*, Philip *le Mercer*,
Reginald de Messingham, Robert de Schintorpe, John de
Waddeword . . . . .

DONECASTRE.

. . . . rent of assize by the year £17. There are at Donecastre
four mills, and at Hextorpe one mill, which are worth by the
year 40 marcs. Market-toll *(tollon' fori)* of Donecastre is worth
twenty marcs; also the Court of Donecastre, 60*s.* Sum, £60.
Of which the lord Peter de Mauley six years ago gave to
Peter his son and heir and Nicholaa his wife[a] for her endowment
(ad ipsam dotand'), £7 10*s.* 9*d.* yearly; and so there remained
in his hands at the time of his death, £52 9*s.* 3*d.*

ROSINGTON.

Joan, daughter of Nicholas of Rosington, holds one bovate
for half a marc; William de Fram[ton] one toft for 18*d.*; the
parson of Rosington, one toft for 12*d.* ; . . . . one toft for 12*d.*;
the heirs of Robert de Vipont for the town of Bautre for . . . .
Sum, 12*s.* 2*d.*
There are four carucates and half a bovate of land in the
hands of bondmen, to wit, thirty two bovates and a half (the
bovate 10*s.* 10*d.*). Sum, £17 12*s.* 1*d.*
Fifteen cottars yield yearly 17*s.* 10*d.*
There are in the hands of bondmen at will of the lord
47 acres of the lord's demesne (at 5*d.*), and other 69 acres in
their hands (at 4*d.*). One croft yields 4*s.* 6*d.*, another 12*d.*, and
a plot of meadow, 16*s.* Sum, 64*s.* 1*d.*
The mill of Rosington 26*s.* 8*d.*, the fishery at the mill gates
6*s.* 8*d.*, and fishery in the marsh 12*s.* 4*d.* Sum, 45*s.* 8*d.*
Sum total of Rosington by the year £24 11*s.* 10*d.*, without
the advowson of the church.
The church of Rosington is worth by the year £12.

[a] Nicholaa, daughter of Gilbert de Gaunt, senior, and one of the sisters and
coheirs of Gilbert de Gaunt, junior *(De Banco Roll*, Trin., 8 Edw. II., m. 259, and
Ibid., Mich., 9 Edw. II., m. 428 *d*, quoted in *The Antiquary*, N.S., vol. ii., pp. 137,
140).

HEXTORP AND BALLEBY.[a]

The lord of Loversalle[b] renders for Loversale, that is to say, the fourth part of one fee, 12*d.*; the township of Balleby for herbage, 12*d.*; . . . *le Rede* for one toft and two and a half acres of land, 16*d.*; Alan de Karhus' for one toft and four and a half acres of land, 2*s.*; William Tock for one rood of land, 1*d.*; Anabilia Vinter for half an acre, 2*d.*; the Hospital of S. James for one acre, 4*d.*; Richard Dilman for half an acre, 2*d.*; Nicholas *le Mercer* for an acre and a half, 1½*d.* by the year, or one pound of cumin.   Sum, 6*s.* 2½*d.*

There are in Hextorpe and Balleby 5½ bovates (the bovate of 24 acres, and worth 10*s.*), 55*s.*; and two bovates (each 24 acres, at 8*s.*), 16*s.*

There are three cottages, 2*s.*; 21 acres of demesne in the Holme (at 6*d.*), 10*s.* 6*d.*; and three acres of meadow (at 18*d.*), 4*s.* 6*d.*   Sum, 17*s.*

WAITELE.[c]

The lord of Waitele renders yearly for the land which he holds in Waitele, 24*s.*

SCHINTORPE.[d]

The lordship *(dominicum)* of Schintorpe renders yearly 18*s.*, whereof Maud *(Matild')* de Schintorp has in dower a third part, and there remains to the lord's use, 12*s.*

Sum total of the lands in the hand of the lord Peter, except the advowsons of Rosington and Schintorp, £83 11*s.* 3*d.*

The lord Peter de Mauley who now is (son and heir of the lord Peter, deceased), and Nicholaa his wife, hold by the gift of the father 124½ acres of the demesne of Hextorpe (at 5*d.*); ten and a half acres of meadow (at 18*d.*); 19*s.* 6*d.* rent from two bovates in Hextorpe; 20*s.* 6*d.* rent of freemen in Hextorpe and Balleby; 56*s.* 8*d.* rent of freemen in Waitele; the town of Sandalle, which was extended for £11 4*s.* 2*d.*; rent of the lord of Loversalle, for the vill of Loversalle, 2*s.*; and £7 10*s.* 9*d.* of the rent of Donecastre as appears above in the extent of Donecastre.

Sum, £27 1*s.* 7*d.*

---

[a] Hexthorpe and Balby, near Doncaster.

[b] In 1284-5 Jordan le Vavasur held Loversalle, in the name of his wife's dower, of Peter de Mauley, for the fourth part of a knight's fee (Kirkby's *Inquest*, p. 5). Loversall is three miles south of Doncaster.

[c] Wheatley, near Doncaster. Also spelt Watelage, Watelag, Waythelach, and Watelay.

[d] " The site of this lost vill has been well ascertained by Mr. Bower and Mr. Wrightson, to have been in some closes between Cusworth and Newton, where are still certain unevennesses of the surface indicative of buildings having formerly existed in that place " (Hunter's *South Yorkshire*, vol. ii., p. 490).

FEES.

Knights' fees.

The heirs of Robert de Vipont hold in Bautre and Ouster-
feud^a .   2
Richard de Barneby in Barneby^b   ½
Hugh de Langethauit in Langethauit and Thils^c   ¼
John de Bosseville in Loveresalle   ¼
Baldwin Wake in Bramham and Clifford   .   .   2
Adam *de Novo mercato* in Schintorpe   .   .   ¼
Peter de Waddeuord in Waddeuord^d   .   .   ¼
John de Vescy in Roderham, Picburne, and Hoton Livet,^e
of which Custance Livet is wont to hold two fees   .   3½

The lord Peter de Mauley, son and heir of the lord Peter,
deceased, is of full age, namely, thirty years.

He held Donecastre of the King with his other lands by
the service of riding with the King, together with two knights,
when his peers shall so ride. He held Rosington of the fee of
Peverel, and not of the fee of Donecastre, but the service by
which he holds all his lands is that of riding with the king.^f

---

CXIII. MARGERY, DAUGHTER AND HEIR OF JOHN DE
ANLANBY. *State of Mind.*

[7 EDW. I. No. 72.]

Writ of *certiorari* directed to Thomas de Normanville, the King's Steward.
Inquiry to be made as to the state of mind of Margery, daughter and
heir of John de Anlanby, and in the meantime the custody of her
person and property to be committed to William de Beverley, her
kinsman. And as Robert de Stoteville has taken her son and heir away
from his mother, the boy is to be recovered and given into the custody
of the same William. Dated at Nottingham, 9 Sept., 7th year (1279).

INQUISITION taken at York, before Thomas de Normanvyle,
in eight days of S. Michael 7 Edw. (6 Oct., 1279), by Robert
Salveyn, Thomas de Houeton, John de Anlanby of Cotingham,
John Lygard of Anlanby, William de Middelton of the same,
John Thothe of Northcave, Robert de Boscehale of Heyton,

^a Bawtry and Austerfield.
^b Barnby-upon Don.
^c The parish of Langthwaite with Tilts, in the parish of Doncaster.
^d Wadworth.
^e Rotherham, Pickburn, in the parish of Brodsworth, and Hooton Levet, in the
parish of Maltby.
^f " Item dicunt quod tenuit Donecastre de domino Rege cum aliis terris suis
per servicium equitandi cum domino Rege cum duobus militibus in servicio domini
Regis, quando pares sui equitaverint. Item dicunt quod tenuit Rosington de feodo
de Peverel, et non de feodo Donecastre, set tenet de domino Rege cum aliis terris,
et serviciis, cum alio servicio suo equitandi cum Rege, per [quod] servicium tenet
omnes terras suas."

William de Melton, Walter de Dodemere, Gilbert son of William of Wilmerfosse, William *le Vavasour*, William Faceben,[a] and Alan of Saint James *(de Sancto Jacobo)*, who say upon their oath that Margery, daughter and heir of John de Anlanby, deceased, who held of the Abbot of S. Mary, York, by the service of two marcs yearly, as free farmer, for all service save two suits at the Abbot's court to be made by reasonable summons, is so incapable that she is not of sound mind or in any wise sufficient for the rule of her property, lands, and tenements. The said Margery holds her land by hereditary right of the said Abbot by the service aforesaid, and that land is worth by the year thirteen marcs less four shillings. She began to be ill *(cepit egrotari)* a fortnight before the feast of the Purification of the Blessed Mary last (2 Feb., 1278-9), after which term came Robert de Stotevylle of Cotingham, of whom she holds and claims to hold nothing, and to whom she does no service, and without any authority took away John her son and heir from her, and has detained, and yet detains him most unjustly.

CXIV. PETER DE BRUS.[b] *Extent of Knights' Fees.*

[7 EDW. I. No. 32.]

[M. 1.]

The King to Thomas de Normanville, his Steward. Whereas we have not yet caused to be divided the knight's fees which belonged to Peter de Brus, deceased, who held of us in chief, amongst the heirs and partners of the same inheritance, on account of which, at the suit of Margaret de Ros,[c] sister and one of the heirs of the said Peter, we have often commanded Walter de Faucumberge and Agnes his wife, and the other coheirs and partners of the aforesaid inheritance, that they should on certain days and places appear before us for the purpose of receiving their shares of the aforesaid fees; and whereas they have taken no trouble to come according to our order for that purpose, we command you to inquire what, and how many fees the said Peter held, and how much they may be worth by the year. In the meantime letting the heirs and partners aforesaid know, that they be then present there to receive their shares in the aforesaid fees, warning them that whether they come or not, we shall not neglect to cause to be assigned to the aforesaid Margaret, as may be just, the share falling to her in this part. Dated at Westminster, 7 July, 7th year (1279).

[M. 3.]

INQUISITION of knight's fees held by Peter de Brus in the bailiwick of Holdirnesse, made by John de Carleton, Simon

---

a The reading of this word is doubtful. In 1284-5, William Faceben' or Fateben held seven bovates of the Templars in South Cave (Kirkby's *Inquest*, p. 85).

b See No. LXXXII.

c Widow of Robert de Ros, of Wark. In the spring of 2 Edw. I. (1273-4) she paid the King a fine of £10 that the Escheator beyond Trent might take her oath in those parts, that she would not marry without the King's leave. It is added she had lands in Yorkshire *(Rot. Fin.* 2 Edw. I., m. 24).

de Gousil, Henry de Preston, Stephen de Ouistwyke, Walter de
Flinton, William *de la Chaumbre*, Roger de Lundo, Simon de
Lundo, John de Dringhou, William de Grimeston, John
Bernard, and John de Fitlinge, who say that Peter de Brus held
nothing in demesne of the King in Holdirnesse, but Herbert de
Saint Quintin held in Rolliston[a] and Mapilton 12 carucates of
land, in Dringhou and Ulleram five carucates, in Ouistwyke three
carucates, of the heirs of Roger de Merley, by knight's service,
whereof 23½ carucates make one knight's fee. The heirs of
Roger de Merley held the same of Peter de Brus, who held of
the King after the decease of the lady Avelina, heir of William
de Fortibus formerly Earl of Albemarle. Peter did suit at the
Wapentake [court] of Holdirnesse for the same, and homage to
the Earl of Albemarle with knight's service, as they believe.
He held no tenements of others in this bailiwick.

_____

[M. 4.]

INQUISITION of fees held by Peter de Brus in the North
Riding, East Riding, and Clarhoue, taken on Sunday after
the feast of S. Luke the Evangelist, 7 Edw. (22 Oct., 1279), by
William de Mumbray, William de Bovington, John de Lesingbi,
Robert de Scudirschelf, Matthew de Glaphoue, Walter de
Thorpe, Robert de Collebi, Thomas de Waxsant, John de
Kirkebi, William de Thorinton, Alan de Mautebi, and Geoffrey
de Tocotes, who say upon their oath that Peter de Brus held
of the King in chief sixteen knights' fees: whereof Roger de
Merlay held two fees in Burtone-Annes[b] and elsewhere; William
Esturmi and his parceners *(participes)*, two fees in Fayceby[c]
and elsewhere; Robert de Lascelles, one fee in Bordilbi[d] and
elsewhere; William and John Mauleverer, three fees in Gerbor-
debi, Alverton,[e] and elsewhere; Robert Ingram, three fees in
Erneclive, Heslerton,[f] and elsewhere; William de Perci of

[a] Rowlston, Mappleton, and Dringhoe, in the parish of Skipsea, Ulrome, in
the parishes of Skipsea and Barmston, and Owstwick, in the parishes of Garton
and Roos.

[b] Burton Agnes, near Bridlington.

[c] Faceby, a small parish near Stokesley.

[d] The site of Mount Grace Priory. The founder, Thomas de Holland, Duke
of Surrey, endowed the Priory in 1397 with his manor of Bordelby, on the borders
of Cleveland, and willed that in future it should be called the house of Mount
Grace of Ingleby, a name it retains to the present day.

[e] Garraby, or Garrowby, in the parish of Kirby Underdale, and Allerton
Mauleverer. The former place is called Geruezbi and Gheruenzbi, in *Domesday*,
and Germandeby and Garmanby, in Kirkby's *Inquest*.

[f] Ingleby Arncliff, near Northallerton, and East and West Heslarton, near
Malton.

Kildale, three fees in Kildale, Crathorne,[a] and elsewhere; William Loring, half a fee in Caldengilbi[b]; William de Thocotes, half a fee in Thocotes[c] and elsewhere. The said Peter held Danebi for one fee in demesne, and of the Constable of Chester two fees, whereof Ambrose de Chamera and Geoffrey Maucovenaunt hold one in Esington[d] and elsewhere, and Robert de Neyvile one in Hemillington[e] and elsewhere. The same Peter held of the Bishop of Durham one fee in Herternesse,[f] which Robert de Brus held of him (Peter). Others held of Peter eleven knights' fees, one carucate and a half of land, where ten carucates make a knight's fee, in many places by the particles under written, namely: Richard Malebisse, in Morton[g] and elsewhere, half a fee; Robert de Buttirwyk, in the same[h] and elsewhere, one fee; Robert Fossard, in Otirington,[i] one fee; Richard de Grimiston, in the same[j] and elsewhere, one fee; William de Roselle, in Ascilbi,[k] three-quarters of a fee; William Buscelle, in Bollebi,[l] half a fee; Robert de Pothou, in Hilton,[m] one quarter of a fee; William de Picton, in the same,[n] the fourth part of one fee, one carucate and a half of land; Adam de Seton, in the same[o] and elsewhere, four carucates and a half; Richard de Normanbi, in the same,[p] two carucates; Richard de Hoton, in the same,[q] seven carucates; Robert Scarbot, in Skelton[r] and elsewhere, one carucate; Richard de Lakenebi, in the same,[s] half a carucate;

[a] Kildale and Crathorne, parishes in Cleveland.

[b] Cold Ingleby, otherwise Ingleby Loring, in the parish of Stainton-in-Cleveland.

[c] Tocketts, in the parish of Guisborough.

[d] Easington, in Cleveland.

[e] Hemlington, in the parish of Stainton-in-Cleveland.

[f] Hartness, the district around Hart and Hartlepool, at this time held by a junior branch of the Brus family, which a few years later gave a King to Scotland.

[g] Morton, in the parish of Ormesby.

[h] Probably Butterwick, in the parish of Barton-le-Street, in Ryedale.

[i] There is nothing to shew whether North or South Otterington is the place intended.

[j] North Grimston, near Malton.

[k] Aislaby, in the parish of Whitby.

[l] Boulby, in the parish of Easington.

[m] Hilton, near Yarm.

[n] Picton, in the parish of Kirklevington.

[o] Seaton Hall, in the parish of Hinderwell, a mile N.E. of the village. A place of some importance in *Domesday* times, when it was a manor and possessed a church. (Atkinson's *History of Cleveland*, vol. i. pp. 213, 216).

[p] Normanby, in the parish of Ormesby.

[q] Hutton Lowcross, in the parish of Guisborough. Sir Joseph Pease's seat, Hutton Hall, is in this township.

[r] Skelton-in-Cleveland.

[s] Lakenby, in the parish of Wilton.

William de Bovington, one fee and half a carucate of land in Acclum[a]; Marmaduke de Twenge, in Morsum[b] and elsewhere, one carucate and a half; Roger de Neusum, in the same,[c] one fee; William de Boyvill, in Thormotebi[d] and elsewhere, one fee; Conan de Liverton, in the same,[e] half a fee; the Prior of Giseburne and William Humet, in Lofthus,[f] half a fee; William de Bovington and his parceners, in Levingthorpe,[g] half a fee; Matthew de Galaphoue, in the same,[h] half a carucate of land.

They know of no more fees of the said Peter; of their value they are ignorant, except fees belonging to the manor of Thorpe Arch *(de Archis)* and Carleton. [i]

[On a small strip of parchment three lines to this effect :—]

Also in Aynesty there are five knights' fees appertaining to the manor of Thorpe of Arches, which John de Bellew *(Bella aqua)* holds. Karleton in Balne is held in socage of the fee of Paynel.[j]

[a] Acklam, near Middlesborough.

[b] Moorsholme, in the parish of Skelton.

[c] Newham, in the parish of Marton, or perhaps the vill of Neusom or Newsholm, now depopulated, nearly adjoined to that of Bempton the S.W. (Kirkby's *Inquest*, pp. 54 *n.*, 55).

[d] Thornaby, near South Stockton.

[e] Liverton, a chapelry dependent on Easington, in Cleveland. The owner is also called Conan Fitz Henry, and Conan de Manfield or Kelkfield.

[f] Loftus-in-Cleveland.

[g] Linthorpe, near Middlesborough.

[h] Wrongly identified by Mr. Scaife (Kirkby's *Inquest*, pp. 132, 235) with Waupley, anciently Wapelho, in the parish of Easington. It really is a farm called Glaphow, in the parish of Skelton, no great way from Stanghow, going by the road from Lockwood-beck towards Skelton, after passing the turn to Stanghow, Glaphow lies on the right hand side.

[i] Thorpe Arch and Carlton, in the parish of Snaith, called below Karleton in Balne.

[j] Besides the foregoing, there is a mutilated membrane (m. 6) which repeats apparently the particulars set out in the inquisition taken 22 Oct., 1279, but (as well as can be made out) worded rather differently. For example—the town of Daneby with forest for one knight's fee. *(Et villam de Daneby cum foresta pro uno feodo militis).* There is also an inquisition of knights' fees in the County of Westmoreland (m. 5), taken before Sir Thomas de Normanvile, on the Sunday after Michaelmas day, 7th year (10 Oct., 1279). It is here found that Peter de Brus held of the King in chief by the service of the moiety of one knight's fee and a half, a moiety of all lands and tenements which were of William de Lancaster at the time of his death, amounting in yearly value to two hundred marcs. Mem. 2 contains the knights' fees in Lancashire.

CXV. FOR THE FRIARS MINORS IN YORK. *Ad. q. d.*

[7 Edw. I. No. 54.]

Writ dated at Westminster, 9 Nov., 7th year (1279).

INQUISITION made on Friday after the feast of S. Lucy Virgin, 8 Edward (15 Dec., 1279), before Ranulf de Daker, Sheriff of Yorkshire, and John Sampson, Mayor of the City of York, by Robert *le Blund*, John de Cantbrig', William de Clervaus, Roger de Boville, Thomas de Eskrike, Adam de Wixtouue, Simon *del Weuele*, Hugh *le Tailur*, Robert de Dunde, William Durant, Robert de Hedon, and Hugh de Wyrly, if it would be to the damage of the King, or annoyance of the City of York, or of any other whomsoever, if the King should grant to the Friars Minors dwelling in the said City, that they may enclose that street which is between their site and the land of Alan Brian. They say that it would not, and that the street contains in length 23½ perches, and in width, eighteen feet in one place, and fifteen feet in another.

CXVI. JOHN DE BOLTON.[a] *Inq. p. m.*

[8 EDW. I. No. 26.]

Writ dated at Windsor, 26 Nov., 8th year (1279).

INQUISITION made before the Sheriff of Yorkshire, at Bolton, by William *de Camera* of Wilton, Geoffrey Coltbayn of Fangefosse, John *le Alblaster* of Geveldale, Walter de Quixlay of the same, Ralph de Mikelfelde of Bolthon, Roger son of Hugh of the same, Walter son of Beatrice of the same, John *le Archer* of Japum, John de Barton of Hoton, Henry de Barton of the same, Nicholas Dod of Swintan, and John son of Hugh of the same, who say upon their oath that John de Bolthon (in the writ Bóulton) held of the King in chief the manor of Colswan-hoton[b] together with the launds *(una cum landis)* of Sandburne

---

[a] On 26 Nov., 1279, orders were given by the King, then at Windsor, to Thomas de Normanville, senior, to seize the lands of which John de Boulton died seised in chief. On 5 June in the next year, in consideration of the good and laudable service done by Thomas de Boulton, deceased, in his lifetime to the King, and for a fine of £20, which Robert, son and heir of the said Thomas, made with the King, the King pardoned him all amercements from whatever causes, in which his father had been amerced before the Barons of the Exchequer, or the Justices assigned for the custody of the Jews, or the Justices when last itinerant in Lincolnshire, or the Justices of the King's Bench *(Rot. Fin.,* 8 Edw. I,, mm. 19, 9*)*. This last entry shews that Robert, the brother and heir of John de Bolton, was the son and heir of a Thomas de Bolton, which is confirmed by No. LXXXIV. There is an is an account of this family in Kirkby's *Inquest*, p. 257 *n.*

[b] Hutton-on-Derwent, or Low Hutton. Sandburn and Carlton are near York.

and Carleton by the service of the fourth part of one knights'
fee; and it is worth by the year £17 12s. 5d. He held the
manor of Bolton^a of Robert de Gray for homage and service of
three-pence yearly, and it is worth by the year £10 12s. 2d. He
held also of John Painel the manor of Yarpesthorpe^b with the
appurtenances, for his homage and doing foreign service to the
King, and it is worth by the year £23 12s. 4d.

Robert de Bolton, brother of John, is his next heir, and of
full age.

And be it known that this Inquisition was made on
Saturday after the feast of S. Thomas the Apostle, in the eighth
year of the King's reign (23 Dec., 1279).

CXVII. ROBERT DE CREPPINGES. *Inq. p. m.*

[8 EDW. I. No. 11.]
[M. 1.]

Writ dated at Winchester, 4 Jan., 8th year (1279-80).

[M. 2.]

WAPENTAKE OF OSEGOTECROSSE.

EXTENT made of the lands and tenements which were of
Robert de Crippellings (in the writ Creppinges) in the
Soke of Snayt, by Henry de Hecke, John de Goldale, Eadmund
de Goldale, Alexander de Wytelay, Richard de Roceholme,
Henry son of Walter of Newland *(de nova terra)*, William
Despenser, John Clerk *(cleric)* of Derlington, William Vendi-
locke, Adam *de la More* of Hethensale, Adam son of John of
Polington, Alexander Dilcocke.

	Annual value.		
	£	s.	d.
In Snayt^c eight bovates of land, and they yield yearly	0	19	9
In Goldale twenty-four bovates	2	9	0
In Hethensale eleven bovates	1	2	5½
In Hecke eight bovates	0	16	4
In Wytelay twelve bovates	1	2	5½
In Berlay and Burton eleven bovates	0	11	0
In a certain assart at Snayt fifty acres	1	18	0
A suitors' Court	1	1	0

Sum total, £10.

---

^a Bolton, near Yapham.

^b Easthorpe, near Malton.

^c Snaith, Gowdall, Hensall, Heck, Whitley, Barlow, and Burton, in the parish
of Brayton.

He held the Soke in chief of the King in the name of serjeanty, and used to render to the King while he held the Soke entirely half a marc, but now the King has in his hand eleven bovates of land in Hansay[a] appertaining to the Soke of Snayt. John de Crippellinges[b] is son and heir of Robert, and aged twenty-eight years.

[M. 3.]

WAPENTAKE OF HERTEHIL.

INQUISITION made before Sir Thomas de Normanvile and Sir Ranulf de Dak[re], of the lands and tenements which Robert de Crippelings held, by John Thothe, William son of Gamel, William *de la Gorge*, Laurence de Cardoil, Thomas de Hundegate, William Tardcurtays, Robert Baty, Richard de Maule, Walter *le Granger*, William de Gremmesby, Richard de Kokerington, and Thomas de Seton.

He held in the town of Yapom[c] one carucate of land, worth by the year six marcs; in Barneby 5s. rent; in Wappelington 2s. rent by the service of archery, to be done at the gate of York Castle in time of war by one man. The said lands and rent he held in chief of Robert *le Chaumberleyn*. Sum total, £4 7s.

John de Crippelinges is son and heir of Robert, and aged twenty-eight years.

[M. 4.]

> Another writ referring to the insufficiency of the inquisition, because no mention is made therein of how much land of the Soke of Snayth is held by serjeanty, and commanding further inquiry to be made and returned in fifteen days from Easter-day. In the meantime the heir to be permitted to cultivate the lands inherited from his father, and to receive the rents and issues, subject to security being received to satisfy the King for such rents and issues hereafter, if required. Dated at Lyndhurst, 20 Jan., 8th year (1279-80).
>
> [*On the back of the writ.*] The sum of the rents and other issues, forthcoming from lands and tenements which were of Robert de Creppinge, deceased, from the day of receiving the writ is eight marcs 2s. Sir John de [He]ton, Henry de Hec, John de Goldale, Edmund his brother, Thomas the Clerk (*le Clerc*) of Goldale, and William de Couwyc, are manucaptors of John, son and heir of Robert de Creppinge, to satisfy for the aforesaid issues.

[M. 5.]

INQUISITION made at Snayd before the Escheator, concerning the lands and tenements which were of Robert de Crip-

---

[a] Perhaps for Hethensale, or is it a form of Haddlesay?

[b] His homage was taken by the King at Westminster, 26 May, 1280 (*Rot. Fin.*, 8 Edw. I., m. 10). John de Creppyng' was Sheriff for the first three quarters of 1 Edw. II. (1307).

[c] Yapham, near Pocklington, Barmby-on-the-Moor, and Waplington, in the parish of Pocklington.

plinges on the day of his death in the soke of Snayd, by John de Heton, Henry de Hecke, John de Goldale, Eadmund of the same, Alexander de Wytelay, Michael of the same, Hugh son of Alan of Goldale, Adam de Hethensale, William Despenser of Rouclef, William Vendilocke of Hethensale, Reginald of the same, and William de Couwicke, who say by their oath that Robert de Cripplinges held of the King in chief in the Soke of Snayd on the day of his death, 74 bovates of land·with the appurtenances by great serjeanty; and they are worth by the year together with the Court in all issues, £10, and he rendered to the King yearly for all services 40d., because the King recovered from the said Robert £10 of land in Hansay of the aforesaid serjeanty. And they say that John de Crippelinges, son of Robert, is his next heir, and aged twenty-eight years.

CXVIII. WILLIAM DE HERTLINGTON.[a] *Inq. p. m.*

[8 Edw. I. No. 12.]

Writ dated at Lindhurst, 20 Jan., 8th year (1279-80).

INQUISITION made at York, on Saturday after the feast of S. Peter in the chair, 8 Edward (24 Feb., 1279-80). before Thomas de Normanvile, the King's Steward, concerning the lands and tenements of which William de Hertlington was seised in fee on the day of his death, by Sir Roger Tempest, Sir Robert de Stiveton, William de Cestrehunte, Everard Fauvel, Elias de Kyghelay, John of the same, Alan de Katherton, Adam de Plumlunde, Elias de Stretton, Walter de Rymington, Richard de Kyghelay, and Henry *le Mazon* of Skipton, who say upon their oath that the said William held one carucate and six bovates of land in Hertlington and Appeltrewyc,[b] of the tenure of Skipton, which was formerly of the Earl of Albemarle and is now in the King's hand, for 16d. to be paid yearly to the King; he owed homage and suit at the Court of Skipton from three weeks to three weeks, and the whole land is worth by the year 70s.

He held also:

	Annual rent.		Annual value.		
	s.	d.	£	s.	d.
In Hertlington of Sir Robert de Nevile three carucates	12	0	6	0	0

[a] On 26 March, 1280, the King, then at Down Ampney *(Dunamen')*, took the homage of William, son of William de Hertlington, for the lands his father held in chief *(Rot. Fin.,* 8 Edw. I., m. 15*).* There is a notice and pedigree of the Hartlington family in Whitaker's *Craven.*

[b] Hartlington and Appletreewick, in the parish of Burnsall in Craven.

	Annual rent.		Annual value.		
	s.	d.	£	s.	d.
In Danlithe[a] of William Mauleverer three carucates	16	0	7	4	0
In Rilleston of Sir Roger Tempest one carucate, to whom are due ward and relief			1	16	0

Sum total, £18 10s.

William de Hertlington, son of the said William, is his next heir, and aged thirty years and more.

CXIX. NICHOLAS DE STAPELTON.[b] *Extent of Lands in custody.*

[8 EDW. I. No. 43.]

Writ of *certiorari* directed to Thomas de Normanville, the King's Steward, and dated at Seleburne, 7 July, 8th year (1280).

EXTENT at Westehathelsay,[c] before the Sheriff of Yorkshire, of the lands and tenements which Nicholas de Stapelton has to keep *(custodienda)* by the King's commission in the said town, made by Robert le Pavelly, John de Birne, John de Wridelesforde, James de Berlay, Richard Clerk *(clericum)* of Carleton, Roger de Bethhale, Alan Damet of Brayton, Richard son of Alan, Robert Tailor *(cissorem)*, Thomas de Capella, William de Camellesforde, and Peter Pateman, who say upon their oath that the capital messuage is worth by the year 6s. There are five bovates of land in villenage (every bovate 13s.), and free tenants, viz: Peter de Hathelsay who holds three bovates, and pays yearly 3s. 6d., Ydonea, wife of Ralph *le Vyer*, and Siyerria,[d] wife of Gilbert, hold one bovate for 14d. John Warde holds one bovate for 5s. 2d, and eight acres of land for 2s. William de Camellesforde holds two and a half acres for one pound of pepper, and five acres for 9d. Roger de Bethalle, seven acres for 9d.. Richard Ayr, four acres of land and one

---

[a] A mistake for Hanlithe, now Hanlith, in the parish of Kirkby Malhamdale. In 1302-3, Sir Henry de Hertlington held of William Malleverer three carucates in Hahmlith (Kirkby's *Inquest*, p. 191).

[b] According to the pedigree of the Stapletons of Richmondshire *(Yorkshire Archæological Journal*, vol. viii., pp. 85, 86*)*, Sir Nicholas de Stapelton was one of the Judges in the reign of Edward I., and died in 1290, having married a daughter of Milo de Basset, who had lands in West Haddlesey. On 14 Nov., (1275), he had a grant from the King for £40 for the marriage of the heirs of William de Wyndes[ore], deceased, who held in chief *(Rot. Fin.* 3 Edw. I,, m. 2*)*.

[c] West Haddlesey is in the parish of Birkin.

[d] Probably to be read, " Sitherria."

27

acre and a half of meadow, for 3s. Robert Pavely, three acres of meadow for one pair of gloves, price one penny. Robert Tailor *(cissor)*, one toft and two acres of land for 2d. There are also fifty-five acres of land which are approved from the waste, and yield by the year 55s., and forty acres of meadow, of which every acre is worth yearly 18d. The herbage and a certain fishery are together estimated at 10s. by the year. There is nothing beyond the extent.   Sum, £10 13s. 4d.

CXX. EARL OF CORNWALL AND ISABELLA DE FORTIBUS, COUNTESS OF ALBEMARLE.

[8 EDW. I. No. 82.]

Mandate to H. de Kendale and W. de Odiham, that, having inspected the transcript of an inquisition made before Master Thomas de Sodington, which transcript the bearer will exhibit to them, and having heard from him the plaint concerning the injuries done to his lady, the Countess of Albemarle, they provide a remedy. Dated at Rhuddlan *(Rothelanum)*, 25 June [no year].

THE King sent to Master Thomas de Sudinton his writ. Whereas Edmund, Earl of Cornwall, and Isabel de Fortibus, Countess of Albemarle, have granted in the King's Court that the variance between them concerning the wood of Swindon,[a] which the Countess asserts to appertain to her manor of Harewode, be heard and determined by him, he is commanded to inquire into the truth of the matter by the oath of knights and other lawful men of the neighbourhood of Harewode and Kirkeby. Dated at Westminster, 28 May, 8th year (1280). The Sheriff was commanded to cause to come at this day, to wit, Monday after the feast of S. James the Apostle (29 July, 1280), twelve, etc. At which day come the Earl and Countess by their attorneys.

The Countess says (by attorney) that Margery de Redvers *(Ripar')*[b] her grandmother (whose heir she is), was seised as of fee and right of Swindon wood, as appertaining to her manor of Harewode, by the metes and bounds underwritten, namely: beginning from the bank *(riparia)* of the Werf, and so ascending by the beck which runs through the town of Witheton, between the wood of Rigton and of Swindon, inclosing Holker, and so by the said beck *(rivulum)* up to the ditch *(sikettum)* which runs through the middle of the town of Waleton, and so descending

[a] Swinden, in the parish of Kirkby Overblow, bordering upon Harewood parish.

[b] See Nos. XLVIII. and LIV.

between the covert of Swindon wood from the field of Kirkeby, as far as the bank of the Werf, taking all the esplees thereof forthcoming from the said wood, as in herbage, pannage of hogs, as well demesne as foreign, minerals found, honey and wax, animals said to be waifs, if any chance to be found, and eyries of birds of prey *(aerias omnia avium de preda)*, to take, give, and sell estovers at will, and all other esplees which appertain to the same wood, without view or livery of any forester of the said Earl or of his ancestors, and doing all other things as of her own demesne wood. And that the said Earl or his ancestors ought not to have anything in the wood, save hunting and attachments of the same, and this within the metes and bounds aforesaid. She says also that the foresters of the Earl or of his ancestors had not puture, corn in autumn, bonepeny, or anything else from the tenants of herself or her ancestors, nor ought the tenants to come to his Court of Knaresburge, for any inquisition to be made for hunting or other things, and they never did until Richard, formerly King of Germany *(Almann')* father of the Earl, whose heir he is, by one William de Ireby, his Steward, unjustly occupied the said wood, while the King was in parts beyond the sea ; and that the said Edmund yet detains it in occupation. And this she is ready to verify as the Court shall consider, and prays that it be inquired into, etc.

And the said Earl comes by attorney and acknowledges that the wood is the right of the Countess, but says that she ought to have there only reasonable estovers, namely, to burn and . . . . husbote and heybote, and by view and livery of his foresters of Knaresburge, and that the said wood is within the metes of his forest of Knaresburge. He says also that he, his ancestors, and others holding the manor of Knaresburge from the time of King John, grandfather of the now King, have had in the said wood, herbage, pannage, minerals, honey, wax, animals which are said to be wayfs, eyries of birds of prey, attachments, amercements, and all other things appertaining to the wood, saving nevertheless to the Countess her reasonable estovers, and this by the view and livery of his foresters. He says also that his foresters ought to have puture, bonepeny, and corn in autumn from the tenants of the Countess, and these tenants ought to come to the Earl's Court when summoned to make inquisition, and they have been used to do so from the time aforesaid. And this he prays may be inquired into, and the Countess likewise, etc.

Richard de Stolkelde, Peter Becard, John Mauleverer of Linton, Richard de Staxtone, William *de la Sale*, Peter de Hoperton, Richard de Wigedon, Adam Ward of Colethorpe,

Matthew de Braem, Roger de Cressewell, William de Stubhous, and William de Midelton, sworn and elected by the consent of the parties, say upon their oath that Margery de Redvers *(Ripar')*, grandmother of the Countess, whose heir she is, held the wood of Swindon as appurtenant to her manor of Harewode by the metes and bounds aforesaid, taking therein herbage, pannage as well of her own hogs as of others whomsoever, attachments of wood, minerals *(mineram)*, honey, wax, animals which are called wayfs, and all things forthcoming from the said wood as though of her own demesne, and therefrom may sell and give at her own will, without view and livery of the Earl's foresters, saving nevertheless to the Earl, hunting, and attachments and amercements of the same. They say also that the Earl's foresters ought not to have puture, corn in autumn, or bonepeny from the tenants of the Countess, nor ought her tenants to come to the Earl's Court of Knaresburge for making inquisition concerning hunting or other things, save within the metes and bounds aforesaid of the wood, nor used they to do so before the occupation made by William de Ireby, Steward of Richard, formerly King of Germany *(Alemann')*, father of the said Edmund, Earl of Cornwall, whose heir he is. They say also that the said Earl yet detains in occupation the premises in the manner aforesaid.

Therefore it is considered that the Countess should recover her seisin of the said wood, by the metes and bounds aforesaid. And that the said Earl has not anything in the wood, save only hunting, with attachments and amercements of the same. And that his foresters henceforth may not have puture, corn in autumn, or bonepeny from the tenants of the Countess, serf or free, nor shall her tenants henceforth come to the Earl's Court of Knaresburge for making any inquisitions; but, when inquisitions are made by the said tenants, they shall be for hunting or for trespass of hunting within the metes and bounds of the said wood, as is aforesaid.[a]

---

[a] The original of the verdict is as follows:—Dicunt super sacramentum suum quod Margeria de Ripar', avya predicte Comitisse, cujus heres ipsa est, tenuit predictum boscum de Swindon' tanquam pertinens ad manerium suum de Harewode per metas et divisas predictas, capiendo in eodem bosco herbagium pannagium tam de propriis porcis quam aliorum quorumcumque, atach' de bosco, mineram, mel, et ceram de eodem bosco, vendere, dare pro voluntate sua sine visu et liberacione forestariorum predicti Comitis, salvis tamen eidem Comiti venacione et atach' et amerciamentis ejusdem. Dicunt eciam quod forestarii dicti Comitis non debent habere puturam, bladum in autumpno, nec bonepeny de tenentibus ipsius Comitisse, nec eciam debent ipsi tenentes Comitisse venire ad Curiam ipsius Comitis de Knaresburg' pro inquisicione facienda de venacione nec aliis, nisi infra metas et divisas predictas predicti bosci, vel quod hoc . . . . facere solebant ante occupacionem predictam, factam per Willelmum de Ireby, Senescallum Ricardi quondam Regis Alemann', patris predicti Edmundi Comitis Cornubie cujus heres ipsa est.

CXXI. JOHN, SON OF WALTER DE ABBREFORD
(ABBERFORTH).

[8 Edw. I. No. 4.]

Writ dated at Newstead *(Novum locum in Shyrewode)*, 3 Aug., 8th year (1280).

INQUISITION made on Monday after the Assumption B.V.M., 8 Edward (19 Aug., 1280), before the Sheriff of Yorkshire, by Nicholas de Okelestorpe, William de Langethwayth, John de Lede, clerk, Elias de Neuton, clerk, John de Oscom, Hugh de Brinkall, Robert Marshal *(marescallum)* of Tadechastre, Thomas *le Lardiner* of the same, Simon de Cokesforthe, Richard Mileshouer of the same, Batheman de Saxton, William son of Henry of Tadechastre, who say on their oath that John, son of Walter de Abberforth, held nothing in chief of the King, but he held one carucate of land of Gilbert de Neville by the service of homage and of scutage when it shall fall; whereof nine carucates make the fee of one knight.

The manor[a] with garden and curtilage is worth by the year 6s. There are in demesne 32 acres of arable land, worth 32s., and many small parcels of meadow which yield yearly 8s. Two granges at the town-end *(ad exitum ville)* yield 4s. There is annual rent of one mill, 13s. 4d., and of free men, 8d.

Sum, 64s.

John is dead, and Isabel *(Ysabella)*, his sister, is his next heir; and she will be fifteen years old at Easter next (13 April, 1281).

Dicunt eciam quod predictus Edmundus omnia premissa modo quo predictum est, adhuc detinet occupata. Et ideo consideratum est quod predicta Comitissa recuparet seysinam suam de predicto bosco per metas et divisas predictas cum omnibus suis pert., absque hoc quod predictus Comes aliquid habeat in predicto bosco nisi tantum venacionem et atach' et amerciamenta de tenentibus ipsius Comitisse, servis, vel liberis; nec tenentes ipsius Comitisse de cetero veniant ad Curiam ipsius Comitis de Knaresburg' pro aliquibus inquisicionibus faciendis, set cum inquisicio facta fuerit per eosdem tenentes pro venacione vel pro transgressione venacionis, fiat infra metas et divisas bosci predicti, sicut predictum est.

[a] The manor of Aberford, eleven miles E.N.E. of Leeds.

CXXII. ROBERT, BISHOP OF DURHAM, *v.* JOHN DE AVERANGE
AND JOHN DE THORPE.

[8 EDW. I. No. 40.]

Writ directed to the Sheriff of Yorkshire, concerning a plea lately moved in
the King's court, between [Robert], Bishop of Durham,[a] of one part,
and John de Averange and John de Thorpe of the other part, and commanding him to take with him two Knights of the County, and to
inquire by the oath of twelve men of the parts of Skipwhyt[b]—of whom
six to be chosen by the Bishop (if he will), and the other six by John
and John—what are and ought to be the right bounds and divisions
between the Bishop's wood of Blakewode and the tenements of John
and John in the moor of Skipwhyt, and before the octave of S. Michael
now instant (6 October), to cause such bounds and divisions to be made,
and to remit the result of the inquiry, together with the writ. Dated at
Stocton [near Durham], 20 Sept., 8th year (1280).

THE Sheriff, having taken with him Sirs Geoffrey Aguyllun
and Henry son of Conayn, went in person to the place, on
Thursday after the feast of S. Michael, 8 Edward (3 Oct., 1280),
and inquired by the oath of Robert de Balliol, William Burdun,
Peter de Hathilsey, John de Pothow, John *de Castello,* and
Thomas de Luceby, chosen by the Bishop, and by the oath of
Robert de Osgodeby, Walter de Elmeshey,[c] William de Moreby,
Robert Anvers, Robert *le Lung* of Kelkefeude, and Alexander
Burdun, chosen by John de Averenches[d] and John de Thorpe,
who, being sworn, say upon their oath that the right bounds and
divisions between the Bishop's wood of Blakwode and the
tenements of John and John in Scipwhit moor, begin in a place
called Anvers pit towards the east, and extend in a line up to
another place towards the west, which is called Burdun pit, and
from that place, to wit, Burdun pit, as far as another place
which is called Moreby pit, towards the west in a line, and so
from place to place westwards, as far as the bounds of Rikale.
In witness whereof the Sheriff's seal and the seals of the two
knights who were present with him are appended to this
inquisition.[e]

[a] Robert de Insula, Bishop of Durham, 1274 to 1283.

[b] Skipwith, near Escrick, south of York.

[c] Called Walter de Hemelsay in the next inquisition.

[d] Called above, John de Averange. He derived his name from Avranches in
Normandy.

[e] There are now no seals, of course, the document being cut clean off at the
bottom. The original of the verdict is as follows:—Qui Jur' dicunt super sacramentum suum, quod recte bunde et divise inter boscum ipsius Episcopi de Blakwode
et ten' ipsorum Johannis et Johannis in mora de Scipwhit incipiunt in quodam loco
qui vocatur Anuers pit versus orientem, et extendit *(sic)* se linealiter usque ad alium
locum versus Occidentem qui vocatur Burdun pit. Et de illo loco, scilicet Burdun
pit, usque ad alium locum qui vocatur Moreby pit versus occidentem linealiter.
Et sic de loco in locum linealiter versus occidentem usque ad divisas de Rikale.

CXXIII. DAVID DE CAWUDE, GRANDSON AND HEIR OF
JOHN DE CAWUDE. *Of the Bailiwick of the
Hay of Langwath.*

No Writ.

[8 EDW. I. No. 49.]

INQUISITION[a] of twelve Jurors between Use and Derewent,
namely, Robert de Menthorph, William de Moreby, Robert
de Osgoteby, Walter de Hemelsay, Conan de Kelkefelde,
William Darel, John *de Castello*, Robert *le Lung* of Kelkefelde,
Walter *le Serjaunt* of the same, Philip son of Hauwis of the
same, Robert de Henlay, and John son of Eva of Osgoteby,
about the Hay of Langwathe and the forestry *(forestarie)*
between the waters of Use and Derewent, in the 8th year,
before Thomas de Normanville, Steward of the King; who say
on their [oath], that John de Cawude, grandfather of David de
Cawude who now is, held the bailiwick of the Hay of Langwath
on the day he died, but not the forestry between the waters . . .
. . . . but held the bailiwick of that forest before the forest had
been disafforested, and this by the service of guarding the aforesaid bailiwick by grant . . . . . of King Edward that now is,
and it ought by hereditary right to belong to the said David, as
grandson and heir of the said John de Cawude . . . . of
Langwath is now in the hand of the Archbishop. The bailiwick
of the Hay of Langwath was worth five marcs a year, and the
bailiwick of the forestry [between the waters of Use] and Derewent, before it was disafforested, was worth 100s. a year. And to
this inquisition the aforesaid Jurors have set their seals.

CXXIV. THE MEN OF HEDON. *Ad. q. d.*

[9 EDW. I. No. 45.]

Writ[b] directed to Thomas de Normanvyle, and referring to a petition of the
men of Hedon that they might have the town to farm. Inquiry is
therefore commanded to be made as to the value, &c. Dated at Westminster, 30 Nov., in the ninth year (1280).

INQUISITION before Sir Thomas de Normanville, made by Sirs
John de Carleton, William de Faukenberge, John Passemer,
Henry de Preston, knights, John de Drynghou, John de Camer-

---

[a] In parts ragged. On 17 Aug., 1280, the King, then at York, informed the
Barons of the Exchequer that David de Cawode was to pay by annual instalments
of 40s. the sum of £10, which he was fined for marrying without the King's licence,
being under age and in the King's custody *(Rot. Fin.,* 8 Edw. I., m. 5). See No.
LIX.

[b] On the dorse, "per J. de Kyrby."

yngton, Alexander de Holme, William de Grymestone, Simon de Lunde, William de Hoton, Henry de Wyveton, and William de Holme, who say upon their oath that, things being as they are now *(quod rebus se habentibus ut nunc)*, the town of Hedon is worth by the year forty pounds with reprises reckoned, to wit, yearly, to one bailiff, 20*s.*; to two under bailiffs with clerk, 20*s.*; in keeping up two bridges, a mill, hall, and gaol, 20*s.*, if the town were in the King's hand.

They say also upon their oath that the men are straitened and poor *(tenues et pauperes)*. As to whether it be to the advantage or damage of the King if the town be let in fee farm, they believe that if it be so demised to them, it may in course of time be improved; if not demised to them, it may in a short time be deteriorated in value; because many wish to move away on account of their being talliated here every year, and they have near this two other towns, Ravensered[a] and the Hul,[b] with two good harbours, growing from day to day, where they can dwell without tallage.[c]

CXXV. ADAM DE EVERINGHAM. *Inq. p. m.*

[9 EDW. I. No. 5.]

Writ[d] directed to Thomas de Normanville, and dated at the Tower of London, 8 Dec., 9th year (1280). *

INQUISITION made on Monday the feast of S. Hilary (13 Jan., 1280-1), by Thomas de Graystoke, Peter de Hathelsay,

---

[a] More usually Ravenserod. The termination being the Norse *oddr*, a point, still preserved in the phrase " odds and ends."

[b] Soon afterwards incorporated as Kingston-upon-Hull.

[c] Dicunt eciam super sacramentum suum quod homines predicte ville tenues sunt et pauperes. An sit ad comodum seu ad dampnum domini Regis si predicta villa dimittatur in feodi firmam, credunt quod si eisdem dimittatur in feodi firmam, potest per spacium temporis meliorari, et si non dimittatur eis in feodi firmam, credunt quod potest per parvum temporis deteriorari, eo quod multi se volunt amovere a villa quia quolibet anno talliantur, et quia sunt prope predictam villam due ville, scilicet, Ravensered et le Hul, cum duobus bonis portubus de die in diem crescentibus, et ibidem possunt manere sine tallagio.

[d] At the back is a memorandum, that this writ came to "me" at London, on Wednesday before the Conversion of S. Paul (22 Jan., 1280-1). The writ for Lincolnshire is endorsed with a note that the said Adam died on the day of the Conception of the Blessed Virgin (8 Dec., 1280)—" et dictus Adam obiit die Concepcionis Beate Marie anno nono." Both these dates present difficulties. The first may be explained by supposing the endorsement to have been made by the official in London, on receiving the inquisition and writ sewn thereto from the Escheator. As to the date of Adam de Everingham's death, it is difficult to give any satisfactory explanation, unless he died in London, and the writ was issued the same day. This solution seems negatived by the date of the death being endorsed on the Lincolnshire writ, giving one to believe that his death took place in that

German Hay, William *le Conestable*, Robert Salvayn, Thomas de Gunneby, knights, William de Schyrburne, Roger Sleghtte, Richard de Herlethorpe, Roger de Hugate, William Sturmy, and Walter de Ruddestane, who say upon their oath that Adam de Everingham held of the King in chief in the County of York one knight's fee, to wit, in Brampton, Besakre, Heyhelleres, and Gayte,[a] which fee Philip de Vermaylles held of him (Adam) by knight's service. He held of the Archbishop of York the manor of Everingham[b] with the appurtenances, which is worth by the year in all issues £23 9s. 8d., doing suit therefor at the Archbishop's Court of Wylton[c] from three weeks to three weeks ; and of the Earl of Lincoln the manors of Farburne[d] (worth by the year £18 2s. 6d.), and Havercroft[e] (100s.), by doing suit at the Earl's Court of Pontefract from three weeks to three weeks, and scutage when current *(quando currit)*. He held also the manor of Kibbelingcotes[f] (worth 100s. by the year) of the Provost of Beverley, doing suit at his Court at Beverley from three weeks to three weeks, for all services.

Robert de Everingham, his eldest son and next heir, is aged twenty-four years.[g]

County. Adam de Everingham was the son and heir of Robert de Everingham, by Isabel, sister and heiress of Thomas de Birkin, and daughter of John de Birkin, son and heir of Adam Fitz Peter, with whom he got large estates, including the forest of Sherwood *(Excerpta è Rotulis Finium*, vol. i., pp. 116, 162, 206, and *Rievaulx Chartulary*, p. 388). He paid homage for his mother's lands on 12 Aug., 1252 *(Excerpta è Rotulis Finium*, vol. ii., p. 136). On 9 Sept., 1279, the King gave him leave to hunt the fox in the royal chaces and warrens in Holderness, excepting during the fence-months *(Patent Rolls,* 7 Edw. I., m. 9 (17), abstracted in 48*th Report of Dep. Keeper of Public Records*, p. 67). He died, as appears above, in the autumn or early winter of 1280. His son and heir, Robert, paid homage at Desenigg', on 9 Feb., 1280-1, for the lands held in chief *(Rot. Fin.,* 9 Edw. I., m. 17).

a Brampton, Bessacar, High Ellers, and Gate, all in the parish of Cantley.

b Everingham, in the East Riding, near Market Weighton.

c Bishop Wilton, near Pocklington.

d Fairburn, in the parish of Ledston.

e Havercroft, in the parish of Felkirk, near Barnsley.

f Kiplin-Cotes, near Market Weighton.

g There are two other inquisitions, taken in the Counties of Lincoln and Nottingham, by which the finding as to the heir and his age is the same.

CXXVI. WILLIAM DE CHAUNCY.[a]   *Inq. p. m.*

[9 EDW. I. No. 25.]

Writ dated at Wodestoke, 9 April, 9th year (1281).

INQUISITION made at York, on Wednesday, the eve of the
Apostles Philip and James (30 April, 1281), before Thomas
de Normanville, by William de Knapton, Robert *le Turnur*,
Robert Page of Tocwyht, William *del Hill* of Bilton, William
de Berdene of the same, Simon *du Parke* of the same, Philip
son of Ralph of Munketon, Hugh Prodhome of Merston, Robert
Fox of Angrum, Henry Fraunceys of Merston, and Thomas
Turpyn, who say on their oath that William de Chauncy held
no land in the County of York of the King in chief, but he held
in this County, in the town of Munketon,[b] of John Paynel, one
messuage with garden, the fruit of which, with herbage, is worth
by the year 5*s*., and eleven bovates and a half of land (each
bovate containing four acres, and worth 4*s*.), 46*s*. There is an
assart which contains 56 acres of land (the acre, 9*d*.), worth 42*s*.;
also five and a half acres and one rood of meadow (the acre, 4*s*.),
23*s*. There is a plot *(platera)* of meadow, worth 10*s*.; and a
wood of 36 acres, the herbage and underwood of which are
worth yearly 10*s*. There is an uncultivated plot *(quedam platera
friscar')*, the agistment of which is worth by the year 3*s*. Of
rent of assize, one free tenant there pays 13*s*. 6*d*., and certain
tenants of Wyvelestorpe,[c] for having common in the pasture of
Munketon, 12*d*. The whole of the aforesaid tenements he held of
John Paynel by knight's service, doing homage and foreign service
(when it falls due), as much as appertains to so much land.

He had a son and heir, Philip by name, who at the feast of
S. Martin-in-winter, in the 9th year (11 Nov., 1281), will be
eighteen years old.[d]

[a] See No. LX. On 16 Feb., 1282-3, the King, then at Rothel', in consideration
of one hundred marcs, granted the custody of the land and heir of William de
Chauncy, deceased, with his marriage, to Geoffrey de Neville *(Rot. Fin.*, 11 Ewd. I.
m. 21). On 6 Jan., 1289-90, the King, for a fine of 10 marcs, gave Isabel, widow
of William de Chancy, leave to marry whom she would *(Ibid,* 18 Edw. I., m. 21).

[b] Moor Monkton, near York.

[c] Wilstrop, a township in the parish of Kirk Hammerton.

[d] There is a writ of *certiorari*, with the *teste* of the King at Deseninge, on the
11th of Feb., in the ninth year (1280-1), which relates to a complaint made by
Isabel, who was wife of William de Chauncy, that, although her late husband at
her marriage endowed her at the church door with the manor of Wylweton
(Willoughton), and she ought to have it according to law and custom of the realm,
the King's Steward, Richard de Holebroke, had taken it into the King's hand, and
yet detained it. An inquisition is thereupon taken in Lincolnshire (undated), by
which it is found that William endowed Isabel with this manor at the church door.
Mention is here made of William having received for the term of his life, by the
hand of Lucy *(Lucie)* de Chancy, out of the manor of Swynhop, ten marcs yearly.
The jury find Philip to be son and heir, and that he will be eighteen years old at
the feast of S. Martin-in-winter (11 Nov., 1281).

CXXVII. THE CANONS OF HOWDEN. *Ad. q. d.*

[9 EDW. I. No. 62.]

Writ[a] directed to the Sheriff of Yorkshire, concerning a petition from the Canons of the church of Howden (here, *Houedene*), that they have a quarry in Tevesdale,[b] and cannot conveniently lead stone therefrom for the fabric of their church, on account of a nook of the King's quarry adjoining. Dated at Westminster, 29 May, 9th year (1281).

INQUISITION upon the articles contained in the writ, made by Robert *le Marescall* of Tadecastre, Thomas de Goderomgate, Adam Cardon, Thomas *le Keu*, Robert *le Gardiner* of Stutton, Geoffrey de Thorneton, Henry son of Gera *(fil' Gere)*, Thomas de Kereby, Hugh de Brinkill, Elias *le Clerke* of Neuton, John de Oskumbe, and Richard de Malesoueres, who, being sworn, say upon their oath that it would not be to the annoyance or damage of anyone, if the King were to grant to the Canons of Houedon the nook *(nokam)*, but to the damage of the King, because the king now has more of the quarry than that nook, which is accounted to be one acre; and an acre in the quarry is worth to sell, six marcs. And whereas a certain part of that nook is being carried for the fabric of the King's castle, they estimate the residue at five marcs. Therefore they say that it would not be to greater damage than of five marcs, because if the King wish to do any works in stone, he can have in the same quarry an acre which is worth more, for . . . .[c] In witness, etc.

[a] A strip of parchment (7 inches long by ¾ wide) with these words :—" Les Chanoignes de ly Glyse de Houedone pryent a nostre seignur le Rey sa grace de ceste chose al overeigne de lur Eglyse."

[b] In the neighbourhood of Tadcaster. The stone for York Minster came from the same quarry. Robert le Vavasour granted to St. Peter's, York, for the health of his soul and of Juliana, his wife, a way-leave in Thevedale, which was part of his freehold, for getting stone for building and repairing the Minster *(York Fabric Rolls, p. 147)*.

[c] Here the parchment is torn off at the beginning of the last line, and one or two words are missing. On the back of the inquisition is a memorandum to this effect :—Let Thomas de Normanville be commanded to view that quarry, and inquire into the truth concerning damage to the King.

CXXVIII. ABBOT OF CITEAUX. *Ad q. d.*

[9 EDW. I. No. 52 A.]

Writ, directed to Thomas de Normanville, and commanding inquiry to be made, whether it would be to the damage of the King, or to the annoyance of his town of Scardeburge, if he should grant to the Abbot of Citeaux,[a] that he and his successors, Abbots of that place, might hold a messuage which had been granted by John Lomb to the Abbot and to his church of Scardeburge, and had been taken by the bailiffs of town into the King's hand by reason of the Statute of Mortmain. Dated at Westminster, 10 June, 9th year (1281).

INQUISITION made at Skardeburge, on Sunday after the feast of S. James the Apostle, 9 Edward (27 July, 1281), before Thomas de Normanvile, by Emery *(Emericum)* Edwyne, Alan Beaufrunt, Henry *le Caretter*, Henry de Roston, Robert Beaufrunt, John Gerarde, John son of William, Simon de Roston, Henry de Bromton, Adam Hutred, Robert de Northfolke, Roger Farman, and Roger Haldan, who say upon their oath that it would be to the damage of the King, if that messuage were to come into mortmain, because he would so lose an escheat; and that it would be to the annoyance of the town, because the Burgesses have the King's charter,[b] that no messuage, burgage, land, rent, or any possession within the limits of the borough, shall be given, sold, assigned, bequeathed, or otherwise aliened, to any religious men without the assent and will of the commonalty of the said borough.

They say also that John Cattesbak, father of John Lambe, bought that messuage of Simon, son of Thomas of Lindeberge, to hold of the Abbot and Convent of Citeaux, and the said John procured a quit-claim from Simon to the Abbot and Convent of all the right he had in the said messuage, and afterwards himself (John) took the messuage of them, to hold to him and his heirs or assigns by the service of 12*d.* only yearly.

---

[a] *Cicestr'.* A mistake for *Cisterc'.* The church was given by Richard I. to the Abbey of the Cistercians at Albemarle, to which it was appropriated, and a Vicarage ordained therein in 1321 ; and on the dissolution of that Alien Monastery, it was, temp. Henry IV., given to the Priory of Bridlington, to which it was appropriated (Lawton's *Collection,* p. 309).

[b] See *Charter Roll,* 53 Hen. III., m. 1., for a charter granted to the Burgesses of "Eschardeburge," in which these words occur :—"Et quod nullum mesuagium, burgagium, terra, redditus, aut aliqua possessio infra l[imites ejusdem burgi] legitur vel aliquo modo alienetur aliquibus vivis religiosis sine assensu et volunate ejusdem Burgi." Dated at Windsor, 20 Jan. (1268-9). Henry confirmed on the same day the charter of Henry II. (his grandfather) made to the same Burgesses. See *Tower. Cartæ Antiquæ.* NN. 60, 61. To the Bailiffs and Burgesses of Scarborough. Allowance of 50 marcs in the favour of their town, having paid the sum a second time, as part of the fine of 60 marcs, for a charter of liberties. Westminster, 8 Jan., 1256-7 *(Close Roll,* 4 Hen. III., m. 11*).*

That messuage is of the fee of Saint Mary's Church in Scardeburge, as they understand, but who first conferred it upon the Church they know not. John Cattesbak held it of the Abbot and Convent aforesaid for twenty years. And they say that the King has no right in the messuage, as they believe.[a]

CXXIX. WILLIAM DE FEUGERS. *Inq. p. m.*

[9 EDW. I. No. 17.]

Writ directed to Thomas de Normanville, and dated at Westminster, 10 July, 9th year (1281).

INQUISITION made by Geoffrey de Toccotes, Walter de Thorpe, Hugh de Hoton, Henry *le Venur'*, Geoffrey de Piketon, Peter Ragott',[b] Walter de Hurthewrd, Alan de Mauteby, Stephen Guer, Richard Clerk *(Cler')*, Robert de Hoton in Middelton, and Robert son of Weila *(fil' Weile)*, who say upon their oath that William de Feugers[c] held of the King in chief the town of Castelleuigton[d] by the service of half of one knight's fee. The capital messuage there is worth by the year one marc. There are in demesne forty-one bovates, each worth by the year with meadow appertaining, 12s., also demesne meadow, 7s. Eleven cottages, each worth yearly 16d. Demesne wood, about 20 acres, worth, after waste and destruction made, half a marc yearly. Two water-mills are worth by the year five marcs. Rent of assize of free tenants, 17s.

Andrew, son of the said William de Feugers, is his next heir, and aged fifty years.

Done at Stokesley, on Tuesday before the feast of S. Bartholomew in the ninth year of the reign (19 Aug., 1281).

---

[a] Endorsed. "Inquisicio de uno mesuagio in villa de Scardeburghe."

[b] This name is open to doubt.

[c] On 10 July, 1281, the lands of which William de Feugers died seised in chief, were ordered to be seized into the King's hand by Thomas de Normanville, the King's Steward *(Rot. Fin.* 9 Edw. I., m. 7*)*.

[d] Castle Levington, near Yarm, in the parish of Kirk Levington. It derives its distinctive name from an imposing prehistoric fortification, with a massive rampart, finely situated on the summit of the steep banks of the Leven.

CXXX. PETER OF SAVOY. *Extent of Lands.*[a]

[10 EDW. I No. 28.]

No writ.

[M. 13.]

COUNTY OF YORK.

EXTENT of the lands belonging to the Honour of Riche-
munde, in the County of York, made before Thomas de
Normanville, [Adam de Wynton], Drogo de Fere, and John de
Croxleghe, on Friday before the feast of S.S. Tiburtius and
Valerian· . . . . year (12 April, 1280),[b] by the oath of Halnath
de Halnakeby,· Henry Lespring, William de Skargile, Robert de
Witeclive,[c] knights, Geoffrey de Ha . by,[d] [Robert de] Appel-
garthe, Peter Groseteste, Stephen de Bowes, Hugh de Langeton,
Walter de Ulvigton, Symon de Multon, and [William de]
Bernigham, Jurors of the Wapentake of Gillinge.

GILLINGE.

A capital messuage worth 2*s.*; 133 acres of arable land in
demesne (at 12*d.*), £6 13*s.*; 13 acres of meadow (at 5*s.* 2*d.*),
67*s.* 2*d.*; 11 acres of meadow of the same demesne, 11*s.*; three
acres of meadow of the same demesne, 9*s.*; an assart and nine
acres of arable land, 8*s.* 10*d.*; and a water-mill, £10. Twenty
bondmen holding 20 bovates of land, each bovate containing
16 acres by the perch of 20 feet, £20. Thirteen cottars, 21*s.* 6*d.*
Perquisites of court, 20*s.*   Sum, £43 12*s.* 6*d.*

FORSETH.[e]

A capital messuage worth by the year 3*s.*; 252 acres of
arable land in demesne (at 12*d.*), £12 12*s.*; and four acres of
meadow and one forland, 19*s.*; herbage of vivary 6*s.*; and one
watermill, worth yearly £4. There are 33 bond tenants holding

---

[a] The following is the list of the documents contained under the heading 10
Edw. I., No. 28:—M. 1. Writ illegible, but probably relating to Cambridgeshire;
M. 2. Writ for the Counties of Lincoln and Notts., dated 9 Dec., 1280; M. 3.
Cambridgeshire; M. 4. Herts.; MM. 5, 6. Lincolnshire; M. 7. Notts. (apparently);
MM. 8, 9, 10. Lincolnshire; MM. 11, 12. Norfolk; MM. 13, 14, 15. Yorks.; M.
16. Notts.; M. 17. Norfolk. These are all very mutilated, and exceedingly difficult
to decipher. There is a contemporary transcript of the extents throughout in the
Chapter House Books, A$\frac{4}{22}$. The additions in square brackets are from the
transcript.

[b] This date is given on the assumption that the regnal year is the eighth, as in
the extent next following.

[c] Wycliffe. In *Domesday*, Wicliue.

[d] Probably Hanby. In 1284-5, Geoffrey de Hanby held six bovates of land in
Yafforth, near Northallerton, of the Earl of Richmond (Kirkby's *Inquest*, p. 176).

[e] Forsett, in the parish of Gilling, three miles south of Gainford Station.

33 bovates (each containing 12 acres by the perch as above and worth 10s.), £16 10s.; and six cottars who pay yearly 13s. 4d. Free tenants yield 10s., and the perquisites of courts are worth by the year 13s. 4d.   Sum, £36 6s. 8d.

MULTON.[a]

A capital messuage worth by the year 3s. 4d.; 267 acres of arable land in demesne (at 15d.), £16 13s. 9d.; 13 acres three roods of meadow (at 6s.), £4 2s. 6d. The Canons celebrating divine service in Richmond Castle are now enfeoffed of the said meadow by John de Britany. A water-mill is worth by the year 66s. 8d. There are 41 bovates of arable land (each 18 acres by the perch as above and worth 12s.) with meadow appertaining to the same, £24 12s., and the Canons aforesaid are enfeoffed of eight bovates of this land by the said John. Eleven cottars yield yearly 20s. 4d. There are free tenants who hold half a carucate of land for 5s. A smith (faber) pays yearly for five acres 2d.; the Abbot of Fountains for the site of Couton Grange,[b] 10s.; the Templars,[c] for one carucate of land, 10s. The perquisites of Courts are worth by the year 13s. 4d.   Sum, £51 17s. 1d.

BOWES.

There is a castle which is in the keeping of Gwichard de Charrun, with demesne lands by the feoffment of Peter of Savoy; 66 acres of arable land in demesne, worth by the year 66s.; 23 acres of meadow, 47s. 6d. A watermill and an oven (furnum) are worth by the year £11 6s. 8d. There are 48 bovates of land (each 12 acres by the perch as above, at 6s.), worth £14 8s. Ten cottars pay yearly 30s. Of assart by the year 12s. From three tenants called gresmen (qui vocantur gresmanni), 4s. 6d. yearly, and from other tenants in Cassiflat[d] and Staynhoukelde,[e] 40s.; from Cougeld and Schirnegeld by the year 6s. 0½d. From herbage, agistment, turbary, and heath, 40s. yearly. The market-toll is worth £33 6s. 8d. From one pound of cumin 1½d., and from escapes of cattle (escapiis

---

ᵃ Moulton, in the parish of Middleton Tyas.

ᵇ Cowton Grange, in the parish of Middleton Tyas, two and a half miles S.E. of the village.

ᶜ Mikel Couton in Kirkby's Inquest, called Temple Couton in 1316, and now East or Long Cowton (Kirkby's Inquest, p. 177 n).

ᵈ Perhaps Casey Green, in New Forest, commemorates this place called Gratsiflat in Inq. p. m., 13 Edw. I., No. 23.

ᵉ Called Stande Howkefeld, temp. Hen. VIII., and Stoneykeld, 30 Car. II. (Plantagenet Harrison's History of Yorkshire, vol. i., pp. 331, 339). Now Stone-how, on the Greta, west of Bowes.

averiorum) of Bringenhale and Stredforde,[a] 16*s*. yearly. Free tenants yield by the year 13*s*. 5*d*., and the hospital of Staynmor, 26*s*. 8*d*.

BULRUN AND BOWES.[b]

Twelve bovates of land which Robert de Appelgarth holds by the feoffment of John de Britany, are worth by the year £7 4*s*. (the bovate 12*s*.). One water-mill is worth 53*s*. 4*d*.; two cottars pay yearly 6*s*.; and the perquisites of Courts are worth by the year 50*s*.   Sum, £86 16*s*. 11*d*.

ARKELGARTH,[c] with the New Forest.

There are 30 cottages which yield yearly 30*s*., and one house, 6*s*. 8*d*. One close which Robert de Appelgarth holds by the year, is worth by the year 40*s*. The agistment of pasture[d] is worth by the year 40*s*. And divers pastures in Helwathe, Hallegate, and Kexthwayt,[e] are worth by the year £13 6*s*. 8*d*.; in Langethwayt, £4; in Exkerlede, 66*s*. 8*d*.; in Stirkthwayt, £4; in Kiwawe, £4 13*s*. 4*d*.; in Fagardegile, £6 3*s*. 4*d*. One new enclosure, 26*s*. 8*d*.; in Specchohues, 60*s*., and in Hep (or Hepe), £6.[f] Pleas and perquisites are worth by the year 40*s*.

Sum, £55 13*s*. 4*d*.

ALDEBURGH.[g]

A capital messuage worth by the year 6*s*. 8*d*.; 164 acres of arable land in demesne (at 18*d*.), £12 6*s*; 16 acres of meadow (at 5*s*.), £4. A water-mill is worth yearly £6 13*s*. 4*d*. There are 31 bovates of land (each eight acres, at 14*s*.), £21 14*s*. From two pounds of pepper and one pound of cumin, 13*d*. Eight cottars pay yearly 26*s*. 6*d*., and free tenants, 12*s*. The perquisites of courts are worth by the year 6*s*. 8*d*. Hasculf de Cleseby is enfeoffed of the aforesaid land for the term of his life by John de Britany.   Sum, £47 6*s*. 3*d*

---

[a] Brignall and Startforth.

[b] Boldron, in the parish of Startforth, two miles S.W. of Barnard Castle.

[c] Arkengarthdale.

[d] Here some words have been omitted in the transcript, and the writer has passed to " pasture " in the line below.

[e] Helwith, Hallgate, Kexwith, in the township of New Forest, in the S.W. of the parish of Kirkby Ravensworth.

[f] Langthwaite, a little north of Arkle Town. High and Low Eskeleth, higher up the Arkle Beck. Storthwaite, a little lower down on the opposite side. Kiwawe gerhaps Whaw, on the Arkle Beck between Low Eskeleth and Faggergill. Fagardegile now Faggergill, near the source of the Arkle Beck. Specchohues, not identified. Hep or Hepe, now East and West Hope, two farm houses about five miles N.N.E. of St. Mary's Church, Arkengarthdale.

[g] Aldbrough in the parish of Stanwick, three miles S.S.E. of Piercebridge Station.

The garden appertaining to Richmond Castle, with herbage and fruit, is worth by the year 16s. The lands of the servants *(terre servient')* of the Castle, are worth 45s. 1d. The output *(exitus)* of the lead mine is worth yearly £10. The pleas and perquisites of the Court of the Honour of Richmond, are worth by the year £10. Certain foreign free tenants yield by the year 30s. 6d. Sum, £20 11s. 7d. Sum of the sums aforesaid, £342 4s. 4d.

[Here there is in the original inquisition a space which is followed by :]

By the oath of Robert[a] de Lascels, Hervey de Waterlosus,[b] knights, Roger Tysel,[c] Thomas de Thornton, John de Rythe, William de Burgh *(Burgo)*, Robert de Hacceforde, Alexander de Haukeswelle, Richard de Wodyngton, Thomas de Swynwayt, John de Thornton, and Thomas de Crakhale.

BEYNBRIGGE.[d]

A capital messuage worth with curtilage 4s. The township of this manor holds the demesnes at the will of the lord, viz. : 34 acres of arable land, 200 acres of meadow, one watermill, one oven with brewery *(unum furnum cum braceria)*; and they yield by the year £66 13s. 4d. There is a park containing 17 acres, the herbage of which is worth yearly 40s.

VACCARY in the forest.

The vaccary in Constansate[e] is worth by the year £13 6s. 8d.; in Mouresgate, £13 6s. 8d. ; in Stalunluske, £9 6s. 8d. ; in Beredale £4. ; in Beutresate, £10; in Seldalegile, £13 6s. 8d. ; in Appeltresate, £9 13s. 8d. ; in Snaysum, £6 ; in Mussedale,

---

[a] These names are taken from the Chapter House Book, in which the original is not followed exactly. For instance the first surname is there written " Laceles."

[b] *Sic* in the Chapter House Book. A form of Watlous (Kirkby's *Inquest*, p. 154), where Hervey de Watlous held lands in Thornton and Watlous of Robert de Tatersale.

[c] Perhaps an error for Oysel. In 1284-5, Roger Oysell held lands in Aysgarth, Burton in Bishopdale, and Thoralby *(Ibid.*, pp. 150, 151, 162*)*.

[d] Bainbridge, in the parish of Aysgarth.

[e] Most of these names appear again in 13 Edw. I., No 23, under the heading of Bainbridge. Constansate, there Cuntelsatte, is now Counterside. Mouresgate, there Moursette, is Marsett. Stalunluske, there Balunbusc, is Stallingbusk. Beredale, which does not vary, is lost. Beutresate or Bertresatte, Buttersett. Seldalegile or Sleddalegayle, now Sleddale Gayle. Appeltresate, now Appersett. Snaysum, now Snaizholm. Mussedale or Mosedale, Mossdale. Setebukste, Fossedale, and Cotterdale, which are not repeated in the later inquisition, are now Sedbusk, Fossdale, and Cotterdale. Sundestan is perhaps Simonstone, a hamlet close to Fossdale, where Lord Wharncliffe has his shooting box. Quelpesetehoues, which reappears under the form Welpesattehowe, seems to defy identification.

29

£4 13s. 4d.; in Setebukste, Sundestan, Fossedale, and Cotter-dale, which are in the hand of Abbot of Jerveaux, by feoff-ment of John of Britany, and are worth by the year £39 6s. 8d.; and in Quelpesetehoues which is in the hand of Halnath de Halnakeby by feoffment of John of Britany, is worth by the year 26s. 8d. There is a vivary, called Semerwater,[a] worth yearly 40s. The agistment of cattle is worth £6; the sale of wood, and the iron mine, 20s.; pleas and perquisites of Courts, escapes and attachments, £12 by the year. Sum, £213 17s. 4d.

KATERK.[b]

A capital messuage worth by the year 5s.; 32 bovates of arable land in demesne (each bovate six acres, at 8s.), £12 16s.; 31½ bovates held by bondmen (of 10 acres, at 13s. 4d.), £21. Fifty-six acres, called Plusweynlondes (at 16d., are worth 74s. 8d. Gresmen *(gresmanni)* hold 32½ acres, 42s. Two bovates which contain 24 acres, and 32 acres, called Forland, are worth by the year 74s. 8d. There are cottars, who yield yearly 6s. 5d.; and two forges *(due forgie),* 6d. From rent of a pond and of a mill, 33s. 4d. The pleas and perquisites of Courts are worth by the year 26s. 8d.   Sum, £46 19s. 3d.

ESTBOULTON.

From rent due in the same, 9s. 1d.

[M. 13ᵈ.]

Knights' Fees which owe ward (guard) to the Castle of Richmond in the County of York.

The Abbot of Fountains for the third part of one knight's fee in Anderbyvesconte,[c] renders' to the castle-guard of Rich-mond 2s. 3d.[d]

The Abbot of Jervaulx *(Girovall')* for half a fee in Rok-kewyt,[e] 3s. 4d.[d]

Ralph de Rougemond for the third part of one fee in Sutton Rugemond,[f] 2s. 3d.[d]

ᵃ Seamerwater, near Hawes.

ᵇ Catterick.

ᶜ Ainderby Quernhowe, in the parish of Pickhill in Halikeld. This place has no distinction addition in *Domesday* or Kirkby's *Inquest.*

ᵈ In the Chapter House Book the word " Hangest " is written here at the end; but this is not found in the original. It is wrongly added.

ᵉ Rookwith, in the parish of Thornton Watlas, two miles south of Jervaulx Station. This place is Hang East.

ᶠ Sutton Howgrave, in the parish of Kirklington in Halikeld, five miles north of Ripon.

The Abbot of Fountains for the third part of one fee in Sinderby,[a] 2s. 3d.[b]

Stephen de Coverham for two fees in Warlanby,[c] one marc.

Robert de Musters for two and a half fees in Kirtlington,[d] 16s. 8d.[b]

Walter de Eggelclive[e] for two fees in Berdene,[f] one marc.

Geoffrey le Noreys and Emma de Bereforde for one fee in Bereforde,[g] half a marc.

Henry de Ripon for one fee in Neuton Morel,[h] half a marc.

Roger de Ingoldby and Nicholas de Wandesleghe for one fee in Wandesleghe,[i] half a marc.

Simon de Multon for the tenth part of one fee in Henham and Multon,[j] 10d.

William de Bernigham for the fourth part of one fee in Little Hoton,[k] 20d.

Robert de Wiclife for one fee in the same,[l] half a marc.

Edmund Fyton for one fee in Holteby and Enderdeby,[m] half a marc.[n]

William de Brettevile for one fee in Jaford,[o] half a marc.

Edmund Fyton for one fee in Great Couton,[p] half a marc.

The same Edmund for the fourth part of one fee in Brompton,[q] 20d.

[a] Sinderby, in the parish of Pickhill, now a station on the line between Northallerton and Melmerby junction.

[b] In the Chapter House Book the word " Hangest " is written here at the end ; but this is not found in the original. It is wrongly added.

[c] Warlaby, in the parish of Ainderby Steeple, two miles S.W. of Northallerton.

[d] Kirklington, in Halikeld, a mile west of Sinderby Station. The arms of the Musters or de Monasteriis, a church, is still to be seen in one of the windows of Kirklington Church.

[e] Eglesclive in A$\frac{4}{22}$.

[f] Barden, in the parish of Hawxwell and wapentake of Hang West, three miles N.E. of Leyburn.

[g] Barforth, on the river Tees, in the parish of Gilling, nearly opposite Gainford.

[h] Newton Morell, in the parish of St. John Stanwick, four miles S.E. of the church.

[i] Wensley, the parish in which Leyburn is situated.

[j] Henham seems lost. Moulton, in the parish of Middleton Tyas, is two miles north of Scorton Station on the Richmond line.

[k] A mile and three quarters S.E. of Wycliffe.

[l] Wycliffe-on-Tees, four and a half miles E.S.E. of Barnard Castle.

[m] Holtby and Ainderby Myers, in the parish of Hornby and wapentake of Hang East, a few miles north of Bedale.

[n] " Hangest " added here in the Chapter House Book.

[o] Yafforth, a mile and a half N.N.W. of Northallerton.

[p] East or Long Cowton, also called Mikel and Temple Cowton, a parish and station on the line between Northallerton and Darlington.

[q] Patrick Brompton, a parish in the wapentake of Hang East.

The Abbot of Jervaulx for the fourth part of one fee in Hoton Hang,[a] 20*d.*

Brian fitz Alan and William de Lasceles for one fee in Suthcouton and Northcouton,[b] half a marc.

Edward Charles for one fee in Brigenhale,[c] half a marc.

Hugh fitz Henry for three fees and the sixth part of one fee in Kirkeby Raveneswathe, 21*s.* 1½*d.*

Robert de Tateshale for half a fee in Westwitton, 40*d.*

The same Robert and Mary de Middelham for six fees in Middelham, 40*s.*

Humfrey de Bassingburne for two fees in Thornton Stiward, one marc.

Avice Marmyon for two and a half fees in Tanefelde, 16*s.* 8*d.*

John de Romundeby[d] for one fee in Ergom, half a marc.[e]

John le Bretun and Henry de Ripon for the fourth part in Colebron, 20*d.*[f]

Avice Marmyon and Henry Conan[g] for two fees in Manefelde, one marc.

Hugh de Aske for one fee in Aske and Marige,[h] half a marc.

Rouald *le Constable* for thirteen fees in Burton,[i] four pounds half a marc.

Thomas de Burgh *(Burgo)* for two fees in Hacforde,[j] one marc [whereof Hengest, 12*s.* 4*d.*].

Matthew de Kerkham[k'] for the sixth part of one fee in Estlaton, 13½*d.*

Osbert and Odart for the sixth part of one fee in Gillinge, 13½*d.*

[a] Hutton Hang, one mile S.W. of the village of Fingall, in the wapentake of Hang West.

[b] North Cowton and South Cowton, to the south of Moulton Station.

[c] Brignall, a mile S.W. of Greta Bridge.

[d] Rouneby A$\frac{4}{2^{1}}$. In 1284-5 Richard de Romondby held six carucates in Ergom, now Eryholme, a parish on the Tees below Croft, in the wapentake of Gilling East (Kirkby's *Inquest*, p, 178). He derived his name from Romanby, close to Northallerton Station.

[e] "Hangest" added here in the Chapter House Book.

[f] "Hangest" added in A$\frac{4}{2^{1}}$. Colburn, in the parish of Catterick and wapentake of Hang East, between Richmond and Catterick.

[g] Generally called Henry Fitz Conan.

[h] Aske, now Lord Zetland's seat, and Marrick, farther up the Swale.

[i] Roald fitz Roald held Burton Constable at the time of Kirkby's *Inquest*, of John, Earl of Richmond.

[j] Hackforth, in the parish of Hornby and wapentake of Hang East, three miles south of Catterick.

[k] A mistake for Kerkan, now Carkin, in the parish of Gilling. East Layton is six miles north of Richmond.

Brian fitz Alan, John le Bretoun, and Hugh fitz Henry, for two and a half fees in Kilverdeby, Askham, Appelby, and Fencotes,[a] 16s. 8d. [whereof Hangest in Fencotes.][b]

Simon de Furneus for one fee in Enderby,[c] half a marc.

Roger de Lasceles for two and a half fees in Scorueton,[d] 16s. 8d.

Brian fitz Alan for three fees and a sixth part in Bedale, 21s. 1½d.[b]

Roger de Mounbray for one fee in Masham, half a marc.[b]

The Abbot of Jervaulx, the Abbot of Saint Agatha, and Roger de Waldeby, for a sixth part in Tunstale,[e] 13½d.

Nicholas de Stapelton and the Abbot of Saint Agatha for one fee in Stapelton,[f] half a marc.

Sum, £20 19s. 10½d., viz. : from 62½ fees, a fourth part, and an eighth part.

Sum of the sums of Beynbrigge and within, £282 5s. 6½d.

Sum of the whole Honour of Richmond with the borough, £668 13s. 10½d.[g]

EXTENT[h] of the town of Richmond made before Sir Thomas de Normanville, Adam de Wynton, Drogo de Fere, and John de Croxleghe, assigned by the King to make it, by the oath of Thomas son of Geoffrey, Richard Dyer *(tinctoris)*, William de Lythe, William Blund *(blundi)*, Thomas Longespey, Alan de Ulvshou,[i] Roger de Ellyngton, William Payben, Eude son of Henry, William de Dunskere, Peter son of John, and William de Spytelgate, on Thursday before Palm Sunday, in the eighth year of Edward (11 April, 1280).

---

[a] Killerby, two miles S.W. of Catterick. Askham may be a mistake for Aiskew, close to Bedale. Appleby, now Eppleby, a village three miles S.W. of Piercebridge Station. Great and Little Fencote, in the parish of Kirkby Fleetham, five and a half miles west of Northallerton.

[b] "Hangest" added in A 2⁄4⁄2.

[c] Ainderby Steeple, two and a half miles S.W. of Northallerton, called in Kirkby's *Inquest*, Ainderby Fourneux, and Ainderby with Steeple.

[d] Scruton, four and a half miles W.S.W. of Northallerton. *Domesday*, Scurueton.

[e] Tunstall, two miles S.W. of Catterick.

[f] Stapleton on the Tees, west of Darlington.

[g] Below, the sum total amounts to a sovereign more.

[h] This extent is not found in the file of inquisitions, numbered 10 Edw. I., No. 28.

[i] Written Vlushov. No doubt the Ulveshowe or Elueshou of Kirkby's *Inquest*. "The vill of Ulveshowe has disappeared. It stood, probably, not far from Ulshaw Bridge, near Middleham, and about three miles and a half E.S.E. of Wensley (Kirkby's *Inquest*, p. 158n).

The borough of Richmond with demesne lands, fairs, markets, tolls, amercements, pleas, and other issues appertaining thereto, is worth by the year in common years £40.

The dye-house[a] of Richmond, which Thomas son of Geoffrey holds by charter of the Earl, is worth by the year in common years £4.

One house in Bergate, which was an escheat of the Earl by reason of the felony done by Geoffrey the fuller (*fullonem*), is now in the hands of the Canons celebrating in Richmond Castle, by the gift of John of Britany, and is worth yearly 4s.

Sum, £44 4s.

[M. 12.]

EXTENT of the lands belonging to the Honour of Ryche-munde, in the County of York, and other Counties . . . . appears below.

COUNTY OF YORK.

Place.	Annual value.		
	£	s.	d.
Borough of Rychemunde with the demesnes and other appurtenances . . .	44	4	0
Gillinge . .	43	12	6
Forsete . . .	36	6	8
Molton	51	17	1
Bouwes and Bulerun . . .	86	16	11
Appelgarthe[b]	55	13	4
Aldeburge	47	6	3
Lead mines (*minera plumbi*), with rent of garden and perquisites of the great Court.	20	11	7
Baynebrigge with the vaccary in the forest . .	213	17	4
Caterice[c]	46	8	4
Ward of the Castle of Rychemunde . .	20	19	10½
Sum, £667 13s. 10½d.[d]			

[a] Written "Tincit' iria." Perhaps ·'Tincturaria" with *domus* understood. Observe in the jurors' names Richard *tinctor*.

[b] This should be Arkelgarth.

[c] On p. 226 Catterick is said to be £46 19s. 3d.

[d] On p. 229 the sum for Richmondshire is given as £668 13s. 10½d. The sum given above agrees with the items.

Writ[a] dated at Westminster, 1 Dec., 10th year (1281), and directed to Thomas de Normanville, Escheator beyond Trent, commanding him in the presence of one of the attornies of our most dear mother, Alianora, Queen of England, whom she might choose to associate with him, to diligently inquire by the oaths of just and lawful men of his bailiwick, by whom the truth may be better known, what were the fees held of the Honour of Richemond, wherever they be in his bailiwick, and who holds them, and how, and in what manner, and who of them hold elsewhere in chief, and to cause all those fees to be diligently and faithfully extended, as to how much they may be worth a year in all outgoings, as in homages, services, rents, wardships, reliefs, marriages, advowsons of churches, and all else belonging to the same fees; and to send the same inquisition and extent clearly and plainly made under his own seal, and that of the attorney of our said mother, and those by whom the inquisition and extent were made, and this writ.[b]

[M. 14.]

EXTENT made at Richemunde, on Saturday next after the feast of S. Luke the Evangelist, in the eleventh of the reign of King Edward, beginning (24 Oct., 1282), by the oath of William de Burgh, Osbert de Pykehale, Henry de Torp, Thomas de Disforde, Thomas de Gaytanby, Thomas de Crachale, Thomas de S . . th . , Richard de Wodigton, Thomas de Hey, Michael de Layton, John de Couton in Caldewelle, and Robert Warde of . . . . . , who say on their oath that :—

Sir Robert de Tadersale[c] holds in chief of the Earl of Rychemunde three fees and a half by homage, and pays scutage when it is current *(quando currit)*, namely : in West Wytton and Welle, Crachale and Thorraldby,[d] and they are worth as in demesnes, capital messuages, demesne meadows, woods, pastures, free services, bondages *(bondag')*, cottars *(coterell')*, rents, mills, free courts, and other rents of all kinds, £200. Of marriage when it happens according to the value of the lands or . . . . . The advowson of two churches, Welle, worth £50, West Wytton £20. He holds elsewhere of the King in chief in Norfolk, of ancient demesne. Sum, £200. The advowson of two churches.

Lady Mary de Nevile, Lady of Middilham, holds etc., three fees in Middilham, Snape, Carleton in Coverdale, etc., value of holding, £200. Of marriage as above. She has the

---

[a] On fol. 12 (or page 25) immediately preceding the extent made at Richmond, on Saturday after the feast of St. Luke the Evangelist, in the 11th year (24 Oct., 1282), there is this writ, which is not found in the file of inquisitions 20 Edw. I., No. 28. On p. 39 is a writ directed to the Sheriff of Cambridgeshire, commanding inquiry to be made as to what fees appertain to the Honour of Richmond. Dated at Dyvises, 3 April, 10th year (1282).

[b] The terms of this writ show clearly that the extent which follows was made thereupon in answer.

[c] This entry is given in full. The following ones are much abstracted. It is unfortunate the notice about marriage is imperfect in this first entry, and given afterwards only in an abbreviated form.

[d] Thoralby, a hamlet a mile south of Aysgarth.

advowson of two churches, Aykescharth, worth £200, and Middilham, 20 marcs. She holds elsewhere of the King in chief, namely, in Norfolk of the ancient (feoffment).
Sum, £200. Advowsons of two churches.

Sir Thomas Burgh (de Burgo) holds, etc., two fees in Hackeford,[a] Hapelton and the other Hapelton,[b] Burton and Bissopdale,[c] and elsewhere, etc., value of holding £68 6s. 8d. Of marriage as above. He has the advowson of the church of Langeton,[d] worth £20. He holds of the King by reason of the escheat of the Earl of Chester, of the new (feoffment).
Sum, £68 and half a marc. The advowson of one church, £20.

Sir Roald de Burton holds, etc., 13 fees in Burton, Caldewelle,[e] Croft, and elsewhere, etc., value of holding, £76 4s. 2d. Of marriage as above. Sum, £76 4s. 2d.

Sir Brian fitz Alan holds, etc., six fees and the sixth part of one fee in Bedale, Aykescothe, Burel, Frytby,[f] and elsewhere, with the members, etc., value of holding, £200 6s. 8d. Of marriage as above. He has the advowson of three churches, Bedale, worth £100, Melsandeby, £20, and Rockeby,[g] £10.
Sum, £200 and half a marc. Advowson of three churches, £130.

Sir Roger de Lasseles holds, etc., two and a half fees in Scrueton,[h] with the members, etc., value of holding, £120 5s. 6d. Of marriage as above. He has the advowson of two churches, Kyrkeby Wiske, worth 100 marcs, and Scrueton, worth £20.
Sum, £120 5s. 6d. Advowson of two churches, £80 and 10 marcs.

Sir Gilbert de Gaunt holds, etc., four fees in Helath in Swaldale,[i] with the members, etc., value of holding, 100 marcs 6s. 8d. Of marriage as above. He holds elsewhere of the King of the ancient (feoffment). Sum, 100 marcs and half a marc.

Sir John le Breton holds, etc., the fourth part of one fee in Colburne, Aynderby,[j] with the members, etc., value of holding,

---

[a] Written Backeford in A.$\frac{4}{2\frac{1}{2}}$.

[b] Appleton East and West, a township two miles south of Catterick.

[c] Burton in Bishopdale or West Burton, a hamlet a mile and a half S.E. of Aysgarth.

[d] Great Langton, or Langton-on-Swale, a village and parish five miles N.W. of Northallerton.

[e] Caldwell, a mile and a half south of Gainford.

[f] Bedale, Aysgarth, Burrill, and Firby (Domesday, Fredebi), near Bedale.

[g] Melsonby, and Rokeby on the Tees, below Barnard Castle.

[h] Scruton.

[i] Healaugh on the Swale, above Reeth.

[j] Probably Ainderby Myers.

£19 15s. 3d. Of marriage as above. He has the advowson of the church of Finkhale,[a] worth £30.

Sum, £19 15s. 3d. Advowson of the church, £30.

Henry de Ryppon holds, etc., half a fee in Colburne and Appelby,[b] etc., value of holding, £13 16s. 1d. Of marriage as above. £13 16s. 1d.

Nicholas de Wandeslay holds, etc., half a fee in Wandeslay,[c] etc., value of holding, £16 3s. 1d. Of marriage as above.

Sum, £16 3s. 1d.

Sir Roger de Ingoldby holds, etc., half a fee in Wandeslay, etc., value of the holding, £20 2s. Of marriage as above. He has the advowson of the church of Wandeslay, worth £70.

Sum, £20 2s. Advowson of one church, £70.

Stephen de Coverham holds, etc., half a fee in Coverham, etc., value of holding, 66s. 8d. Of marriage as above.

Sum, five marcs.

William le Scurop[d] holds, etc., the twelfth part of one fee, etc., value of holding, 60s. Of marriage as above. Sum, 60s.

Walter de Berdene holds, etc.; one fee in Berdene,[e] with the members, etc., value of holding, £20 6s. 8d. Of marriage as above. Sum, £20 and half a marc.

Edmund de Killum holds, etc., one fee in Daneby,[f] etc., value of holding, £15 3s. 4d. Of marriage as above.

Sum, £15 3s. 4d.

Sir Umfred de Bassengburne holds, etc., two fees in Thornton Stiwarde, with the members, etc., value of holding, £45 6s. 8d. Of marriage as above. Sum, £45 and half a marc.

Roger de Waldby holds, etc., the fourth part of one fee in Tunstal,[g] etc., value of holding, 60s. Of marriage as above.

Sum, 60s.

Sir Henry fitz Conan holds, etc., the third part and the ninth part of one fee in Fletham,[h] etc., value of holding, £13 14s. 4d. Of marriage as above. Sum, £13 14s. 4d.

[a] Fingall, a station on the Northallerton and Leyburn line.

[b] Eppleby.

[c] Wensley, *Domesday*, Wendreslaga.

[d] A corruption of Scrop. In 1284-5, William le Scrop held a sixth part of a knight's fee in East or Low Bolton, near Redmire, in the parish of Wensley (Kirkby's *Inquest*, p. 152).

[e] Barden, near Leyburn.

[f] Danby-on-Yore, in the parish of Thornton Steward, two miles west of Middleham, on the opposite side of the river.

[g] Tunstall, two miles S.W. of Catterick.

[h] Kirkby Fleetham.

John Coleman holds, etc., the third part and the ninth part of one fee in the same vill of Fletham, etc., value of holding, £11 6s. 1d. Of marriage as above.   Sum, £11 6s. 1d.

Sir William Giffard holds, etc., the third part and the ninth part of one fee in the same vill of Fletham, etc., value of holding, 78s. 8d.   Sum, 78s. 8d.

Lady Avice Marmion holds, etc., four fees and a half in Tanfelde, with the members, and in Manefeld, with the members, etc., value of holding, £80 14s. 2d. Of marriage as above. She has the advowson of the churches of Tanefeld, worth 40 marcs, Wat,ᵃ worth 50 marcs, and of Manefeld, worth 60 marcs.

Sum, £80 14s. 2d. Advowson of three churches, 150 marcs.

Robert de Musters holds, etc., two fees and a half in Kertligtonᵇ with the members, etc., value of holding, £31 4s. 2d. Of marriage as above. He has the advowson of the church of Kertligton, worth £50.

Sum, £31 4s. 2d. Advowson of one church, £50.

Ralph de Rogemunde holds, etc., the fourth part of one fee in Sutton Hougrave, etc., value of holding, £13 4s. 2d. Of marriage as above.   Sum, £13 4s. 2d.

Sir Hugh Fitz Henry holds, etc., three fees and the sixth part of one fee in Ravensvat, Cutherston,ᶜ and the other members, etc., value of holding, £112 0s. 4d. Of marriage as above. He has the advowson of the church of S. Roumald,ᵈ worth £120. He holds elsewhere of the King after the decease of P. of Savoy, by reason of the Countess of Albemarle.ᵉ

Sum, £112 0s. 4d. Advowson of one church, £120.

Sir John de Romundesby holds, etc., one fee in Ergum,ᶠ etc., value of holding, £15 9s. Of marriage as above.

Sum, £15 9s.

Walter de Musters holds, etc., the twelfth part of one fee in the same vill of Ergum, etc., value of holding, 65s. Of marriage as above.   Sum, 65s.

Sir William de Schargel holds, etc., the fourth part of one fee in Scargel,ᵍ etc., value of holding, £6 17s. 6d. Of marriage as above.   Sum, £6 17s. 6d.

ᵃ Wath.

ᵇ Kirtlington.

ᶜ Ravenswath and Cotherstone.

ᵈ Romaldkirk.

ᵉ Aveline de Fortibus, Countess of Albemarle, wife of Edmund Plantagenet, brother of Edward I.

ᶠ Eryholme.

ᵍ Scargill, four miles south of Barnard Castle.

Edward Charles holds, etc., one fee in Brigenhale, etc., value of holding, £42 9s. 2d. Of marriage as above.

Sum, £42 9s. 2d.

Sir^a *(Dominus)* Hugh de Aske holds, etc., one fee in Aske and Marrike, etc., value of holding, £40 10s. Of marriage as above.

Sum, £40 10s.

Sir *(Dominus)* Edmund Fytune holds, etc., two fees in Couton, with members, etc., value of holding, £20 8s. 6d. Of marriage as above. He holds elsewhere of the King, viz.: in the Counties of Blakeburne and Bolin, but it is not known in what manner.

Sum, £20 8s. 6d.

Geoffrey Norays of Berforde holds, etc., one fee in Berforde,^b etc., value of holding, 107s. 4d. Of marriage as above.

Sum, 107s. 4d.

Thomas Gretheved holds, etc., the third part of one fee in Manefelde, etc., value of holding, 54s. Of marriage as above.

Sum, 45s.

William de Lindesay holds, etc., the fourth part of one fee in Middilton,^c etc., value of holding, £15 13s. 4d. Of marriage as above.

Sum, £15 13s. 4d.

Henry de Middilton holds, etc., the fourth part of one fee in Middilton, etc., value of holding, £10 5s. 2d. Of marriage as above.

Sum, £10 5s. 2d.

Alan de Cneton holds, etc., the fourth part of one fee in Kneton^d and Middilton, etc., value of holding, £11 3s. 4d.

Sum, £11 3s. 4d.

Simon de Mulketon holds, etc., the tenth part of one fee in Multon,^e etc., value of holding, 54s. Of marriage as above.

Sum, 54s.

Odard de Gillinge holds, etc., the twelfth part of one fee in Gillinge, etc., value of holding, 40s. Of marriage as above.

Sum, 40s.

Osbert de Gillinge holds, etc., the twelfth part of one fee in Gillinge, etc., value of holding, [40s.]. Of marriage as above.

Sum [40s.].^f

---

^a Here (after Edward Charles), in the original (which is defective and difficult to read), the names are continued on the dorse of the membrane (14) with the heading repeated, viz.:—" Extenta feodorum Honoris de Richemunde in Comitatu Ebor. facta per Thomam de Normanville et Johannem de Crokesle in Richemundshire." In the Chapter House Book the same heading is written, and the names are continued (p. 29) in the same form as before.

^b Barforth.

^c Middleton Tyas.

^d Kneeton, a small hamlet, a mile N.E. of Middleton Tyas.

^e Moulton.

^f Omitted in the Chapter House book, but discernible in 10 Edw. I., No. 28.

John de Hertforde holds, etc., the third part of one fee in the same,ᵃ etc., value of holding, £13 6s. 8d. Of marriage as above.   Sum, 20 marcs.

Stephen de Bernyghamᵇ holds, etc., the twelfth part of one fee, and is a free farmer. He does no homage, nor does he render scutage; and after his death nothing shall be done to the Castle, save the doubling of his farm *(et post decessum ejus nichil faciet castro nisi duplicacionem firme sue)*.

William de Bernygham holds in chief of the Earl of Richmond, the fourth part of one fee in Little Hoton by homage, and renders scutage when current. Value of holding, 100s. Of marriage as above.   Sum, 100s.

Robert de Furneus holds, etc., one fee in Aynderby,ᶜ etc., value of holding, £24. Of marriage as above. He has the advowson of the church of Aynderby, which is worth £40.

Sum, £24. Advowson of a church, £40.

In Danebyᵈ with Mount Sorel, there are three parts of one fee which used *(solebant)* to do homage and render scutage when current, but they are now in the hand of the Earl of Richmond. The present value in demesne to the Earl's use, as in capital messuages, demesne lands, etc., is £30; and there is the advowson of the church of Daneby, which is worth by the year £40.

Sum, £30. Advowson of a church, £40.

The Abbot of Egleston holds the fourth part of one fee in Egleston by homage, and renders scutage when current. What he holds in demesne as in capital messuages, etc., is worth nothing, because not any profit to the Earl.

The Abbot of Fountains holds in chief of the Earl of Richmond, two parts of one fee in Ainderby Vecounteᵉ and Synderby, etc. Value of holding, etc. (as Egleston).

The Abbot of Saint Agatha holds, etc., half a fee and the eighteenth part of one fee in Stapelton and Tunstal, etc. Value of holding, etc. (as Egleston).

The Abbot of Jervaulx holds, etc., half a fee, the third part and eighteenth part of one fee in Rokewyke,ᶠ Hoton Hange, and in Tonstal, etc. Value of holding (as Egleston).

ᵃ Hartforth, one and a quarter miles N.E. of Gilling.

ᵇ In 1284-5, William de Bernyngham held two carucates in Barningham (Kirkby's *Inquest*, p. 166).

ᶜ Ainderby Steeple.

ᵈ Danby Wiske.

ᵉ Ainderby Quernhowe.

ᶠ Rookwith.

Sum of fees of those who hold nothing elsewhere of the King in chief—35 fees which are worth by the year £553 14s. 1d.

Memorandum, that there are 27 fees, the tenants of which hold elsewhere of the King in chief.[a]

CXXXI. BALDWIN WAKE.[b] *Extent of Manors.*

No writ.

[10 EDW. I. No. 26.][c]

[M. 1.]

EXTENT of the manor of Aton in Clivelonde, of which Baldewin Wake was seised in his demesne as of fee on the day of his death, made on Monday the morrow of Palm Sunday *(in crastino Palmarum)*, 10 Edward I. (23 March, 1281-2), at Aton, before Henry de Bray, by Sir John de Meynil, Sir Robert de Scotherskalfe, knights, William de Mumbray, Robert de Pothou, John de Kerkeby, Thomas de Waxsont, William Tosti,

---

[a] At the end of m. 17 are some figures which (bad to make out) seem to indicate the whole value of Richmondshire. The following is a copy of this portion, as well as can be made out:—" Summa Agen' ij^m vj^c xix*li.* vs. vjd. in sterling. Summa in Turron' x^m ccccl xxvij*li.* ijs., et sic excedit summa de Agen' in sterling., summam Richemund' in sterling., viij^c xiij*li.* . . . . s. viijd." This entry will be understood by referring back to No. LXXVII, where it was agreed that John de Brittany, Earl of Richmond, should have the Agenois until he could get the County of Richmond. From this entry it appears that the Agenois exceeded the value of Richmondshire by over £813. The two totals given, the first on p. 230, £667 13s. 10½d., and the one above, £553 14s. 1d., make in all £1221 7s. 11¾d. The rents derived from the parts of the Honour in other Counties must have made up the difference.

[b] Son and heir of Hugh Wake and Joan de Stuteville (No. XCVII). He married Hawise, daughter, and ultimately sole heiress of Robert de Quency, as her only sister Joan, wife of Sir Humfrey de Bohun, died without issue *(Cal. Gen.* vol. i., pp. 111, 346). On 10 Feb., 1281-2, the King, then at Cirencester, ordered Thomas de Normanville, the Escheator beyond Trent, to seize the lands which Baldwin de Wake, deceased, held in chief *(Rot. Fin.,* 10 Edw. I., m. 16). On 13 April following, being then at Devizes, he ordered the manor of Hykam, extended at £17 10s. 3d., to be assigned to his widow, Hawise, in dower, she paying the annual rent to the Crown of £7 9s. 4d., for which the Sheriff of Lincolnshire was to be answerable to the Escheator *(Ibid.,* m. 13). On 20 May in the same year, the King, then at Worcester, granted to Henry de Bray, clerk, to be held at the King's pleasure, the manor of Skeldinghope, which belonged to Baldwin Wake deceased, who held in chief, and which was in the royal custody by reason of John, son and heir of the aforesaid Baldwin, being under age and in the custody of the King *(Ibid.,* m. 12). His widow, Hawise, died before 27 March, 1285, the date of the writ of *diem clausit extremum* directed to the Escheator *citra Trentam (Ibid.,* 13 Edw. I., m. 15).

[c] The following is a list of the contents of the extents comprised under the heading 10 Edw. I., No. 26.:—M. 1. Yorks. (Aton) ; M. 2. Cumberland ; M. 3, 3^d. Yorks. (Cotingham) ; MM. 4, 5, 6, Lincolnshire ; MM. 7, 7^d, 8, 8^d. Yorks. (Botercram, Kirkby Moresheved) ; M. 9, Lincoln ; M. 10. Yorks. and elsewhere.

John Marchant, Richard de Fenton, John de Leysingby, Semon de Tay, Robert de Thormotby, and Robert de Lindeshe, who say by their oath that the said manor is held in chief of Sir *(domino)* Nicholas de Meynil for half a knight's fee, yielding 3*s.*, for foreign service called Fine of Wapentake *(de forinseco quod vocatur Finis Wapent').* The capital messuage, the buildings of which are badly *(debiliter)* constructed, together with the garden, curtilage and other easements, is valued by the year at 20*s.*

There are in demesne eleven score and 18 acres of land (at 6*d.* the acre), 119*s.*; also in demesne 30½ acres of meadow (at 2*s.*), 61*s.*; and pasture, demesne and several, in which 12 oxen may be kept, worth yearly 3*s.* There is a plot *(placea)* called Ergum,[a] which is sometimes ploughed, and worth 6*d.* A wood called Wystendale contains in length the fourth part of a league, and in width one quarentel *(unam quarentelam),* the yearly profit of which is 2*s.* A grove, called Elmerege, is worth by the year 2*s.*, and not more, because the lady of Hemelington[b] has twenty waggon loads of wood, both for plough-timber and for the hearth, and beyond this, housbote and heybote, by view of the lord's forester. There is a water-mill, called Westmulne, worth by the year 106*s.* 8*d.*, also the fourth part of another mill called Estmulne, valued at 27*s.* 8*d.*

Five free tenants pay yearly 22*s.* 10½*d.* and two pounds of cumin (at 1*d.*), 23*s.* ½*d.* Two tenants for a term of years pay for a tenement, 18*s.* 4*d.* There are 21 bondmen *(bondi)* who yield by the year £15 16*s.* 9*d.*; and 26 cottars, £4 2*s.* 2*d.* A forge yields yearly 12*d.* The township of Aton renders for toll of oven and brewing, 5*s.* 6*d.* *(pro tolneto furni et bracin'),* and for Wapentake-fine, 5*s.* 9¾*d.* The agistment in the common pasture is valued at 2*s.*; merchets, heriots, fines, pleas, and per-quisites, at 13*s.* 4*d.* Sum total, £40 9*s.* 9¼*d.*

Afterwards it is found that the said lord Baldewin and Hawyse, his wife, were jointly enfeoffed by Roger de Mosegrave, to hold to them and their heirs for ever, in 12 bovates and 12 acres of land, and the fourth part of a watermill with the appurtenances; all of which are valued by the year at £6 1*s.* 8*d.*

Nicholas de Meynel holds one carucate of land in Aton; Robert de Thormodeby, six bovates in Thormodeby;[c] John Marchand, one toft and four bovates in Aton; Robert de Merton, four bovates in the same; and Robert *le Taylour,* one toft in

---

[a] Airy Holme, a farm house in the parish of Ayton-in-Cleveland, on the south side of Roseberry Topping.

[b] Hemlington, in the parish of Stainton, four miles N.E. of Ayton.

[c] Thornaby, south of Stockton.

the same. These owe suit and foreign service *(debent sect' et forinsec')*. The Prior of Geseburne holds one carucate, and the Master of S. Leonard, York, half a carucate of land in Aton in frank almoigne. The lady of Hemelington holds the manor of Hemelington,[a] and 12*s*. 2*d*. annual rent in Aton, in dower, out of the lands which were of Robert de Stoteville, formerly her husband; and they are valued at £21 by the year.

The Abbot of Wetheby[b] holds the church of Aton to his own uses *(in proprios usus)*.

[M. 3.]

EXTENT of the manor of Cotingham, made on Thursday in Easter week, at Cotingham, 10 Edward (2 April, 1282), before Henry de Bray, by James de Frivile, John de Meus, Peter de Saunton, Robert de Cave, German Hay,[c] knights. Laurence de Eton, John son of Ellen *(fil' Elene)* of Brentingham, John Kent of the same, Nigel de Waldeby, Robert Freman, Alan of S. James *((Alanum de Sancto Jacobo)*, Alan Moigne of Hesele, John de Cave, John Taket,[d] John de Hanlanby, Nigel *le Parker*, Laurence Curteys, and John de Hedon, who say by their oath that the capital messuage of Cotingham is well constructed with a double ditch enclosed by a wall, and is worth, with easement of the necessary houses, in herbage, fruit of the garden, and fishery of the fosses, £7 16*s*. 8*d*. by the year, that is to say: the easement of the necessary houses is valued at 30*s*., if the demesnes of the manor be entirely let to any tenant; but if not, then nothing. The herbage and fruit of the garden are valued at 60*s*.; the fishing of the fosses *(fossatorum)*, at 66*s*. 8*d*.

Sum, £7 16*s*. 8*d*.

DEMESNES.

There are in demesne eight carucates of arable land, containing 1,061½ acres, by the perch of 17½ feet, which lie in certain ploughed lands *(culturis)*, thus called: Wyndgarthe, Pertreflat, 39 acres (at 18*d*.), 58*s*. 6*d*.; Molcastreflattes, 18 acres (at 12*d*.), 18*s*.; Pelnarthe, Lorteleghe, Suthe Derningham,

---

[a] Perhaps Emma, daughter of Richard Malebisse, and widow of Robert de Stuteville. Her husband gave a serf to Guisborough, called Ralph, son of Roger of Hemelington. There was another Robert de Stuteville, son of the above named Robert and Emma, whose widow (if he married) may be the person in question *(Guisborough Chartulary, Cott. MSS.; Cleop. D. ii., fo. 254[d])*.

[b] The church of Ayton was given to Whitby Abbey by William de Stuteville, in the latter part of the twelfth century *(Whitby Chartulary, vol. i., pp. 48, 68)*.

[c] Each of the five names is preceded by " dominum."

[d] Takel on the dorse.

Northe Derningham, Neubreke, Molcastreflattes, and Haven-
flattes,ᵃ 656 acres (at 8*d*.), £25 17*s*. 4*d*.; Safrundale and Westlathes, 13 score six acres (at 6*d*.), £6 13*s*.; Westlathes, five score
five and a half acres (at 4*d*.); and in the same *(in eadem
cultura)* 57 acres (at 2*d*.), 44*s*. 8*d*.   Sum, £38 11*s*. 6*d*.ᵇ

MEADOWS.

There are in certain meadows, called Saltenges and Pelnarthe, 15 score 19 acres, at 3*s*. the acre, £47 17*s*.

SEVERAL PASTURE.

There are these pastures, namely: Estlandes, worth by the
year £12; Wythes, £9 12*s*.; Someryonge, £9 6*s*. 8*d*.; Saltenges,
53*s*. 4*d*.; . . . . hus, £4 11*s*. 6*d*.; Little Derningham, 53*s*. 4*d*.;
. . . . crofte, 30*s*.; other small several pastures, valued at
113*s*. 10*d*. by the year.   Sum, £48 0*s*. 8*d*.

PARK.

There is a park well enclosed, containing in circuit *(pro-
cinctu)* four leagues, in which the game are estimated at 500
(D. ferarum), whose pasture with that of 35 [? mares] is worth
by the year £13 0*s*. 6*d*.   A wood, called Suthewode, herbage
worth 33*s*. 4*d*.; another, Northwode, herbage 6*s*. 8*d*.   The
underwood of the park without waste or destruction is worth
yearly £6; the underwood of Suthewode, £12 10*s*.; of Northwode, 116*s*. 8*d*.   The underwood of Northwode, which was of
Reginald Pratte, is worth by the year, without waste or destruction, 41*s*. 8*d*.   The pannage of the park and of the woods
aforesaid is worth 53*s*. 4*d*.   Sum, £44 2*s*. 2*d*.
There are three water-mills and one wind-mill, worth
yearly twenty marcs.
The rents of 74 free tenants are yearly £24 14*s*. 6*d*.; of
62 tenants at will, £48 1*s*. 1*d*.   There are 92 bondmen who
yield in services and rent £99 1*s*. 2*d*., and 137 cottars *(coterii)*,
who yield £31 13*s*.   Thirty tenants of sheepcotes *(tenentes bercarias)* upon Nauendike, pay 75*s*.   The cottars and bondmen
render yearly of custom, called *Turfpeny* and *Grundpeni*, 48*s*.
10*d*.   The men of Skipwythe for *Grundpeny* of twelve acres of
meadow in Illemere, four [shillings] at mowing time.   There are
small herbages after the corn and hay are carried which are
called *Averinge*, and are worth yearly 100*s*.   The agistment
of foreign cattle *(averiorum forinsecorum)* in the common
pasture of Cotingham, is worth by the year 20*s*.   The men of

ᵃ Reading doubtful.
ᵇ The total here is affected by an error above of £4, in the item of 656 acres,
which at 8*d*., are worth £21 17*s*. 4*d*., and *not* £25 17*s*. 4*d*.

Swinlonde[a] and of Miton[b] for watering their cattle in Derning-amdike, yield yearly 10s.; the men of Braythueyt[c] for theirs in Ragwelle water, 6s.; the men of Sokene for pontage of Saltenges, 7s.

Pleas, perquisites, fines, gersomes *(geresume)* and merchets *(marchette)*, are worth by the year £12; faldage, 7s.

Sum total, £435 2s. 3d.

[M. 3ᵈ.]

KNIGHTS' FEES BELONGING TO THE MANOR OF COTINGHAM.

The heirs of Adam de Traneby hold half a fee in Hesel' upon Humber, in the County of York.

Henry de Eton half a fee in Etton, in the County of York.

The heirs of Grace de Insula hold two fees and a half in Donington, Hemyngby, Nauenby, and Glentham, in the County of Lincoln.

John de Meus holds three parts of one knight's fee in Wytheton[d] and Northcave, in the County of York.

The same holds half a fee in Willardeby, Wlfreton, and Scolecotes,[e] in the County of York.

John de Kente holds the twelfth part of one fee in Branting-ham, in the County of York.

John de Pateshulle holds the fourth part of one fee in Alstonwike,[f] in the County of York.

John de Skipwike and his parceners *(participes sui)* hold one fee in Skipwike, Wicheton, in the County of York, and in Thorpe in Lindsey *(Lindes')*, in the County of Lincoln.

John Takel holds the fortieth part of one fee in Cotingham.

ADVOWSONS OF THE CHURCHES BELONGING TO THE MANOR OF COTINGHAM.

The church of Cotingham is worth by the year 200 marcs.

The church of Roule[g] is worth by the year 100 marcs, and belongs *(spectat)* to the manor of Cotingham.

The church of Etton is worth by the year 50 marcs, and belongs *(spectat)* to the manor of Cotingham.

[a] Swanland, in the parish of Ferriby.

[b] Myton, near Hull. Lost.

[c] Coupled with Swanland and Feriby, in Kirkby's *Inquest* (p. 263), the editor of which was unable to identify it.

[d] Little Weighton, near Cottingham. In *Domesday*, Wideton, in Kirkby's *Inquest*, Witheton, Wychton, and Wytheton.

[e] Willerby, Wolfreton, in the parish of Kirkella, and Sculcoates.

[f] Elsternwick, in the parish of Humbleton, near Hedon.

[g] Rowley.

BOTERCRAM.

[M. 7.]

EXTENT of the manor of Botercram, in the County of York, made on Thursday after the feast of the Annunciation of the Blessed Mary, in the 10th year (26 April, 1282), before Henry de Bray, by Robert de Barnneby, Roscelin de Skreingham, John de Barton, Richard de Stoketon, John de Stoketon, Nicholas Rossel of Hoton, Thomas de Dunstapel, John Torny of Touthorpe, Galfrid *le Heyr*, Henry de Barton, Richard *le Fremon*, and William Malfey of Skreingham, who say on their oath that Baldewyn Wake held the manor of Botercram of the King in chief, and was thereof seised in his demesne as of fee on the day he died. There is there a certain capital messuage, consisting of diverse houses *(de diversis domubus)*, both necessary and others, well built; which messuage with the garden is extended at 20*s.* The site of another messuage without building *(sine edificio)* in a place called Skreingham is extended at 10*s.*

Sum, 30*s.*

Demesne. In demesne 661 acres and one rood of arable land by the greater hundred *(per majus C.)*, extended at 6*d.* an acre. Sum, £16 10*s.* 7*d.*

Meadow. Forty acres of meadow in demesne (at 3*s.*).

Sum, £6.

Several Pasture. A certain pasture full of thorns *(spinosa)*, called Rokelond, extended at 20*s.* Certain herbages and several pastures *(herbagia et seperabilia)*, lying in divers places, extended at 14*s.* 8*d.* Sum, 34*s.* 8*d.*

Free tenants. Robert Borad holds four bovates in Skreingham at 6*d.* Sum, 6*d.* Henry, son of Laurence holds one toft and croft in Botercram at 2*s.* Sum, 2*s.* Dernory[a] holds one toft with croft in the same, for the term of life, at 4*s.* Sum, 4*s.* Nicholas Clerk holds one toft with croft in the same at 12*d.* Sum, 12*d.* William Cossing holds one toft with croft in the same at 14*d.* Sum, 14*d.* Robert, son of *(omission)* holds one toft in the same at 12*d.* Sum, 12*d.* Peter Pessunt holds one plot *(placeam)* of land in augmentation of his charge *(in aumentacionem cure sue)*, at 1*d.* Sum, 1*d.* Alice, daughter of Elena, holds three acres and a half of land in Ouegate Sutton[b] at 1*d.* Sum, 1*d.* William Pessun [holds] certain land in Ouegate Sutton, at 1½*d.* Sum, 1½*d.* William Bate holds a certain plot in Botercram at ½*d.* Sum, ½*d.* Nicholas, son of James, a meadow containing three roods at 1*d.* Sum, 1*d.* Richard Bolloc holds one acre of

---

[a] Perhaps Dervory.

[b] Probably Sutton-on-the-Forest (p. 9), or possibly Full Sutton, three miles S.S.E. of Scrayingham.

meadow in the same at 1*d.* Sum, 1*d.* 'Roger de Stransale holds one acre and a half of meadow, and pays for works from the same. Sum, 6*d.* Theobald de Skel' holds three acres of land in Barneby[a] at 1*d.* Sum, 1*d.* Mary de Coleville holds 100*s.* of land for the term of her life at 1*d.* Sum, 1*d.*

Free tenants at the will of the lord.[b] There are six free tenants *(libere tenentes)* holding six bovates of land, at the will of the lord, in Skreingham, at 42*s.* Sum, 42*s.* There are six tenants holding eighteen acres in Grouthorp Mure,[c] at the will of the lord (14 acres at 10*d.* and four acres at 8*d.*). Sum, 14*s.* 4*d.* Geoffrey *le Heyr* holds six and a half acres of forlonde in Skreingham at 3*s.* Sum, 3*s.* There are eleven tenants who hold thirteen tofts at the will of the lord, and pay 39*s.* Sum, 39*s.* There is a smith who holds a certain house for his workshop in the King's highway[d] at 4*d.* Sum. 4*d.* Two tenants holding four bovates of land at 28*s.* 4*d.* Sum, 28*s.* 4*d.* Thomas de Wolberfos holds one toft and four and a half acres of land at 4*s.* Sum, 4*s.* There are seven tenants holding eight bovates ·of land, and also twelve tenants holding twelve tofts of the . . . . . .[e] in the last circuit *(iter)* of the Justices at York, of the Earl Marshall, and are extended at 110*s.* 6*d.* Sum,· 110*s.* 6*d.*

Pepper. Gwydo de Skreingham holds two bovates of land and pays one pound of pepper, which is extended at 8*d.* Sum, 8*d.* Roger Clerk of Barneby holds one toft and pays one pound of pepper, and it is extended at 8*d.* Sum, 8*d.*

Cumin. The Abbot of Sent Agas,[f] Thomas *del Boure*, John de Hoton, and William *del Coudrey* pay five pounds of cumin, and a pound is extended at 1*d.* Sum, 5*d.*

Free tenants' works.[g] Henry de Ouegate Sutton holds one carucate of land containing eight bovates, and shall plough at winter sowing *(arrabit ad semen hyemale)* for one day, and at Lent sowing *(ad semen quatr')* for one day, a day's work is extended at 4*d.*; shall reap one day in autumn with fifteen others *(se sextodecimo)*; the work of each day is extended at 1*d.*; shall carry corn for one day, which is extended at 4*d.*; shall do suit to the court and to the mill, and shall carry building

---

[a] Barnby, in the parish of Bossall, on the opposite side of the river from Scrayingham.

[b] *Tenentes ad voluntatem domini libere.*

[c] Gowthorpe Common and Gowthorpe Field, in the parish of Fangfoss, about four miles S.S.E. of Scrayingham.

[d] *Ad fabricam suam in regia strata.*

[e] *De perquis'* . . . . .

[f] The Abbot of St. Agatha of Easby, near Richmond.

[g] *Libere tenentes facientes opera tantum.*

material *(meremium)* for making the mill and dam *(stangnum)*. Sum, 2*s*. 4*d*. Henry de Folkerthorpe holds half a carucate of land by doing a moiety of the above services. Sum, 14*d*. William Bate holds one bovate of land in the same manner as the said Henry, and does the eighth part of the service. Sum, 3½*d*. Richard, son of Osebert, holds one carucate of land by doing service as the said Henry, and also does summonses of court. Sum, 2*s*. 4*d*.[a] Richard Fremon holds two bovates of land, and shall reap for one day with five others *(se* vj.*)*, shall plough once a year and carry for one day. The works are extended at 14*d*. William Malefey holds two bovates of land and does works as the aforesaid Richard, and they are extended at 14*d*. Sum, 2*s*. 4*d*.[b] Geoffrey *le Heyr* holds the third part of one carucate of land, shall reap for one day with five others *(se* vj^{to}*)*, and carry for one day. Sum, 10*d*.

Bondmen. Peter son of Adam holds two bovates of land, and pays 15*d*. at Easter and Michaelmas. The same pays 12*d*. at Christmas, which is called *Yolstoch*, and one quarter and a half of barley-malt *(brasei orgei)*, the quarter being extended at 3*s*., and two fowls worth 3*d*. at Christmas, and 40 eggs at Easter, worth 1¼*d*.; shall plough one day, extended at 4*d*., and shall plough half an acre, this work is extended at 2½*d*.; shall find one workman with his horse and cart *(unum operarium cum equo suo et carecta)*, if need be, from Whitsunday to Martinmas for four days a week, for everything he shall be commanded to do, without food except for four days in autumn, and the work of each day is extended at 1¼*d*. After Martinmas and in Lent *(quatr')* he shall harrow and make cartings with his horse, and those works are extended at 16*d*. and no more, because he shall give each day two loaves, 13 score of which are made of a quarter.[c] He is talliated at the will of the lord, and shall give pannage. Sum, 19*s*. 9¾*d*. There are fourteen other bondmen who pay and do all the aforesaid works just as the aforesaid Peter. Sum, £13 17*s*. 4½*d*.

Cottars. William Ravene holds one toft and croft and pays 8*d*. at the aforesaid terms; shall maintain the thatch of the houses,[d] and carry water for making the wall, shall hoe, toss hay, reap three days in autumn, and shall have two loaves of the price aforesaid; shall make the mill dam. These works are extended at 16*d*. a year. Sum, 2*s*. There are there seven cottars besides the said William, who do the same works, and

---

[a] js. iiij*d*.

[b] Sic.

[c] *Quia dabit quolibet die ij panes, quorum xiij*^{xx} *fiunt de quarter'*.

[d] *Serviet cooperatorium domorum*.

their works are extended at 14s. Sum, 14s. There are 48 cottars there who pay yearly 52s. 8d. Each of them shall reap three days, and the work of each day is extended at 1d., and shall turn hay in the meadow called Borghenge in common,ᵃ extended at 12d.; shall make the mill dam, and give aid with the bondmen. Sum, 65s. 8d. Six other cottars there paying 5s. 8d., and their works in autumn are extended at 6d. Sum, 6s. 2d.

Mills. Two water-mills, extended at £8, with the suit appurtenant. Sum, £8. Richard de Barneby pays half a quarter of corn *(frumenti)* for multure, extended at 2s. William son of Robert pays one strike *(estr')* of corn, and half a strike of wheat *(siliginis),* extended at 8d. Sum, 2s. 8d.

Passage and Fishery. Passage of the bridge, extended at 10s. Fishery of the water of Derwent, extended at 10s. Sum, 20s.

Pannage and Aid. Customary pannage,ᵇ extended at 12d. Aid of the natives *(nativorum),* extended at 40s. Sum, 41s.

Perquisites. Fines, merchets, gersumes, pleas, and perquisites, extended at 40s. Sum, 40s. Sum total, £71ᶜ 7s. 4¼d.

[M. 7ᵈ]

KNIGHTS' FEES.

KNIGHTS' fees appurtenant to the Manor of Buterkram.

Alan de Walkingham holds one knight's fee in Bolteby, Ravenesthorpe, and Thirneby.ᵈ

Jordan Folyet holds two knights' fees in Cowesby, Nesse, Stivelingflete, Rippelingham, and Brantingham.ᵉ

William de Lasceles holds the third part of one knight's fee in Calueton.ᶠ

John de Bossale holds three parts of one knight's fee in Bosdale and Claxton.ᵍ

John de Vescy holds one knight's fee in Schyreburne.ʰ
The same holds one knight's fee in Langet'.ⁱ ˌ

ᵃ *In communi.* Perhaps "in the common [field]."
ᵇ *Pannagium de consuetudine.*
ᶜ First figure doubtful.
ᵈ *Thirneby,* now Thirleby. These places are situated E. and N.E. of Thirsk, under the Hambleton Hills.
ᵉ Cowesby, five and a half miles N.E. of Thirsk, and East Nesse, in the parish of Hovingham. Stillingfleet, Riplingham, and Brantingham, are in the East Riding.
ᶠ Cawton, two miles east of Gilling-in-Ryedale.
ᵍ Bossall, and Claxton, in the parish of Bossall.
ʰ Sherburn, in the East Riding, near Malton.
ⁱ Langton, near Malton.

Geoffrey de Upsale holds one fee in Upsale, Kilventon, and Thorneberge.[a]

Robert (?) Chambard holds one knight's fee in Slengeby.[b]

Walter (?) Boneface and Lucas de Flathewathe hold half a fee in Flathewathe and Toraldethorpe.[c]

William de Mortimer *(de Mortuo mari)* holds the fourth part of one fee in Toraldethorpe.

Sibilla, widow of Geoffrey de Mortimer *(de Mortuo mari)*, holds the fourth part of one fee in the same vill.

Robert de Grey holds half a fee in Stivelingflet.

The heirs of Anketin Malore hold half a fee in Clifford.[d]

The heir of Richard son of Maurice holds the tenth part of one fee in Skrengham *(sic)*.

Richard de Dunstaple, the tenth part of one fee in Flaxton.

P . . s . . *(fil')* of William *le Bretun* holds the twentieth part of one fee in Skrengham.

Reginald de Cap[t]oft, the eighth part of one fee in Barneby.

Richard de Barneby, the tenth part of one fee in the same.

[M. 8.]

KERKEBY MORESHEVED.

EXTENT of Kerkeby Moresheved, in the County of York, made on Tuesday, the vigil of the Annunciation of the Blessed Mary, 10th year (24 March, 1281-2), before Henry de Bray, by Sir Robert de Boleforde, knight, John Abraham, Robert *le Barun*, William de Middelton, Richard de Fadmore, James de Holm, Walter de Habbeton, Reginald de Boterwyke, William *en* [*le Wrae*], Ralph Smith *(fabrum)*, William Brounig, William Nissaunt,[e] Richard Graundvale,[f] Nicholas Guiond, and Adam Forester *(forestarium)*, who say on their oath that Baldewin Wake held Kerkeby Moresheved, in the County of York, of Roger de Munbray, and was thereof seised in his demesne as of fee on the day he died. There is there a capital messuage consisting of diverse houses *(de diversis domubus)*,

---

[a] Upsall, South Kilvington, and Thornbrough, north of Thirsk.

[b] Slingsby, near Malton.

[c] Flawith and Tholthorpe *(Domesday,* Turoluestorp, Turulfestorp), N.N.W. of the village of Alne.

[d] Clifford, in the West Riding, one and a half miles north of Bramham. See No. xcii.

[e] Nussaunt below.

[f] *Graundvalvale.* Written Graundvale below.

both necessary and others, well built, one grange in bad repair *(debili)* only excepted. The messuage with garden and croft adjoining is extended at 20s. Sum, 20s.

Demesne. In demesne 207 acres of arable land by the greater hundred *(per majus C.)*, extended at 6d. an acre. Sum, £6 3s. 6d. And 122 acres of land, extended at 4d. Sum, 47s. 4d. . . . . *Meadow.* 128½ acres of meadow, extended at 2s. an acre. Sum, £14 17s.

The Park. A park containing one league in circuit, in which there are estimated to be seven score beasts, beyond the maintaining *(sustentacionem)* of which the herbage of the same park is extended at 13s. 4d. The sale of underwood which 'may be made there yearly without waste, is extended at 7s. 6d. The pannage of the same park is extended at 6s. 8d., and not more, because there are few oaks in the same. Sum, 27s. 6d.

Pasture. A several pasture, in which 64 oxen or cows can be maintained *(sustentari).* The pasture of each beast is extended at 2d. Sum, 10s. 8d.

Wood. A wood called Westwode containing more than one league in length, and less than half in breadth, the herbage of which wood is not extended because the free tenants *(liberi)*, bondmen, and cottars have common of pasture there with their beasts. The sale of underwood which may be made there without waste, is extended at 40s. Sum, 40s.

Free Tenants at will.[a] Three tenants holding three sheepfolds *(bercarias)* at the will of the same lord, and paying 30s. 8d. a year. Sum, 30s. 8d.

Rents of the Free Tenants.[b] Richard, son of Robert Nussaunt holds one toft and two bovates of land, pays at two terms of the year 3s. 4d., at Easter 20d., and at Michaelmas 20d., and does suit to the court and to the lord's mill, and foreign service. Sum, 3s. 4d. Robert Nussaunt holds one messuage and one bovate and three acres of land, and pays 3s. 4d. at the terms aforesaid, and does service as the aforesaid Richard. Sum, 3s. 4d. Roger *le Huntere* holds one plot of land, and pays 2s. at the same terms, and does etc. Sum, 2s. Nicholas, son of Robert Nussaunt holds one messuage and one great close *(j magnam clausturam)* in Braunsedale,[c] and pays one arrow at Easter for all service. Richard Graundvale holds one messuage and two bovates of land, and pays one penny at Easter for all service as long as he shall live, but his heirs shall do suit of court. Geoffrey, son of Christiana, holds one messuage, and

---

[a] *Liberi tenentes ad voluntatem.*
[b] *Redditus libere tenencium.*
[c] Bransdale.

pays by the year six fowls at Christmas, extended at 6*d*. Sum, 6*d*. Henry Levedimon holds one messuage, and pays by the year one pound of cumin at Christmas, extended at 1*d*. Sum, 1*d*. Adam *le Messer* holds one messuage, and pays two pounds of cumin at the same term, a pound extended at 1*d*. Sum, 2*d*. Aubricia,[a] relict of Bennet *(Benedicti)*, holds one messuage, and pays one pound of cumin, extended as above. Sum, 1*d*. Richard *del Clif* and Juliana *del Clif* hold two messuages, and pay two pounds of pepper, a pound extended at 8*d*. Sum, 16*d*. Adam de Gilimor[b] holds one messuage and two bovates of land, and ought to keep the foreign wood[c] of the lord and the moor. That service is extended at 6*s*. 8*d*. Sum, 6*s*. 8*d*. Stephen, son of William, holds one messuage and one croft, and pays yearly 12*d*. at the terms as above, and does suit to the court and to the lord's mill, and foreign (service),[d] and shall give pannage, that is every tenth pig, and if he shall have less than ten pigs, shall give for every pig over one year old *(superannato)*,[e] 1*d*., and for every pig not over one year old, ½*d*. Sum, 12*d*. William *en le Wrae* holds one toft and one croft, and pays 4*s*. at the terms aforesaid, and does all the services as the aforesaid Stephen. Sum, 4*s*. Ralph Smith *(faber)* holds two tofts and one croft, and pays 6*s*. at the terms as above, and does all the services as the aforesaid Stephen. Sum, 6*s*. Robert Scote holds one toft, and pays 2*s*. 6*d*. at the terms aforesaid, and does, etc. Sum, 2*s*. 6*d*. William Brounig holds one toft and one croft, and pays 5*s*. at the said terms, and does, etc. Sum, 5*s*.

Tenants at the will of the Lord. There are nine tenants holding twelve bovates of land at the will of the lord, and each of them pays for each bovate of land by the year 6*s*. 8*d*. at the terms as above, and each of them pays two strikes *(estr')* of nuts at Martinmas, price of each strike 3*d*.; and one fowl at Christmas, called *le Wodehen*, price of the fowl 1*d*. Sum of nuts, two quarters and two strikes, extended at 4*s*. 6*d*. Sum of fowls, nine, extended at 9*d*. Sum, £4 5*s*. [3]*d*., and not more, because the nuts and fowls are paid in respect of their messuage, and not in respect of the bovate of land. And thus it is to be understood about all the nuts and fowls paid in the whole manor. Osebert *de la Wodehouse* holds one messuage, called *la Wodehouse*, and one croft at the will of the lord, and pays 10*s*. Philip *le Forester* holds a certain great close *(quemdam*

---

[a] Aubric'a.
[b] Now Gillamoor.
[c] That is the wood outside the demesne. See *Domesday* of S. Paul, LXV.
[d] *Forinsecum*.
[e] Old enough to be separated from the mother.

magnum clausum) at the will of the lord, and pays 6s. at the terms as above. Sum, 16s. There are five tenants holding certain waste plots *(quasdam wastas placeas)*, namely: in the places called Coteflat, Loftischo,[a] Godefr' . . , Harlonde,[a] and beneath Gillemore Clif, at the will of the lord, and paying 27s. at the terms as above. Sum, 27s.

Natives.[b] In a certain dale called Farndale, there are four score and ten natives, not tenants by the bovate of land, but by more and less,[c] whose rents are extended at £38 8s. 8d. Each of whom pays at Martinmas two strikes of nuts, four of the aforesaid tenants only being excepted from the rent of nuts, from which four, one strike of nuts. Price of nuts as above. Sum of nuts, two and a half quarters and one strike. Sum in money, 43s. 9d. Of whom four score and five shall give a harrowing in Lent *(herciar' in quatr')*, according to the size of his holding, that is, for each acre of his own land a ½d. worth of harrowing *(unum obolatum herciature)*. Those works are extended at 29s. 4d. They ought to be talliated and give pannage as above. Sum, £1 . . 10 . . 1d.[d] There are there three tenants in certain waste places called Arkeners and Swenekelis, holding ten acres of land, and paying 10s. a year, and giving nuts worth 18d. The harrowing is extended at 5d. They are serfs *(servi)* as the aforesaid ones of Farndale. Sum, 11s. 11d.

Bonàmen. In a certain dale called Brauncedale there are twenty-five natives *(nativi)*, whose rents are extended at £4 14s. 3d. They shall give nuts and fowls, and do harrowings, and ought to reap in autumn. The works are worth 21s. 2d. Sum, [£5 15s. 5d.]. William Gondi holds one messuage, and one bovate of land, which *(que)* with meadow contains fourteen acres, and pays yearly at Easter 2s. 6d., and at Michaelmas 2s. 6d. And his three neighbours with their oxen, joined to himself and his oxen, shall plough for one day at the winter sowing[e] *(semen hyemale)*, and his work is worth a penny, and he ought to harrow for two days at the same season, and the work of each day is worth 1d. He shall plough at Lent sowing *(ad semen quatrag')* for two days in the manner as above, that

---

[a] Loskay House and Harland are farms in the parish of Kirkby Moorside, one and three quarter miles and two miles north of the village.

[b] *Nativi.*

[c] *Per bovatam terre non tenentes, set secundum majus et minus.*

[d] *Summa,* x . . . *li.* x . . jd.

[e] " Et tribus vicinis cum bobus suis sibi et bobus suis adiunctis arrabunt per j diem." This sentence is not very clear, but it seems to mean that William Gondi had to join with three neighbours in providing a team of oxen, and that he received some payment or allowance for the services of himself and his oxen.

work is extended by the day's work *(per dietam)* at 1*d.*, and shall harrow for two days, each day's work *(quelibet dieta)* is worth 1*d.*, and ought to hoe for one day (work, a halfpenny), to mow for one day and a half (a day's work *(dieta)* worth 2*d.*), to turn hay for one day (worth ½*d.*), shall carry hay for one day (worth 3*d.*), shall reap in autumn for nine days (the work of each day worth 1*d.*), ought to carry corn for one day in autumn (day's work *(dieta)* worth 3*d.*), shall give one fowl at Christmas (worth 1*d.*), which fowls are called *Wodehennes*, and shall give two strikes of nuts at Martinmas (each strike worth 3*d.*), and ought to be talliated at the will of the lord. He shall give every tenth pig for pannage, as is aforesaid, and he shall do service . . . . . the day, and is not valued because he is not bound to do that service unless the lord be personally present in the manor. And be it known that the abovesaid works are not otherwise extended, because the food is deducted from him in which the lord is bound to him in each of the abovesaid works.[a] The same William holds another bovate of land without a messuage, for which he pays and does in all as before, except the nuts and fowls, which are deducted for want of the second messuage. There are 29 other bondmen holding 29 messuages and 55 bovates of land, for which messuages and bovates of land they pay yearly and do the customary works and services, as the aforesaid William. Sum of messuages, 29. Sum of bovates of land, 55. Sum, £21 6*s.* Certain of the aforesaid natives *(nativis)* hold certain parcels of land called *forlonde*, and pay yearly 18*s.* Sum, 18*s.*

Cottars. John Botermouthou holds one toft, and pays 12*d.* at Easter and 12*d.* at Michaelmas, and shall mow for one day, and hoe for one day, and turn hay for one day, and reap in autumn for three days, and give two strikes of nuts and one fowl. These works, nuts, and fowl are extended at 13*d.* There are 24 cottars whose rents are extended at 40*s.* 8*d.*, and they do works and customs, which are extended with the works of the said John at 26*s.* Sum, 68*s.* 8*d.* Six other cottars whose rents are extended at 9*s.* 6*d.*, and the works and customs at 3*s.* 6*d.* Sum, 13*s.* Eighteen other cottars, who pay yearly 46*s.* 1*d.* at the terms as above, and do no works or customs. Sum, 46*s.* 1*d.* A cottar, namely, Peter Skinner *(pelliparius)*, pays 12*d.* a year, and does one work extended at 1*d.* Sum, 13*d.* Ten cottars, holding of the church, do works and customs extended at 4*s.* 2*d.* Sum, 4*s.* 2*d.*

[a] " Et facit servicium . . . . . . diem, et non apreciatur quia non tenetur illud servicium facere, nisi dominus personaliter steterit in manerio. Et sciendum quod operaciones supradicte ideo aliter non extenduntur, quia subtra[h]itur ei cibus ad quem dominus ei tenetur in singulis operibus supradictis."

And be it known that all the beforesaid tenants, both bond-men and cottars, ought to be talliated every year at Michaelmas, and shall give merchet for their daughters, and gersume, and do suit to the lord's mill, and shall give the tenth pig, although the lord shall not find them pannage, and the beforesaid aid *(auxilium)* is extended by the year at 100s.   Sum, 100s.

Five water-mills extended at £23 8s. 8d.   Sum, £23 8s. 8d.

The customary pannage *(pannagium de consuetudine)* is extended at 30s.   The herbage of the moor is extended at 6s. 8d.[a]   Sum, 36s. 8d.[a]

The oven of the vill of Kirkeby *(furnus villate de Kerk')* pays 20s.   The toll of the market of the same is extended at 46s. 8d.   ' Sum, 66s. 8d.

Merchet, gersumes, fines, pleas, and perquisites are extended at 100s.   Sum, 100s.

Sum total, £154 4s. 1d.

[M. 8ᵈ.]

KNIGHTS' fees belonging to the manor of Kyrkeby More-sheved.

John de Vescy holds one fee in Berk', Musecotes, and Wymbelton.[b]

The heirs of Roger Pa . . lf hold one fee in Newebaud, Cossefford, and Lalleford, in the County of Warwick.

The heirs of Thomas de Wapenbir' hold four fees and a half in the Counties of Northants, Leicester, Warwick, and Bucks.

The heirs of Roger de Wywelton hold five fees and a half in Whywelton, Staureton, Grimescote, in the County of North-ants, and elsewhere in the County of Sussex.

Gilbert de Wittelebur' holds the manor of Brinckelowe, in the County of Warwick, by paying yearly one sore sparrow-hawk *(j esperverium sorum)*, at the feast of S. Peter *ad vincula* (Aug. 1.), or 2s., for all service.

Nicholas Wake holds one knight's fee in Cropton and Middelton, in the County of York.[c]

ᵃ The sum of shillings in both these places is doubtful.

ᵇ Unless Berk' be a mistake for Berg', now Great Barugh, a hamlet two miles west of the village of Kirkby Misperton, it is difficult to suggest what place is meant. Muscoates is in the parish of Kirkdale, a mile and a half N.E. of Nun-nington. Wymbelton, now Wombleton, a hamlet in the parish of Kirkdale, two and a half miles S.E. of Kirkby Moorside.

ᶜ Cropton, a hamlet, four miles N.W. of Pickering, and Middleton, a village and parish near Pickering to the N.W.

Roger de Wrelton and his parceners *(participes)* hold half a fee in Wrelton, Aselakeby,[a] and Middelton, in the County of York.

Eustace de Per[t] holds the eighth part of one knight's fee in Wrelton.

[M. 10.]

THE goods and chattels of Baldewyn Wake, which were found in his manors on the day of his death.[b]

MANORS WHICH ARE IN THE KING'S HAND.

LIDEL. Sum of money of the goods and chattels found at Lides *(sic)*, £46 13s. 3d.

BOTERCRAM. Sum of money of the goods and chattels found at Botercram, £95 9s. 1d.

COTINGHAM. Sum of money of the goods and chattels found at Cotingham, £631 0s. 20d.

BRUNNE (Co. Linc.). Sum of money of the goods and chattels found at Brunne, £54 12s. 6d., and thereout was paid for the burial of the said Baldewyn £19 12s. 2d., and so there remains clear, £35 0s. 4d.

SCHELDINGHOPE (Co. Linc.). Sum of money of the goods and chattels found at Scheldinghope, £88 8s. 4d., and thereout was paid for the burial of the said Baldewyn, £41 11s. 2d., and so there remains clear, £46 16s. 10d.

Sum total remaining clear, £855 0s. 14d.

---

[a] Wrelton and Aislaby *(Domesday,* Aslachebi, Aslachesbi), hamlets in the parish of Middleton, N.W. of Pickering.

[b] Whereas by inspection of the rolls of the Exchequer it is found, that Baldwin Wake was on the day of his decease bound to the King in £724 18s. 4d. and four horses of clear debt, by reason of which after Baldwin's death the King caused seizure to be made of all goods and chattels found in the manors of Lidel in Cumberland, Aton, Kirkeby Moresheved, Buttercram, and Cotingham, in Yorkshire, and in other of Baldwin's manors in divers Counties of England, now the King gives power to his clerk, Master Henry de Bray, to deliver to Thomas de Normanville, Escheator beyond Trent, such goods and chattels as amount to the value abovenamed by appraisement made, or (if necessary) to be made, if they reach that sum. If they are found after sale to exceed the debt to the King, the surplus is to be delivered without delay to Hawise, Baldwin's widow, in order that she may satisfy her late husband's poorer creditors of the debts due by him to them at the time of his death. Dated at Worcester, 20 May (1282) *(Rot. Fin.,* 10 Edw. I., m. 12). On 18 Feb., 1281-2, the Sheriff of Lincolnshire was commanded that, of Baldwin Wake's goods and chattels seized (by reason of his debts due at the time of his death) into the King's hand, he caused to be raised without delay £100 for delivery to Hawise, his widow, for expenses incurred by her about the burial of her late husband. A further sum of £40 to be raised and given to her of the King's especial grace by reason of her relationship to himself (cui eas racione consanguinitatis Rex concessit de gracia Regis speciali) *(Ibid.,* m. 16).

MANORS BELONGING TO LADY WAKE.

ATON. Sum of money of the goods and chattels found at Aton, £36 . . .s. . . .d.

KERKEBY MORESHEVED. Sum of money of the goods and chattels found at Kerkeby, £99 4s. . . . .

HICHAM (Co. Linc.). Sum of money of the goods and chattels found at Hicham, £11 12s.

KELLEBY (Co. Linc.). Sum of money of the goods and chattels found at Kelleby, £42 10s. 9d., and thereout was paid for the burial of the said Baldewyn, £14 11s. [8]d.,ᵃ and so there remains clear, £26 19s. 1d.

DEPINGE (Co. Linc.). Sum of money of the goods and chattels found at Depinge, £105 11s., and by payment for the burial of the said Baldewyn . . . . , and so there remains clear, £41 . . . . 8d.

STEVENTON. Sum of money of the goods and chattels found at Steventon, £24 5s. 4d.

COLLE QUINCI. Sum of money of the goods at Colle Quinci, £20 12s. 2d.

S[um total which] remains clear, £261 10s.

And be it remembered that the lady received for the burial of the said Baldewyn, £ . . .9 1 . . . 3d.,ᵇ as is above specified, except the sums . . . .

CXXXII. AVICE DE MARMION.ᶜ *Ad q. d.*

[10 EDW. I. No. 37.]

Writ dated at Devises the first of April, 10th year (1282), that, whereas Avice de Marmyun, notwithstanding the Statute of Mortmain, had petitioned for leave to assign six marcs worth of land and rent for the support of a chaplain, to celebrate at Westanfelde, the King, being anxious to encourage her laudable purpose, commands inquiry to be made as to what damage (if any) will arise by granting her petition.

INQUISITION made at York, on the morrow of S. Matthew the Apostle, 10 Edw. (22 Sept., 1282), before Sir Thomas de Normanville, the King's Steward, by Henry de Thorpe, Thomas de Gaytenby, Andrew Ferthynge, Roger F . k . . ng of Mildeby, Adam de Frytheby, Richard *del Hou*, Ralph Freman of Norton, Walter Serjaunt of the same, Hugh Broune of Neuton, Nissant

ᵃ This amount should be £15 11s. 8d.

ᵇ . . . . xix*li*. ᴧ . . . . . iij*d*.

ᶜ Avice, daughter of John, Lord Marmion, of Tanfield, sister and heir of Robert Marmion. She married John Grey, Lord Grey of Rotherfield, and had two sons, John and Robert, who assumed the name of Marmion. Elizabeth the daughter of the latter, carried the estates into the Fitzhugh family.

(Nissantum) of the same, John de Pykehall, and Henry de
Eskelby, whether it would be to the damage of the King if he
should grant to Avice Marmion leave to give and grant six
marcs worth *(sex marcatas)* of land and rent with the appurtenances in Westanfeld and Nosterfeld,[a] for the support of a
chaplain celebrating divine service at Westanfeld. They say
that the said land and rent are held immediately of John de
Britany, Earl of Richmond, by knight's service; and that the
King can lose nothing save ward, if ward there chance to be
(nisi wardam de warda si acciderit).

CXXXIII. ROBERT DE NEVILL.[b] *Inq. p. m.*

[10 EDW. I. No. 18.]

Writ dated at Rhuddlan *(Rothelan)*, 20 Aug., 10th year (1282).

INQUISITION made at York, on Monday after the feast of
S. Michael, 10 Edward (5 Oct., 1282), before Thomas de
Normanvile, and John de Lythegreinnis, then Sheriff of York-
shire, by Peter de Rotherfeld, Andrew de Neivile, Henry de

---

[a] Nosterfield, a hamlet in the parish of West Tanfield, six miles N.W. of
Ripon.

[b] Grandson of Robert Fitz Meldred (No. xxxviia.), and Isabella, sister and
heiress of Henry de Neville *(Excerpta è Rotulis Finium*, vol.˙i., p. 156). His
father, Geoffrey, assumed the name of Neville. In 1254 Robert de Neville paid to
the Queen's garderobe £15 6s. 3d. for his relief *(Ibid.*, vol. ii., p. 185). He married
Ida, widow of Roger Bertram, as appears from the inquisiton taken at Newcastle-
upon-Tyne, on Sunday after the feast of S. Denis *(Dionisii)*, 10 Edw. (4 Oct., 1282),
which finds that Robert de Nevill held no lands or tenements in the County of
Northumberland except one hundred pounds *(libratas)* of land, which he had by
reason of the dower of the lady Ida, his wife, who was formerly wife of Roger
Bertram, in Mitford and Felton. The finding in this inquisition as to the heir and
his age is the same as that given above in Yorkshire. By writ dated at Denbigh
(Dynbeghe), 23 Oct., 10th year (1282), the King commands Henry de Normanvile,
his Escheator beyond Trent, that, having taken the oath of Ida, who was wife of
Robert de Nevyle, not to marry without the King's leave, he is to assign dower to
her out of the lands and tenements of her late husband. There is a similar mandate
(of the same date) to the Sheriff of Lincolnshire concerning the assignment of dower
in that County to the same Ida. His son and heir, Robert, married Mary, one of
the daughters and co-heirs of Ralph Fitz Ranulph, of Middleham (No. LXVII.).
He predeceased his father and was buried at Coverham Abbey. He left a son
Ranulph, who as is mentioned, was his grandfather's heir. On 14 May, 1283,
Thomas de Normanville, the Escheator beyond Trent, was ordered by the King,
then at Glintlugathe, to allow the friends of Ranulph de Neville, grandson and
heir of Robert de Neville, deceased (who held in chief), who was under age and in
the King's custody, to plough and harrow *(arrare et rebinare)* the lands in his
bailiwick of the said Robert, and which were the inheritance of the said Ranulph
(Rot. Fin., 11 Edw. I., m. 15). Thomas de Normanville accounted to the King
for issues of the lands of Robert de Nevill, from 20 Aug., 10th year (1282), to
11 Jan., 12th year (1283-4), before the said lands were delivered to Ranulph, son
and heir of Robert *(Exchequer Accounts ultra Trentam* ³⁄₄). The extent of knights'
fees belonging to Robert de Nevill will be found below (No. CXXXVIII).

Watehous, Robert de Buneyike, William Burdun, Roger Grimet, William Daniel, Henry de Kynmeslawe, Paulin de Lillinge, Nicholas de Grimston, knights, Thomas de Gaitinbe, Thomas de Spenigthorp, John de Ritthe, Roger de Tornthorne, William Thorni of Wiginthorp, John de Wolton, and William Thorni of Tiverinton, who say upon their oath that Robert de Neuvile held the manor of Raskelf and the town of Sutton, in the County of York, of the King in chief by the service of two knights.

RASKELF.

The capital messuage with fruit of the garden and herbage, is worth by the year half a marc. There are seven score and ten acres of arable land (8*d.* the acre), 100*s.*, forty acres of meadow (12*d.*), 40*s.* Annual rent of free tenants, 27*s.*, bondmen £9 18*s.*, cottars, £9 2*s.* 3½*d.* From two mills (one a watermill, the other a windmill), 60*s.*, pannage, one marc, pleas and perquisites of Court, half a marc. Sum total, £31 13*s.* 11½*d.*

SUTTON.[a]

Rent of free tenants, 20*s.* 5*d.*, bondmen, £29 5*s.* 8*d.*, cottars, £4 11*s.* 11*d.*, pannage, one marc. Sum total, £35 11*s.* 4*d.*

HOTON VIC'.[b]

He held Hotonscireve of Peter de Mauley in chief by the service of five knights, the capital messuage of which is worth by the year with fruit and herbage, 10*s.* Pleas and perquisites of Court, one marc. Annual rent of free tenants, £9 6*s.* 7*d.*; of bondmen, £10 11*s.*; of cottars, 71*s.* Rent of a windmill and of a watermill, two marcs. Rent of free tenants of West Lillinge,[c] 10*d.*; of free tenants of Tiverinton,[d] 10*s.* Rent of the town of Bridale,[e] 12*s.*

There are in demesne three hundred and forty-five acres of arable land, by the great hundred (the acre 12*d.*), £20 0*s.* 5*d.*; and of meadow in demesne two hundred and five score acres,[•] by the great hundred (the acre, 2*s.*), £34. Sum, £81 11*s.* 5*d.*[f]

Ranulf, son of Robert de Neiville the younger, is his next heir; and he will be aged twenty years on the day of S. Luke the Evangelist, in the tenth year (18 Oct., 1282).

[a] Sutton-on-the-Forest.
[b] Sherriff Hutton.
[c] West Lilling, a mile south of Sheriff Hutton.
[d] Terrington.
[e] Burdale, in the parish of Wharam Percy.
[f] The sum total does not agree with the items.

CXXXIV. AGNES DE ATHEWYKE. *Inq. p. m.*

[10 EDW. I. No. 10.]

Writ dated at Rhuddlan *(Rothelanum)*, 9 Oct., 10th year (1282).

INQUISITION made at Poclington, on Sunday after the feast of S. Edmund the King, 11 Edward (22 Nov., 1282), before Sir Thomas de Normanville, by Adam Arundel, William de Yedingham, Adam de Dugelby, Richard *le Waleys,* John Puterel, William de Dalton, Peter de Breddale, Robert de Crohem, John *del Hill,* Roger *le Paumer,* William de Freston, and William de Barton *en Housum,* who say on their oath that Agnes de Athewike held nothing of the King in chief; but she held for the term of her life, in the town of Bugethorp, one messuage and seven bovates of land of Sir Walter de Grey; and after his death she did the service appertaining to the land to Sir Thomas de Chauncy, as chief lord. The messuage is worth by the year 13*s.* 4*d.*, and every bovate, 12*s.* She held the land of the said Sir Thomas de Chauncy by the service of scutage, and died without an heir of her body, because she held of the aforesaid Sir Walter de Grey for the term of her life.

CXXXV. THOMAS DE FLIXTON, *a Felon. Of year and day.*[a]

[10 EDW. I. No. 51.]

Writ dated at Rhuddlan *(Rothel')*, 12 Oct., 10th year (1282).

INQUISITION—whether four bovates of land with the appurtenances in Scalleby, held by Thomas de Flixton, who committed felony, have been in the King's hand for a year and a day, or not—made before John de Lythegraynes, Sheriff of Yorkshire, by Thomas de Edbriston, Bartholomew de Scalleby, William de Everle, William de Yrton, Robert de Wyern', Roger de Wrelton, Roger de Morpath, Bernard de Bergh, Roger Haldan, William de Thormoteby, Geoffrey son of Bartholomew

---

[a] "If the outlawed persons have freehold land it is to be seized immediately into the hand of the lord King, and to be held for a year and a day, and it is to return to the chief lords after that term, if he has held it from any other than the King himself; in this latter case it shall be an escheat of the King himself . . . . The cause why the land shall remain in the hand of the King seems to be this, because in truth, when a person is convicted of any felony, he will be in the power of the King to pull down his buildings, to root up his gardens, to plough up his meadows. And since such things would turn to the great damage of the lord, in the common interest it has been provided that buildings and gardens *of this kind* should be preserved, and that the lord the King on such account should have the profits of the whole of that land for a year and a day, and so everything in its integrity should return into the hands of the chief lords."—Bracton, *De Legibus Angliæ*, Rolls edition, vol. ii., p. 343.

de Scalleby, and Hugh *le Brun*, who say upon their oath that the four bovates have now been in the King's hand for one year and one day, and that the said Thomas held that land of the lord Edmund, the King's brother. Bartholomew de Scalleby holds two bovates out of the four, the other two lying unculti- vated *(frische)*; and he has had a year and a day of those two, whereof he ought to answer to the King. Robert de Conseline(?), bailiff of lord Edmund for the manor of Piker[ing], has had the two bovates remaining uncultivated and he has sold the meadow for 5*s.*, whereof he ought to answer to the King.

CXXXVI. ᵢROGER DE CLIFFORD.ᵃ *Inq. p. m.*

[11 EDW. I. No. 36 A.]

Writ dated at Rhuddlan, 12 Dec., 11th year (1282).

INQUISITION taken at Maltheby, on Innocents' day, 11 Edw. (28 Dec., 1282), before Sir Thomas de Normanvile, by Sir Henry de Tynisloue, Ingermut' de H . . . . . . de le Scolys,ᵇ Peter de Wodeword, Alexander de Scouceby, Peter de Lounedir, Peter Lemynge, Richard de Souteby, Richard de Pikeburne, Oliver de Wyckirislay, Alan Bacum of Waythe, John de Wyck- irislay, sworn, who say upon their oath that Sir Roger de Clifford held nothing in chief of the King of his own inheritance in the County of York, but he and Sir Roger de Leyburne held the manor of Malthebyᶜ with the appurtenances of the Castle of T[y]keil, for the service of one knight when scutage is current *(scutagium currit)*, and this by reason of their wives who were daughters and heirs of Robert de Vipont *(Veteri ponte)*. There pertain to the manor of Maltheby six knights' fees and a half, each of which renders in the name of ward *(nomine warde)*, by the year 10*s.* 8*d.*

ᵃ He married Isabel, daughter and heiress of Robert de Vipont (No. LXIV.), and was killed in the Welsh wars in the lifetime ₒof his father. On 4 Feb., 1282-3, the King took at Rhuddlan the homage of Isabel, widow ·of Roger de Clifford, junior, daughter and one of the heirs of Robert de Vipont, for all the lands which the said Roger and Isabel held of the King in chief of the heritage of the said Isabel on the day Roger died *(Rot. Fin.,* 11 Edw. I., m. 22*)*. Her son, another Roger de Clifford, was summoned to Parliament, and was slain at Bannockburn, in 1314.

ᵇ In Inq. p. m., 12 Edw. I., No. 17, which is the inquisition on the death of Roger de Leyburne, the husband of the other co-heir, amongst the jurors Ingram de Ulcotes and Richard de Scales occur, who may be the persons represented by the imperfect names above.

ᶜ Maltby, near Tickhill.

33

The manor with two gardens is worth by the year 5s., the dovehouse, 2s. There are eight score acres of arable land (at 4d.), and meadow, 10s., mill, 66s. 8d., herbage and cutting of woods, 3s. by the year. There are six bondmen holding six bovates of land, they pay yearly 71s. 11d. There are 28 cottars (coterelli) who pay 71s. 1¾d. There are six free tenants who render yearly 18s. 11d. Perquisite of Court (perquisicio Curie) is worth by the year 6s. 8d. The customary tenants render yearly twenty-nine hens.   Sum of the whole, £19 0s. 4¾d. The advowson of the church of Maltheby pertains to the same. Roger de Clifford has one son, his heir, named Robert, aged nine years.

CXXXVII.   SIR WILLIAM DE EBOR.,[a] KNIGHT.

[11 EDW. I. No. 6.]

Writ dated at Rhuddlan (Rothelan'), 11 Jan., 11th year (1282-3).

INQUISITION made at Swyne, on Tuesday before the feast of the Annunciation B.V.M. (16 March, 1282-3), by Walter de Flinton, John de Fitteling', Henry de Wyueton, Walter de Apelton, John de Sauce, Thomas Lygearde, Sayer Copyn, John Northe, Simon Wyttike, Simon son of Hugh of Swyne, Peter le Mumer, and William de Cotome, who say upon their oath that William of York (de Ebor') knt., held nothing of the King in chief in Holdernesse on the day of his death, but he held in Eske[b] in Holdernesse six bovates of land of William of York (de Ebor'), Rector of the church of Patringeton by knight's service; and they are worth by the year in all issues, £8 0s. 2d. He also held the manor of Hebbedene in Craven by homage and service of the Abbot of Fountains and his predecessors, worth in common years £14. His heir is his son William, who will be nineteen years old at the feast of Saint Martin, in the year above said (11 Nov., 1283).

ª Son and heir of Sir Nicholas de Ebor., brother to William, Provost of Beverley and Bishop of Salisbury (Kirkby's Inquest, p. 20 n.).

ᵇ Eske, in the parish of St. John, Beverley.

CXXXVIII. ROBERT DE NEVILL.[a] *Extent of Lands.*

[11 Edw. I. No. 41.]

Writ dated at Rhuddlan, 10 Feb., 11th year (1282-3).

E XTENT of lands and tenements, knights' fees, and advowsons of churches, which were of lord Robert de Nevill, in the County of York, made before Thomas de Normanville, and John de Lytegrenes, Sheriff of the County.

RASKELF.

Robert de Nevill held of the King in chief the manor of Raskelfe and the town of Sutton with their appurtenances, by the services of two knights' fees. The capital messuage of Raskelf with fruit of the garden and herbage, is worth by the year half a marc. There are in demesne seven score and ten acres of arable land (at 8*d.*), worth by the year 100*s.*, and forty acres of meadow in demesne, 40*s.* Of annual rent of free tenants, 27*s.*; of bondmen, £9 18*s.*; of cottars £9 2*s.* 3½*d.* Two mills, one a watermill, the other a windmill, worth by the year 60*s.* Pannage of the forest, one marc, and pleas of Court, half a marc. Sum of the value, £31 13*s.* 11½*d.*

SUTTON.

In Sutton, annual rent of free tenants, 20*s.* 5*d.*; of bondmen, £29 5*s.* 8*d.*; of cottars, £4 11*s.* 11*d.* Pannage of forest there, by the year one marc. Sum of the value of the manor,[b] £35 11*s.* 4*d.*

SCHIREVEHOTON.

The same Robert held the manor of Schirevehoton of Peter de Mauley by the service of five knights' fees. The capital messuage, with fruit and herbage of garden, is worth by the year 10*s.* There are in demesne 350 acres of arable land by the long hundred *(per majus centum)*, £20 10*s.* (acre 12*d.*), and demesne meadow 17 score acres, £34 11*s.* 5*d.* (acre 2*s.*). Two mills, one a watermill, the other a windmill, are worth by the year two marcs. Rent of free tenants, £9 6*s.* 7*d.*; of bondmen, £20 11*s.*; of cottars, 71*s.* Rent of free tenants in West Lilling and Tyverington[c] and . . . . dale, 22*s.* 10*d.* Pleas and perquisites of the Court one marc.

---

a See No. CXXXIII.

b Sutton is called a manor here—" Summa valoris predicti manerii."

c The remainder is illegible. The loss is the less important as the information is very much the same as that given in No. CXXXIII.

CXXXIX. RALPH SALVAYN.[a]

[11 EDW. I. No. 74.]

Writ directed to Thomas de Normanville, Escheator, upon the complaint of Ralph Salvayn, who held certain lands and tenements in Dalton,[b] by the law of England, in right of Margery his deceased wife, which he had demised to Anketin his son; after whose death the Escheator had taken them into the King's hand and withheld the same from him (Ralph). Inquiry to be made. Dated at Rhuddlan, 3 Feb., 11th year (1282-3).

INQUISITION made at Haumelake,[c] on Thursday before the feast of S. Mark the Evangelist, 11 Edw., (22 April, 1283), in presence of Sir Thomas de Normanville, by William Burdun, William de Torny of Tyverington, Ralph son of James of Stitenhum, William son of Adam of Galmethorpe, Alan *le Gras*, Peter de Ros of Barton, William de Thouthorpe, Robert de Barneby, John de Torny, Ralph son of Elias of Schowesby, Elias Lokenhand of Queneby,[d] and Geoffrey Bret, who say upon their oath that Ralph Salvayn enfeoffed Anketin, his son, of all lands and tenements which he (Ralph) had by the law of England, by reason of his marriage with Margery his wife, to hold to him and his heirs for 5*s.* to be paid to the King in Ralph's name at Michaelmas, and 1*d.* to Ralph for life at the [feast of] the Nativity of S. John the Baptist. The lands and tenements of Dalton are held of the King in chief by serjeanty, and five shillings yearly to be yielded as aforesaid for all things.

CXL. WILLIAM, SON OF THOMAS THE MARSHAL OF CARLETON. *Of year and day.*

[11 EDW. I. No. 43.]

Writ directed to the Sheriff of Yorkshire, and dated at Aberconewey in Snaudon, 7 April, 11th year (1283).

INQUISITION made at Carleton, by Richard de Roceholme, Richard Clerk *(clericum)* of Carleton, Peter at the Hall *(ad aulam)* of the same, Thomas *(de Capell')* of the Chapel of the same, Henry son of Walter of Drax, William Marscall of the same, Peter de Sayl, Adam de Hyrst, Adam Clerk *(clericum)* of Carleton, Henry son of Robert of the same, Henry son of

---

a See No. XCII.
b North Dalton.

c Helmsley.
d Whenby.

William of the same, and William son of Agnes of the same, whether William son of Thomas the Marshal *(le Marescal)* of Carleton, who was outlawed for felony, held one messuage in Carleton.[a] They say upon their oath that he held one messuage, and not a bovate but twenty-two acres of arable land. He held also ten acres of pasture, one acre one perch and the third part of a perch of meadow. These are yet in the King's hand, because a year and day[b] have not gone, but will expire before *(citra)* the feast of S. Michael, in the eleventh year of the reign (29 Sept., 1283). He held all the aforesaid tenements of lord John de Bellew *(Bella aqua)* except two acres of land held of Sir Walter de Bucketon.

The messuage with waste is worth 20s. Every acre of the twenty acres of land held of John de Bellew, is worth 4d. a year. Sum, 6s. 8d.; saving the service due to the chief lord of the fee. Every acre of pasture is worth 12d., saving service, etc., 10s. The meadow is worth 12d., save as above. The two acres of arable land held of Walter de Bucketon are worth 6d., saving service to the said Walter.

The lord John de Bellew will answer to the King for 37s. 8d. for waste and the tenements held of him, and Walter de Bucketon will answer to the King for 6d. for the lands held of him.

[a] Carlton, in the parish of Snaith.
[b] See *ante* page 256, for note as to year and day.

APPENDIX I.

The following Inquisitions, not being attributed to Yorkshire in the printed Calendar, were passed over.

I. JOHN DE LUNGVYLERS, KNIGHT. *Extent of Lands.*[a]

[39 HEN. III. No. 39.]

BRERELAY.[b]

At Brerelay there is a capital messuage containing by estimation one acre, yearly 2*s*.

Sixty acres of arable land in demesne, by the perch of 20 feet, each acre yearly 3*d*.

Six (?) acres of meadow in demesne, at 16*d*. the acre.

A wood half a league long containing by estimation 60 acres, pannage and herbage of the same, half a marc yearly.

Ten bondmen who hold ten tofts and . . . acres of land, and they pay yearly in money at Martinmas and Pentecost 45*s*. They do works which are extended at 3*s*. 4*d*. yearly.

Two cottars who hold two tofts and one bovate of land, pay yearly at the said terms 8*s*.

Two tenants who hold one bovate of land, and pay yearly at the said terms for all 10*s*. They answer for foreign service (*respond' de forins'*).

William de Brerelay holds two bovates of land by knight service; he does nothing but foreign [service]; worth yearly 10*s*.

Richard Jurdan holds half a bovate of land by the same service, and answers for foreign service; it is worth 6*s*. yearly.

Ralph son of Ralph holds . . . acres of land by the same service, and answers for foreign service; it is worth yearly 5*s*.

Thomas son of Richard holds 60 acres of land by the same service, and answers for foreign service; it is worth 2*s*. 6*d*. yearly.

Sum of the whole extent of this manor of Brerelay,

£4 17*s*. 11*d*.

[a] See p. 44. Owing to the bad light which prevailed when this inquisition was originally copied, it was impossible to decipher the latter part. It has now been transcribed by Mr. Paley Baildon, to whose kindness the Society are indebted for this and the other omitted inquisitions.

[b] Brierley, in the parish of Felkirk.

COLLING.ᵃ

There is at Colling a capital messuage containing by estimation half an acre, and it is extended yearly at 3s.

Thirty acres of arable land, each acre yearly 4d.

Two acres of meadow in demesne at 8d. the acre.

A wood and a moor, a league and a half in length and a league in breadth; there are three pastures within the said wood . . . . . herbage for 70 cows with their calves of two years old, and the herbage and pasture of each cow with its calves is extended yearly at . . . . Pannage and perquisites of the wood, yearly 6s. 8d.

Nine tenants hold nine tofts and 74 acres at the will of the lord, and pay yearly . . . . . .

Sum of the whole extent of this Manor of Colling, 78s. 11d.

Sum total of the whole extent of the lands which were of Sir John de Lungevilers, in the County of York.

£49 12s. 10½d.

FEES WHICH ARE HELD BY KNIGHT SERVICE IN CRAVEN.

Walter de . . . . . holds three carucates in Heton,ᵇ and does nothing but foreign [service]; worth yearly 100s.

Henry de . . . . . holds in the same by the same service three carucates of land; worth [yearly] 100s.

John le . . . . holds two carucates of land in Geregraveᶜ by the same service, and one and a half carucates in Akeworthe; worth yearly half a marc [?].

Adam de Neusum holds half a carucate of land in Neusumᵈ by the same service, and it is worth yearly one marc.

Walter [?] de Farnhil holds in the sameᵉ one and a half carucates of land by the same service; worth yearly 36s.

Elias de . . . . . holds five bovates of land in the same by the same service; worth yearly one marc.

William . . . . . holds four carucates of land in Cuniglayᶠ by the same service, and pays yearly on S. Oswald's day 2s. 9d.; worth yearly half a marc.

Alexander de Farnhyl holds in the same half a carucate of land by the same service; worth yearly 10s.

ᵃ Cowling Hill, in the parish of Kildwick.
ᵇ Hetton, in the parish of Burnsall.
ᶜ Gargrave and Oakworth in the parish of Keighley.
ᵈ Newsholme, in the same parish.
ᵉ Farnhill, in the parish of Kildwick.
ᶠ Cononley, in the same parish.

. . . . . . daughter of Adam holds in Farnhyl two bovates of land by the same service; worth yearly 5s.

William de Bramton holds in Geregrave half a carucate of land by the same service; worth yearly 20s.

. . . . holds in Farnhyl and Cuniglay one carucate of land, and pays yearly on S. Oswald's day 3s. 7d.

. . . . . de Esseton holds in the same[a] half a carucate of land by the same service; worth yearly 20s.

. . . . . . holds·half a carucate of land in Esseton by the same service, and answers for foreign [service].

. . . . [Lunge]vylers held of Edmund de Lascy the ·manor of . . . . . and of Farnelay with the appurtenances, and of . . . . . . with the appurtenances by . . . . .

. . . . . . next after the feast of S. . . . . in the 37th year [1252-3], and that John de Lungevylers, son of Sir John . . . .

II. WILLIAM LE SCOT. *Inq. p. m.*

[45 HEN. III. No. 17.]

Writ dated at S. Paul's, London, 27 May, 45th year (1261).

INQUISITION made by John de Batelay, Jordan *de la Wodehale,* Simon son of Walter of the same, Robert de Presselay, Thomas son of Maude of Bramlay, Gilbert Marescall of Presselay, Henry de Honelay, John de Scolecroft, William Atteclyff(?) of Armelay, Adam de Schafton of Clerkeswelle, Geoffrey Luvekoke of Kalverlay, Jordan Attegren in Pudessay, and John son of Nicholas of Hecmundeswyk, who say on their oath that William *(le) Scot* held of the fee (late, *writ*) of Edmund de Lascy on the day that he died 40 acres of land, 4d. the acre, and four marcs rent, and pasture price 3s., and a watermill and half another mill which are worth 40s. yearly, and a capital messuage worth 2s. yearly. Sum, 111s. 8d.

He held no land of any other; he held his land of the said Edmund for half a knight's fee for all service.[b]

John le Scot is his son and next heir, aged 22 on the vigil of the Apostles Peter and Paul, in the 45th year (June 28, 1261).[c]

[a] Eshton, in the parish of Gargrave.

[b] In 1284-5, the Abbot of Kirkstall, Roger de Ledes, and John Scott of Calverley, held one knight's fee of the Honour of Pontefract in Headingley, and Altofts, in the parish of Normanton (Kirkby's *Inquest,* p. 33).

[c] In July, 1261, William le Latimer, the Escheator beyond Trent, was commanded to give back to John le Scot, son and heir of William le Scot, being of full age, the lands which his father held of Edmund de Lascy, whose land and heir were in the King's custody, and to take security for the payment of 50s., as his relief, before the feast of All Saints *(Excerpta è Rot. Fin.,* vol. i., p. 356).

III.   WILLIAM SELISAULE.[a]

[52 HEN. III. No. 42].

Writ dated at York, 18 Sept., 52nd year (1268).

INQUISITION—whether William Selisaule, detained in the King's prison at York for the death of Adam de Hauern' (Auwerne, in writ), killed him by misadventure or by malice aforethought, etc.—taken before John de Oketon, by Robert de Langethwait of Brimham, William . . . . . of Langethwait, Hugh Gernun of Brimham, Robert de Cliffor[d], . . . Brinkil, John de Oscom, Bate . . . . of Saxton, John de Lede, clerk, William . . . . , Paulin de Sutton, and William *le Serjaunt* of Sutton, who say on their oath that a certain stranger had married *(nupserat)* a woman, and brought her along and certain others who were present at the same time, ... by the King's highway to one end of the town of Byrun.[b] William Selisaule, perceiving this, came up [and demanded] from them a ball *(quandam pelotam)*, which is given by custom. And they having no ball committed to him a pair of gloves by way of a pledge for the ball ; and he, taking the gloves, went back home. And certain other men of the town of Byrun, not known (?) to the said William, coming out and hearing of the said passing through,[c] demanded that a ball should be given to them according to custom; and the said passers through[d] said that they would not give them a ball, because they had delivered a pledge for a ball to a certain man of the town of . . . And the said men of Byrun, not believing this, still demanded a ball. And so a contention arising (?) between them, the said [wedding party] who were somewhat drunk *(aliquantulum inebriati)*, assaulted the men of Byrun with hatchets, and bows and arrows, and wounded very many. William Selisaule, hearing the strife between them, run up with a staff so that he might calm the contention, thinking that it was about the said ball for which he had taken pledge. And when he got near to them, one William, son of Ralph of Roal, drew an arrow at him, and struck him in the breast, so that it was thought he would die of the blow. And the said William, son of Ralph, still not content would have drawn again upon him. William Selisaule, seeing that he could not avoid the blow of the arrow unless he struck him so that he could not draw, ran at him, wishing to hit him on the arm so as to hinder the flight *(ictus)* of the arrow, by misadventure struck

---

[a] A portion of the centre of the document is quite illegible, and part of the right margin is torn off.

[b] Byram, in the parish of Brotherton, near Ferrybridge.

[c] " Audientes de transitu predicto," *i.e.* of the wedding party.

[d] "Transeuntes," the wedding party.

the aforesaid Adam, who had inadvertently placed himself between them, so that he died of the blow. The jurors say that in truth he did not kill him by felony or malice aforethought, but by misadventure.

IV. OF THE OFFICES OF FORESTER, CONSTABLE, ETC., OF THE EARL OF RICHMOND, AND OF THE MANORS, LANDS, ETC., HELD OF THE SAME.

[Incert. temp. HEN. III. Appendix. No. 99].

INQUISITION made by twelve knights sworn of the Wapentake of Gilling, to wit, William de Musters, Michael son of Michael, ... aneby, John Colun of . . . . , John de Hertford, Alan de Scaregile, William de Suton, Thomas de Bileton, John de . . . . , Hugh de Scorton, Alan de . . . . . .

They say that Henry, son of Ranulf, ought to be Forester of fee of the Earl of Richmond, to wit, of Arkilgarth and in Hope. The Earl has the Forestship *(forestar')* in his own hands.

They say that Elyas de Richemond, Stephen, the Serjeant *(serviens)* of the·same, Adam de Jafford, and Walter Arundel, hold two carucates of land in the town of Richemond by service of serjeanty by making the summonses . . . . . to the Earl's Court . . . . . it was alienated, as it is contained in the inquisition of the Burgesses of Richemond.

They say that Robert Arndecan of Multon holds one half carucate of land in Multon, by the service of being the keeper of the larder *(larden')* to the Earl of Richemond as of fee; for that service he now yields 10s. yearly to the Earl, and does no service. They know not who changed the service nor by what warrant.

They say that Roald Fitz Alan ought to be Constable of Richemond Castle as of fee, and ought to keep *(servare)* the Castle in consideration of the ward belonging to the same. The Earl now has it in his own hand and takes the ward for his own use.

They say that Alan de Hertford ought to be the Sheriff of Richemond, by rendering yearly to the Earl 20s. Alan is neither Sheriff nor does he pay the 20s.

They say that William de Roulous, a stranger, held the manors of Brunton, Croft, Kypling, and Scytheby[a] in chief of

---

[a] Brunton, probably Brompton-on-Swale, Croft, Kipling, and Skeeby. In 1205, Roald, son of Alan, Constable of Richmond, gave the King £100 and two palfreys to have the lands of William de Rolles, in Brumton, Kilphing', and Crofton, and for a mill and two carucates in Schiteby, and half a carucate in Walemur, which was of his fee, and which belonged to Hasculf, son of Hasculf, who at the time of his death was with the King's enemies in Brittany *(Rotuli de Oblatis et Finibus,* vol. i., pp. 253, 266).

the Earl of Richemond. Roald Fitz Alan recovered the said manors in the King's Court as his inheritance and right, in the time of King John, and while they were in the King's custody saving the rights of anyone.

Alan de Kneton holds 12 librates of land in Kneton and Midelton,[a] doing foreign service and yielding 10s. yearly to the Earl. And that land does service of drengage, to wit, to feed the dogs, puppies (? *pullanos*) . . . . (*nutrices*) . . . . . . of the Lord Earl. The said Alan gave to Henry Mansel, with Agnes his daughter, two bovates of land in the town of Midelton, worth 20s. yearly. Also he gave to Gilbert de Neuton, with Cecily his daughter, two bovates of land in the town of Midelton, and a messuage, worth 26s. yearly. Also to Walter his son he gave two bovates of land in the town of Kneton, and eight acres, worth 28s. yearly. Also he gave to Ralph his son a bovate of land and a toft and croft, worth 10s. yearly. Also he gave to Thomas his son six acres and a toft, worth 6s. yearly. Also he gave to the chapel of Kneton, for having a chantry, a bovate of land; the parson of Midelton holds the same; it is worth 10s. yearly.

They say that Henry de Midelton holds 12 librates of land of the Earl in the town of Midelton, by such service as Alan de Kneton holds his land. (The Abbot of) Fountains has 12 acres of the gift of Henry's grandfather, worth 12s. (yearly).

They say that Roger de Aske ought to be the Earl's warrener as of fee . . . . . [The remainder is torn off].

V. WAPENTAKE OF HALIKELDE.[b]

[Incert. temp. HEN. III. No. 266.]

No writ.

NAMES of twelve knights of Halikelde:—John de Dounou, Bartholomew de Eskelby, Pygot de Neuton, Robert Arundel, Alan de Eskelby, Hugh de Balderby, Geoffrey de How, Elias de Thanefeld, Peter de Disford, Thomas Drepedewyl. This is the verdict of the twelve knights. Ranulf de Sules was in the King's mercy for the forest, and held nine librates of land in Thorneton Cundale[c] and would not pay the amercement

[a] Kneeton and Middelton Tyas.

[b] The date of this inquisition must approximate very closely to that of No. IV., which was taken in the spring of 1245-6. Six of the jurors acted on both inquisitions. Hugh de Bardelby of No. IV. is more correctly written here Hugh de Balderby, John de Dounou, the first juror, was perhaps a relative of Thomas de Aunou of No. IV.

[c] Thornton Bridge, near Cundall. In 1284-5, James de Nerff or Norff', on doubt forms of Norfolk, held six carucates here of Geoffrey de Nevill (Kirkby's *Inquest*, p. 185).

and the King took those nine librates into his hand, and gave
[them] to Hugh de Newile (they know not whether by charter
or not), and Hugh married his daughter to one . . . . de Nore-
folk with the said nine librates of land.

Lady Maude de Morwile gave Robert de Vipont in Cares-
thorp,[a] 15 librates of land of her dower that she might marry
where she would.

The Bishop of Karlisle takes those moneys because of the
son of John de Vipont, who is in ward to the King . . . . . .

Thomas Craune of Ayderby-vecunt[b] held of the Earl of
Richemond six carucates of land for a foreign tenement,[c] whereof the Abbot of Fountains and the *Hopitelers* hold the said
land. And Thomas enfeoffed the Abbot and the *Hospitalares*
in the time of King Henry who now is. Wherefore the lord
P[eter de Savoy] loses the relief and ward of that land.

VI. DAVID LE LARDINER.

[Incert. temp. HEN. III. No. 279.]

No writ.

I NQUISITION[d] made by John de Hamerton, William de Harum,
Simon de Lillinge, Robert de Elkint', William de Avering',
William de Skipwith, Robert Chaumbard, Thomas son of
William, Geoffrey de Thorney, Robert de Hakeford, Richard de
Thorny, John de Cawode, William Marsh *(de Marisco)*, John de
Merston, William *le Stabler,* Ralph *de Camera,* and Richard de
Morers, who say on their oath that the ancestors of David *le
Lardiner* had these liberties, that they ought to make the King's
larder, and keep the prisons of the King's forest, and that they
had measures of the King's corn at any time, and that they
were the King's sellers *(venditores)*, and that they took daily 5*d.*
from the King's purse, whereof they have charters.

They say also that David's ancestors had these liberties
always, that they were wont to take every Saturday, from the
window of every baker selling bread, one loaf *(panem)*, or ½*d.*;
from every brewer one gallon of beer, or ½*d.*; from every

---

[a] Carthorpe, in the parish of Burneston.

[b] Ainderby Quernhowe, in the parish of Pickhill.

[c] Pro forinseco tenem'.

[d] See Nos. x., xiv., and lxix. The date of this inquisition must be very
nearly the same as that of No. xxxiii., that is about 1252. Simon de Lilling,
Robert Chaumbard, Richard de Thorney (in No. xxxii.), Thorner, William le
Stabler, and Ralph de Camera, occur as jurors in both inquisitions.

butcher's window a pennyworth *(denarat')* of meat, or a penny; from every fish cart at Fosse bridge four pennyworth of fish for his 4*d.*, as they were bought at the sea, by the faith of the carters; from each horse load of fish carried, one pennyworth of fish for his penny, as it was bought at the sea. And they say that they were wont to make distresses within the City of York for the King's debts, and to take 4*d.* for each distress made, and they were aldermen of the minstrels [*aldremanni fuerunt de menestrallis*].

These liberties David's ancestors used in the time of King Henry, the grandfather of Lord Henry, now King of England, and in the time of the Lord King Richard, until they were interfered with *(impediti)*. They say also that they used all the said liberties in the name of the serjeanty which they had of the King

---

VII. INQUIRY CONCERNING WOOL SHIPPED AT HEDON CONTRARY TO THE ROYAL PROCLAMATION.

[2 EDW. I. No. 83.]

Writ dated at Westminster, 3 June, 2nd year, 1274.

INQUISITION—if Henry Kenibaud, Stephen Wyles, and other men and merchants of Hedon, caused a certain ship to be loaded at Hedon with wool and other merchandise, before the King's prohibition was proclaimed in the County of York, to wit, that no wool should be carried out of England by any person, and on what days and in what places they caused the ship to be loaded, and to be taken to Sandwich [*Sandwicum*], and on what day the Bailiffs of Hedon received the prohibition and published it—made by William Grete, Robert de Skyreburne, Laurence Pavay, Stephen *le Poter*, Henry Webster *(textor)*, Peter de Neuton, Ralph de Westland, Simon Gylt, William Lambekyn, William Tyrel, William Kyffe, and Philip Abot, who say on their oath that on the first Sunday in Lent, in the 2nd year (18 Feb., 1273-4), in the port of Hedon, the merchants loaded the ship, and the same day they caused her to be taken towards Sandwich. In the said ship were 15 sacks of wool, 24 cart loads of lead, and one last of ox-hides. The Bailiffs of Hedon received the prohibition on the Saturday after Mid-Lent in the same year (10 March, 1273-4), and published it the same day. And they say that the merchants knew nothing of the prohibition until they were seized at Har . . . and taken to Sandwich.

APPENDIX II.

ORIGINAL INQUISITIONS.

I. ROBERTUS LE MOYGNE, CAPELLANUS. *Ad. q. d.*

[33 HEN. III. No. 12.]

INQUISICIO[a] si esset ad dampnum Civitatis Ebor. an non, si Dominus Rex concederet Roberto le Moygne Capellano quandam venellam, que vocatur Patricpol, ad elargiand' quandam placeam suam in Ebor.; et si esset ad dampnum, ad quod dampnum, et si, quod absit, incendium contingeret in finibus illis, utrum aqua posset adeo compe[n]diose deferri aliunde ad extingendum illum ignem quam per illam venellam, facta per Hugonem de Menthorpe, Walterum fratrem eius, Hobekinum, Martinum Carnificem, Radulfum le Seler, Jordanum Aurifabrum, Robertum de Driffelde, Ricardum de Sceltona, Johannem de Scocia, Hugonem de Clerevall', Rogerum Hayrun, et Willelmum de Ottelay, qui dicunt super sacramentum suum, quod opcuracio illius venelle, que vocatur Patricpol, quantum placea Roberti le Moygne Capellani juxta dictam venellam se extendit, non est ad dampnum Civitatis Ebor., quia si ignis contigeret in finibus illis, conpediose posset aqua deferri per aliam venellam quam per illam, quia ita profunda est et inusitata quod nemo potest transire per illam.

II. DE STATU CASTRI DE SCARDEBURG'.

[44 HEN. III. No. 28.]

H. Dei gracia Rex Anglie, Dominus Hibernie, et Dux Aquitanie, Vicecomiti Ebor., salutem. Precipimus tibi quod assumptis tecum xij. discretis et legalibus hominibus de visneto de Scardeburg', in propria persona tua accedas ad castrum nostrum de Scardeburg', ad videndum in quo statu Gilbertus de Gaunt castrum illud dimisit, et in quo statu dilectus et fidelis noster H. le Bygod, Justiciarius Anglie, illud ex commissione nostra recepit. Et quid inde inveneris, nobis sub sigillo tuo et sigillis predictorum xij. sine dilacione mittas et hoc breve. T. me ipso apud Westm' xx. die Maii anno regni nostri xliiij.

[a] The writ says "quamdam venellam in Ebor. que appellatur Patricpolle ad elargiand' placiam suam in Ebor. Et si est ad dampnum, ad quod dampnum. Et si, quod absit, incendium contingeret in finibus illis, vtrum aqua posset adeo compendiose deferri aliunde ad extinguendum illum ignem quam per illam venellam."

INQUISICIO facta apud Scardeburg' die Sabati proxima post festum S. Trinitatis anno regni Regis Henrici filii Regis J. xliiij^{to}, coram domino Johanne de Oketon', Vicecomite Ebor., in quo statu dominus Gilbertus de Gaunt castrum de Scardeburg' dimisit, et in quo statu dominus H. le Bigot, Justiciarius Anglie, illud ex dimissione domini Regis recepit. Que quidem inquisicio facta est per Willelmum de R(o)ston, Radulfum filium Petri de eadem, Willelmum de Everle, Robertum de Careby, Ricardum de Nevill', Adam de Rouceby, Radulfum de Loketon', Reginaldum de Haterberg', Rogerum filium Ricardi de Aton', Alanum filium Martini, Johannem le Campion, et Thomam de Helm, qui dicunt super sacramentum suum, quod mang[n]a aula et mang[n]a camera cum warderoba per plura loca sunt discoperta, et mangna indigent reparacione. Coquina cum tresoncia sunt fere discoperte *(sic)*. Stabulum vero omnino discopertum est, et maniure fracte, et unum hostium deficit. Parietes autem domus molendini fracte sunt, nec est ibi molendinum. Granarium vero debile est. Aula infra clausum· turris omnino est discoperta, et quidam de tingnis fracti sunt, et minatur ruinam. Item duo pontes castri et pons accinctus turris debiles sunt, et putrefacte pro mangna parte. Quatuor vero walve duarum januarum interiarum omnino deficiunt, et menia ultra dictas januas decasui preparantur, et in mangna parte ceperunt decasum. In mangna vero turri septem hostia et viginti novem fenestre omnino deficiunt. Planchiatura vero quatuor turriolorum in summitate turris fere putrefacta est et deficit. Murus autem turrim attingens per plura loca prosternitur, et residuum minatur ruinam. Janua vero turris exterior debilis est. Kernelli et alure muri castri versus villam per plura loca deteriorantur, et mangna indigent reparacione. Unus turriolorum copertus plumbo per diversa loca discopertus est. Planchiatura trium turellorum in accinctu meniarum castri fere putrifacta est. Kernelli vero et alure barbecani exterioris per plura loca prosternuntur, et deteriorantur, et mangna indigent reparacione. Parva autem janua barbecani debilis est. In dicto vero castro est omnino defectus balistariorum, quarellorum et omnimodorum armorum municioni castri necessariorum.

III. QUEREMONIA BURGENSIUM DE SCARDEBURG'.

[Incert. temp. HEN. III. No. 152.]

SUPER et aliis conqueruntur Burgenses de Scartheb' de Simone de Hal, Vicecomite Ebor. et ejus servientibus. Inprimis de vinis, et blado, et sale, et omnibus aliis mercandiis, que

veniunt in portum Regis de Scartheb', tam de extraneis, quam
eis in villam manentibus, capiunt per talliam ad dimidium precium
quam vendi posset sine consessu mercatorum; et cum terminus
venerit aliquibus aliquid vel parum pacant, et aliquibus nichil;
unde mercatores portum Regis adeo vitant, quod firmam domini
Regis perficere non possunt, nec villam sustinere. Item capiunt
in portu a piscatoribus, tam extraneis quam aliis, allec sine foro
per quatuor lastas, et tres, et duas, de navi; et quando lasta
venditur pro viginti solidis, pacant decim, et quandoque minus.
Item Vicecomes in propria persona venit in portum, et voluit
capere totum allec de piscatoribus de Scartheb' et aliis sine foro,
et si quis contradicit ei, minatur inprisonare eum et comburere[a]
domum suam; et postea capit vi allec suum, et quando vendunt
pro decem et octo solidis, pacat tantummodo novem solidos, et
aliquando minus. Et prohibet, omnibus audientibus, ne aliquis
caretarius, nec aliquis mercandus in villam domini Regis aliquod
mercandium afferat, vel extraducat, et minatur, si aliquis mercandium afferat, per ballivam suam inprisunare eum, et auferre[b]
ei catalla sua. Et ideo nullus mercandus in villam redire audet,
unde domini Regis firmam amittimus, et villa remanet destructa.
Item quando carnifices de Scartheb' eunt per baillivam Vicecomitis ad emendendum[c] avaria ad mactandum, servientes Vicecomitis auferunt eis avaria sua, partim occidunt, partim retinent
vi donec redimantur. Item Castellani cum Vicecomite ceperunt
de Burgensibus de Scartheb', sicut Justiciariis domini Regis
ultimo errantibus monstratum fuit, in pane et carne, servisia et
pisce, blado et sale, pannis et aliis catallis, ccc*lib.*vj*sol.*et iiij*d.*, unde
nichil reddiderunt, nec reddere[d] volunt, unde aysiati pauperes
devenerunt, et postea villam vacuerunt, unde villa ad tantam
paupertatem redacta est, quod timent ne dominus Rex amittat
auxilium de villa et hominibus suis, cum opus fuerit, quia non
possunt dare domino Regi quod alii vi et injuste extorserunt.
Item monstrandum domino Regi et consilio suo, quod quando
Vicecomes velit habere aliquod mercandium in villa, et aliquis
mercandium ad libitum suum non vult dare, m[ina]tur villam
inflamare. Et ad[e] adventum domini G. de Novill', Camerarii,[f]
faciet capere meliores ville, et in Castellum inprisunare, de
omnibus terris suis et rebus dissaisiare, unde deprecamur diligen-
tissime dominum Regem et ejus consilium, ut hiis supradictis
impendant consilium et auxilium. Item Vicecomes ponit
dominicum servientem[g] suum, sicut nunquam affuit in portu

---

[a] *Comburre.*	[e] *Quod.*
[b] *Aufere.*	[f] *Camerarium.*
[c] *Emendum.*	[g] *Servientum.*
[d] *Redderre.*	

nostro; et idem serviens prohibet omnibus mercatoribus, ne vendant mercandias suas, antequam Vicecomes ceperit quid habere voluerit, quod est contra consuetudines[a] regni et libertates nostras. Item naves et mercatores, cum veniunt apud Scartheb' cum mercandis suis, poscunt lisenciam intrare in portu de baillivis domini Regis de Scartheb' et salve cum mercandis suis; et cum in portu venerint Vicecomitis venit serviens, et capit mercandias suas ad libitum suum. Et quia baillivi eis dant lisenciam salve intrandi, et Vicecomes nec serviens eius nolunt aquietare res quas ceperint, naves de Scartheb' et homines, cum in portubus eorum venerint, debitum Vicecomitis aquietare distringunt, unde precamur consilium et auxilium pro amore Dei.

IV. De Terra de Agenois data in escambium pro Comitatu de Richemonde.

[Incert. temp. Hen. III. No. 175.]

SACHENT tous ceus ki ces presentes lettres verrunt ou orrunt, que come le noble Ber, Johan, Conte de Bretaine, demandast e requeist a noble Ber, Henris, par la grace de Deu Roys de Engleterre, la Conte de Richemunt e les aportenances, la quele ces auncestres avoient autre fies tenue, et demaundast la dite Conte come son heritage, e cil Rois eust done la dite Conte a sire Peres de Savoie, son uncle, de ki mems il ne la poett nene voleit retraire; icelui Roy dona en eschaunge de la Conte de Richemunt ou dit Johan Conte de Bretaine, a avoir e a tenir a lui e a ses heirs par num de heritage, la terre de Agenois, ou les deniers ke li Rois de France Looys li doit doner e rendre pur cele dite terre de Agenois, iesque la value de la dite Conte de Richemont e des aportenances, ke li auncestres du dit Conte tindrent, 't sera prisee bien e leaument a drette value de terre par an par deus chevalers, eleuz a fere le pris de la dite Conte de Richemont; e li uns des chevaliers sera mis de par le dit Rois de Engleterre, et li autre par le dit Conte. E si li uns, ou li dous de ces chevalers moreient, pus ke il sereint esleuz, devant ke li pris de la dite Cunte de Richemont fust fete, li Rois et li Conte mettroient autres en lor luis, chescun le son, si come il est dit par de sus. E si il aveneit ke til deu chevaler devantdit ne se pussent acorder a feire le pris de cele Conte de Richemont, li tierz sera eleu par la noble dame Margar', par la grace de Deu Royne de France, en teu maneree ke ceo a quei le tierz s'acordera de pris de la Conte de Richemont aveques un de eaus soit garde et tenu.

E li devantdit Rois de Engleterre est tenuz a destreindre ceus
ke li chevaler devantdit vodrunt apeler a faire la prisee de la
dite Conte de Richemunt, e a aus aider e conseiler leaument par
lor seremenz. E ceste prisee doit estre faite dedenz l'an ke
Johan li esnez fiz e heir du dit Conte de Bretaine, e damisele
Beatriz, fille du dit Rois de Engleterre, seront esposez e asem-
blez par non de mariage. E li dit Conte de Bretaine avera la
terre de Agenois devauntdite, ou les deniers ke li Reys de
France rendra chescon an au dit Rois de Engleterre par la
reison de la terre de Agenois, en teu manere ke si la terre de
Agenois, ou les deners valoient plus ke le pris de la Cunte de
Richemunt fet par les chevalers avantdiz, li Roys de France
rendra a celui Rois de Engleterre le plus ; e si mens valoient, le
Rois de Engleterre deit parfere au dit Conte iesque la value du
pris de la Conte de Richemont, e a seer en ses terres plus pre-
cheines a la terre de Agenois, ke li sont donees e rendues par le
Roi de France. E ceste eschaunge devantdiz vot e otroie li dit
Rois de Engleterre a celui Conte en teu manere, que li dit Conte
prenne e tiengne totes ces choses bien e en peis come son heritage, dou Roi de France, e l'en face homage, jesque a taunt ke
li Rois de Engleterre li ait assis la value du priʒ de la Cunte de
Richemont, si come il est devauntdit en reame de France ou en
reame de Engleterre. E cest assise li doit faire ʼt achever li dit
Roi d'Angl' dedenz siʒ anz puis la date de cestes letres al
esgard de deus chevaliers avantdiz, ou du tierz ovesques un des
deus, si li deus ne se poent acorder, ʼt ausi doit li dit Rois
asseurer totes cestes choses al esgard de ces chevaliers.

V. MAGISTER ET FRATRES HOSPITALIS S. NICHOLAI EBOR.

[3 EDW. I. No. 55.]

ET Robertus de Crepping', ad hoc vocatus per predictos
Gwychardum [de Charrum] et Willelmum [de Northburgo],
dicit quod dum ipse fuit Vicecomes Ebor., vidit quod predicta
acra prati et dimidia abbuttabat super vivarium domini Regis de
Fosse, ita quod ad quamlibet superundacionem aque coopertum
erat pratum illud, et quia vidit quod si dominus Rex vellet
molendina sua sub Castello existencia amovere, et capud vivarii
sui predicti exaltare, superundaretur pratum illud omni hora
anni. Credebat ipse, et ut datum fuit ei intelligi per aliquos de
Wappentagio de Bulmere, quod illud pratum pertinebat ad
dominum Regem, et ea racione seysivit illud in manum domini
Regis, et illud tenuit quamdiu fuit Vicecomes istius Comitatus,

et omnes Vicecomites istius Comitatus similiter fecerunt hucusque. Et facta est inquisicio predicta, tam per homines de Civitate predicta, quam de suburbio ejusdem, viz., per sacramentum Walteri de Grymeston, Johannis Verdenel; Willelmi de Malton', Willelmi de Roston', Petri Walding, Alexandri Cissoris, Nicholai filii Hugonis, Thome de Nafferton, Simonis Everard, Johannis de Dalton, Willelmi le Lung et Thome Clerici, qui dicunt super sacramentum suum, quod predicta carrucata terre et pratum non sunt, nec fuerunt, de antiquo dominico corone domini Regis, nec unquam fuerunt arrentata ad Scaccarium domini Regis. Et dicunt quod Matild' Imperatrix, quondam Regina Anglie, emit predictam carucatam terre et pratum cum pert., et dedit illa predicto Hospitali et Fratribus ejusdem tali condicione, quod ipse imperp. invenirent omnibus leprosis ad predictum Hospitale venientibus in vigilia Sanctorum Petri et Pauli victualia subscripta, scilicet panem et cervisiam, muluellum cum buttiro, et salmonem undecumque eveniret, et caseum. Et tali servicio et non alio tenent predictam car. terre et pratum. Et quesiti utrum predictum pratum pertineat ad predictam car. terre, dicunt quod sic. Dicunt eciam quod predicta car. terre valet singulis annis sex marcas et dim., et pratum valet singulis annis unam marcam.

VI. MAGISTER ET FRATRES HOSPITALIS S. NICHOLAI EBOR.

[3 EDW. I. No. 76.]

INQUISICIO facta inter Dominum Regem ex una parte, et Magistrum et Fratres Hospitalis S. Nicholai Ebor. ex altera, per Walterum de [Gryme]stona de Ebor., etc., jurati, per sacramentum dicunt quod Matild' bona Regina Anglie dedit predictis Magistro et Fratribus dicti Hospitalis unam car. terre cum una acra prati et dim. in campis suburbii Cyvitatis Ebor., et confirmat' per Regem Stephanum, ad pascendum omnes leprosos de Comitatu Ebor. ibidem de consuetudine venientes in vigilia Apostolorum Petri et Pauli, pro animabus omnium antecessorum eorum et successorum. Et fuerunt in saysina predicti prati a tempore predicte bone Regine Matild' usque ad secundum tempus quo Robertus de Crepping' fuit Vicecomes Ebor., qui eos de predicto prato dissaysiavit et tenuit ad opus equorum suorum, et sic quilibet Vicecomes post alium illud pratum detinuerunt. Et valet illud pratum dimidiam marcam per annum. Et spacium dicte dissaisine continet viginti annos et plus.

ADDENDA ET CORRIGENDA.

Page 4. No. v. At the Assizes held at York, at Easter, 30 Hen. III. (1246), Elena, widow of William de Percy, claimed against Robert de Brus the third part of ten librates of land and 20s. rent in Tattecastre; against the Prior of Helagh Park the third part of two marcs rent in the same town; against Wymund de Raleg' the third part of ten librates of land in Wandesforde and Nafferton; against Robert de Percy the third part of four bovates of land in Oxton; against Walter de Haulay the third part of three bovates of land in Foston; and against Robert de Dighton the third part of two bovates of land in Nafferton, as her dower. Robert and the others came and sought a view of the lands (*petunt inde vis'*), which was granted them. Elena appointed Robert de Twenge or Richard Kalle, her attorney. The defendants called to warranty Henry de Percy, son and heir of William de Percy, who was under age and in ward to the King, by charters of feoffment of the said William, which they produced. The case was adjourned to Michaelmas Term, at Westminster. In the meantime they were to speak with the King. The defendants, except the Prior, appointed as their attorney, William de Arundelle or Walter de Haulay. The Prior appointed as his attorney, brother Nicholas, a canon of his house. She further claimed her dower against the Abbot of Sallay, Laurence Chamberlain (*Camerarium*), Richard Calle, Thomas Marshall (*Marescallum*), Ingram de Percy, William de Percy, Alan de Percy, Joscelin de Percy, Jordan *del Estre*, Thomas *le Lardiner*, Walter de Duvedale, Reyner de Stockelde, and Henry de Percy, who all satisfied her concerning her dower without leave of the Justices, therefore all in mercy. (*Yorkshire Assize Rolls*, N. I. 1—5, m. 4 or 5a.)

Page 8. No. ix. According to the Helagh Park Chartulary (*Cott. MS., Vespasian*, A. iv., fo. 1), this Alice Haget had the following children: Euphemia, Prioress of Sinningthwait, Richard de S. Maria, *ob. v.m.*, Elizabeth (who had Richard *le Waleys*, Stephen, and Richard, *sic*), and Nicholaa (who had Alice, wife of John *le Vavasour*.)—W. P. B.

Jordan de S. Maria and Alice his wife confirm the gift of Geoffrey Haget of lands in Helagh, and give other lands there. Test., John de Birkin, Hugh de Lelay and Robert his brother, Alan de Catherton, and others; *s.d.*, but *circa* 8 Henry III. (*Chartulary*, fo. 5.)—W. P. B.

Alice, widow of Jordan de S. Maria, confirms. Test., Sir Brian Fitz Alan, Alan de Catherton, Giles de Catherton, and others; *s.d.* (*Ibid.*, fo. 6.)—W. P. B.

Page 10, line 5. 52 Hen. III., 1267-8. John, son of Nigel de Stockeld, summoned Mathew de Brame and Agnes his wife, to acquit him of the service which William de Ros requires for the free tenement which John holds of them in Nordicton. John holds 12 bovates 2 acres by the service of 15*s.* yearly for all service. But by the default of Mathew and Agnes, de Ros demands suit at his court of Suthdicton, and has distrained for the same. (*Assize Roll*, N. 1. 2—1, m. 12.)—W. P. B.

Page 10, *note* b. In 1205, Hillaria Trussebut paid the King ten marcs to have her reasonable share of the land of Branteston in Northants, which had belonged to Albrea de Harecurt, her mother. The Sheriff was ordered, after taking security for the payment of the ten marcs, to cause her to have full seisin ; saving to the King the chattels William de Albeny had there from the King. (*per Regem*), and the rent for Easter Term last past. (*Rotuli de Oblatis et Finibus*, p. 288.)

Page 13. Line 4 from end of No. xiv. for *goal* read *gaol.*

Ibid. Line 5 of No. xv., for *Phillipa* read *Philippa.*

Page 15, *note* a. The information given in the earlier portion of this note is incorrect. The skeleton pedigree given below, which is chiefly taken from the one printed in the *Yorkshire Archæological and Topographical Journal*, vol vii., p. 268, will serve to shew the true descent :

```
                    Adam Fitz Sweyn Fitz Alric
 ┌──────────┬──────────────────────────────────┐
Maud    Amabel,─1. Simon de Crevequor.─2. William de Neville, 1202.
         1202.
         ┌───────────────────────┐        ┌──────────────────────
      Cecilia de C.,─Walter de Neville.  Sarra,─1. Thomas de Burgh.
      1207-8.                            1207-8.─2. Simon Fitz Walter,
      ┌──────────────────────────┐                1207-8.
   ─Alex. de N., 1218-19.  Inq. p. m., 1249.
```

1207-8, Cecilia de Crevequor owes £100 and two palfreys for having her reasonable part, *cum eisnecia*, of all the inheritance of Amabel, her mother, wife of William de Nevill.

Simon Fitz Walter and Sarra owe the same for Sarra's reasonable part, saving to Cecilia de Crevequor, her sister, her *eisnecia.* (*Pipe Roll*, 9 John.)

1218-19. Alexander de Neovill, heir of Cecilia de Crevequer, renders an account of £37 and one marc and two palfreys, for having a reasonable part, &c., as above. (*Pipe Roll*, 3 Hen. III.) —W. P. B.

3 Hen. III. (1218-19). The assize found that Alexander de Nevill had unjustly, &c., disseised Adam de Mirefeld and Margery

ADDENDA ET CORRIGENDA.

his wife of common of pasture in Mirefeld. (*Assize Roll*, Various Series, No. 91, m. 10.)

NOTE. This disposes of Mr. J. C. Brook's theory as to the origin of the Mirfield family (*ante* p. 15, note a). This Adam de Mirfield was the son of Uctred, who was the son of Ravenkill.— W. P. B.

Page 18. No. xx. 1275. Theobald *le Botyller* demands against Agnes Bacun one carucate in Edelynton, of which one Maude, his ancestor was seised in the time of King John, and from her it descended to Theobald as son and heir, and from him to another Theobald as son and heir, and from him to Theobald, the demandant, as son and heir. Agnes vouched to warrant Fulk, son of Fulk Fitz Warin, who vouched John le Vavasur, who said that one Robert his ancestor gave that land to the said Maude in marriage, but that she subsequently gave it back to him. Great Assize. (*De Banco*, Mic., 3 & 4 Edw. I., No. 13, m. 29.)—W. P. B.

Page 19. No. xxii., *note* a. 1224. William de Lascells complains that Legarda, widow of Herbert de Blaungy, had disseised him of half the ford [*passagium*] of Pagula, which belongs to him in respect of his free tenement there, of which William de Otringham, his father's uncle, was seised in the time of Henry II. From William it descended to Agnes as sister and heir, and from her to John as son and heir, and from him to William, the plaintiff, as son and heir. (*Curia Regis*, No. 85. Mic., 8 Hen. III., m. 28.)— W. P. B.

Page 23. No. xxvii. Amongst the pleas on the Yorkshire Assize Roll for Easter, 30 Hen. III. (6 April, 1246), is an action by Emma Wastehueose against John, son of Hugh, about a quarter of a bovate of land in Kuwic (Cowick), which was adjourned until the defendant came of age. At the same time she brought other actions against Hugh de Stertebrigge and Milisant his wife, and against Henry, son of Simon, about two half bovates of land in the same vill, of which her father, Alan, had been seised in demesne in the reign of King John, and which had descended to her as her father's heir. She lost both these actions. Henry only claimed his half bovate in right of his mother, Maud, who held the same in dower, a fact Emma could not deny. Hugh and Milisant called to warranty for their half bovate Adam de Tydewurthehag', who in his turn called Emma herself to warranty, producing a charter of feoffment by her father, by which he enfeoffed Geoffrey Clerk, Adam's grandfather, whose heir he was in the said half bovate. Finally Adam gave half a marc for licence to agree, Anthony Dawtrey (*de Alta ripa*), being his surety. By this agreement Emma granted the half bovate to Adam, he doing all services, and she warranting (*Yorkshire Assize Rolls*, N. 1. 1—5, m. 11 or 12 *b*). She also had suits concerning land in Duffeud (Duffield). Final agreement with Reginald *le Buler* to whom she granted 8s. annual rent for his life. (*Ibid.*, m. 10.)

Page 29, line 4. For 1250 read 1251.

Page 40, *note* b, line 1. 1196-7. Eudo de Lungvilers owed five marcs for disseisin. (*Pipe Roll,* 8 Ric. I.)—W. P. B.

"Out of Bolton Leiger." Elias de Stiveton grants to Robert his brother those two bovates in Gargrave, which Richard his brother had of the gift of Eudo de Longvillers. (*Harleian MS.*, 804, fo. 55 *d.*)—W. P. B..

1226-7. Thomas de Burgo v. Richard de Alencun respecting the church of Penigheston. Richard says that a fourth part of the advowson belongs to a fourth part of the manor of Penigheston, which is divided into four parts, which belong to these persons, namely: one part to Thomas de Burgo, the plaintiff; one part to Richard de Alencun, the defendant, by reason of Joan, daughter and heir of Alexander de Nevill, who is in his ward; one part to Eudo de Lungvillers, and one part to Geoffrey de Nevill, by reason of their wives. And he says also that the last presentation was made by all of them.

The jury say that Simon Fitz Walter presented the last parson, one William, to half the church; and immediately after he was admitted, came Alexander de Nevill. father of Joan, and presented one Robert to a fourth part. Robert impleaded William before the Archbishop, and William gave him two marcs yearly for peace sake. One John, son of Swane, who had the advowson of the whole church, sold one half of it to William de Nevill, who was father of Sarra, mother of Thomas de Burgo (whose heir Thomas is), and by reason of that sale, the said Simon Fitz Walter, formerly husband of Sarra, presented. John, son of Swane, sold the other half to Roger de Montbegon, whose heirs are the wives of Eudo de Lung-villers and Geoffrey de Nevill. Thomas is adjudged to have his presentation to one half the church, and Richard is in mercy. (*Curia Regis*, No. 97, 11 Hen. III., m. 14.)—W. P. B.

1232. Geoffrey de Neovill and Mabilia his wife against Clemencia de Lungvilers, to do service for the free tenement which she holds of them in Brerley, by right of esnecy. Clemencia vouches to warrant the Earl of Lincoln, of whom she says she holds. The Earl comes and warrants, and the plaintiffs withdraw their writ. (*Curia Regis*, No. 111, Mic., 16 and 17 Hen. III., m. 11).—W.P.B.

1242-3. Lancashire. John de Lungvilers demands against Hubert de Burgo, Earl of Kent, and Margaret his wife, the manors of Horneby and Melling as his right. The defendants say that the Abbot of Croxton holds one carucate in those manors, in which carucate they have no interest. John says that Roger de Montebegon held those manors entire, and Henry de Montebegon, his heir, after him, and he enfeoffed the Earl and Margaret. The defendants vouch to warrant Henry de Mungedon. (*Coram Rege*, Hen. III., No. 61, m. 1 *d.*)—W. P. B.

1275. Geoffrey de Nevill and Margaret his wife demand against William de Lungvilers land and rent in Gayrgrave, of which John de Lungvilers, grandfather of Margaret (whose heir she is) was seised.

William says that John, a long time before his death, enfeoffed him, William. Jury. (*De Banco*, Trin., 3 Edw. I., No. 12, m. 46.) —W. P. B.

1344. Thomas de Lungvylers, chivaler, demands against Robert de Nevill of Farneley, chivaler, the manor of Gergrave and 5 messuages, land, and 40s. rent in Armeley, by writ of formedon. (*De Banco*, Hil., 18 Edw. III., No. 70, m. 134 *d.*)—W. P. B.

Page 43, line 5 from bottom. Cleckheaton. 1283. Richard de Thornhill *v.* Richard le Fevre of Wyk and others, for taking goods and chattels at Cleck Heton to the value of 5 marcs. (*De Banco*, East., 11 Edw. I., No. 51, m. 9.)—W. P. B.

Page 48, line 12. 1260. Clemencia de Knoll vouches Elias, son of Elias de Knoll, to warrant the third part of a messuage and land in Neweton, which Juliana, widow of William de Neweton, claims in dower. (*Curia Regis*, No. 166, East., 44 Hen. III., m. 36.) —W. P. B.

Page 50, line 2 from bottom. Helmeshal probably means North and South Elmsall, both of which formed part of the Lascy fee. See No. LV. (p. 99), and *Kirkby's Inquest*, pp. 5, 363.

Page 51, lines 1 and 7. On Aug. 18, 1257, the King, then at Chester, granted to Edmund de Lacy a market on Wednesdays, and a fair on the eve, day, and morrow of the Holy Trinity, at Tanshelfe, in his manor of Pontefract. (*Charter Roll*, 41 Hen. III., m. 3.)

Page 63, line 17. Roda is no doubt some *royd* or clearing, in North Yorkshire a *ridding*, which can no longer be identified.

Page 66. No. XLVI. 1252. Henry de Percy *v.* William de Geyrgrave and Maude his wife, to warrant a messuage and 16 acres of land in Austeneby. (*Curia Regis*, No. 148, Mic., 36 and 37 Hen. III., m. 23 *d.*)—W. P. B.

Page 74, at end of the *note*. An entry on the *Close Roll* for 44 Hen III. (Part i., m. 19), under the year 1259, gives the names of the husbands of the four daughters of William *le Fort*. The oldest married Ingram de Percy, the second Peter de Chauvent, the third Imbert de Muntferant, the fourth Laurence Seymour (*de Sancto Mauro*).

Page 97. No. LV. It will be noticed here that the writ is of later date than the extent. It appears from the original, that the writ was addressed to Richard de Schireburne, whilst the extent in Yorkshire was made before Sir Henry Waleys, deputy of Sir Richard de Hemmigton. The latter under the name of Richard de Hemmington, *ad hoc assignatus*, made the extent of the manor of Steventon in Bedfordshire, on Saturday before the Exaltation of the Holy Cross, 48 Hen. III. (Sept. 13, 1264), and also again on Tuesday before St. Denis' day in the same year. He and Richard de Byk' made the extent of the manor of Wadenho, in Northants, on Wednesday before the Exaltation of the Holy Cross, 48 Hen. III. (Sept. 10, 1264).

Page 100, first *note*, line 14. The statement in the note, taken from the *Newminster Chartulary*, that Isabella de Somerville's children died without issue, is incorrect. From the *Inq. p. m.* of Philip de Somerville, son of Isabella, who died on Jan. 23, 1354-5, it appears that his heirs were his daughter, Joan, wife of Rees ap Griffith, knight, aged forty and upwards; and Maud, daughter of John de Stafford (by Elizabeth, his other daughter), wife of Edmund de Vernon, aged thirteen on Christmas day last past (*Inq. p. m.*, 29 Edw. III. (First Nos.), No. 46, mm. 5, 7).

Page 100, *note* a. Time of John. Query date. Herbert de S. Quintin and Agnes his wife demand against Alice de Stuteville, two carucates and 40 acres of land in Burton, as Agnes' reasonable part of the inheritance of Anselin de Stuteville, brother of Alice and Agnes. (*Curia Regis*, No. 68, m. 6).—W. P. B.

1219. Robert de Insula and Rohese his wife, William Fitz Warine and Agnes his wife, and Alice de Stuteville *v.* Herbert de S. Quintin and Agnes his wife, touching the inheritance of Anselin de Stuteville, the brother of Alice and of Agnes de S. Quintin, and the uncle [*avunculus*] of Rohese and of Agnes Fitz Warine. Alice de Stuteville has died since the commencement of the action; Reginald de Merlay is her heir. (*Curia Regis*, No. 70., Mic., 3 and 4 Hen. III., m. 19.)—W. P. B.

On April 18, 1257, the King, then at Merton, granted a charter of free warren to Roger de Merlay in all his demesne lands of Anneys Burton. (*Charter Roll*, 41 Hen. III., m. 5.)

Page 101, line 3 from bottom. Jetengham is no doubt Yeddingham, as appears by the following extract from Burton's *Mon. Ebor.* (p. 286). " Sir Hugh Gubyon, knight, son of Richard Gubyon, for the good of the souls of Roger and William de Merlay, his uncles, and of Richard Gubyon his brother, gave all his land in Yeddingham to the Monastery there, exempt from all suits of court, etc., a priest to celebrate divine service in the Monastery daily for ever. See also the *Newminster Chartulary*, p. 15.

Page 105. No. LIX. 1267-8. 52 Hen. III. Margery, widow of John de Cawode claims dower in Heworth against John de Heworth. (*Assize Roll, Yorkshire*, N.—1—2; 1, m. 68.)—W. P. B.

Page 109. No. LXIII. 1259. Robert de Stopham and Hawise his wife *v.* Alan Sampson. One Roger *le Peytevin* delivered to Alan and one Adam *le Cerf*, the manor of Toueton for £200, which he was to repay at Martinmas, 42 Hen. III., and if it was not then paid the manor was to remain to Alan and Adam, and the survivor of them for life; and they had a deed to that effect. Roger *le Peytevin* afterwards granted the manor in the same way to Robert de Stopham and Hawise, and the survivor of them, for life, on condition that they should pay the £200 to Alan and Adam. This the plaintiffs did and obtained seisin of the manor and of the said deed, when Alan and Adam, at the instigation of Roger *le Peytevin*, snatched the deed from Hawise and broke the seal. (*Curia Regis*, No. 161, Mic., 43 Hen. III., m. 17 *d.*)—W. P. B.

36

1271. Certificate of Assize of Novel disseisin. The assize came to recognize if Robert de Stopham and Ralph his son had disseised Roger *le Peytevyn* of the manor of Toueton (less one bovate and eight acres), Robert and Ralph say that Robert de Stopham was enfeoffed of the manor by Roger *le Peytevyn*, and produce a charter thereof. The jury of assize found that the defendants had disseised the plaintiff, and assessed £60 damages. The King's Court now reverses this, and Robert de Stopham remains in seisin. (*Curia Regis*, No. 204, Trin., 55 Hen. III., m. 28.)—W. P. B.

Page 116. No. LXVIII. 1212-13, 14 John. Juliana, widow of Nigel de Plumpton, demands against Peter de Plumpton her reasonable dower in Plumpton, Gersington, Necfeld, Hidel, and Ribeston. (*Curia Regis*, No. 56, m. 16 *d*.)—W. P. B.

Page 133. No. LXXX. 1241. Master John de Harkestowe was summoned to answer William de Cantilupo, junior, in a plea that he hold to an agreement made between them touching the manor of Bingeleye. They settled the matter on these terms :—If William pays 100 marcs to Master John, at St. Andrew's Priory, Northampton, within a month from Michaelmas next, then Master John shall return the manor to William without any condition, and in the meantime the Master shall hold the manor, and shall allow off the 100 marcs whatever he shall receive therefrom ; if William shall not pay by the time appointed, then Master John shall hold the manor for the term contained in the chirograph made between. (Hil., 25 Hen. III., *Curia Regis*, No. 122, m. 13 *d*.)—W. P. B.

Page 159, *note* d. 1220-1. John Daivill gave a palfrey to have a weekly market on Mondays at Adlingfleet. (*Pipe Roll*, 5 Hen. III.)—W. P. B.

Page 160. At the end of John de Eyville's Inquisition is the following letter, probably from the Justices assigned for the custody of the Jews, to whom the writ dated 27 May, 1275, was addressed : " Ad mandatum vestrum, scrutatis rotulis in custodia nostra existentibus, inventum est quod Johannes de Eyville debet Elie le Blund xx*li*., redditos ad festum Omnium Sanctorum anno Henrici lvij° act' . . . . die Maii anno regni H. xlvj, unde tercia pars est Salam' filii Salam', et altera tercia pars est Mosei filii Elie, et iidem Judei exigunt totum predictum debitum et lucrum. Et idem Johannes debet eidem Elye L marcas, redditas a die S. Michaelis in unum mensem anno regni Henrici xlviij^{to}, act' vicesimo quarto die Maii anno eodem. Tercia pars istius debiti est Magistri Elie, et alia tercia pars est Mossei filii Elie, et iidem Judei exigunt illud totum debitum et lucrum."

Page 173. No. CI. Joan, daughter of William de Dufton or Dustune, was the youngest of three daughters. On their father's death, Walter de Grey, Archbishop of York, had a grant of their marriages. He married Isabel, the eldest daughter, to Walter de Grey, by whom she had a daughter, Isabel ; Roysia, the second, to a person named De Vylli; and Joan, the third, to Mauger le Vavasur. (*Cal. Gen.*, vol i., p. 148.)

Page 177, line 13. For *1272* read *1277*.

Page 179, line 2. For Robert *Lister* read Robert *Webster*.

Page 180, *note* c. 1245-6. John de Curtenay was summoned to warrant to Alexander de Ledes one third of a knight's fee in Kirkeby, which Alan de Aldefeud had claimed against him in the court of Roger de Mubray. (*Assize Roll, Yorkshire*, N.—1—1 ; 5, m. 10 *d.*)—W. P. B.

Page 186, *note* a, line 2. For £200 read £20.

Page 206. No. cxvii. 1279. Nicholas de Stapelton, who sued for the King, claimed against Robert de Everyngham, parson of Byrkyn, a messuage and six bovates of land in West Hathelseye, as the King's right, which King Henry demised to Ingram de Percy and the heirs of his body, and now ought to revert to the King because Ingram died *s. p.* Robert de Creppyng put in his claim to the property (less one bovate), and vouched to warranty William de Percy. The King recovered seisin. (*De Banco*, East., 7 Edw. I., No. 31, m. 27 ; Trin., No. 32, m. 92.)—W. P. B.

P. 221, line 12. For *Ragott'* read *Bagott'*. By marrying a Bagot heiress the Crathornes became wealthy people in the earlier part of the fourteenth century, when they succeeded the Percies of Kildale as lords of the manor of Crathorne.

Page 229, line 24. For *Eude* read *Eudo*.

Page 234, *note* b. For *Kirtlington* read *Kirklington*.

Page 235, line 10. The County of Blakeburne is probably Blackburnshire in Lancashire. The County of Bolin is uncertain, unless, perhaps, for the Honour of Bolingbroke, but this is more than doubtful.

Page 255, *note* e. For *Wharam* read *Wharram*.

Page 258. No. cxxxvii. 1273. William de Ebor. *v.* Robert de Neville, senior, and Elyas de Rylleston, touching the presentation to the church of Bruneshale [Burnsall]. Elyas, as to one half, says that William de Heppeden, the ancestor of William de Ebor., did (as William says) present the last parson, but that he did so in right of Eustace de Rylleston (whose son and heir Elyas is) while Eustace was under age and in ward to Heppedon. Judgment, that the plaintiff do recover this half. As to the other half, Robert says that the plaintiff forfeited his lands in the late war, and that the King gave part of them to him, Robert, and that the plaintiff had never redeemed them according to the Dictum of Kenileworth. Nevile afterwards withdrew his claim. (*De Banco*, Trin., 1 Edw. I., No. 5, m. 35.)—W. P. B.

10 Edw. I. William de Hebden had free warren in all his demesne lands in Hebden, Coniston, Burnsall and Esks. (*Harl. MS.*, 804, fo. 27 *d.*)

1282. Cecily, widow of William de Ebor., claims against Robert de Nevyle, the guardian of the land and heir of William de Ebor., her dower in Thorp, Crakhou, and Brunshale ; and against other defendants, dower in Hebbedon, Haslereg, Wendeslandale, etc. (*De Banco*, Hil., 10 Edw. I., No. 46, m. 67 *d.*)—W. P. B.

Page 268, line 10. For *Ayderby-vecunt* read *Aynderby-vecunt*.

GLOSSARY AND NOTES.

A S some of the subscribers to the *Record Series* are not familiar with many of the words and expressions contained in these Inquisitions, the Glossary has been made more full than would otherwise have been the case, and it is hoped that it will be found useful. Index references are given to most of the words and phrases, and a list of authorities is also given. This list is by no means perfect, but it contains such works as the compiler had access to, and as he has found similar lists of great assistance to him, it is given for what it is worth.—S. J. C.

LIST OF AUTHORITIES.

Atkinson's *Cleveland Glossary*, 1868.
Ayliffe's *Parergon Juris Canonici Anglicani*, 1726.
Blackie's *Dictionary of Place Names*, 3rd edition, 1887.
Blount's *Law Dictionary*, 1717.
Boldon Buke. Surt.
Bosworth's *Anglo Saxon Dictionary*, 1838.
Bracton, *De Legibus et Consuetudinibus Angliæ.* R. S.
Catholicon Anglicum. C. S.
Chartularies (Various). Surt.
Coke's *Complete Copyholder*, 1668.
Coke's *Institutes*, I and II., 4th edition, III. and IV., 6th edition.
Cowell's *Interpreter*, 1672.
Cruise's *Digest of the Laws of England respecting Real Property* 4th edition, 1835.
Cruise's *Treatise on the Origin and Nature of Dignities or Titles of Honour*, 2nd edition, 1823.
Cunningham's *Growth of English Industry and Commerce*, 1890; referred to as Cunningham.
Custumals of Battle Abbey. C. S.
Diary of Abraham de la Pryme. Surt.
Digby's *History of the Law of Real Property.* 1876.
Domesday of St. Paul's. C. S.
Du Cange, *Glossarium Mediæ et Infimæ Latinitatis*, 1883—7.
Dugdale's *Origines Juridiciales*, 1671.
Earle's *Handbook to the Land—Charters and other Saxonic Documents (Glossary)*, 1888.
Elton's *Origins of English History*, 2nd edition, 1890.
Eyton's *Domesday Studies* (Dorset), 1878.
General Introduction to Domesday Book. By Sir Henry Ellis, 1817.
Gomme's *Primitive Folk Moots*, 1880.
Greenwood's *Authority, Jurisdiction, and Method of Keeping County Courts, Courts Leet, and Courts Baron—Explaining the Judicial and Ministerial Authority of Sheriffs, also the Office and Duty of a Coroner*, 8th edition, 1722.
Halliwell's *Dictionary of Archaic and Provincial Words*, 9th edition, 1878.
Hazlitt's *Tenures of Land and Customs of Manors (Glossary)*, 1874.
Holyoke's *Latin Dictionary*, 1677.
Household Roll of Bishop Swinfield. C. S.
Introduction to Pipe Rolls, vol iii. P. S.
Jacob's *Law Dictionary*, 1736.
Kelham's *Norman Dictionary*, 1779.

Kemble's *Saxons in England*, 1876.
Kennett's *Parochial Antiquities (Glossary)*, 1818; referred to as Kennett, *Glossary*.
Kitchin's *Courts Leet, Courts Baron, &c.*, editions of 1587 and 1663.
Lee's *Glossary of Liturgical and Ecclesiastical Terms*, 1877.
Lewis's *Ancient Laws of Wales*, 1889.
Littleton's *Latin Dictionary*, 1678.
Lucas's *Studies in Nidderdale, (Glossary)*, about 1882.
Lyttleton's *Tenures*, edited by Tomlins, 1841.
Madox, *Baronia Anglica*, 1741.
    ,,   *Firma Burgi*, 1726.
    ,,   *Formulare Anglicanum*, 1702.
    ,,   *History of the Exchequer*, 1711.
Manchester Court Leet Records. Chet. S.
Manipulus Vocabulorum. C. S.
Manwood's *Forest Laws*, 1st edition, 1598; referred to as Manwood.
Martin's (C. Trice) *Record Interpreter* 1892.
Miege's *French Dictionary*, 1688.
Nelson's *Lex Maneriorum*, 1726.
Northumberland Assize Rolls. Surt.
Palmer's *Folk Etymology*, 1882.
Parker's *Concise Glossary of Architecture*, 1882.
Piers Plowman, edited by Rev. Professor Skeat, with *Glossarial Index and Notes*, Clarendon Press, 1886
Pike's *History of Crime in England*, 1873.
Promptorium Parvulorum. C. S.
Reeves' *History of English Law*, edited by Finlason, 1869.
Rules for the Interpretation of Deeds, with a *Glossary*. By Elphinstone, Norton, and Clark. 1885.
Scriven on *Copyholds*, 5th edition, 1867.
Scrutton's *Commons and Common Fields*, 1887
Seebohm's *English Village Community*, 3rd edition, 1884.
Selden Society's Publications.
Shillibeer's *Ancient Customs of the Manor of Taunton Deane*, 1821.
Skeats' *Concise Etymological Dictionary*, 1882.
Smith's (Toulmin) *English Gilds.* E. E. T. S.
Spelman's *Glossary*, 1664.
Statutes at Large, Ruffhead's edition.
Stephen's *Commentaries on the Laws of England*, 9th edition.
Stratmann's *Middle English Dictionary.* 1891.
Streatfield's *Lincolnshire and the Danes (Glossary)*, 1884.
Stubbs, *Constitutional History of England*, 8vo edition, 1880.
Stubbs, *Select Charters*, 4th edition, 1881.
Taylor's (Rev. Isaac) *Words and Places*, 6th edition, 1878.
Termes de la Ley, 1721.
The Law French and the Law Latin Dictionary, collected out of the best authors, by F. O., 1701.
The New English Dictionary.
Thorpe's *Ancient Laws and Institutes of England (Glossary)*, 1840.
Thorpe's *Diplomatorium Ævi Saxonici (Glossary).* 1865.
Vinogradoff's *Villainage in England*, 1892.
Visitations of Southwell Minster. C. S.
Watkins on *Copyholds*, 1797.
West's *Symboleography*, 1632.
Wilkins' *Leges Anglo Saxonicæ, Ecclesiasticæ, et Civiles (Glossary)*, 1721.
Wright's *Anglo Saxon and Old English Vocabularies*, 1884.
Wright's *Court Hand Restored*, 8th edition, 1846.
Wright's *Provincial Dictionary.*
Year Books, 15 *Edward III.* R. S.
York Volume of the Archæological Institute.
Yorkshire Archæological Association, Journal.
    Ditto,   ditto   *Selby Coucher Book.* Record Series.

ABBREVIATIONS.

C. S.	Camden Society.
Chet. S.	Chetham Society.
E. E. T. S.	Early English Text Society.
P. S.	Pipe Roll Society.
R. S.	Rolls Series.
Seld.	Selden Society.
Surt.	Surtees Society.
Y.A.A., J.	Yorkshire Archæological Association, Journal.
Y.A.A., R.	Yorkshire Archœological Association, Record Series.

The Arabic numerals immediately after the leading words refer to the page, and the Roman numerals immediately after the leading words refer to the Inquisition where the word may be found.

Advowson of a church (83, 104, 108, 116, 169, 231—6, 241). The right of patronage, *i.e.*, the power of presenting some fit and proper person to the Bishop or Ordinary for institution into a vacant benefice. See Kennett, *Glossary*, also Ayliffe's *Parergon*, pp. 410—17.

Advowson of a religious house (114, 128, 148—151). The right of patronage acquired, sometimes by the founder of the house, and sometimes by a powerful neighbour, who was chosen by the house as advocate, patron, or champion. Sometimes the patron had the sole nomination of the abbot or prior, and sometimes he granted a *congé d' élire* or licence of electing to the members of the house. See Kennett, *Glossary*, also Freeman, *Norman Conquest*, vol v., p. 501.

Aferus, *affrus* (169). A horse or ox for farm service.

Agist, agistment (29, 218, 223—6). "The taking in the beasts and cattle of every person being an inhabitant within a forest that may for their money have common of herbage there for such beasts as are commonable within a forest ; and this manner of taking in of cattle to pasture or feed by the week or by the month or otherwise is called agisting of beasts or cattle, and the common of herbage that they have there for their beasts is called agistment. But it is to be understood that agistment is most properly the common of herbage of any kind of ground or land or woods, or the money that is received or due for the same." Manwood, c. 11, s. 1. See "Agister."

Agister (111). An officer of the forest whose duty was to take in beasts to agistment, that is, to pasture within the forest, or to feed on the pannage, and who was answerable to the king for the money and profit arising from such agistment. Manwood, c. 11, s. 1. See "Agist."

Aid, *auxilium* (4, 80, 146, and elsewhere). A pecuniary contribution made by a tenant to his lord, originally levied at the will of the lord, but by Magna Charta limited to three special occasions, viz. :—1. To make the lord's eldest son a knight ; 2. To marry his eldest daughter ; 3. To ransom his person when taken in war. Aid was due to the Crown from its immediate tenants, and likewise to inferior lords from their immediate tenants. Madox *(Hist. Exch.*, c. 15) gives instances of several aids levied in early times besides those above mentioned. Aid was nearly allied to scutage, hidage, carucage, and tallage. See Madox *(Hist. Exch.*, c. 15), who amongst other instances says that the aid levied by King Richard I. for the ransom of his person when he was taken and imprisoned on his return from the Holy Land was paid by the tenants *in capite* under the name of scutage, and by tenants in socage or other inferior tenure under the name of hidage or carucage. The Statute of Westminster the First limits the amount to be taken for an aid to twenty shillings for a knight's fee, and twenty shillings for each £20 land held in socage, and so in proportion for more or less. It also prescribes other limitations as to levying aids.

Aldermen of the Minstrels (269). Headmen, rulers, governors, or wardens of the guild of minstrels at York. See *New English Dictionary*, *s. v.* "Alderman." There were guilds of minstrels at both York and Beverley. See also Toulmin Smith's *English Gilds*, p. 294, for mention of the "Gild of the Minstrels and Players" of Lincoln. See also Kennett, *Glossary*, *s.v.*, *Ministrallus*.

Altile (plural *altilia*) (100). A fat fowl.

Allour (72), alour, alure. The walk or passage behind the battlements of a castle or the parapet of a church or other building, the gutter of a roof, a covered passage or cloister, an alley or aisle.

Almoigne or frankalmoigne, *libera elemosina*, free alms (4, 107, 114, 138, 143). The tenure by which religious corporations in almost every instance held their lands. It was subject to no service except that of praying for the soul of the donor and those of his ancestors and heirs, and except up to the date of the Norman Conquest or thereabouts, the *trinoda necessitas*, *i.e.*, the duty of rendering military service, and the building and repair of castles, bridges, and high roads. This tenure could not be created by a subject after the Statute of Westminster the Third, *Quia Emptores*, 18 Edw. I. It differed from tenure by divine service in that lands held by the latter tenure were subject to fealty, &c., and also to distress in case of breach or neglect of the service under which the land was held.

Amercement, amerciament (26, 211, 212, 267). The pecuniary punishment of an offender against the king or other lord in his court, that is found to be *in misericordiâ*, *i.e.*, to have offended and to stand at the mercy of the king or lord. An amercement differed from a fine in that it was arbitrarily imposed at the discretion of the court, but a fine was fixed and certain.

Appeal, to (14). To accuse. Bracton, book iii., treatise ii., chapters 18 to 22 inclusive.

Approve, to, *approviare*, *approvare* (164, 210), to make profit or advantage to oneself. To approve land, was to make the best benefit of it by increasing the value or rent. By the Stat. of Merton, the lord is permitted to approve, *i.e.*, to enclose the waste lands of his manor. *New English Dict.*

Arrare (254, *note* b), probably means to harrow. Du Cange, under the second division of the word, gives the meaning as *fatigare*, *exagitare*, *vexare; quo sensu travailler dicimus*.

Arrentagium (148). Rent. Compare Blount, *Law Dictionary*, *s.v.*, *arrentare*, "arrentation."

Assart (XLV., also 98, 99). Land cleared of wood and rendered arable. To assart land in the forest without licence was a grave offence against the forest laws, inasmuch as thereby the thickets and coverts were plucked up by the roots, and could not grow again so as to afford food and cover for the beasts of the forest. See Manwood, c. 9.

Assise or **Assize**. Jacob (*Law Dictionary*) says, that according to our ancient books, assize is defined to be an assembly of knights and other substantial men, with the justice in a certain place and at a certain time appointed. This word is properly derived from the latin verb *assideo* to sit together, and is also taken for the court, place, or time when and where the writs and processes of assize are handled or taken. And in this signification assize is *general*, as when the justices go their several circuits, with commissions to take all assizes ; or *special*, where a special commission is granted to certain persons (formerly oftentimes done) for taking an assize upon one or two disseisins only. There were five several commissions for a general assize, viz.:—(1) Of Oyer and Terminer, directed to the judges and many other gentlemen of the county by which they were empowered to try treasons, felonies, &c. (2) Of Gaol delivery, directed to the judges and the clerk of assize associate, which gave them power to try every prisoner in the gaol, committed for any offence whatsoever, but none but prisoners. (3) Of Assize, directed to the judges and the clerk of assize, to take assizes and do right upon writs of assize brought before them, by such as were wrongfully thrust out of their lands and possessions. (4) Of Nisi Prius, directed to the judges and clerk of assize, by which civil causes grown to issue in the courts above, were tried in the vacation by a Jury of twelve men of the county where the cause of action arose. (5) A Commission of the Peace in every county of the circuit, and all justices of the peace of the county were bound to be present at the assizes, and the sheriff also, to give their attendance on the judges, or they should be fined. The term assize was likewise applied to a jury where assizes of novel disseisin were tried. The term assize also was used for a writ for recovery of possession of things immovable, *e.g.*, assise of novel disseisin. It also signified a Statute or Act of Parliament, *e.g.*, Assize of the Forest, Assize of Bread and Ale, &c.

Assise of Novel Disseisin (282) was an action for recovery of lands, tenements, rents, common of pasture, common way, or of an office, toll, &c., brought by a tenant in fee simple, fee tail, or for life, who had been put out of possession or disseised.

Attachment (94, 103, 211, 212). The apprehension of a person or seizure of goods, also certain rights and privileges, *e.g.*, of water, underwood, &c. Attachment of the forest was a forest court.

Avallacio anguillarum (81, 82). A take of eels. See Du Cange, *s.v.*, *avalagium*, *avalison*.

Avantagium patrimonii (101). Appears to have been a portion of the family property acquired by a child beyond his or her proper share. See Du Cange, *avantagium* (2)—*præcipuitas*—*patrimonium*.

Aventure, *adventura* (12). Casual profit.

Average, *averagium* (90). The work done by *averia* or beasts of draught or burden. The service done by a tenant for his lord in the carriage of goods by any beast of burden.

Averia (144, 240). Beasts of draught or burden. Kennett, *Glossary*, says the word sometimes includes all personal estate, as *catalla* includes all goods and chattels.

Averinge (240). Small herbages after the corn and hay are carried are so called, *i.e.*, stubble and aftergrass or fog. See " Averish " in the *New English Dictionary*, and in Halliwell's *Dictionary*.

Averpenny. The money paid by a tenant in commutation of the service (*avera*) of performing any work for his lord, by his beasts of draught or burden.

Bailiff, *ballivus* (34). An officer of a manor, next in rank to the steward. His principal duties were to inspect and superintend the works due from the tenants of the manor, and see that they were properly performed. *Domesday of St. Paul's*, xxxv. The name was also given to any officer who was deputed to look after the property of another. The sheriff was the king's bailiff with regard to his county, which was frequently spoken of as his bailiwick.

Bailiwick, *balliva* (32, 148, 201, 202, 215). Under the term was comprised any office, jurisdiction, or territory, committed to the care of a subordinate official.

Bayl (82). Bail, custody, jurisdiction, power; also tribute, toll, duty. The district under the charge of a bailiff. See *New English Dictionary*, also Du Cange, *s.v. Balia*. The 13*s.* 4*d.* arising from the Bayl of Skipse (p. 82) would be a payment in the nature of Castleguard, *q.v.*

Bercaria (138, 145). A sheepfold, also a sheepwalk. See *Domesday of St. Paul's*, lxxix., and 59.

Bercarius (XLV.) A shepherd. See *Custumals of Battle Abbey*, xxv.

Bondage (7, 11, 32, and LIV., CXII.). A kind of servile tenure, a species of villenage, which see.

Bondman (7, 41, 48, and CXII.). Sometimes called a native or serf. A kind of villein, which see.

Bonepeny (211). Probably boonpenny, *i.e.*, a payment in lieu of boonworks.

Boonworks. See *precariæ*.

Boscus forinsecus (248). Foreign wood. A wood not included in the demesne, where other men have common, and in which therefore the lord's rights were limited. See the *Extenta Manerii*, sec. 5, also *Domesday of St. Paul's*, lxv.

Bovate or **Oxgang.** Half a virgate, or yard land of varying measurement. The following measurements appear in these inquisitions, viz.: 5, 6, 7, 8, 9, 10, 11, 12, 15, 16, and 24 acres. A bovate appears to have been the holding of a tenant who contributed one ox to the manorial team of eight oxen. See Vinogradoff, p. 238.

Brachettus (138), *brachetus, bracetus.* A brach or brachet, *i.e.*, a dog which hunts by scent. See Du Cange, *s.v. bracco, New English Dict.*, *s.v.*, brach.

Bracinum, *bracina, braceria* (41, 100, 255, and elsewhere). A brewery, a brewhouse.

Braseum, *brasium, braesium* (244). Malt. Coke, IV. *Inst.*, pp. 262-3, *braseum orgei*, barley malt.

Bruerium, *bruarium* (142). Heather ground.

Bulehil (59). Probably bolehill. A provincial term for the heap of refuse at the mouth of a pit, called a pithill. The heaps of metallic scoria found in the lead mining districts, are called bolehills. Halliwell's *Dict*. The *New English Dict.*, *s.v.* "Bole," says boles or bolestids are places where in ancient times (before smelting mills were invented), miners did fine their lead.

Burgage, *burgagium* (82, 220). A sort of quit rent paid to the chief lord for the houses and tenements in a town or borough.

Burgage tenure is said by Lyttleton (*Tenures*, c. 10) to be the tenure by which lands and tenements within boroughs and towns are holden of a king or a subject by a certain annual rent. And such tenure, he says, is but tenure in socage. The custom of Borough English was an incident of burgage tenure in certain towns and places in England.

Burgenses, burgesses (122, 163, 164, 220). The inhabitants of a town or burgh paying quit rent to the chief lord for the houses or tenements occupied by them.

Burgh, borough, *burgus, burgum,* A.S., *burh* (50, 124, 140, 164, 220, 230). Not only a municipal or parliamentary borough, but also a fortified town, and generally any inhabited place larger than a village. The original meaning appears to have been a fortified place, a stronghold. See the *New*

37

English Dict., also Spelman's *Glossary*, *s.v. burgus*, and Kemble's *Saxons in England*, book ii., c. 7, and appendix C. Stubbs *(Constit. Hist.*, vol. i. p. 105) says "the '*burh*' of the A.S. period was simply a more strictly organised form of the township."

Calcetum (175). A causeway.

Carecta (244). A cart.

Carucate, *carucata*. A ploughland or hide was of uncertain extent, but said to be the extent that could be ploughed by a team of eight oxen in the course of a year. The size varied in different parts of the country and according to the nature of the land. The normal size is said to be 120 acres, but in Kirkby's *Inquest* (Surt.), p. 446, are several examples, varying from 106½ acres to 27¾ acres, and in the *Register of Worcester Priory* (C.S.), a carucate appears to have contained 180 acres. Seebohm *(Vill. Commun.*, p. 37) gives instances of hides varying in area from 240 to 120 acres. Coke *(1. Inst.*, 69 a.) says that a plowland may contain a messuage, wood, meadow, and pasture. See *post.*, "Hide," also Elphinstone, *Interpretation of Deeds*, *s.v.* "Measures of land."

Castleguard (83, 175, 226) is an imposition laid upon such of the king's subjects as dwell within a certain compass of any castle, to the maintenance of such as watch and ward it. It is sometimes used for the circuit itself which is inhabited by such as are subject to this service. *Termes de la Ley.* Tenure by castleguard is to hold of the superior lord by the service of guarding a tower, a door, or some other place of his castle. To hold of the king by castleguard is knight's service *in capite*, but to hold by a certain rent for castleguard is but socage. Lyttleton's *Tenures*, book ii., c. 4; see also c. 20 of *Magna Charta*, 9 Hen. III., as to doing of castle ward.

Chase is generally understood to mean a franchise of a middle nature between a forest and a park. (See "Forest," *post.*). Manwood (c. 1, sec. 4), says, "In these three things doth a forest differ from a chase, that is to say, in particular laws, in particular offices, and in certain courts that are incident unto a forest for the execution of those laws. For a chase hath no particular laws that are proper to a chase only; for all offenders in a chase are to be punished by the common law, and not by the forest law, nor by any other law that is proper to a chase. A chase hath no such officers as a forest hath, but only keepers and woodwards. Chase, *chacea*, also means a road or droveway or driftway, by which a person drives cattle to a pasture.

Chief, to hold in (10, 20, 90, and elsewhere), was to hold lands directly from the crown as the immediate tenant. Such tenure might either be by knight service or in socage.

Compes (75). A fetter.

Coningeria (84). A rabbit warren.

Coopertorium (79). Reeds. Literally a covering, and so reeds, which form a covering or thatch.

Corn in autumn (211). The claim of foresters to gather corn, &c., is limited by c. 7 of the Charter of the Forest, 9 Hen. III., which provides that "No Forester or Bedel from henceforth shall make Scotale, or gather Garb, or Oats, or any Corn, Lamb, or Pig, or shall make any Gathering but by the sight and upon the view of the twelve Rangers, when they shall make their Range."

Cotagium (197). The tenure of a cottar.

Cottar, *cottarius, coterius, coterellus.* A holder of a croft or small plot of land with his cottage or homestead. See "Villein." Sometimes the cottar paid a money rent, as in Inquisitions xx., xlv., cxxx., and cxxxvi., and sometimes he did works in addition to payment of rent, as in Inquisition cxxxi. See also pp. 36, 67, 121, and 138. In the *Custumals of Battle Abbey* there appears to have been a distinction between the *cottarius* and the *coterellus* (Introduction, p. viii.), which cannot be discovered in these inquisitions. See also Kennett, *Glossary*, *s.v. coterellus*.

Cougeld (p. 223). See *post.*, " Kingelde."

County court (118). The chief court of the county, having both civil and criminal jurisdiction, and presided over by the sheriff or his deputy. It dated back to Anglo-Saxon times, and in addition to its ordinary jurisdiction, it transacted various kinds of private business, conducted inquiries directed by the king's writ, raised money for the king's use, transacted the military business of the county, provided for the conservation of the peace, &c., &c. See Stubbs, *Const. Hist.*, *s.v.* " County court," " Shire moot."

Court, *curia*, in these inquisitions generally means the court of the lord of a manor or honour, or else a wapentake or hundred court.

Crossbowman, Service of a, was a species of grand serjeanty. See Inquisition XLIV., p. 46, on the death of William the Arblaster, of Givendale. In vol. cxxiii. of the *Dodsworth MSS.*, in the Bodleian Library, under the heading of Notes of Inquisitions of Tenures in Chief, are some notes about the Arblaster family, of which the following is a summary:

Fo. 131. 2 Ed. II. Ricus le Alblaster held premises in North Geuehale and Est Geuendale in chief by the service of finding the sixth part of one Crossbowman in the Castle of York, at his own expense, for 40 days if there be war in the county.

Fo. 134. 2 Ed. III., No. 30. Robtus Alblaster de North Gueldale held lands in North Geuendale and Est Geuendale. Radus le Alablaster *est filius*.

Fo. 139. Escheats, 18 Ed. III., No. 3. William, son of Robert de North Geuendale, held lands in North Geuendale of the king in chief by fealty and service, rendering to the king's exchequer, by the hands of the Sheriff, 2s. 6d. at Easter and Michaelmas. And John is his son and heir.

Fo. 140 *b*. Escheats, 20 Ed. III., No. 6. Johes l' Archer held lands in Yapum of the king in chief by the service of the 7th part of a certain serjeanty, which serjeanty is held entire of the king in chief by finding one man with bow and arrows in the Castle of York, at his own expense, for 40 days if war shall be in the county, by homage. And John is his son and heir.

Then follows a note in small and difficult handwriting:

" *iste Jo : fil : ob. (seisitus?) de (premissis?)* 24 E. III."

Fo. 144. 23 Ed. III., No. 151. Radus Alblaster held of the king in chief as of his crown *(ut de coronâ)*, by homage and service of the sixth part of a certain serjeanty, certain tenements in North Geuendale and Est Geuenda *(sic)*.

Fo. 154. Escheats, 51 Ed. III., No. 13. Agnes de Geuendale held of the king in chief certain tenements in Est and North Geuendale by finding, with her companions *(cum sociis suis)*, an archer in a certain tower within the Castle of York, for the safe custody of the Castle, for 40 days in time of war.

Culture, *cultura* (52, and elsewhere). A piece of cultivated ground of no determined but of moderate size.

Curtilage (57, and elsewhere). A garden, yard, field, or piece of void ground, lying near and belonging to the messuage. *Termes de la Ley*.

Demesne, to hold lands in (2, 12, 15, 21, 30, 91, 242, and elsewhere), was to hold the same as the demesne lands of the manor. To be seized in demesne, was said of one who held lands for the term of his life. But he who held the same to him and his heirs, or to him and his successors was said to hold in his demesne as of fee. Demesnes were in common speech the lord's chief manor place, and the lands belonging to it which he kept in his own hands. The king's ancient demesnes are the lands and manors which were in William the Conqueror's hands, and in *Domesday* book stated to have been in the possession of Edward the Confessor. See Elphinstone, *Interpretation of Deeds*, and the authorities there cited.

Denarata, *denariata*. A pennyworth. See the example in Inquisition VI. of Appendix I. *Denariata terræ* is said to have been a measure of land containing a square perch. Elphinstone, *s.v.* " Measures of land."

Deraynatus (125), proved. There are many forms of this word.
See Du Cange, *s.v. derationare.*

Dieta (250). The space of a day, a day's work, a day's wage.
Du Cange.

Dower (32, 181, and elsewhere), "by the law of the realm, is a
portion which a widow hath of the lands of her husband, which by the common law is the third part; but by her husband's assignment, by his father's
assent, at the church door, she may have so much of his father's land as is so
assigned, and so of the husband's assignment of part of his own land. And
dower, by the custom of some places, is to have half the husband's land."
Termes de la Ley. See also Lyttleton, *Tenures*, book i., c. 5.

Dower, assignment of (106, 180, 184). See "Dower."

Dower at the church door (181). See "Dower."

Drengage, *drengagium* (100, 131, 142, 267). A servile tenure,
differing from and superior to tenure in villenage in that it was not at the will
of the lord, but fixed and permanent. The services incident to this tenure
were, however, very similar to the services due from a villein. There are
many examples of tenure in drengage in the *Boldon Buke*, and the conclusions
at which the learned editor of that volume, the Rev. Wm. Greenwell, arrives
with regard to the nature of the tenure are to some extent confirmed by the
instances appearing in this volume. It does not, however, seem quite clear
that the dreng was personally free from servile work, as stated by Mr. Greenwell. The examples given in these inquisitions and in the *Boldon Buke*, seem
to dispose of Spelman's statement *(Glossary, s.v.,* drenches, *drengus, drengagium)*, that the drenches were tenants by military service, and that they or
their ancestors had held their lands before the Norman Conquest.

Dreng or drengh, *drengus* (100). One who held his land by
drengage tenure.

Duwa or duva (1). The bank of a ditch. See Du Cange, *s.v.*
duva, douva, doga; French, *douve.*

Eisnecia, eynescie, or **esnecy** (133 *n*, 277), is defined by Jacob
(Law Dictionary) as a private prerogative allowed to the eldest coparcener
where an estate is descended to coparceners, *i.e.*, coheiresses, to choose first
after the inheritance is divided. *Jus eisneciæ* is *jus primogenituræ;* in which
sense it may be extended to the eldest son and his issue. In the *Statute of
Marlbridge*, cap. 9., it is called *Enitia pars hæreditatis.* In p. 133 *n, eynescie*
appears to be used as an adjective, and to signify elder.

Enfeoff, *feoffare* (26). To convey hereditaments to one in fee
simple, fee tail, or for life, with livery of seisin and possession, without which
nothing passed. Delivery of seisin and possession was the essential part of
the transaction, a writing not being required until the passing of the Statute
of Frauds (29 Car. II., c. 3).

Englesher', Englishry (50). The fact of being an Englishman.
Chiefly in legal phrase, *presentment of Englishry:* the offering of proof that
a slain person was an Englishman, in order to escape the fine levied (under
the Norman kings) upon the hundred or township, for the murder of a
"Frenchman" or Norman. The fine of Englishry would usually be paid to
the Crown, but the Lacies claimed to have a liberty within the Honour of
Pontefract or the Wapentake of Osgoldcross (Inquisition LXIII., p. 109), and
probably claimed the right to receive all such fines. Mr. W. P. Baildon gives
the following note on the subject: "Thomas Deyville, keeper of the Castle
and Honour of Pontefract and of other lands and tenements which were of
Thomas, late Earl of Lancaster, and other enemies and rebels in the county
of York," in his account for the 18th year of Edw. II. (1324-5), states that

there is a decay of 13s. 4d. of a certain rent called Englescherie in Wridlesford, because the tenements out of which the said rent was paid came to the hands of Henry, late Earl of Lincoln, and lord of the said Castle and Honour, and were in the hands of the said Earl of Lancaster, after the death of the said Earl of Lincoln, until the time of the Earl of Lancaster's forfeiture, and now they are in the king's hand, on account of that forfeiture, for default of tenants. *Exchequer*, L. T. R. Memoranda, 18 Edw. II. *Common Roll*, Trinity, m. 5.

Escape (223, 226) was of two kinds, voluntary and negligent, and was where one that was arrested came to his liberty before delivery by award of any justice or order of law. The person responsible for the escape was liable to be amerced. See *Termes de la Ley*. There was also an escape of beasts; and any man whose cattle were found within the forbidden limits of a forest was subject to punishment, unless he was *quietus de escapio* by charter.

Escheat, *escaeta, escaetta, escaetum* (6, 23, 24, 220, 230, and elsewhere). An escheat was the determination of a tenure from the extinction of the blood of the tenant, either by his dying without heirs, or attainder for treason or felony. In such cases the land escheated or fell back to the lord of the fee. P. S., vol. iii., *Glossary*

Escheator, eschaetor, escaetor (27, 152, 153, and elsewhere). The escheator was that officer who was accountable for the escheats due to the king in the county wherein he held office. After the deaths of any of the king's tenants, who held by knight service or otherwise, he held an inquisition, which he certified into the Exchequer. In the reign of Henry III. England was divided into two Escheatries, *Citra Trentam* and *Ultra Trentam*. P. S., vol. iii., *Glossary*.

Espervarius (or **spervarius**) **sorus** (180, 251). A sparrow-hawk in his first or golden plumage, a bird of the first year, not moulted. Du Cange, *s.v. saurus*; Bracton, vol. v., p. 83. The term "*sorus*" was also applied to men, *e.g.*, the father of St. Bernard was called *sorus*, *i.e.*, reddish, yellow-haired. See Morison's *Life of St. Bernard*, p. 2, and *note*.

Esplees, *explecia, explectamenta* (183, 211). The full profits which the land yields, as the hay of the meadow, the feed of the pasture, the corn of the arable, the rents, services, and such like issues. Sometimes it signifies the farm or lands themselves.

Estovers, common of (211), was the tenant's right to take wood necessary for the use of his farm or house from his lord's estate. These estovers were known as house-bote, cart-bote, fire-bote, plough-bote, and hay or hedge-bote, according to the purposes for which they were required.

Estrica, *strica*, or *strikq* (245-8-9), a strike or bushel. In the *Domesday of St. Paul's*, pp. lxxi. 17, the strike is considered to equal two bushels, but the examples on pages 248-9 of this volume, show clearly that a strike of one bushel is meant.

Extent (xv., xix., lxxv., lxxvi., lxxxi., and others). The survey and valuation of an estate made upon inquisition or the oath of a jury. The Statute *Extenta Manerii*, which is generally assumed to be dated 4 Edw. I., Stat. 1, gives elaborate instructions for making an extent. The extent or survey of a manor contained an account of the whole condition of the estate, the buildings belonging to it, the fields and stock on the domain, the pasturage, the amount of wood, and the profits of the waste, the mills, fisheries, and so forth. It also enumerated the free tenants, and stated the terms of their tenure; the villeins and cottars, and their services; as well as the patronage and other incidental rights belonging to the manor. See Cunningham, p. 218.

Extend (150, 181). To survey and value a manor, lands, or tenements.

Eyre, Justices in, *Justiciarii itinerantes* (30). The Justices of the Forest were so called, concerning whom see "Eyre of the Forest." The term was also applied to the justices sent with commissions into counties, to hear pleas of the Crown, cases concerning Jews, and certain civil pleas. They were so called to distinguish them from the *Justiciarii residentes, i.e.,* the justices residing at Westminster, or Justices of the Bench, and were eventually supplanted by the Justices of Assize. These Justices in Eyre were originally not justices of any superior court, but were of an inferior order of judges. Coke, Litt., 293 *b* ; Reeve, *English Law*, I., lxxxi. *n.*, and chapters 2 and 4.

Eyre of the Forest (112). The Court of the Justice Seat, held before the Chief Justice of the Forest and his fellows, called Justices in Eyre, who had authority to hear and determine concerning vert and venison, and other pleas of the forest. There were two Chief Justices, one for the forest on this side Trent, the other beyond. See Coke, IV. *Inst.*, c. 73, on Forest Courts ; also Manwood.

Faldage (241). The right of the lord of a manor, or other person, to have all the sheep within his manor, or within a town or other district, folded at night on his land for the purpose of manuring it. Elphinstone, *s.v.* "Frankfoldage," and the authorities there cited. See also *Domesday of St. Paul's*, lxxxiv.

Farm, *firma* (37, 55, 71, and elsewhere). Derived from an Anglo-Saxon word signifying provisions. It came to be used for rent because anciently the greater part of the rents were reserved in provisions until the use of money became more general. Ultimately the word farm came to signify the estate or land held at a rent or farm. As to the farm system, see Vinogradoff, p. 301, *et seq.*

Farm, free; *libera firma.* Lands or tenements changed by feoffment from knight service to a fixed annual rent, and free from homage, wardship, relief, and marriage, and all other services not reserved by the feoffment.

Farm, great and little The distinction between these two kinds of farm is not clear. (See pp. 52, 53). The rent paid by a villein at great farm was more per bovate than the rent paid by a villein at little farm, but the rents were not always the same, *e.g.,* the rent of a villein at great farm varied from 6s. to 8s. per bovate, without any boonworks, and the rent of a villein at little farm was generally 3s. 3½d. per bovate; but one tenant paid 2s. 8½d. per bovate, another paid 3s. 4d. for three parts of a bovate, and two others paid 1s. 11¾d. for three parts of a bovate, and all but those last-mentioned did boonworks.

Faucibus (67) for *falcibus.* Abl. plur. of falx, a hook, bill, scythe, or sickle.

Fealty (119), *fidelitas,* signifies an oath taken at the admittance of every tenant (except tenants in frankalmoigne and tenants at will), to be true to the lord of whom he holds his land, and is due upon every change of the lord. For forms of the oath, both of a freeholder and of a villein, see Blount's *Law Dictionary, s.v.* "fealty." See also Lyttleton's *Tenures*, book ii., c. 2. See also the Statute called *Modus faciendi homagium et fidelitatem,* 17 Edw. II., Statute 2.

Fence Month (29). So called because it was the fawning month, when the does and fawns had protection. It commenced fifteen days before Midsummer and ended fifteen days after Midsummer. The Charter of the Forest, c. 8, provides that the third Court of Swannimote should be held and kept fifteen days before Midsummer, and that at that time all the foresters, verderers, and agisters should meet together to make provision for the quiet and safety of the wild beasts during the time of their fawning.

Feodum (or *feudum*) **Loricæ.** The same as hauberk fee or knight's fee. See "Knight service." Spelman, however, says *(Glossary, s.v. feudum loricatum, loricati, armiger)* that the words sometimes mean the fee held by a squire. [N.B. The inquisition containing this phrase will appear in Vol. II.]

Feoffment (226) is where a man conveys hereditaments to one in fee simple, fee tail, or for life, with livery of seisin and possession. In order to preserve evidence of the transaction it was usual that a charter or deed of feoffment should be executed, but writing was not essential until the passing of the Statute of Frauds.

Ferthepenye (50). This so called custom in Pontefract is probably equivalent to Frithpenny, *i.e.*, the penny paid to the lords of some manors by each freeman within the manor, who appeared at the view of Frankpledge. See *Domesday of St. Paul's*, cv.—cvii., and *note*. It has also been suggested that the custom may have some connection with the ferthefields, frithfields, or common fields of vert. The word frith also means a hedge, a coppice, young underwood. See Halliwell's *Dictionary*. See also page 28 of these Inquisitions, for an instance of a payment by the men of the king's demesne of Pickering, of one half-penny per bovate every year to the foresters, when the latter made livery to them on making their hedges.

Feugera (78). Fern, bracken.

Fine. A payment made by a copyhold tenant to his lord, on admittance to his land; a payment made to procure some privilege, benefit, or immunity. See Madox, *Hist. Exch.*, chapters 11, 12, and 13. A fine is also a fixed pecuniary penalty under some Statute. See *Boldon Buke, s.v. finis,* for a good definition of fines.

Fine of Wapentake (32, 238), appears to have been a payment in commutation of services at the wapentake or hundred court. The services done by tenants of a manor at these courts were called *forinsec* or foreign, because they were done outside the manor, and in course of time they were frequently commuted for a money payment. There was also a payment called hundred penny, in discharge of tallage for the hundred, which may have been akin to this fine. See Du Cange, *s.v. hundredum,* hundredes-penny; also Kennett, *Glossary, s.v. hundredus.*

Foreign Wood of the lord. See *ante*, "*Boscus forinsecus.*"

Forest (28, 29, 31, 32, 111, 114, 144, 145, 211, 215, 225, 267). "A forest is a certain territory of wooddy grounds and fruitful pastures privileged for wild beasts and fowls of forest, chase, and warren to rest and abide in, in the safe protection of the king for his princely delight and pleasure; which territory of ground, so privileged, is meered and bounded with unremoveable marks, meeres, and boundaries, either known by matter of record or else by prescription; and also replenished with wild beasts of venerie or chase, and with great coverts of vert for the succour of the said wild beasts to have their abode in. For the preservation and continuance of which said place, together with the vert and venison, there are certain particular laws, privileges, and officers belonging to the same, meet for that purpose. . . . . . The wild beasts of the forest are five, and no more, that is to say, the hart, the hind, the hare, the boar, and the wolf. The beasts of the chase are also five, the buck, the doe, the fox, the martin, and the roe. The beasts and fowls of warren are the hare, the coney, the pheasant, and the partridge. All these have privilege within the forest." Manwood, c. 1. "A Forest doth consist of eight things, viz.: of Soil, Covert, Laws, Courts, Judges, Officers, Game, and Certain Bounds." Coke, IV. *Inst.*, 289. "The next in degree unto it (a forest) is a liberty of a frank-chase. A chase in one degree is the selfsame thing that a park is, and there is no diversity between them, save that a park is enclosed, and a chase is always open and not enclosed, and therefore the next in degree unto a frank-chase is a park. The last and next in degree unto a park is the liberty and franchise of a free warren. . . . . Every forest is a chase, a park, and a warren, but a chase is not a forest, but a part of it; and in the like sort of a park and a warren." Manwood, as above. The owner of a wood within a forest or chase might not fell timber or cut wood therein, except under certain restrictions. Coke, IV. *Inst.*, 297-8; Manwood, c. 8. Manwood further states that although it is a common opinion that a forest may not be held by a subject, yet there are instances of forests being held by subjects (*e.g.*, the Earl of Lancaster, temp. Edw. II. and Edw. III.), who executed the forest laws therein. (c. 3, secs. 2, 3, and 4).

Forester (28, 30, 111, 211, 266). An officer of the forest, sworn to preserve the vert and venison of the forest, to attend upon the wild beasts within his bailiwick, to watch and keep them safe by day and by night, to apprehend all offenders there in vert and venison, and to present them at the courts of the forest. *Termes de la Ley.* See also Coke, IV. *Inst.*, 293, for the oath of a forester, setting out his duty.

Forland (222, 226), forlande (62), forlant (81), forlonde (250). (1) A plot of land outside the demesne and not included in the common fields of a manor. See Vinogradoff, p. 332; *Domesday of St. Paul's*, lxxii., lxxiv. (2) The headland at the end of a shot or group of selions or strips of land of a common field. Kennett, *Glossary*, *s.v. forera*. Seebohm, *English Village Community*, pp. 4, 20, 108.

Forum (50). A fair, equals *nundinæ, feriæ*. Du Cange.

Fossatum, *foss* (1, 38, 39, 40). A ditch, trench, or moat; also the earthen rampart or bank thrown up round a castle, fortified camp, or other stronghold; also the stronghold itself.

Frankalmoign. See "Almoigne."

Frank chase. See "Chase."

Frank marriage, *liberum maritagium* (3, 86). A peculiar species of estate tail. "Where tenements are given by one man to another, with a wife (which is daughter or cousin to the giver) in frankmarriage, the which gift hath an inheritance by these words "frankmarriage" annexed to it, although it be not expressly said or rehearsed in the gift, the donees shall have the tenements to them and to their heirs between them two begotten. And this is called especial tail, because the issue of the second wife may not inherit." Coke, Litt., book i., c. 2, sec. 17; Lyttleton, *Tenures*, p. 26.

Free warren. See "Warren."

Frischa. Uncultivated land fit for pasturing animals. See Du Cange, who gives many forms of the word.

Friscus and *frischus, a, um* (218, 257). Uncultivated.

Furnage, *furnagium, fornagium* (French, *fournage*). The toll paid by a lord's tenants for the privilege of using the common bakehouse or oven.

Furnus, *fornax* (55, 76, 136, 225, 238). A public bakehouse or oven, at which the lord's tenants were compelled to bake their bread, &c., paying for the privilege a toll called *furnage*.

Gabelage, Latin, *gabulagium* (22, 164). A rent, duty, custom, or service, yielded or done to the king or some other lord. See Du Cange, *s.v. gablum;* also Coke, Litt., book ii., c. 12, sec. 213. There is a payment of langable or landgable mentioned in the *Domesday of St. Paul's* (pp. lxix. and 6), which appears to be akin to gabelage. In Spelman's *Glossary*, it is said to be a payment of 1d. for each house, but in the *Domesday of St. Paul's* it was a payment of sums varying from 2½*d*. to 15*d*. for each virgate. According to Abraham de la Pryme *(Diary,* Surt., p. 125*)*, the custom of paying gabelage or gavelage at Scarborough gave rise to the proverb of "Scarborough Warning." The following is his note on the subject:

"'Scarburg Warning' is a proverb in many places of the north, signifying any sudden warning given upon any account. . . . . This is the true origin. . . . . .
"The town is a corporation town, and tho' it is very poor now to what it was formerly, yet it has a . . . . . , who is commonly some poor man, they haveing no rich ones amongst them. About two days before Michilmas day the sayd . . . being arrayed in gown of state, he mounts upon horseback, and has his attendants with him, and the macebearer carrying the mace before him, with two fidlers and a base viol.
"Thus marching in state (as big as the lord mare of London), all along the shore side, they make many halts, and the cryer cries thus with a strange sort of a singing voyce, high and low,
"Whay! why! whay!
Pay your gavelage, ha!
Between this and Michaelmas day,
Or you'll be fined, I say!
"Then the fiddlers begins to dance, and caper, and plays fit to make one burst with laughter that sees and hears them. Then they go on again, and crys as before, with the greatest majesty and gravity immaginable, none of this comical crew being seen as much as to smile all the time, when as spectators are almost bursten with laughing.
"This is the true origin of the proverb, for this custom of gavelage is a certain tribute that every house pays to the . . . . . when he is pleased to call for it, and he gives not above one day warning, and may call for it when he pleases."

Gaynagium (124), gaynage. The gain or profit of tilled or planted ground. Also a payment made in the produce of the land. Cowell's *Interpreter;* also Du Cange, *s.v. gaagneria.*

Geldable (110). Taxable, liable to pay tax or tribute.

Gersumes, geresume, gersame (241, 245, 251). Any kind of payment in the way of purchase, or reward, or for damages; the fine or premium paid on the grant of a lease, a fine, or amerciament. The word is also used for merchet, *e.g., Gersumam pro filiâ suâ maritandâ.* See Vinogradoff, p. 147, also pp. 441—4.

Gresman (42, 43, 75, 223, 226). A species of villein, classed with cottars in Inquisition XLI. One who pays gersom to his lord. See Vinogradoff, p. 147.

Grundpeny (240), from the example given, was evidently a rent paid for the use and occupation of land.

Gule of August, *gula Augusti* (79). The first day of August, Lammas day, the festival of St. Peter *ad Vincula.*

Hall and Court (14). The lord's court was originally held in his hall, and so was called hallmote or halimote, as well as court baron. The receipts from hall and court would be the fines and amercements imposed at the court.

Harz (28). The meaning of this word is doubtful, it may possibly be the plural of hart, a handle. See the word in Halliwell's *Dictionary.*

Haubergeon, habergeon, or hauberk. A coat of mail. The service of serjeanty of one haubergeon (23), was probably equivalent to the service of one knight.

Haubercke fee (121). Same as knight's fee. See "Knight service." The hauberk or coat of mail formed part of the distinctive armour of a knight.

Hay, haia, haya, haga (28, 111, 112, 141, 215). A hedge, also a park or enclosure.

Haybote, heybote (18, 28, 238). The liberty of cutting wood for making and maintaining hedges and fences.

Herbage, *herbagium* (23, 31, 58, 222, 225), signifies the pasture or fruit of the earth provided by nature for the food of cattle, as distinguished

38

from deer and other wild animals. It is also commonly used for a liberty that a man hath to feed his cattle in another man's ground, as in a forest. The meaning of the word was much discussed in the case of Earl de la Warr *v.* Miles, 17 Ch. D. 535. See also Elphinstone, *Interpretation of Deeds*, and the references there given.

Herciatura (249), harrowing.

Hercia (74), a harrow.

Heriot. The military equipment of a vassal which on his death reverted to his lord. Ultimately it extended to the best chattel of a vassal which was given at his death to his lord. Eventually it was compounded for a money payment, and is now applied to the payment made by a copyholder to the lord of a manor on admission to the copyholds of a deceased copyholder. The difference beween a heriot and a relief is, that a heriot was for the tenant who died, and was out of his goods; a relief was for the tenant who succeeded, and was out of his purse.

Hide. See *ante*, "Carucate." An Anglo-Saxon measure of land of uncertain extent, ultimately considered to be equivalent to a carucate or ploughland. See Kemble's *Saxons in England*, vol. i., Appendix B; Eyton's *Dorset Domesday*, pp. 3—24; and Ellis's *Introduction to Domesday.*

Hiritini. See p. 46 and *note* à. The suggestions there given are all very doubtful. The word seems more likely to be akin to hericia, which Du Cange renders as "Septum quod portis urbium objicitur, seu quodvis repagulum quo locus aliquis occluditur ac munitur." And he gives the following example from the *Reg. feudor, Norman, ex Cod. reg.* 4653. A. fol. 157, viz.: "Homines sui debent reparare unam perticatam de fossatis . . . . . et facere Hericiam supra illam perticatam cum reparata fuerit." The proper translation of hericiam in this instance seems to be a barricade or palisade.

Homage, *homagium* (26, 175, 186, 202, 213). The solemn act by which a tenant acknowledged his lord as him of whom he held his land, and to whom he was bound to render service. It was rendered but once by a tenant on coming to his land, and was due from a freehold tenant only. Lyttleton (*Tenures*, bk. ii., c. 1) says: "Homage is the most honourable service and most humble service of reverence that a frank tenant may do to his lord; for when the tenant shall make homage to his lord, he shall be ungirt and his head uncovered, and his lord shall sit, and the tenant shall kneel before him on both his knees, and hold his hands stretched forth joined together between the hands of his lord, and shall say thus: I become your man from this day forward for life, for member and for earthly honour, and unto you I shall be true and faithful, and bear to you faith for the tenements that I claim to hold of you, saving the faith that I owe unto our sovereign lord the king: and then the lord so sitting shall kiss him." A religious man however, in doing homage is not to say "I become your man, for that he hath professed himself to be only the man of God." There is also a variation in the homage to be done by a woman. See also *Modus faciendi homagium et fidelitatem*, 17 Edw. II., Stat. ². The service of homage was discharged by the Stat. 12 Car. II., c. 24.

Hostium (72). A door.

Husbote, housbote (18, 29, 238). The liberty of cutting wood for building and repair of houses; possibly also for firing, but this is generally called firebote. See page 238, where it is stated that "the lady of Hemelington has twenty waggon loads of wood, both for plough-timber and for the hearth, and beyond this, housbote and heybote." In this example, wood for the hearth, *i.e.*, firebote, is distinct from housebote.

Inquisition is generally understood to mean an inquiry held by the king's sheriff, escheator, steward, or other officer, with or without a jury, under the authority of some statute, commission, writ, or precept of the crown, for the purpose of watching and protecting the king's interests. The majority of the inquisitions in this volume are Inquisitions *Post Mortem*, *i.e.*, inquisitions held on the death of any man of fortune, to inquire into the value of his estate, the tenure by which it was held, and who and of what age his heir was; so as to ascertain the profits due to the king in the way of wardship, relief, &c. There were also many inquisitions under the Statute called *Extenta Manerii*. See the word "Extent" in this Glossary, also "Escheator," and the several kinds of Writ. There was also a mode of procedure by inquisition in the prosecution of offenders against ecclesiastical law, as to which, see Reeve, *Eng. Law*, vol. iii., p. 65.

Instauramentum, also called *Restauramentum* and *Implementum Manerii* (127). The stock of a farm, both live and dead, and ploughings and sowings. In the *Glossary* to the *Boldon Buke*, it is suggested that serfs attached to demesne land were included in the *instauramentum*. Store cattle were cattle let with a farm.

Jewry, Chirographer's chest of, also called *archa jndæorum* or *chirographorum* (159). A chest kept in London and other towns for the deposit of one part of each contract or chirograph (known as the *pes chirographi*), entered into by a Jew with a Christian, and if this counterpart was not found there, when required, the contract was void. These chests were kept with great care and were only opened in the presence of the sheriff, chirographers, and cofferers, or in London, of the Barons of the Exchequer, or other qualified officers. The chirographers were the clerks (commonly Christians and Jews acting together) who wrote the chirographs, and the cofferers were the keepers of the chests. The Jews inhabiting a quarter of a city or town were styled a "*communa*" or commonalty (Pike's *Hist. of Crime*, vol. i., p. 463). For a mention of the commonalty of the Jews of York, see *Select Pleas of the Crown* (Seld.) vol. i., p. 57. Madox *(Hist. of Exch.*, c. 7, *Of the Exchequer of the Jews)*, gives a concise account of the position of the Jews in England from the reign of Hen. II. to the year 1290, when they were expelled from the country. He also gives many illustrations from the Public Records. See also an article by the late Robert Davies, F.S.A., on *The Mediæval Jews of York*, in vol. iii. of the Y.A.A., J., and in the same volume an article by the Rev. J. T. Fowler, F.S.A., *On Certain "Starrs" or Jewish Documents*.

Jewry, Statute of, *Statutum de Judaismo* (155), is of uncertain date, but stated by Stubbs *(Const. Hist.*, vol. ii., p. 578 *n.)* to belong probably to the year 1275. This opinion is to some extent confirmed by the two inquisitions given in this volume, the writs for which are dated respectively 24th and 27th May, 1275 (see pp. 154, 159, and 282 *ante*), and which refer to the Statute. The Statute would therefore probably be passed by the Parliament which passed the Statute of Westminster the First, and which was held at Westminster on the morrow of the Octave of Easter, *i.e.*, 23rd April. Ruffhead gives the date 25th April. The Statute of Jewry made provision for enforcing securities given to Jews. It also enacted that Jews might reside in the king's cities and boroughs where the chirographer's chests of Jewry were kept, and that each Jew should make an annual payment by way of tallage to the king, "whose serf he is," that Jews might live loyally by their merchandise and labour, and that they might have intercourse with Christians in buying and selling; also that they might buy houses and rent lands under certain restrictions. Judaism, or Jewry, was at one time synonymous with mortgage. There are instances of this in the *Selby Coucher Book* (Y.A.A., R., vol. x.). The petition of the barons at the Parliament of Oxford, seeks a remedy against the conduct of the Jews in delivering their debts and the lands pledged to them to the magnates of the realm, who use them for purposes of oppression. Stubbs, *Select Charters*, p. 385-6. For Jewry Debtors, see pp. 109, 154, 159, 282, of these inquisitions.

Jews, Justices assigned for the custody of (159, 205 *n*, 282), were persons assigned to be curators of the revenue of the Jews. In more ancient times they were commonly Christians and Jews appointed to act together, afterwards they were, for the most part, Christians only. They were usually put into their office by the King by letters of the Great Seal, but sometimes the treasurer and barons have appointed a justice of the Jews and other clerks of the Judaism by the king's direction. These justices of the Jews exercised jurisdiction in the affairs of Judaism, viz.: in the accounts of that revenue, in pleas upon contracts made with the Jews, in causes or questions touching their lands or chattels, their tallages, fines, forfeitures, &c. They were looked upon as members or officers of the Great Exchequer, and entitled to the privileges belonging to persons resident there. Madox, *Hist. Exch.*, pp. 159, 160.

Justice of the Forest (28, 29, 30, 111, 162). See "Eyre of the Forest."

Justiciar of England (72). The chief minister of the Norman kings. Stubbs, *Const. Hist.*, vol. i., p. 392 ; *Select Charters*, p. 16. The chief administrator of the law, chief representative of the king in absence, and, while his office lasted, the most powerful subject in the realm. Freeman, *Norman Conquest*, vol. v., p. 432. The title ceased in 52 Hen. III. Reeves, *Eng. Law*, vol. i., p. 533. The *Justiciar* presided in the King's Court *(Curia Regis)* and in the Exchequer. See Dugdale's *Origines Juridiciales*, pp. 20, 38 ; and Madox, *Hist. Exch.*, c. 2.

Kernellus (72), a battlement.

Kingelde. From a custom so called, in Bowes, 6*s.* $\frac{1}{2}d$. This word occurs in the Inquisition *post mortem* of John de Britany, Earl of Richmond, 13 Edw. I., which has been postponed to the next volume of Inquisitions for want of space. It is suggested that "Kingelde" is the same as "Cougeld," which occurs on page 223 *ante*, and that both "Kingelde" and "Cougeld" are corrupt readings of "Congild," as "Schirnegeld" on p. 223 *ante* may be of "Scyragild," both words meaning a society or gild. See "Gildscyra" and "Congildones" *s.v.* "Gilda" in Du Cange. See also Spelman, *Glossary, s.v.* "Geldum;" and Thorpe's *Ancient Laws and Institutes of England.* Du Cange says "Kingeld" was a kind of tribute which might be paid to a king, and if this statement be correct the word would appear to be akin to *Xenia*, which is defined by Spelman *(Glossary)* as the gifts which were offered by the inhabitants of a province to their governors, or to kings and royal personages, and other dignified individuals, when passing through a district. See *Notes and Queries*, 8th series, vol. i., p. 169.

Knight's fee. See "Knight service." The following instances of the varying areas of a knight's fee occur in these inquisitions, viz. :—

9 carucates, pp. 171, 213.	14 carucates, p. 86.	23½ carucates, p. 202.
10 ,, pp. 7, 121, 203.	23 ,, p. 87.	48 ,, p. 153.
12 ,, pp. 85, 86.		

Lac (168). A gift, an offering.

Lardiner (9, 13, 117, 118, 266, 268). The keeper of the larder.

Laund (205). A plain or open place in a wood, an unploughed plain, a lawn.

Leirwite, legerwyte, legewit, letherwit, lechewit (XLI., XLV., CVII.). A fine or payment to which tenants in villenage, and sometimes sokemen, were subject for the incontinence of their daughters and other female relatives. See "Merchet." It was also a fine on violation. See Seld., vol. ii., p. 12.

Librata terræ (192, 195-6, 254 *n*). A librate of land. The examples on pp. 195-6 show that in those cases a librate of land meant land worth £1 a year. A librate was also a measure of land containing 240 acres. See Elphinstone, *s.v.* "Measures of Land" ; also Du Cange, *s.v. Libra terræ.*

Mairemium, *meremium* (244). Wood of any kind available for building. See *Boldon Buke;* also Du Cange, *s.v. Materia.*

Manor. Latin, *manerium.* French, *manoir.* Formerly meant an extent of land granted to some person, for him and his heirs to dwell upon and enjoy, and which was divided into three parts, viz.: (1) The demesne lands, which were reserved for the lord's own use, and cultivated to a certain extent by his own teams and servants, and to some extent by the tenants of the manor who held by prædial services, *i.e.*, by the service of agricultural labour; (2) The assised or tenemental lands, or lands granted or let out by the lord to tenants in consideration of rents or services, or both, and varying in tenure from the freehold of a free tenant to the uncertain tenancies of the various classes of servile tenants, which uncertain tenancies, however, eventually developed into a tenure which, under the name of copyhold, is now practically fixed and certain; (3) The waste lands, which also belonged to the lord, but subject to the common rights of the tenants.

Both the free and the servile tenants were of various degrees. The free tenants included lords of inferior manors held of a superior manor or honour, tenants by knight service, and other classes of free tenants, all of whom were liable for some rent or service to the lord of the manor under whom they held. The servile tenants were also of many classes, and were not the same in every manor. Those mentioned in this volume of Inquisitions are villeins, drenghs, gresmen, cottars, natives, and serfs. Another class of tenants was the sokemen, who were sometimes free and sometimes villein.

Every lord of a manor exercised a jurisdiction over his tenants in the court of the manor, called the court baron; and in some manors was also held a court leet, which had jurisdiction over crimes committed within the manor; the court baron dealing with civil business, especially with matters relating to the freehold. In later times arose the customary court, which dealt with the interests of the copyholders of the manor, and is now frequently called a court baron. Owing to the gradual changes in the position of the tenants of manors, and to the greater security and fixity of their tenures, also to the sales of demesne lands and other possessions of the lords within the districts of their manors, the term manor is now more generally understood to mean the jurisdiction and privileges belonging to and exercised by the lord, than the land comprised within the district of the manor. The term had, and still has, a very comprehensive and varied meaning. In some instances it was synonymous with honour or hundred, and in one instance, at least (viz.: the Manor of Taunton Dene), a manor comprised five hundreds; other manors comprised large districts and several towns, while in other cases there were three or four manors in one township. The term manor was also sometimes applied to a messuage or mansion house only. See further on this subject, Seld., vols. ii. and iv.; Vinogradoff's *Villainage in England;* the *Custumals of Battle Abbey;* the *Domesday of St. Paul's;* Cruise on *Dignities,* c. 2; Digby's *Real Property,* c. 1; Scrutton's *Commons and Common Fields;* and many other of the authorities named at the head of this *Glossary.*

Manucaptor, *mainpernor.* One who takes a man into friendly custody, who otherwise is or might be committed to prison, upon security given for his forthcoming at a day assigned. (Blount's *Law Dict.*). When a debtor had to find sureties for the payment of his debt to the king, such sureties were termed *plegii, obsides,* or *manucaptores.*

Marcata terræ (254), a marc's worth of land per annum. It was also a measure of land containing 160 perches or one acre. See Elphinstone, *s.v.* "Measures of land," also Du Cange, *s.v.* "Marca."

Mensura de granar' (127). Probably *mensura de granario, i.e.,* granary measure, or corn measure. See a note on "Measures" in the *Domesday of St. Paul's,* cxxviii.

Merchet, *marcheta, merchetum* (XLI., XLVI., CVII., CXXXI.). The ransom or fine paid by a villein, and in some manors by a sokeman or freeman, on the marriage of his daughter, granddaughter, or sister, and in some cases of his son, outside the boundary of the lord's dominion. In some manors however, merchet was payable on marriages within the manor. The case given in the *Year Books*, 15 Edw. III., p. 33, shows that merchet was sometimes akin to leirwite (which see). For the many theories as to this payment, and as to the derivation of the word merchet, see Mr. Pike's Introduction to the above mentioned volume of the *Year Books*. The inquisition *post mortem* of Letitia de Kaynes (p. 186, *ante*), shows that sokemen, or at any rate their daughters, were liable to pay both merchet and legerwyte, or leirwite. Many instances occur in the Inquisitions of the liability of villeins to these payments. From the Extent of Lands of Peter of Savoy, we gather (pp. 231-6, *ante*), that in certain parts of the Honour of Richmond, the payment or fine on a marriage, varied according to the value of the lands affected by such marriage.

Mill rent (186). There is nothing to show what was the reason or consideration for this custom. In the *Domesday of St. Paul's*, cxxx., is a note on *multura molendini* and *telonium molendini*, which may be referred to.

Mortmain (220). Dead hand. Lands were said to come into a "dead hand" when they were held by a Corporation, Guild, or Fraternity, whose possession was "immortal," as Coke termed it; whereby the services that were due for the same were wrongfully withdrawn, and the chief lords lost their escheats. The expression was probably first applied to the holding of lands by religious bodies, or persons who, being " professed," were reckoned dead persons in law. It then came to be applied to the holding of lands by Corporations as opposed to individuals, whether the Corporation were ecclesiastical or lay, sole or aggregate. There are numerous Statutes of Mortmain passed for the purpose of regulating and restraining the alienation of lands in Mortmain. The first of such Statutes are *Magna Charta* and the Statute *De Viris Religiosis*, 7 Edw. I; and two very recent and important ones are the "Mortmain and Charitable Uses" Acts, 1888 and 1891.

Multura, *molta, molitura, mulitura*, multure (26). The toll paid for grinding at the lord's mill; sometimes the grist or corn taken to be ground.

Mulvellus (156, 275). A mullet. See Spelman and Du Cange, who both refer to the Empress Maud's grant to the lepers of York.

Namium vetitum (34) An unjust taking the cattle of another, and driving them to an unlawful place, pretending damage done by them. In which case the owner of the cattle might demand satisfaction for the injury, which was called *placitum de vetito namio*. See *post.*, "Withernam."

Namius, *namium, namum* (34, 96). A distress, a pledge.

Native (249). See " Bondman," " Villein."

Nisus mutatus (77). A mewed hawk, one which has moulted, and consequently more valuable than the sore, or unmoulted hawk, *nisus sorus*. In the *Boldon Buke* the value of the moulted sparrow-hawk is put at 5*s.*, and of the sore sparrow-hawk at 1*s.* See the *Glossary* in that Book, *s.v. sparvarius*.

Noka (219). A nook of land, the quantity uncertain, in some places 12½ acres. Martin, *Record Interpreter;* see also Du Cange, *s.v. noca, nocata, nocha, noka*.

Nundinæ (50). A market or fair. See *ante*, "*Forum.*"

Obolatus (249). A halfpennyworth. See Du Cange, *s.v. Obolata terræ.* This latter term was used for a measure of land, sometimes half an acre and sometimes half a perch. See Elphinstone, *s.v.* " Measures of land."

Occasio (127). Disturbance, molestation, hindrance.

Opcuracio (19). A taking in, enclosing.

Operarius. A person liable to do works for the lord. Scrutton, *Commons and Common Fields*, pp. 28—30. *Domesday of St. Paul's, Introduction*, pp. xxiii. to xxviii.

Pannage (4, 28, 29, 31, 259, 263). The running and feeding of swine in the woods, also the price paid to the proprietor of the woods for the privilege of running and feeding swine therein. Ellis, *Introduction to Domesday*, Manwood, c. 12.

Parasceve (134). From the Greek παρασκευή, preparation. The day of preparation for the Jewish Sabbath, *i.e.*, Friday; but more particularly Good Friday. The word is generally declined as in the Greek, but Du Cange gives an instance of the word remaining unchanged as in Inquisition LXXX., p. 134.

Park (66, 124, 141, 143, 225, 240). A piece of enclosed ground stored with beasts of venery, and other wild beasts of the forest and chase, and held by prescription, or the king's grant. A park differs from a chase or warren in that it must be enclosed. See "Chase," "Forest," "Warren."

Pascha Floridum (172). Palm Sunday.

Passagium (124). A ferry, passage, also the right of passage. A payment for the right or liberty of passage, or for the use of a ferry. For other meanings, see Du Cange.

Pelota (265). A ball. Du Cange.

Perquisites of Court (81, 106, 168, 223, and elsewhere). The profits due to the lord for fines, &c.

Pesso (28). The feeding of swine in the woods. Also the mast or food of swine. See Du Cange, *s.v. paisso*.

Placea, *placia* (1, 144, and elsewhere). A place, a plot of ground, the site of a house; hence a house or mansion. Kennett, *Glossary*. See Du Cange for other meanings.

Planchiatura (72). Planking, flooring.

Platera, a plot (218).

Pleas and perquisites of Court (68, 70, 128, 223-6, and elsewhere). The profit arising from proceedings in court, and from fines, amerciaments, &c.

Pleas of the Crown (118), were all suits in the king's name in respect of offences committed against his crown and dignity, or against his crown and peace, *e.g.*, treasons, felonies, misprisions of either, and mayhem. Blount, *Law Dict.*

Plotheland (50). Probably a corruption of ploughland. See *ante*, "Carucate," and "Hide."

Ploughland. See *ante*, "Carucate" and "Hide."

Pomarius bosci (24). An apple tree of the wood, a crab tree. Compare *Pomme de bois*, a crab or wilding. Cotgrave.

Pondfald (124), poundfalde, pondfolde, ponfold. A pinfold. See *Piers Plowman, Glossary.*

Pontage (241). A tax for the repair of a bridge, also toll taken on a bridge.

Potagium (75). Pottage.

Prebend (190). A several benefice rising from some temporal land or church appropriated towards the maintenance of a clerk, or member of a collegiate church, and commonly named from the place from whence the profit ariseth. Blount, *Law Dict.*

Precariæ. Boonworks, *i.e.*, works done for the lord by his tenants at his request. The boondays for ploughing were in winter and spring, and those for gathering in the crops were in autumn. Boonworks were due from both free tenants and servile tenants, and the lord sometimes provided food and drink, or only one or the other, and sometimes neither. There are many instances of boonworks in these inquisitions. See Nos. LIV., LVI., XCVII., CXXXI. See also p. 51. In the Introduction (p. VIII.) to the *Custumals of Battle Abbey* the boonworks are distinguished from the daily works or week-works, the *averagia* or carrying services, and the occasional works, but the distinction is not always clear in these inquisitions. See also *Domesday of St. Paul's*, lxvii., and elsewhere; Vinogradoff, p. 174; and Seebohm, p. 78, and elsewhere.

Pullanus (267). A foal. Martin, *Record Interpreter*. Possibly also a puppy. A horse colt. *Household Roll of Bishop Swinfield*, C.S., p. 151 *n*, and *Glossary*. In the *Promptorium Parvulorum* "*pullus*" is given as the Latin for "colte (or fole), yonge horse." See also Du Cange, *s.v.* "*pullani*."

Purparty (133 *n*). A part or share of an estate, held jointly by co-owners, which is by partition allotted to any one of the owners.

Purpresture (1), is anything done to the hurt of the king's forests, demesnes, or highways, &c., by enclosure or building. When a man takes to himself, or encroaches upon anything, whether it be in lands, franchises, or jurisdiction, it is a purpresture. Purprestures can be committed against the king, the lord of a fee, or a neighbour. See Manwood, c. 10; Spelman, *Glossary*; Coke, Litt., book iii., c. 8, s. 475; II. *Inst.*, 272.

Puture, *putura* (211, 212). A custom claimed by foresters, and sometimes by bailiffs of hundreds, to take food for themselves, their men, horses, dogs, and hawks, gratis from the tenants and inhabitants within the perambulation of the forest or hundred.

Quarentele, *quarentela* (238). The same as "Quarentene," which see.

Quarentene, quarantine, *quarentena* (45). A furlong or forty perches of linear measure. The word also means a space of forty days, and has other meanings, for which see Du Cange.

Rebinare (254, *note* b). To plough a second time. Du Cange.

Reeve, *præpositus* (26, 27, 98, 99). An officer of a manor who was elected yearly, in some cases by the free tenants, and in others by the customary or unfree tenants. His duties varied in different manors, but he seems to have been, in many instances, a foreman of the labourers, and to have had the care of the agricultural work, the cattle, buildings, and stock of a manor. *Domesday of St. Paul's*, xxxvi. He appears to have been originally a villein tenant, and to have been overlooked by the lord's bailiff. *Fleta*, bk. ii., c. 72.

Regarder (30, 111), sometimes called a ranger. An officer of the forest whose duty it was to go through and view the forest before any Court of Justice Seat was held, and to see, inquire into, and report on all trespasses of the forest, all offences concerning vert and venison, and all concealments of any offences or defaults of the foresters and all other officers of the forest. Coke, IV. *Inst.*, p. 292, gives a list of twelve special matters which the regarders were to attend to. The Charter of the Forest prescribes twelve regarders for each forest.

Relief, *relevium* (177, 186, 268). The money paid by the incoming heir, when of full age, to his lord on succeeding to and entering upon his inheritance. See Bracton, book ii., c. 36, and Digby's *Real Property*, pp. 40, and 78.

Reprises (216). The deductions and charges paid and allowed out of the yearly value of an estate, such as rent charges, pensions, annuities, fees of stewards and bailiffs, and such like.

Retroduna (164 *n*). The rear (probably central) mound on which a tower or keep of a castle is built, or it may be the donjon or keep itself. See *Du Cange, s.v.* "Dunum," "Dunjo." Duna also is used for the bank of a ditch or moat, Y.A.A., J., vol. vi., p. 397. It is therefore possible that in this instance *retroduna* may mean the rear bank of the moat of the castle of Scarborough, *i.e.*, the one on the side next the castle. Nets may often be seen drying on this bank at the present time.

Rent is divided into rent service, rent charge, and rent seck, also into rent of assise, white rent, black rent, rent moveable, rent resolute, chief rent, fee farm rent, and rack rent.

Rent service is where a man holds his land by fealty, or other service, and a certain rent, or that which a man reserves to be paid to him on granting a lease to another.

Rent charge is where a man by deed charges his lands or tenements with a sum of money to be paid to the grantee yearly, with a power of distress.

Rent seck, or dry rent is, where a man granting an estate in lands or tenements by deed, reserves a rent without power of distress.

Rent of assise (170, 182, 198), is the certain rent of the freeholders and ancient copyholders, so called because it was assised and certain, and so assised lands were lands let out to tenants, either on payment of an assised or fixed rent alone, or of such a rent combined with fixed services.

White rent, *alba firma,* blanch farm, or *redditus albus,* so called because paid in silver to distinguish it from rents paid in kind, or in services.

Black rent, *redditus niger,* black mail, is rent paid in kind, *i.e.*, in corn, flesh, &c.

Rent moveable, *redditus mobilis.* Farm rent for life, years, or at will, which is variable and uncertain.

Rent resolute, *redditus resolutus.* Said by Coke (II. *Inst.*, p. 19) to be rents issuing of a manor to another lord. Blount (*Law Dict.*) says rents resolute are such rents or tenths as were anciently payable to the crown from the lands of abbies and religious houses, and after the dissolution, these abbey lands being demised to others, the said rents were still reserved and made payable to the crown.

Chief rent, a modern name for a rent charge, and for a rent of assise payable out of freeholds.

Fee farm rent is where land is granted in fee for so much rent as it is reasonably worth, more or less, so it be one fourth (or as some say, one third) of the annual value, without homage, fealty, or other service, except what is specially provided for in the feoffment. Instead of a money rent there might be some special reservation, such as finding a chaplain to sing divine service, &c. Blount's *Law Dict.*.

Rack rent is rent of, or approaching, the full value of the premises out of which it issues.

Salina (140). A salt pit or pan. A tax on salt. Du Cange.

Schirnegeld (223), probably a corruption of "Scyragild." See *ante,* "Kingelde."

Scutage, escuage, *escutagium* (175, 186, 217, 236, 256, and elsewhere), was a duty or service arising out of baronies and knights' fees, for service in the king's army. It denoted *servitium scuti,* the service of the shield, and was wont to be rendered thus, viz.: for every knight's fee, the service of one knight; for every half fee, the service of half a knight; and so in proportion. Baronies were charged with scutage in the same manner, *i.e.*, according to the number of the knight's fees whereof the barony consisted. The service of scutage was performed either personally in the king's army, or else by a pecuniary commutation. The term scutage, however, was generally used in the latter of these two senses, and was understood to be a composition in money for actual military service. In some instances it was nearly allied to an aid, *q. v.* See Madox, *Hist. Exch.*, c. 16; Digby, *Real Property*, p. 116; Stubbs, *Select Charters*, p. 364; also Kennett, *Glossary*, *s.v. scutagium.*

Seisin, *seisina* (26, 27, 153, and elsewhere). Possession; strictly, possession as of freehold, *i.e.*, possession which a freeholder has.

Selda (50). A shop, booth, or stall, also a window where goods are exposed for sale.

Semen hyemale (243, 249). Winter sowing; literally, winter seed.

Semen quatrag, *i.e.*, **Quadragesimale** (243, 249). Lent sowing.

Serf (125, 249). See "Bondman," "Villein."

Serjeanty, Grand, tenure by, was a species of tenure by knight service of the king only, whereby the tenant was bound, instead of serving the king generally in his wars, to do some special honorary service to the king in person, as, to carry his banner or sword; or to be his butler, champion, or other officer at his coronation; or to do some real service, such as keeping the gate of York Castle, or conducting the king's treasure through the county. See "Service" for references.

Serjeanty, Petty, tenure by, was a socage tenure, and consisted in holding lands of the king only by the service of rendering to him yearly some small thing pertaining to war. See c. 27 of *Magna Charta*, 9 Hen. III. See "Service" for references.

Service. The rent return or duty owing from a vassal or tenant to his lord by reason of his tenure or holding. The two great classes of lay services were *free*, or those due from free men, and *non-free*, or those due from villeins and others holding in villenage. Another class of services was those due from tenants in frankalmoign and tenants by divine service. The following are the principal services mentioned in these inquisitions:

Archery to be done at the gate of York Castle in time of war by one man, p. 207.
Barony, pp. 55, 61—3, 133*n*, 137, and elsewhere.
Castleguard, pp. 83, 175.
Conducting the king's treasure through the county, p. 46.
Crossbowman, p. 46.
Drengage, pp. 100, 267.
Free, pp. 161-2, and elsewhere.
Free foreign, p. 154.
Free men, pp. 5, 160.
Free tenants, pp. 15, 43, 48, 71, 92, and elsewhere.
Foreign, pp. 3, 7, 32, 37, 71, 262—3, and elsewhere.
Foreign, called Fine of Wapentake, p. 238.
Great Serjeanty, p. 208.
Gresman, pp. 75-6.
Guarding the bailiwick of the Hay of Langwath, p. 215.
Haubercke fee, p. 121.
Homage and scutage, p. 213.
Homage and service, p. 258.
Homage, 10*s.* for castleguard, ploughing, making one perch upon the causeway of Tykehill. Suit, &c. p. 175.
Homage, suit, and service, p. 175.

Service *(continued)*.
Homage, ward, and relief, p. 176.
Keeping the forest of Pickering, p. 158.
Knight's, pp. 104, 171, 193, and elsewhere.
   One fourth part of a knight's fee, p. 206.
   Third part of a knight's fee, p. 5.
   Half a knight's fee, pp. 90, 188, and elsewhere.
   One knight, p. 257.
   Two knights, p. 259.
   Two knights when the king goes in his army, p. 197.
   Three knights' fees, p. 170.
   Five knights' fees, pp. 255, 259.
   Ten knights, p. 170.
Military, p. 138.
Money rents, and food and labour services, are too numerous to index.
Of being the keeper of the larder, pp. 266, 268.
One arrow at Easter, for all services, p. 247.
One mewed hawk, p. 77.
One pair of gilt spurs, p. 137.
One penny at Easter, for all services, p. 247.
Providing food for lepers, p. 156.
Riding with the king, together with two knights, when his peers shall so ride,
   p. 200.
Royal, p. 10.
Scutage, pp. 213, 256.
Serjeanty, pp. 22, 121, 161, 260, 266, 269.
Serjeanty of one haubergeon in the king's army, p. 23.
Serjeanty of the gate of York Castle, p. 87.
Services due from all the tenants of a manor, free or otherwise, p. 176.
Sufficiently keeping the king's wood of Langwath, p. 105.
Suit at Court of Beverley for all services, and suit at other courts, p. 217.
Suit at Wapentake Court of Heudrenesse, p. 154.
Suit at Wapentake Court of Pikeringe, p. 46.
Suit at Court of Tykhill, p. 176.
Villein services, see Inquisitions XLV., XLVIII., LIV., XCVII., CXXXI.
Villenage, p. 89.
Ward at York Castle, p. 46.
Working one perch of harrowing (? palisading) at Pickering Castle, p. 46.

Service of Barony (55, 61—3, 133*n*, 137). The service due to the
king from the holder of a barony, which was to provide the service of a certain
number of knights, variously stated to be thirteen and a quarter, and twenty,
but the instances given by Madox *(Baronia Anglica)* are much more varied; and
to attend the *Curia Regis*, or king's court, and the great council at the great
festivals and at other times when summoned, and to do homage and fealty.
There were also the same incidents as in tenure by knight service, *i.e.*, aids,
relief, wardship, marriage, &c., Madox, *Hist. of Exch.*

Service of free men, to hold in (5, 103). That is in free socage.
See " Socage."

Service, knight (193 and elsewhere). Tenure by knight service
was esteemed the most honourable species of tenure.   For this tenure a
quantity of land necessary, the area of which was uncertain, but the
annual value of which was fixed at £20 at an early period, probably in the
reign of William the Conqueror (See p. 188 *ante.*)   This holding constituted
a knight's fee, and he who held it was bound to do homage and fealty to his
lord, and to attend him to the wars for forty days in every year if called upon,
which attendance was his *redditus* or return, his rent or service for the land he
claimed to hold.   In lieu of personal attendance, however, a money payment
called scutage or escuage was eventually accepted (See *ante*, " Scutage."

Under the provisions of the Assize of Arms passed in 1181, the holder of a knight's fee must possess a coat of mail, a helmet, a shield, and a lance, and every knight was to have as many of these arms and weapons as he had knight's fees. A tenant by knight service might hold either of the king or of a subject, but in either case he was liable to do homage and fealty to his lord. The tenure drew to it seven incidents, viz.: aids, relief, primer seisin, wardship, marriage, fines for alienation, and escheat.

Service of conducting the king's treasure through the county (46) was a species of grand serjeanty. In the *York Volume of the Archæological Institute*, pp. 21—4, are some interesting notes by the Rev. Joseph Hunter, "respecting Travelling and the Transmission of Treasure, chiefly in the northern parts of the kingdom in the reigns of Edward I., II., and III.

Service, royal or foreign (see "*Service*" for references) *servitium regale vel forinsecum*. So called because it was due to the king and not to the immediate lord, whose service was termed "intrinsic," *i.e.*, *servitium intrinsecum*. See Bracton, vol. i., p. 283.

Sessum juncorum (119). A plot of rushes. See Du Cange, *s.v. sedes*, 4.

Sikettus, *siketus* (30, 31, 210). A small stream or watercourse. A ditch, a sike. Du Cange, *s. v. sica*.

Situs (140). A site or situation, the berth of a ship.

Skeppa, sceppa, esceppa, escheppa, eskeppa (140). A skep or basket. An ancient measure of corn, meal, or salt, the exact size of which is uncertain. See Du Cange; also Kennett, *Glossary, s. v.* "Sceap"; Jacob, *Law Dict., s. v.* "Esceppa," "Sceppa"; and Bosworth, *A. S. Dict., s. v.* "Scep."

Socage (17, 32, 35, 109, 204). Lyttleton (*Tenures*, book ii., c. 5), says that tenure in socage is where the tenant holdeth of his lord the tenancy by certain service for all manner of services, so that the service be not knight's service. As where a man holdeth of his lord by fealty and certain rent, for all manner of services, or else where a man holdeth his land by homage, fealty, and certain rent for all manner of services; for homage of itself maketh not knight's service. Also a man may hold of his lord by fealty only and such tenure is tenure in socage. Socage is so called from *soca* a plough, because in ancient time, great part of the tenants that held of their lords by socage, ought to come with their ploughs, every of the said tenants for certain days in the year to plough and sow the demesnes of the lord. Thereby they were quit against their lords of all manner of services, &c. Afterwards these plough services were changed into an annual rent by agreement between the lord and the tenant, but the name still continued, and free socage or freehold tenure is now the tenure under which by far the greatest portion of the land in England and Wales is held ; the Statute 12 Car. II., c. 24, having enacted that all sorts of tenures, held of the king, or others, be turned into free and common socage, save only tenures in frankalmoign, copyholds, and the honorary services of grand serjeanty. Tenure by petit serjeanty, tenure in burgage, and gavelkind tenure, being all varieties of socage tenure were not abolished by the above mentioned Statute, and continue to the present time. Besides free socage, there were socage in ancient tenure, or ancient demesne, and socage in base tenure, or villein socage, both of which are now merged in copyhold tenure.

Soke, *soca* (207). Jurisdiction. A liberty, privilege, or franchise granted by the king to a subject; also the area or territory within which that franchise is exercised.

Sokemen (74, 186). Tenants holding their lands and tenements in socage, *q.v.* There were various classes of sokemen, *e.g.*, free and villein, and those holding in ancient demesne, and those outside. The free sokemen were in some Extents of manors distinguished from the free tenants (as in page 186), but the distinction between the two classes of tenants is not clear. See Vinogradoff, *s.v.* "Socmen." Also Scrutton's *Commons and Common Fields*, *s.v.* "Socmanni."

Stalla, or *stallum* (50). A moveable stall or stand in a fair or market.

Steward, *seneschallus* (26). The lord's chief officer in a manor, his legal adviser, and the guardian of his rights. It was his duty to hold the manorial courts, and to exercise a general supervision over the manor, its officers, tenants, stock, &c.

Subbang' de la mare (81). Seaweed used for litter and manure.

Superannatus (248). Over one year of age. Applied to animals. See Du Cange, and the examples there given.

Suit of Court, *secta curiæ* (75, 93, 103, 118, and elsewhere). The service of attending at the lord's court which the tenants were bound to do. A note to Lyttleton's *Tenures*, p. 108, says:—" Suit service is to come to the court from three weeks to three weeks by the whole year, and for that a man shall be distrained, and not amerced. Suit real is to come to the court of leet and that is but two times in the year, and for that a man shall be amerced and not distrained." In practice, however, the free tenants were amerced for non-attendance at the court baron.

Tallage, *taillagium, talliagium* (27, 46, 125, 216). A tax or toll paid either to the king or to a subordinate lord. The king's tallage was either levied at his will on the Jews or on his demesnes, escheats, and wardships, and upon the burghs and towns of the realm. When paid out of knight's fees it was called scutage, when paid out of the lands which were not of military tenure, it was called hidage or carucage, and the term was generally applied to a tax on burghs and towns. Madox, *Hist. Exch.*, c. 17. Stubbs, *Const. Hist.*, *s.v.* "Tallage." There are instances of tallage payable to an inferior lord in *Select Pleas in Manorial Courts*, Seld., vol. ii. As to tallage payable by burghs and towns, See Madox, *Firma Burgi*. The latter writer (*Hist. Exch.*, c. 17) says, tallage also means *donum* and *assisa*, and Coke (II. *Inst.*, p. 532), says the word "doth include all subsidies, taxes, tenths, fifteenths, impositions, or other burthens or charges put or set upon any man."

Tallage or **Talliate**, to (77). *Talliare*, to levy tallage.

Talliated (42—4, 46, 77, 79, 216). Taxed by tallage.

Tenure. The mode of holding an estate feudally; the holding itself. The development of tenure seems to have been one of the results of the Norman Conquest. The result was not brought about by any positive enactment, but was due to the introduction of Norman customs and ideas, and their combination with Anglo-Saxon customs and ideas. Thus was produced what is called the feudal system, or the feudal mode of holding lands, the five marks of which were (1) hereditary succession, (2) reliefs, (3) wardship and marriage, (4) aids, and (5) escheats. Stubbs, *Const. Hist.*, vol. i., p. 433*n*. The feudal system seems to have been in full operation in the reign of Hen. I. The spiritual tenures were (1) tenure in frankalmoign, (2) tenure by divine service. The four principal lay tenures were (1) by knight service, (2) by free socage, (3) by pure villenage, (4) by villein socage. The two latter tenures are now merged in copyhold tenure, and tenure by knight service is now by the operation of the Stat. 12 Car. II., c. 24, converted into free socage or the ordinary freehold tenure of the present day. See also *s.v.* "Drengage," *ante*.

Tinctura (69) means primarily a dyeing or staining. Here it seems to be used in place of *tinctoria* or *tincturia*, a dyehouse. See Du Cange, *s.v.* *tinctoria, tincturia*. For another form of the word, see *ante*, p. 230 *n*.

Tingnum, *tignum* (72). A beam or rafter.

Toft (VIII., XLV., XLVI.) By most authorities, legal and others, said to be a piece of ground wherein a house has stood. Thorpe *(Ancient Laws and Customs of England)* says it is a piece of land adjacent to the house of a peasant. See also *Boldon Buke.*

Tolcester or tolcestre (65). A toll paid for licence to brew and sell ale. See *Custumals of Battle Abbey.* Compare "Tollale" in vol. ii., p. 367 *n*, of the *Whitby Chartulary*; see also Blount's *Law Dict., s.v.* "Tolsester," and "Gavelsester."

Tollonium, *teolonium, theoloneum, tolnetum,* toll (79, 81, 136, 198). A payment for liberty to buy or sell on the lord's land; a payment for goods sold in any fair or market within a manor; a payment on the return of unsold cattle from a market or fair; a payment for the privilege of passage over private grounds, ferries, bridges, &c.; a payment for the right of making and vending (*e.g.*, beer, as to which see "Tolcester") or for the privilege of using the lord's oven, which latter payment was called "Furnage," which see; or for the privilege of grinding corn at the lord's mill, as to which see "Multure."

Tresonce, *tresoncia, trisantia* (72). An ante-chamber or recess, but more frequently a passage in a house, castle, monastery, or other place of residence. See Parker's *Concise Glossary of Architecture*, 6th edition, p. 305; *Domesday of St.Paul's*, xcix.; and *Promptorium Parvulorum, s.v.* "Tresawnce," and the note thereto.

Trespasses made of vert and venison (112). Offences against the forest laws with regard to vert and venison. See Manwood, c. 5 and 6. Before the making of the Charter of the Forest, the punishment of a man taken offending within the king's forest in killing his deer was very severe. The 10th chapter of the Charter considerably modified the punishment. Any man cutting down or destroying vert, or even dry boughs, or doing anything which caused waste or destruction in woods or grass within the precincts of a forest, appears to have been considered a trespasser in vert, and "put to his fine."

Turbary, common of (66, 223), is a right to dig turves (*i.e.*, peat, not green turf) in another man's land, or in the lord's waste, for fuel to burn in the house. Elphinstone, *Interpretation of Deeds;* also Du Cange, *s.v.* *turba, turbagium;* and Spelman, *Glossary, s.v.* *turba.*

Turf peny (240). Probably a payment for the privilege of cutting turf.

Vaccary (49, 115, 138, 225, 230), *vaccaria.* Pasture for cows. A cow pasture, sometimes a cow house.

Vasculum. A vessel or measure. See *note* a, p. 76.

Venison (112). "A word of art proper to beasts of forest and beasts of chase, and none other. And therefore, by this word venison, it is to be understood, that it is, and must be always one of the five beasts of forest, or one of the five beasts of chase, or else the same is not to be called venison." Manwood, c. v., s. 1.

Verderer (29, 30, 111, and elsewhere). A judicial officer of the forest, chosen in full county by force of the king's writ. His office was to observe and keep the assizes or laws of the forest, and to view, receive, and inrol the attachments and presentments of trespasses of the forest of vert and venison. There were generally four verderers in each forest.

Vert (29, 112) is every tree, bush, or the like, which is of the nature of wood or underwood, and bears green leaf which may hide or cover a deer under it. Manwood (c. 6, s. 1) says there are three special causes why the forest laws have so carefully provided for the preservation of the vert of the forest. I.—To provide covert for the beasts of the forest. II.—To provide food for them. III.—For ornament. Vert was divided into over vert, or hault boys, and nether vert, or south boys; the former comprising great trees, and the latter all underwood, bushes, thorn, gorse, and the like. "The forest lawyers have also a third sort of vert, which they do call special vert, which is every tree and bush within the forest that doth bear fruit to feed the deer. . . . . . and the reason why they do call the same special vert is, because the offence in destroying of such vert is more highly punished than the offence in the destruction of any other vert." Manwood, c. 6, s. z.

Vesture, *vestura terræ*. The profits of the land, *i.e.*, the corn, grass, underwood, sweepage, or mowing, and the like.

View, *visus* (18, 238). Inspection, also judgment.

Villein or villan, *villanus* (XLV., and elsewhere), is a term to which it is difficult to give a precise and definite meaning in a few words. Stubbs (*Const. Hist.*, vol. i., p. 486) says "the *villani* of *Domesday* are no doubt the ceorls of the preceding period, the men of the township, the settled cultivators of the land, who in a perfectly free state of society were the owners of the soil they tilled, but under the complicated system of rights and duties which marked the close of the Anglo-Saxon period had become dependent on a lord, and now, under the prevalence of the feudal idea, were regarded as his customary tenants, irremoveable cultivators, who had no proof of their title but the evidence of their fellow ceorls. For two centuries after the Conquest the *villani* are to be traced in the possession of rights, both social and to a certain extent political, and they . . . . . . were in the possession of considerable comforts." They were safe in the possession of their homes, they had a remedy against the violence of their masters, and they could obtain the rights of free men by renouncing their holdings and taking refuge in a town; and they could also obtain manumission, which, however, was not an unmixed blessing. Villeins are sometimes said to have been divided into villeins regardant and villeins in gross. The former were bound to the vill or manor in which they lived, and seem to have been also called *nativi* or natives, and *bondi* or bondmen, of whom many instances occur in these inquisitions. See pp. 99, 169, and 249, also Inquisition XLV. throughout. Their holdings were of considerable extent, the examples appearing in these inquisitions varying in size from half a bovate to six bovates. They were said to hold these lands at the will of the lord, and subject to certain services of a servile character, of which instances appear frequently in this volume. These servile services were in course of time commuted for a fixed money rent, and the tenure of a villein became the modern copyhold tenure. It will be noticed that many of the villeins named in this volume hold at a money rent. Villeins in gross seem to have been merely *servi*, or slaves, whom the lord could sell and dispose of as he thought fit. They seem to have had no proprietary rights. Villeins are also said to be divided into natives, or bondmen by blood, and villeins by tenure, *i.e.*, free persons of low degree who held land upon performing servile offices for the lord. Cottars also and gresmen, who appear as separate classes in these inquisitions, seem to have been subject to base services, and they were gradually confounded with the villeins as were also the bordars and others. See further on this subject, Stubbs, *Const. Hist.*, vol. i., p. 484, vol. ii., p. 493, and a learned note by Mr. Finlason in his edition of Reeves' *English Law*, c. iii.; also Lyttleton's *Tenures*, bk. i., chapters 10 and 11, and Vinogradoff's *Villainage in England*, and the many authorities quoted by him.

Villenage, *villenagium* (2, 3, 12, 14, 209, and LXXXII., &c.), was a base tenure of lands or tenements, whereby the tenant was bound to do such base or villein services as his lord commanded, or as were fit for a villein to perform. Villenage was divided into pure villenage and villein socage. By the former the tenant was bound to do whatever service his lord commanded; by the latter he was bound to the performance of services agreed on between him and his lord, such as ploughing, reaping, mowing, carrying, &c.

Virgate, or yard land. Said by some writers to be the typical holding of a serf or villein in the open fields of a manor, but this statement does not hold good for the North of England, where the bovate or oxgang appears to have been the unit of the bondman's holding (Inq. XLV., and also p. 249 *ante*). The virgate was of varying measurement but normally about 30 acres (10 acres in each of the three fields in scattered strips). So called from the land being measured out with a rod, *virga*, into acres four rods wide. See Seebohm, pp. 60, 171, 389, and Vinogradoff, pp. 148, 238.

Vivary (7, 222, 226). A place in land or water where living things be kept. A park, warren, or fishpond.

Vouch to warrant, further vouch (184). When an action for the recovery of property was commenced against a man, who alleged that he had acquired it from a third person, he could vouch that third person to warranty, *i.e.*, call upon him to defend the title to the property. The person vouched could in his turn further vouch another person. These terms were for centuries well known in connection with the fictitious action for barring an estate tail, called a Common Recovery.

Waif, *waivium* (211) is properly a wandering flock that no one seeks, follows, or protects. Du Cange. They belonged to the lord of the franchise where they were found, but he was under obligation to have them cried and published in the markets and churches near about, so as to establish a title against the owner. "The jury say that a cow has come as a waif, and is in the Abbot's Court." Pleas in the Manor Court of Elton of the Abbot of Ramsey, vol. ii. *Seld. Soc.*, p. 93. Waif, weif, wayf, gwayf, *weyvium*, *waivium*, meant also a thing lost, and also the goods which a thief having stolen, leaves behind him in his flight. The term is also used of the goods of a man which being pursued as a felon he leaves behind in his flight. These waifs also became the property of the lord under certain conditions.

Waldcroft (145). Probably a croft or enclosure of woody ground. See Du Cange, *s.v. gualdus.*

Wallura (28). Walling.

Walwa, *valva* (72). A leaf or fold of a door or gate.

Wapentake Court or hundred court (118, 154, 202). The court of the wapentake or hundred having both civil and criminal jurisdiction, and dating its origin to Anglo-Saxon times. Eventually in many instances it became identical with the court of a large manor or honour. See Stubbs, *Const. Hist.*, vol. i., c. 5. The hundred court belonged to the crown of common right, and could only be acquired by a subject by grant from the crown or by prescription.

Ward (257, 266,), was the custody of a town or castle, which the inhabitants or tenants were bound to keep at their own expense. Also the same as "Wardpenny," which was a payment made as a commutation for the duty of keeping guard in a town or castle, or as a tax in aid of the cost of keeping watch and ward. See Du Cange, *s.v.* "Warda," "Wardpeni"; also *Domesday of St. Paul's*, lxxviii.—lxxxi. Compare "Castleguard."

Wardship (16 *n*), Ward (41, 209, 268). An important incident of feudal tenure. At the death of a tenant by knight service, his heir male being under the age of twenty-one years, the lord had the lands held of him during the heir's minority. Where the heir was a female, the wardship ceased at her age of fourteen or sixteen, according as she might be married or unmarried at the death of her ancestor. Lyttleton, *Tenures*, bk. ii., c. 4. Where the tenure was in socage, the next friend of the heir to whom the inheritance could not descend, had the wardship of the land and of the heir until the latter attained the age of fourteen years. But the profits of the land were for the heir's benefit. Lyttleton, *Tenures*, c. 5.

Warrecta (78). Fallow ground.

Warren (83, 129). A franchise or place privileged either by prescription or grant from the king to keep beasts and fowls of warren, which are hares, conies, partridges, and pheasants. A warren need not be enclosed. See " Chase," " Forest," " Park."

Wayda (50). Woad.

Withernam (34) " is the taking or driving of a distress to a hold, or out of the county, so that the sheriff cannot upon replevin make delivery thereof to the party distrained, in which case a Writ of Withernam is directed to the Sheriff for the taking of as many of his beasts that did thus unlawfully distrain, or as much goods of his, into his keeping, until he hath made deliverance of the first distress. Also if the beasts be in a fortlet or castle, the sheriff may take with him the power of the county, and beat down the castle, as appears by the Statute of Westminster the First, c. 20." *Termes de la Ley.* See also Coke, II. *Inst.*, 140, 141. See *ante*, " *Namium vetitum.*'

Wodehenne, le Wodehen, *gallina silvestris* (248, 250). Seems to have been a fowl given to the lord for licence to gather wood. Vinogradoff, p. 290. See " Woodgeld " in Blount's *Law Dict.*, and Coke, IV. *Inst.*, c. 73, p. 306. See also the note on " *Gallinæ de Bosco* " in the *Whitby Chartulary* (Surt.), vol. ii., p. 365. Compare " Woodsilver," which was a payment in lieu of the service of carrying wood. *Domesday of St. Paul's*, lxix.

Wreck of the Sea (147—9) is defined by the Statute of Westminster the First, c. 4. The following is Ruffhead's translation. " Concerning wrecks of the sea, it is agreed, that where a man, a dog, or a cat escape quick out of the ship, that such ship nor barge, nor anything within them, shall be adjudged wreck ; (2) but the goods shall be saved and kept by view of the sheriff, coroner, or the king's bailiff, and delivered into the hands of such as are of the town where the goods were found ; (3) so that if any sue for those goods, and after prove that they were his, or perished in his keeping, within a year and a day, they shall be restored to him without delay, and if not, they shall remain to the king, and be seised by the sheriffs, coroners, and bailiffs, and shall be delivered to them of the town, which shall answer before the justices of the wreck belonging to the king ; (4) and where wreck belongeth to another than to the king, he shall have it in like manner ; (5) and he that otherwise doeth, and thereof be attainted, shall be awarded to prison, and make fine at the king's will, and shall yield damages also ; (6) and if a bailiff do it, and it be disallowed by the lord, and the lord will not pretend any title thereunto, the bailiff shall answer, if he have whereof, and if he have not whereof, the lord shall deliver his bailiff's body to the king." See also the Statute *De Officio Coronatoris*, 4 Edw. I., Stat. 2.

Writ of certiorari (150, 187, 200) is generally understood to mean a writ for the removal of proceedings from an inferior to a superior court. The examples given in this volume, are writs directing enquiries of various kinds.

40

Writ of right (34) was a form of real action, the object of which was to determine a disputed right of property in the land. Digby's *Real Property*, p. 71.

Writ of novel disseisin. A form of real action for recovering seisin of lands and hereditaments. Commonly called an assize of novel disseisin. Digby's *Real Property*, c. ii., sec. 9. See also Bracton, book iv.

Writ of quo warranto is a writ that lies against him who usurps any franchise or liberty against the king. Blount, *Law Dict.*

Writ of diem clausit extremum (237 *n.*) was a writ that issued out of the chancery to the escheator of the county upon the death of any of the king's tenants *in capite*, to inquire by a jury of what lands he died seised, and of what value, and who was his next heir. Blount, *Law Dict.*

Writ of ad quod damnum (187) is a writ that lies to the sheriff to inquire what hurt it may be for the king to grant a fair or market in any town or place; or for the king or any other person to grant any lands in fee simple to any house of religion or other body politic. For in such case the land so given is said to fall into a dead hand, so that the chief lords lose all hope of heriots, service of court, and escheats. Blount, *Law Dict.*

Year and day (19, 256, 260). See *note* page 256.

Yolstock (244). The payment of 12*d.* at Christmas, called "Yolstock," was probably a payment in lieu of the service of carrying wood, and may therefore be the same as "Woodsilver," as to which see *Domesday of St. Paul's*, lxix. This payment differed from "Woodgeld," which was a payment for the privilege of cutting wood in a forest. Blount, *Law Dict.*. Spelman, *Glossary.*

INDEX OF NAMES AND PLACES.

45

ROBERT WHITE, PRINTER, WORKSOP.

YORKSHIRE

Archæological and Topographical

ASSOCIATION.

THE RECORD SERIES,

For the Publication of Documents and Abstracts and Indexes
of Documents relating to the County of York.

Volume I., for the year 1885, contains

(1) *A Catalogue of the Inquisitions Post Mortem for the County
of York, for the reigns of James I. and Charles I., in the
Courts of Chancery and of Wards and Liveries.*

(2) *A Catalogue of the Yorkshire Wills at Somerset House, for
the years* 1649 *to* 1660, compiled by Dr. COLLINS, with a
copious Index.

Price to Subscribers, £1 1s.

Volume II., for the year 1886, is the first of four volumes of *Yorkshire Feet of Fines of the Tudor Period*, and has been compiled, with a full Index of Names and Places, by Dr. COLLINS.

Price to Subscribers, £1 1s.

The object of these volumes of *Fines* is to place in the hands
of those interested in the Topography and Genealogy of Yorkshire,
a complete Index of the Names of all Persons and Places in the
Feet of Fines for that County during the Tudor Period, together
with a short Summary or Abstract of each *Fine*. Their value,
therefore, to those interested in Family or Local History is very
great.

Volume III., for the year 1887, contains

(1) *The Proceedings in a Dispute between the Council of the North and certain Justices of the North and West Ridings.*

(2) A *Transcript of the two earliest known Sessions Rolls of the West Riding* (159⅞ to 1602), presented by the late E. HAILSTONE, ESQ., F.S.A., and edited by JOHN LISTER, ESQ., M.A.

Volume IV., for the year 1887, contains

An Index, compiled by Dr. COLLINS, *to Wills proved in the Exchequer and Prerogative Courts of York, from* 1636 to 1652, all of which are still in bundles and untranscribed.

Price of Volumes III. and IV. to Subscribers, £1 1s.

Volume V., for the year 1888, contains another instalment of the *Tudor Fines.*

Volume VI., for the year 1888, contains

An Index, compiled by Dr. COLLINS, *of the Early Wills in the York District Registry, from the year* 1389 *to the year* 1514, together with a List of Peculiars and other Courts which formerly claimed jurisdiction in matters of Probate.

The interest in these *Wills* extends over the whole of the Province of York and the County of Nottingham, which was formerly included in the Province.

Price of Volumes V. and VI. to Subscribers, £1 1s.

Volumes VII. and VIII., for the year 1889, contain the remaining parts of the *Tudor Fines.*

Price of the Two Volumes to Subscribers, £1 1s.

Volume IX., for the year 1890, contains

Abstracts of Wills in the time of the Commonwealth, at Somerset House, chiefly illustrative of Sir William Dugdale's Visitation of Yorkshire in 1665-6—Edited by J. W. CLAY, ESQ., F.S.A.

Volume X., for the year 1890, is

The first volume of the *Coucher Book of Selby Abbey*, from the Original MS. in the possession of THOMAS BROOKE, ESQ., F.S.A., to which is prefixed *Historia Selebiensis Monasterii*, reprinted from Labbe.

The volume contains four plates of the Abbey, and of Seals of the Abbots, and it has been edited by the REV. J. T. FOWLER, M.A., F.S.A. who has added an Historical Introduction.

Price of Volumes IX. and X. to Subscribers, £1 1s.

Volume XI., for the year 1891, contains

An Index, edited by Dr. COLLINS, *of the Wills in the York Registry, from the year 1514 to the year 1553*, to which Dr. COLLINS has added *two Appendices*, viz. I. An Index of all such Administration Acts in the Act Books, from 1514 to 1553, and of all Probate Acts, from 1514 to 1521, in the same, as have not been entered in the Registers. II. Additions and Corrections to Vol. VI., owing to the discovery of a portion of the earliest Act Book of the Deanery of Harthill.

Volume XII., for the year 1891, contains

Abstracts of Yorkshire Inquisitions of the reigns of Henry III. and Edward I., giving much information, not only of a genealogical nature, but also as to the condition of Yorkshire and its inhabitants in the latter half of the 13th century, edited by WILLIAM BROWN, ESQ., M.A.

Price of Volumes XI. and XII. to Subscribers, £1 1s.

Volume XIII. (now in the press) for the year 1892, is

The second volume of the *Coucher Book of Selby Abbey*, edited by the REV. J. T. FOWLER, M.A., F.S.A.

Price to Subscribers, £1 1s.

Other volumes of the *Index of the York Wills* are being prepared by Mr. A. GIBBONS, of Lincoln, and will be issued yearly if the funds of the Society permit.

Subsequent volumes of the Record Series will contain *Notes relating to Yorkshire Monastic Houses, extracted from the Plea Rolls, by W. Paley Baildon, Esq.; Subsidy Rolls for the North and East Ridings and the City of York, temp. Edward I.*, edited by WILLIAM BROWN, ESQ.; *Abstracts of the Royalist Composition Papers for Yorkshire; Abstracts of the Rolls of the more important Manor Courts of Yorkshire; Early Yorkshire Fines*, and other documents of great interest.

The Subscription to the RECORD SERIES is £1 1s. per annum, and is not confined to Members of the Association.

Back volumes will be supplied to New Subscribers at Subscription Prices.

The Names of Persons desirous of subscribing to the RECORD SERIES should be sent to the Honorary Secretary for the Series, S. J. CHADWICK, F.S.A., Church Street, Dewsbury.

New Subscribers are urgently needed to enable the work of this branch of the Association to be carried on with vigour and effect.

October, 1892.